*Java 2 Micro Edition*

# Java 2
# Micro Edition

*Java in Small Things*

JAMES WHITE
DAVID HEMPHILL

MANNING

Greenwich
(74° w. long.)

For online information and ordering of this and other Manning books,
go to www.manning.com. The publisher offers discounts on this book
when ordered in quantity. For more information, please contact:

Special Sales Department
Manning Publications Co.
209 Bruce Park Avenue        Fax: (203) 661-9018
Greenwich, CT 06830          email: orders@manning.com

Manning Publications Co.          Copyeditor:  Lois Patterson
209 Bruce Park Avenue            Typesetter:  Martine Maguire-Weltecke
Greenwich, CT 06830           Cover designer:  Leslie Haimes

ISBN 1-930110-33-2
Printed in the United States of America
1 2 3 4 5 6 7 8 9 10 – VHG – 06 05 04 03 02

*To my wife, Kelly*
J.W.


*To my wife, Amy Votava and my daughter, Olivia Hemphill*
D.H.

# contents

# *preface*

Fifteen to twenty years ago, anyone familiar with the computer industry did not question the impact personal computers would have on our society. The only question was how quickly could PCs be made available at a reasonable price in order to begin this new age. Today, with personal computers in three of every four United States households and with the ubiquity of the Internet associated with all those PCs, the Information Age has arrived. Nearly everyone is connecting to and using information resources in ways exceeding the wildest dreams of early PC visionaries.

**RCA 8TS30 (1943)**
*Courtesy of*
*www.harryposter.com*

Our personal computers are on the same path of technical progression. They are getting smaller while at the same time doing more for us. This should not surprise us since small computers and microchips are already assisting and controlling more of our daily lives. Our cars, home appliances, and entertainment systems probably already have mini-computers that help their associated products give you better service. Now, personal digital assistants (PDA), such as those from Palm Inc. or Compaq, allow you to download your electronic calendar, address book and other personal information from your PC and take them with you when you are away. Is a Palm a personal computer? Many PDAs have more memory storage and processing power than PC's of a few years ago.

Simultaneously, our communications devices have been getting more powerful. When is the last time you used a rotary-dial telephone? More likely, you have been using a cellular digital telephone. This little device can not only place your call from virtually anywhere, but it can also help you remember whom you have to call and provide their home or office telephone numbers. In fact, you have probably programmed it so that you no longer have to know the telephone numbers any more. You simply tell your little phone to ring the person with whom you want to have a conversation. The cell phone contains an electronic address book and other personal information just like your PC.

**Sony Watchman**
**Color TV (2001)**
*Courtesy of Sony Electronics, Inc.*

**Western Electric's
202 Desk Phone (circa 1927)**
*Courtesy of Play Things of Past, Cleveland OH*

If you are fortunate enough to have a two-way pager, you may have it set up to receive and send your email messages among its other duties. In many ways, the numerous communication and information devices such as cell phones and two-way pagers are taking over for your PC when you are away from it.

So, if you have not been paying attention lately, you may want to take a closer look at the electronic devices around you. Your PC, digital assistants, and communication devices are starting to look and behave more and more alike, at least in terms of the conveniences they provide. Again, the natural progression is for technology to do more with less. What is interesting is that the technologies are migrating toward each other. Computers are shrinking and doing more communicating, while other information and communication devices are growing more powerful and providing more personal computer-related services. How soon before everyday appliances like our automobiles, televisions, microwaves, and other appliances start to become a highly connected and powerful network of computing devices that help us live our lives?

**Motorola's StarTAC
(circa 2000)**
*Courtesy of
Motorola, Inc.*

**The merging of technologies**

While the make and type of these systems are still quite diverse, we want the same conveniences and capabilities that these information devices provide us anywhere and at anytime. Providing these capabilities and conveniences is at the heart of any computer system, no matter how large or small the software. This is making the software engineer's job most difficult. How does one provide many of the same capabilities like email, calendaring, address tracking and scheduling across a very diverse, and seemingly growing, set of products? These software capabilities are just the start.

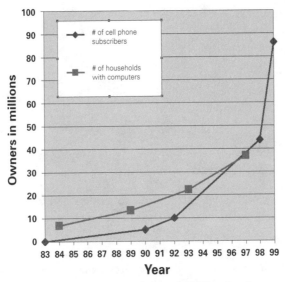

Census Bureau statistics and FCC estimates on number of household PCs and cellular phone subscribers in the United States.[1]

How soon until we have invoicing and billing capability on our cellular telephones? How soon will our refrigerator be able to tell our PDAs that we are out of milk (the inventory is low) and we get a restocking reminder on the way home from work? Is there a write once, run anywhere software solution that allows the software engineer to simply and easily provide many of the same capabilities to this diverse set of devices? We contend that there is a solution, or at least the makings of a solution, in Java and in particular the Java 2 Micro Edition.

If you thought the diversity in the number and type of computer systems was challenging, imagine trying to write software that operates in the "information appliance" arena that includes pagers, cellular phones, PDA's, television set-top boxes, point-of-sale terminals, and other consumer electronics. There are over a dozen cell phone manufactures alone. Each has different characteristics and interfaces.

As we will explore, the Java programming language has generally fulfilled the wish of software engineers looking for a means to write a single application that runs over all types of computer systems. Writing a single code base application that works on an Apple PC, Intel-based PC, Sun Microsystems Workstation, IBM mainframe, etc. is now possible. As you might imagine, the portability of a Java application across an even deeper and more diverse set of information appliances has attracted many to the possibility of running a once-written application on multiple types of systems.

What's more, there are an estimated 100 million cellular telephone users in the United States, with an estimated 530 million cellular telephone users worldwide by 2002. That compares to an estimated 50 million households with personal computers today. The exchange of information and ideas across this number of platforms is truly staggering. Imagine having some of the application capabilities of the Internet and our personal computers on a platform the size of a small cell phone. Imagine further that this transfer of capabilities is relatively seamless!

Of course, the challenge is to compact enough of Java's essentials into a very small package. This is the world of the Java 2 Micro Edition (J2ME). While it is still in its infancy, the convergence of the many technologies and resources surrounding these devices makes the advancement of J2ME as likely as it is necessary.

---

[1]  http://www.census.gov/population/www/socdemo/computer.html

# acknowledgments

Books do not write themselves, and, as we have come to understand all that is involved in putting one on the shelf, we now know that it takes much more than just the authors.

We would like to extend a special thank you to our publisher, Marjan Bace, and to the staff at Manning Publications who have contributed to this effort, as well as to the many people who took time out of their schedules to provide peer reviews, suggestions, and assistance. The reviewers included Carl Baldys, Mike Chan, Perry Dillard, Jon Eaves, Boran Gogetap, Lee Miles, Peter Mortier, Bryan Nehl and Tim Panton. Your work has not gone unnoticed and the final result is a reflection of this combined effort. Thank you.

JAMES WHITE

A lot of energy and time goes into writing a book, and a great number of people have influence on its outcome. Some are directly responsible for its delivery. To this end, I would like to first and foremost thank my co-author David Hemphill. His dedication and loyalty go beyond this single endeavor. He is a quiet yet steady friend that I have come to rely on for guidance on the roughest of days, not to mention, he's pretty darned smart. Thank you David. I would also like to thank the folks who spent hours reviewing the manuscripts in various stages and forms. In particular, I would like to thank Jan Emter and Carl Baldys for their evaluations and assistance. It's not a fun job, but they did it very well. We also owe a special thanks to the folks at esmertec who supported us with the use of their product and the reviews of the material on their product. A big thanks to Jon Eaves for his meticulous technical review. Finally, I would like to thank the editors and staff at Manning (Lianna Wlasiuk and Lois Patterson in particular) for allowing this dream to become a reality.

There are a number of other people who are indirectly responsible for this book's delivery. These are the people who have and will continue to shape my life on a daily basis, sometimes without knowing how much they do so. First, I would like to thank my parents, Ann and Jim White. Both teachers by profession, they have raised the eternal student. They have given me three gifts: life, enjoyment and satisfaction in hard work, and the unquenchable thirst to learn more. Thank you Mom and Dad. Second, I would like to thank my family, good friends, co-workers and colleagues who supported me in the efforts of this book, and in all else as well. In particular, I would like to thank Mike (my brother), Angie and Laura (sisters), Jim St. Aubin, Mike Carson, Phil and Kelly Davis, Todd Lauinger, and Larry Marchman. I would also like to thank Scott King. Forever the optimist, Scott would never let me say die, on this project or in any professional endeavor. Thank you Scott for your friendship and belief in me.

Last, but by all the laws that govern everything that is good and just, not least, I owe my deepest appreciation and devotion to my wife Kelly. I have never met a person so giving and caring in all my life. To say that she has carried me through this book, my career and adult life would be a vast understatement. Without her, this book and everything I do would hold no meaning. Thank you and I love you Kelly.

## DAVID HEMPHILL

When starting out on this project to co-author a book, I was concerned about the amount of time it would take and what life would be like during the months of writing the book. Well, as to how much time it takes, the answer is a rather simple one: all of it. As to what life is like, let's just say that if I did not have such a loving, supporting, caring and understanding family, this could have been painful. That said, I owe my deepest appreciation and gratitude to my wife, Amy Votava. Amy, thank you so much for all of your love and support during this last year. You mean a great deal to me and this last year has shown me the power and strength of our partnership. I truly appreciate how you have stood by me and helped me to see this dream to the end. Thank you. I love you.

I would also like to thank my daughter, Olivia, who, at age two, was unable to assist with editing and reviewing the book, but provided me with an ample supply of hugs and kisses as well as necessary distractions such as make-believe tea breaks with fresh "yellow" pie, spontaneous dancing and daily readings of *The Lorax* and other nontechnical literature.

A list of acknowledgments would not be complete without a word or two directed toward the guy who started all of this in the first place. This would be my co-author, friend, business partner and fellow software engineer Jim White. This project has been as enjoyable as it has been challenging and I am glad for the opportunity to have undertaken it with someone I have come to trust and respect more than just about anyone I have worked with. Jim, thank you for all of your hard work and dedication to this project.

I would also like to extend a special thank you to my parents Karen Stewart and Gary Hemphill. Dad, throughout the writing of this book I often heard your voice in my head saying, "Go the last mile and see it through." and Mom, thank you for driving up to Minnesota to help me find more time to write and to allow Amy and me to get reacquainted from time to time.

In addition, I owe thanks to the rest of my family: my sister, Julia Helbach, my stepparents John Stewart and Carol Hemphill and my in-laws James and Kathryn Votava. You have all provided me with love and inspiration during this last year, Amy and Olivia directly and indirectly many times over.

# about this book

*Java 2 Micro Edition* was written with the developer in mind. It is meant to be a guide that will serve as an introduction to J2ME technology, as well as a reference to more complex issues surrounding mobile/wireless computing. Our intent is to provide a practical overview of the J2ME programming environment by guiding the reader through detailed programming examples and tutorials. A basic understanding of Java programming is all that is required, in addition to a need for or interest in developing applications for mobile and wireless devices.

## INTENDED AUDIENCE

This book is intended, largely, for software engineers interested in writing Java applications. It turns out that if you know Java, you know enough to start writing applications for consumer electronics and embedded devices with a little help.

## ASSUMPTIONS

Throughout this book, applications will be developed in the Microsoft Windows environment. This will not affect the outcome of the product. However, if you choose to develop on another J2ME development platform, such as Solaris, Macintosh, or Linux, you will have to translate all applicable development instructions.

Readers of this text should have a fundamental knowledge of Java. The basic Java syntax is the same for J2ME as it is for other Java environments, including the familiar Java 2 Standard Edition (J2SE). However, the API for many Java classes, even those as basic as String, is diminished relative to the J2SE API. For those familiar with J2SE, we will explain our use of certain types and methods in code examples where a more common J2SE type or method would ordinarily be utilized.

We will also use the Unified Modeling Language (UML) to depict some of the application design. If you are not an object-oriented analyst, you should not be concerned. Our diagrams are pretty simple and merely help provide a picture of some of the structure in the application and how they relate to the classes and interfaces J2ME provides.

# ORGANIZATION

The book has fifteen chapters organized into four parts, followed by four appendices. We begin the book with an introduction to J2ME tools and technologies and then guide the reader through the development of a tutorial application.

## PART 1  Developing with J2ME

The first part of this book focuses on introducing the Java 2 Micro Edition.

Chapter 1 describes how J2ME fits into the larger picture of the Java 2 platform. The case for why J2ME is necessary and useful is discussed as well as the origins from which J2ME has sprung. Chapter 2 describes how J2ME is put together. This provides a context for how J2ME might be used to develop applications for consumer electronics and Internet appliances. This chapter provides a comprehensive, yet high-level tour of J2ME. Finally, before delving into the particulars of developing J2ME applications, chapter 3 offers a quick introduction to development environments, covering the particulars of how to obtain various J2ME development tools and technologies, as well as describing the example application that will be used throughout the book.

## PART 2  Developing for cellular phones and pagers

In chapters 4 through 7, we explore the CLDC and MIDP APIs in a tutorial application that was initially described in chapter 3. The tutorial application allows a customer to use a cell phone or two-way pager to obtain and view stock or mutual fund quotes. The tutorial allows us to see the major aspects of a J2ME application, namely the user interface, event handling, data storage, input/output, and network connectivity.

## PART 3  Developing for PDAs

In chapters 8 through 10, we explore using KJava with the CLDC API. KJava was originally created as a test and demonstration API by Sun for demonstrating the CLDC and KVM on Palm OS devices. Lacking a profile for PDA devices, companies, such as esmertec, have provided commercial implementations with their IDEs for developing Palm OS applications using KJava. Part 3 explores PDA development using the now familiar stock quote application. As in part 2, the tutorial application allows us to examine the major aspects of building a Palm OS application using KJava. This part of the book covers PDA features such as user interface, event handling, data storage, input/output, and network connectivity.

## PART 4  Developing for the enterprise: beyond the specifications

In chapters 11 through 15, we explore the more complex issues of putting together mobile and wireless applications. Chapter 11 leads off by examining the characteristics of a mobile and wireless architecture, focusing on using mobile and wireless devices in conjunction with enterprise technologies. The following chapters explore mobile and wireless computing for the enterprise, paying special attention to integrating the ability to communicate with servlets, JSPs and XML data sources. A more thorough examination of the network communication protocols is provided along with an in-depth look at the J2ME virtual machines and how they differ from the J2SE virtual machine. Finally, we spend some time reviewing related technologies, such as commercial, third-party J2ME solutions as well as non-J2ME solutions.

### Appendices

In the back of the book, four appendices offer an overview of J2ME tools, resources, history, and the J2ME Wireless Toolkit provided by Sun Microsystems.

## SOURCE CODE

Source code for all the programming examples in this book, including the examples in the tutorials, is available for download from the publisher's web site, www.manning.com/white.

### Code conventions

Courier typeface is used to denote code, as well as methods, objects, variable names, and class names. Code annotations accompany many segments of code. Certain annotations are marked with chronologically ordered bullets, such as ❶. These annotations have further explanations that follow the code. Code line continuations are indented.

## AUTHOR ONLINE

Purchase of *Java 2 Micro Edition* includes free access to a private web forum run by Manning Publications where you can make comments about the book, ask technical questions, and receive help from the authors and from other users. To access the forum and subscribe to it, point your web browser to www.manning.com/white. This page provides information on how to get on the forum once you are registered, what kind of help is available, and the rules of conduct on the forum.

Manning's commitment to our readers is to provide a venue where a meaningful dialog between individual readers and between readers and the authors can take place. It is not a commitment to any specific amount of participation on the part of the authors, whose contribution to the AO remains voluntary (and unpaid). We suggest you try asking the authors some challenging questions lest their interest stray!

The Author Online forum and the archives of previous discussions will be accessible from the publisher's web site as long as the book is in print.

# about the cover illustration

The figure on the cover of *Java 2 Micro Edition* is a "Muger Arabe Azanaghi," an Azanaghi Arab Woman from a region in the northernmost section of present-day Mauritania. The illustration is taken from a Spanish compendium of regional dress customs first published in Madrid in 1799. The book's title page states:

> *Coleccion general de los Trages que usan actualmente todas las Nacionas del Mundo desubierto, dibujados y grabados con la mayor exactitud por R.M.V.A.R. Obra muy util y en special para los que tienen la del viajero universal*

Which we translate, as literally as possible, thus:

> *General collection of costumes currently used in the nations of the known world, designed and printed with great exactitude by R.M.V.A.R. This work is very useful especially for those who hold themselves to be universal travelers*

Although nothing is known of the designers, engravers, and workers who colored this illustration by hand, the "exactitude" of their execution is evident in this drawing. The Azanaghi Arab Woman is of course just one of many figures in this colorful collection. Their diversity speaks vividly of the uniqueness and individuality of the world's towns and regions just 200 years ago. This was a time when the dress codes of two regions separated by a few dozen miles identified people uniquely as belonging to one or the other. The collection brings to life a sense of isolation and distance of that period—and of every other historic period except our own hyperkinetic present.

Dress codes have changed since then and the diversity by region, so rich at the time, has faded away. It is now often hard to tell the inhabitant of one continent from another. Perhaps, trying to view it optimistically, we have traded a cultural and visual diversity for a more varied personal life. Or a more varied and interesting intellectual and technical life.

We at Manning celebrate the inventiveness, the initiative and the fun of the computer business with book covers based on the rich diversity of regional life of two centuries ago, brought back to life by the pictures from this collection.

# Developing with J2ME

The first part of this book focuses on introducing the Java 2 Micro Edition. Chapter 1 describes how J2ME fits into the larger picture of the Java 2 platform. The case for why J2ME is necessary and useful is discussed as well as the origins from which J2ME has sprung. The second chapter describes how J2ME is put together. This provides a context for how J2ME might be used to develop applications for consumer electronics and Internet appliances. Chapter 2 also provides a comprehensive, yet high-level tour of J2ME. Finally, before delving into the particulars of developing J2ME applications, chapter 3 provides a quick introduction to the development environments, covering the particulars of how to obtain various J2ME development tools and technologies as well as describing the example application that will be used throughout the book.

**C H A P T E R   1**

# Introduction

If you are involved in the development of software systems, and in particular software written in the Java programming language, yet do not know much about J2ME, you probably have many questions. What is J2ME and where did it come from? How does it relate to the Java I know and have come to enjoy? On what kinds of small things does Java run? Why is Java on small devices important? Where is J2ME going? We attempt to answer these questions and more in this introductory chapter.

## 1.1   SO WHAT IS J2ME ANYWAY?

Java 2 Micro Edition or J2ME is a development and runtime environment designed to put Java software on consumer electronics and embedded devices. As with many things in life, one size does not always fit all. Likewise, a single serving size of Java that fits and runs on every thing from a mainframe to a cellular telephone is impractical.

Java has become one of the most popular programming languages of our time. This is due, in no small part, to Java's ability to run on virtually any platform. J2ME is about making the Java programming language available on an even larger and more diverse set of platforms. In particular, J2ME brings Java to the world of personal information, communication, and computing devices. Usually, these devices are smaller and less powerful than traditional computing devices. As such, J2ME technology is an effort to condense and reduce standard Java into as small a footprint as possible.

The development of J2ME was initiated by Sun Microsystems, but is now supported by some of the biggest consumer electronics and embedded device manufacturers in the world. In particular, many of the world's mobile and wireless technology vendors are either exploring or actively participating in J2ME technology, or they are working on competing products. Those that support J2ME do so under a community process developed by Sun to standardize and guide the future direction of all aspects of the Java Platform. This process is called the Java Community Process (JCP) and it is an important part of the advancement of Java and J2ME, as will be discussed later in this chapter.

While Java runs on everything from mainframes to laptops, it was not until relatively recently that Sun began to re-entertain the idea of putting Java back into small devices. We say re-entertain because Java was initially developed to assist Sun developers in assembling a network of digitally controlled consumer devices (TV, VCR, video disc players, and so forth).

Java's rebirth, through J2ME, as a programming language and software platform for small things is significant in that the sheer number of these devices will far exceed the number of computer systems in the near future. As a young or reborn technology, J2ME is still evolving and the base of support for J2ME is still growing. However, J2ME and other Java-based competing solutions offer a great deal of hope to the software engineering community that is faced with the need to support an overwhelming number of platforms in the future.

### 1.1.1 Where is J2ME being applied?

J2ME is a technology that has found its way into many consumer electronic and embedded devices, some of which you use on a daily basis. It is a young technology that is working its way into even more items that we will use daily. In fact, J2ME is a technology with which we will likely come in contact more often than standard Java or other programming language software. This is because J2ME software applications are destined for very personal devices on which we humans have become dependent. How soon will this occur? A number of cellular telephones already contain J2ME technology.

J2ME software applications will likely control or provide some type of service on our cellular telephones, pagers, personal digital assistants (PDAs), televisions, VCRs, wristwatches, home appliances, electronic entertainment systems, and so forth. J2ME applications will help us make telephone calls and order products. They will help us communicate with friends and neighbors. They will help us find our favorite television show or remind us to feed the dog, and it may be a J2ME game that you play when it comes time to relax. Of course, J2ME applications will also help business too. J2ME applications are helping to extend corporate enterprise systems (both data and applications) to wireless and mobile computing devices. Inventory and customer management, order entry and tracking, and sales force automation may soon be driven by J2ME applications literally running from devices in the palms of employees' hands.

## 1.2 WHAT IS A SMALL DEVICE?

Up to this point, we have tried to refer generically to the platform running a J2ME or other competing Java application as a "device." In fact, we refer to these devices even more generically in the subtitle of this book as "small things." In a few instances, we have used the phrases: information device, consumer electronics, embedded device or our favorite, small device. It is important that we define the vast array of "small devices" and make you aware of which devices in this array J2ME targets. As will be discussed in chapter 2, it is important to know where J2ME is applied since such target devices often define the various pieces and structure of the J2ME architecture.

### 1.2.1 The vast consumer space

Exactly what is a device? Sun claims that J2ME is meant to address "the vast consumer space which covers the range of extremely tiny commodities, such as smart cards or a pager, all the way up to the set-top box, an appliance almost as powerful as a computer."[1] Let's define some of these terms: A *smart card* is a credit card-sized plastic device with an integrated circuit built inside. A *set-top box* is a consumer electronic device that produces output to a conventional television while also connected to a communications channel to allow the user or, more appropriately, television viewer, to interact in some way.

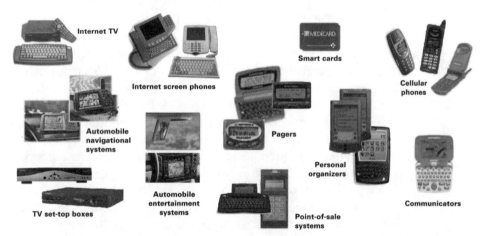

**Figure 1.1   The picture above provides a glimpse of some of the devices encompassing the vast consumer electronics and embedded device space. While Java, through J2ME, may not be available on all of these platforms today, it offers the hope of providing a single programming language to support this vast array of devices in the future. As a programming language designed to run on any platform, Java has been used for developing software on all of these devices and J2ME technology has been applied to a predominance of these devices. However, as we will discuss, J2ME's applicability at the fringes of this vast space can be confusing based on additional Java technologies and specifications such as Java Card and EmbeddedJava.**

---

[1]   http://java.sun.com/j2me/

The "vast consumer space" is filled with devices that include:

- pagers
- cellular telephones
- personal digital assistants or organizers
- point of sale systems
- pocket communicators
- Internet screen telephones
- automobile navigation and entertainment systems
- Internet television sets

Figure 1.1 shows many of these devices.

## 1.2.2   Consumer electronic and embedded devices

While Sun and others associated with the development of J2ME applications still hold to the statement that J2ME is "targeted at consumer electronics and embedded devices,"[2] questions arise as to whether this includes the entire consumer electronics and embedded device space. Sun's own web sites offer conflicting information. For example, many of Sun's web pages on J2ME indicate that J2ME technology includes smart card technology, while Java Card web pages claim that Java Card technology is a complementary technology to J2ME.[3]

Generally, J2ME addresses devices with minimal memory, communications bandwidth, power, and user interface capabilities. Therefore, J2ME is usually considered to address Java programming needs in devices that are larger than smart cards but smaller than personal computers. A term often used for these sorts of devices is *information appliance*. Information appliances provide less computing power than a personal computer and are considered to have a special function. In many cases, these devices are more personal in nature, that is, they are owned and operated by a single individual. Furthermore, unlike a laptop, these computing devices are almost always carried with their owner, in a pocket, purse or coat pocket, also making them more personalized.

As a separate technology, Java for smart cards (Java Card technology) has its own specification. For devices with more memory, power, and capabilities, there is, of course, the Java 2 Standard Edition (J2SE) specification that dictates Java as it is used in personal computers.

We disagree with including "embedded" devices in the group of devices supported by J2ME. While the issue is minor and the distinction will be discussed later in a review of other technologies with respect to J2ME (chapter 15), the whole space of embedded devices is also covered by a separate Sun specification and technology called EmbeddedJava. Therefore, for the purposes of this book, the term "device" will refer

---

[2]   http://java.sun.com/products/cldc/faqs.html
[3]   http://java.sun.com/products/javacard/datasheet.html

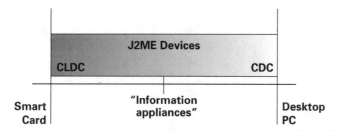

**Figure 1.2** Devices that are specifically supported by J2ME fall between the Smart Card and the desktop or laptop computer. These devices, often referred to collectively as information appliances, include, but are not limited to cell phones, pagers, PDAs, set-top boxes, and Internet phones. CLDC and CDC are specifications that define J2ME at opposite ends of the device spectrum. More information on these specifications is provided in chapter 2.

to the array of electronic devices and information appliances that range from just below the personal computer down to, but not including, the smart card.

You can, and will undoubtedly, find individuals who disagree with this demarcation. However, we find it to be the general consensus and will stick to this definition of a device throughout the remainder of the book.

## 1.3 *J2ME'S ROLE IN WIRELESS AND MOBILE APPLICATIONS*

J2ME is often referred to as Java for wireless and mobile devices. While J2ME technology is used in many wireless and mobile devices, J2ME is not used exclusively in these environments. We do not want to diminish J2ME's role and importance in mobile and wireless applications. However, it is important to realize that J2ME is about more than mobile and wireless applications.

### 1.3.1 Is J2ME mobile?

Mobile devices are defined as those computing devices that are small enough to be easily carried and used while in transport. They provide users with a portion of computing capabilities and information that is available from fixed information systems at home or their place of business. In general, most mobile devices allow themselves to be synchronized with the fixed systems for software and data updates.

As an example, an office may have a customer management application that can provide sales force personnel with information on customers. A mobile device would likely allow a sales person to download a limited amount of customer data for a limited number of customers to use while on the road. Updates to any data on the mobile device would need to be reconciled with the office's customer management system on the sales person's return.

Given this kind of definition, the term mobile is subject to change. In fact, there was a time when we may have called a twenty-pound laptop mobile. Certainly, many, but not all, of the devices that J2ME targets can be considered mobile. PDAs, cell phones, and so forth can certainly be considered mobile platforms when they are provided with software and data. However, set-top boxes, for example, are not meant to be mobile devices. While these devices can run J2ME programs, they are not mobile.

Furthermore, many other Java technologies, J2SE and Java Card included, are running in mobile systems. So while J2ME is an important Java technology for mobile platforms, it is not *the* Java technology for mobile platforms. And Java is not the only solution. There are several technologies that provide mobile applications and data for mobile devices. In fact, many organizations provide tools for downloading a slice of corporate data to a personal device for use while not at the office. These are mobile solutions.

The term "mobile" simply defines the capability or state of the device. So is J2ME mobile? Because mobile devices are usually smaller and more resource constrained, J2ME is a viable development solution for these constrained devices. Therefore, J2ME can and often does play an important role in mobile devices, but the term mobile does not categorize all J2ME applications.

## 1.3.2    Is J2ME wireless?

A wireless device is simply a device capable of communicating or networking without wires or cable. Many J2ME devices are wireless. Cellular telephones, pagers, and pocket communicators are just some of the wireless communications devices that can use J2ME technology. The list of such devices is ever expanding. Many of today's laptops and PDAs provide wireless communication adapters to allow these devices to work in a wireless fashion.

Wireless devices are intended to behave as if they were directly connected to the network with a wire. From a user's perspective, it should appear that any data or application is local to that device or directly connected to the device providing the data or application. For example, a sales person could use a cell phone to look up information on a customer from a customer management system back at the office. To the sales person, it might appear that the data and/or application obtaining and displaying the information is local to the phone when in reality, the data has merely been wirelessly transmitted to the sales person's device.

However, there are several devices that J2ME targets that are not wireless. Again, set-top boxes, Internet screen telephones and televisions are usually wired. In fact, as we will see in future discussions, a large portion of J2ME is set aside for systems that are expected to have a reliable, rich, and high fidelity network connection, which today usually means having connectivity through a wire or cable. The J2ME technology supports many wireless devices, but it is not *the* Java technology for wireless computing. In fact, other technologies such as the Wireless Access Protocol and the Wireless Markup Language are meant to provide wireless capabilities to devices without necessarily providing mobile applications (chapter 15).

Wireless defines the type of communications used by the device. J2ME, therefore, can be and often is an important part of a wireless solution. But while Java and J2ME may be used in wireless devices and applications, not all J2ME applications are wireless.

### 1.3.3   Wireless vs. mobile

The terms wireless and mobile are often used congruently. Erroneously, these adjectives are automatically applied to J2ME applications. Because J2ME devices are often small and can hold a certain amount of data and applications, which are easily transported, J2ME can be and often is used in mobile systems. Likewise, because J2ME is often used in applications that communicate information back and forth across a wireless network, J2ME can be and often is used in wireless systems. Again, however, this does not mean that J2ME applications are all wireless and mobile.

A PDA device holding a small amount of customer data and an application to view and update the customer data is mobile, but not necessarily wireless. If the user is required to connect the device up to a network or other device with some sort of cord in order to get new data or download updated data, then it remains a mobile but wired device.

Alternatively, a cell phone could be equipped with a small browser that allows the device to pull down special or mini-web pages. This device is now considered wireless, but it is not mobile. In order to be mobile, the device must provide some value, in the form of data or application function, when not connected to other systems.

Much of the confusion between wireless and mobile exists because many J2ME applications are designed to work in both a mobile and wireless fashion. Say, for example, the customer information application built for a PDA device is also equipped with a means to call up and ask for new or updated customers that can then be transmitted to the device wirelessly and stored on the device for later retrieval. Now the PDA device is both mobile and wireless.

In this book, we examine J2ME technology that can help make mobile and wireless applications.

## 1.4   *THE JAVA 2 EDITION TRILOGY*

Like all development environments and programming languages, Java has evolved. Many features and capabilities have been added to Java since its initial release. It has also been improved in terms of its performance, efficiencies and reliability. Thus, the "2" in Java 2 refers to its current major version. Sun Microsystems, the creator and manager of Java, has grouped the Java 2 version into three editions:

- Standard Edition (J2SE)
- Enterprise Edition (J2EE)
- Micro Edition (J2ME)

Each edition addresses the Java needs of a particular set of applications. J2ME is the third and latest of three editions of the Java 2 version.

One of the most common exclamations on the part of new Java developers is: "Wow, look at all those packages and classes." One of Java's selling points is the fact that it ships "out of the box" with a rich set of tools, classes, and application programming interfaces (APIs) that provide many common, foundational application components. In theory, these classes and APIs provide the basic frameworks that allow applications to be developed faster. There are over 5,000 classes in the standard download of the Software Development Kit (SDK). Database connectivity, various input/output mechanisms, exception/error handling, and user interface classes are just a few of the many basic functions that come with your standard Java development environments.

As the Java development environment has grown and expanded to fulfill numerous application needs, the number of available Java packages and classes has expanded. Most notably, Java support has spread to include networking, interoperability, and distributed components and processing.

Because the needs of the Java community have broadened, and the sheer number of APIs has grown, Sun established three editions of the Java platform to better address the needs of each general community of application developers. This split in editions occurred at the time Sun released Java 2. The editions do not really provide any additional Java functionality. Instead they are a repackaging of Java technology into logical groupings based on typical developmental use.

There have been claims that another reason for the split in editions is that Sun has used this mechanism for generating revenue. The argument goes that the development environment or JDK (now SDK) and Java Runtime Environment (JRE) have always been free products. The other editions of Java, which fall under different license agreements, allow Sun to recoup some of the revenue lost on the base, no-cost products.

Whatever the real reason for the separation, Java developers must now be aware of the three editions of the Java platform and how they can be applied to their particular development problems. Fundamentally, the three editions are still very similar. The language syntax and base architecture of each edition is generally the same. However, as their names suggest, each edition now offers developers unique features applicable to the size of devices for which the edition was built.

### 1.4.1    J2SE

The Java 2, Standard Edition (J2SE) is the basic Java environment. Its implementations provide the core Java classes and APIs that allow for the development and runtime of standard client and server applications, including applications that run in a web browser.

### 1.4.2    J2EE

The Java 2 Enterprise Edition (J2EE) is a grouping of several Java APIs and non-Java technologies. It is generally used for creating multi-tiered and potentially distributed applications. J2EE technologies can serve as the guts as well as the glue that bring today's large multi-tiered, heterogeneous applications together. J2EE is often described as middleware or server side technologies, but this is a bit limiting. In fact, J2EE includes technologies that are or can be used in all layers of information systems. Take JDBC for example. It may be used to access data from a client Java applet, a middle tier Java servlet or a backend Enterprise JavaBean. Remember that J2EE includes some technologies that are not controlled by Sun and are not necessarily directly connected to Java, such as XML and CORBA. J2EE is another Java technology that can fill dozens of books. Please see other publications, such as *Distributed Programming with Java* by Qusay H. Mahmoud, *Server-Based Java Programming* by Ted Neword and *Java Servlets by Example* by Alan Williamson, Manning Publications, for information on these and other related J2EE technologies.

### 1.4.3    J2ME

Sun introduced Java 2, Micro Edition (J2ME) in June 1999 at the annual JavaOne convention. J2ME is designed to address the Java needs of the consumer electronics and embedded devices community. Initially, J2ME was built for devices with limited power, network connectivity (often wireless), and graphical user interface capabilities. Today, as we shall see, J2ME technology has expanded to cover a somewhat wider array of devices from pagers up to, but not necessarily including, the personal computer.

### 1.4.4    Why we need J2ME

Since Java was initially intended for consumer electronic devices, a natural question may be why another edition? Why not just use the standard Java for small devices? Beyond the issues of needing to separate the multitude of APIs into three distinct editions for better organization and, possibly, Sun's need to recapture revenue, there is another, more compelling, reason for introducing another Java edition: the devices for which J2ME is targeted have specialized needs.

These devices have different software requirements than larger application software environments. In general, the software must have a small footprint. In some cases, the total memory allotted to the device for the Java application, Java classes, and virtual machine is measured in hundreds of kilobytes. That's small!

Furthermore, software applications destined for these consumer electronics and embedded devices usually have unique deployment mechanisms. For example, PDA devices often have what is known as a device "cradle" that is attached to a desktop computer for downloading applications and data.

Finally, these devices have user interface, networking and other needs that cannot be addressed with an all-encompassing (i.e. sizeable footprint) Java API. Java's Swing package for user interface development could certainly be enlarged to include components for building graphical user interfaces for small screens such as those found on cellular telephones. But could that package then fit in the memory of a cell phone?

J2ME addresses the fact that a one-size-fits-all Java environment does not really make sense for all devices. The same principles of platform independence, language syntax, security, and reliability are adhered to in all editions of Java, including J2ME. However, the separate edition addresses the specific needs inherent in the range of small devices that the J2ME edition covers.

It is worth noting, however, that Sun considers upward scalability from J2ME to another edition of Java (namely the J2SE or J2EE) an important feature of J2ME.

Should your application ever grow beyond the confines of a small device, the transition up to a larger, more powerful Java environment may be possible depending on your application's architecture.

## 1.5    THE CASE FOR JAVA

Before we get too deeply into the benefits of J2ME, perhaps we should step back and ask an even more fundamental question: specifically, why is the Java programming language important to software developers for consumer electronics and embedded devices? If you have already worked with Java, this discussion probably won't cover any new ground. However, if you are new to Java, it's worthwhile to review some of the reasons why Java is a popular programming language and why it is a solid contender in the small device arena.

### 1.5.1    Is Java right for small devices?

As has already been mentioned, Java was first designed and built as a common platform to support software development for a set of networked consumer electronic devices. Given Java's initial reason for being, it would seem only natural and appropriate that it return to its roots to be used in a heterogeneous collection of small information devices.

The key term here is heterogeneous! If you are targeting a particular information device, you may find that another programming language or development environment meets your needs just as well if not better than Java. For example, many of today's PDA manufacturers supply programming development kits that produce applications for their systems. These kits often take advantage of features for the specific platform and typically perform better on the target device than programs developed with more generic programming languages such as Java. Furthermore, Java may not have as small a footprint in comparison to many proprietary development environments or other programming languages. As has been discussed, Java has a rich set of classes and APIs that come with the base environments. A device manufacturer does not have to offer such a rich environment. Because many of these programming environments and languages produce executable code such as C, unused features are eliminated at compile time. In contrast, Java's runtime environment must be ready to interpret any and all supported instructions.

So where is your application going to live? Will it run on a variety of small information devices such as pagers, PDAs, cellular phones, and maybe even a set-top-box? If so, you want portability. You are going to want to write the application as few times as possible. Programs written in manufacturers' proprietary development environments or other programming languages will almost certainly not port to such a wide range of devices.

Choosing your programming language is a relatively straightforward issue. Do you want to write an application once and run it on a variety of platforms? If so, Java's

Write Once, Run Anywhere (WORA) platform independence mantra should certainly make it a candidate programming language for you to consider.

Are there other reasons for using Java in small things? Well, in some cases, Java may be the only way to deploy an application to a device. For example, some cell phone manufacturers support only Java.

When considering what programming language to use for applications that run on small devices, you may also want to consider what programming languages you already use on the larger devices and systems. If you already have Java applications running on your servers and desktop systems, putting Java in small devices eliminates the use of another language in your development environment. Furthermore, it may also lead to some code reuse opportunities.

### 1.5.2    Java's beneficial features

Java has a lot to offer. Beyond Java's platform independence, it has a number of features that make it an attractive programming language. These features make Java a likely candidate for software applications regardless of the size or shape of the target platform.

#### Secure

Security was a concern to the designers and developers of Java from the beginning. Even in the development of a programming language initially intended for consumer electronic devices, the developers knew that these devices were going to be networked and therefore vulnerable to malicious attacks from other systems on the network. As Java came to be the programming language of the Web, and because security was built into Java from the beginning, it is well suited to address the security issues associated with the Internet.

#### Reliable

Java's reliability stems from not having to manage some of the lower-level resources such as memory and pointers. Developers are then able to manage information as an object or set of objects, in a manner more akin to how it is done in the real world. Low-level resources like pointers tend to be the often forgotten, memory-busting programming items that cause memory leaks and inadvertent memory access in software applications. Java places the burden of managing references to memory on a garbage collection system where these memory references will be more methodically maintained than in languages such as C++ where the burden is on the programmer.

#### Object-oriented

Java is considered a true object-oriented language. Why is being an object-oriented language important? For starters, object-oriented applications are considered easier to build and maintain. This is because object-oriented programming structures actively encourage developers to organize applications into easy-to-understand, manageable pieces. Large complicated applications are then tackled by assembling many smaller and more digestible pieces. These pieces or, more appropriately objects, contain both behavior and data. Keeping the data and the behavior in an object helps insure that only the code responsible for the data can change the data.

Finally, objects, as representations of things in the real world, tend to allow more people to take part and understand the inner workings of the application. In other words, objects tend to be self-documenting in nature. A businessperson may not understand what a two-page function or procedure does, but he or she may have a pretty good idea of what a `Savings_Account` object does.

### Free

Everyone likes free stuff. Programmers and managers of programmers are no exception. The basic Java development and runtime environments are free. A reference implementation of the J2ME and set of development tools are available from Sun's Java web site (www.java.sun.com).

This is not to say that all Java development and runtime environments are free. Sun maintains control of Java. They offer the basic reference implementations, development tools, class API, and runtime environment for free. However, should you require features outside of the basic environment, you may find yourself outside of the free license agreements. Furthermore, integrated development environments (IDE), server systems, test tools, and a myriad of other tools and products that a development team may want to have in order to make themselves more productive and provide a better quality product are usually not free. The important point, though, is that learning the language, and developing your first application in Java costs little or nothing.

### Simple

Java is simple. This statement always troubles us a bit and bears a little explaining. Java is simple in that if you are familiar with almost any other object-oriented programming language, Java's syntax will seem relatively straightforward and easy to learn. Java's syntax is closely aligned with C++ and includes many of the beneficial features found in other programming languages. The off-hand comment by many experienced programmers is that Java is C++ done right. For example, Java is statically typed. This allows the compiler to catch many coding errors. Also, memory and garbage collection are handled by the Java virtual machine. This capability is usually music to the ears of anyone who has spent many a late night trying to find a memory leak in a C++ or C program. These features of course come at a price, which includes the cost of running the application inside of a virtual machine.

What is not so simple about Java are the nuances of object-oriented development, the multitude of pre-built Java classes that are available with even the most basic of Java environments, understanding the features and aspects of Java that make it perform well or poorly, and many other aspects of Java that make mastering it more of a lengthy project. So, take the claims of simplicity with a grain of salt and base them on your own personal background and experience.

### Other useful features

There are many features that make Java an ideal programming language. Some of the reasons may or may not apply to your given application needs. Multi-threading, exception/error handling, dynamic binding, and performance are just some of the additional reasons why Java is a good programming environment.

Many of the positive features associated with Java originate from the language's beginnings. Throughout its history, Java has expanded to more platforms and environments. Ironically, as has already been alluded to, Java started as a programming language for consumer electronic devices.

## 1.6   ORIGINS OF J2ME

There was a time when "Java" was known as a nickname for the favorite morning drink. For anyone else familiar with or engaged in software development, it's hard to image that the term "Java" has another meaning that is not inexorably tied to today's most popular programming language. Java has become one of the most popular solutions in the holster of "silver bullets" that many of today's software developers use in creating Internet, e-commerce, enterprise-wide and mission critical applications. How did Java come into being? You might find it interesting that Java did not start out as the programming language to control the Internet. Java had humble beginnings that started with small things, namely consumer electronics. In the last few years, Java has had a rebirth of sorts to address the software needs of a burgeoning set of personal computing devices coming to the world marketplace.

### 1.6.1   Java's origins

Java was born in the early 1990's. It was initially called Oak and it was developed for a project that was attempting to develop a set of networked consumer electronic devices that could be programmed from a handheld device similar to a personal digital assistant. At the time, no single programming language was available to address the software needs of the various digitally controlled consumer devices such as televisions, video recorders and disc players, etc. Thus Java had humble beginnings as a means to network and program home entertainment equipment. In a way, early J2ME was the start of the whole Java effort.

Oak, renamed Java after it was discovered that another programming language was already called Oak, saw new life and an expanded role in software development as the Internet began to emerge in the mid-1990s. The requirement, born of the Internet age, for reliable and secure software applications that could be written once for an undetermined number of potential computer systems fit perfectly with Java's original design for consumer electronic devices. With a foothold in its use for the Internet and the World Wide Web and a renewed reason for being, Java expanded to serve in almost every nook and cranny of current software development. Its versatility, many features, and, of course, platform independence have made Java a major component of modern software technology.

### 1.6.2 The return of Java in small devices

Throughout Java's history, Sun and other organizations have used Java in many sizes and shapes of computing devices. However, special attention and focus for using Java on small and often personal computing devices was not organized (and guided by specification) until the late 1990s. As more powerful computing and communication devices have recently been packed into smaller and more personal computing devices, a renewed interest has been placed in Java for these systems. In June of 1999, at the 1999 JavaOne conference, Sun introduced the three platform editions of Java: the J2SE, J2EE, and J2ME. As part of its unveiling of J2ME, Sun also introduced the first J2ME virtual machine, namely a preview version of the KVM or K Virtual Machine. The official return of Java in small devices was complete.

For a more detailed look at Java's history and evolution and J2ME's place in this history, we encourage the interested reader to visit appendix C.

## 1.7 THE J2ME COMMUNITY

It should come as little surprise that some of the biggest supporters of J2ME technology are the manufacturers of small devices like cell phones, pagers, and PDAs such as Motorola, Ericsson, Nokia, Research In Motion, Palm, Siemens, and others. Supporters also include members of the home, office and automobile electronics manufacturers such as Fujitsu, Hitachi, Matsushita (Panasonic), Mitsubishi, Samsung, Sharp, and SONY. Traditional software vendors like Oracle are also participating.

Many of these organizations have directly participated in one or more of the various JCP expert groups that developed or revised the numerous J2ME specifications. Others have endorsed and supported J2ME specifications by adopting J2ME technology in many of their product offerings.

J2ME is not the only game in town. Companies such as IBM and Hewlett-Packard have developed their own Java environments for smaller and embedded devices. While these companies may be developing competing Java products, it is clear that all of these organizations see the benefit of bringing Java to the consumer electronic and embedded device platform.

### 1.7.1 J2ME's guiding light, the Java Community Process

Supporters of J2ME participate in the improvement and advancement of specifications through the Java Community Process. We briefly mentioned the Java Community Process (JCP) earlier in this chapter. It is a formal process established by Sun Microsystems to develop and revise Java technology specifications in cooperation with the Java user community. Each specification developed in the JCP must go through a well-defined process.

The process starts with a request from the Java community at large to develop a new specification or revise an existing specification. The request can then be accepted or rejected by Sun's Process Management Office.

If accepted, the Process Management Office forms an expert group to work on the specification. This group develops a participant's draft specification. The expert group reviews and refines their draft for a period of time and then promotes the draft to that of public draft. The public draft is then opened to the Java community at large for public review and comment. On sufficient review and updates to the public draft, the Process Management Office will promote the draft to that of final release of a specification, post the release, and disband the expert group. At this time, a specification enters maintenance. Various portions of J2ME stand in all phases of this process. As you become more involved in J2ME or Java development, following (or maybe even participating in) the JCP becomes a professional routine.

## 1.8    *J2ME PRODUCTS AND ALTERNATIVES*

While Sun has led many of the developments in Java, it does not have a lock on the technology. This is perhaps most evident in the world of small consumer electronics and embedded devices where other organizations have made products available before J2ME was released.

J2ME is not an implementation but rather a specification (or more precisely a series of specifications). Sun has implementations of some of the specifications, but so do other organizations. Why offer another implementation of J2ME? Well, Sun has not always been the best implementer of the specifications that they have fostered and led. For example, it is generally considered throughout the Java community that IBM provides a much faster and superior Java compiler called Jikes. Likewise, other organizations are building Java virtual machines and APIs that satisfy the J2ME specifications but which have smaller footprints and better performance than the SUN implementations.

There are other Java competitors to J2ME that run in the same general environment, but do not comply with J2ME specifications. Discounting Sun's early efforts with Java on consumer electronics, J2ME is a very young technology. It also addresses a very difficult problem. Namely, this problem is how to write software in a single programming language for devices as diverse as a pager and a television set-top box. Other organizations have decided to focus on providing Java to a less diverse set of target devices. Still other organizations have taken an approach that allows developers to use the Java programming language without removing concerns over target device peculiarities. In other words, they are placing more responsibility on the programmer to insure applications are truly platform-independent.

Of course, another alternative to J2ME is not using Java at all, but instead using another programming language such as C/C++ or using a device manufacturers provided in a software development kit. We have already discussed the issues associated with using and not using Java. In general, Java provides the degree of platform independence that is important to software producers for a wide range of devices. Platform independence may not, however, be important to single-device developers, in which case using another programming language may not only be a valid choice but may be preferred. In chapter 15, we examine technologies that compete with J2ME, and technologies that play a supporting and ancillary role to J2ME.

## 1.9    SUMMARY

In this chapter, we introduced and defined J2ME. As J2ME is also a part of Sun Microsystems's entire Java 2 platform, Sun has positioned J2ME with relation to the other Java 2 editions, namely J2SE and J2EE. We also looked at why another edition of Java is necessary and what Java has to offer to developers of software for consumer electronics and embedded devices. Through an examination of Java and J2ME's history, we saw that Java has really come home again to the small device as Java was initially intended to help bridge common software needs in the consumer electronics market. The JCP has played an instrumental role in organizing the Java community in efforts to improve and advance not only J2ME, but all of the various Java technologies and APIs. In order to help specify where J2ME is actually used, we provided our definition of the "small device" which roughly ranges noninclusively between the smart card and a laptop computer. Finally, we closed this chapter with some discussion on J2ME's relationship to terms such as wireless and mobile as well as to J2ME products.

Many of the topics mentioned in this chapter will be addressed in more detail throughout this book. In the next chapter, we look at the organization and structure, commonly termed the architecture, of J2ME.

# CHAPTER 2

# J2ME architecture

In this chapter you will be introduced to the fundamental pieces that make up J2ME. These include configurations, profiles, and virtual machines. However, before delving into these pieces of the architecture, let us first discuss the goals of the J2ME architecture.

## 2.1  GOALS OF THE J2ME ARCHITECTURE

J2ME has a much different set of goals when compared to J2SE and J2EE, resulting in a much different architecture. The following is a summary of key goals driving the J2ME architecture:

- Provide support to a variety of devices with different capabilities. These devices often vary in the areas of user interface, data storage, network connectivity and bandwidth, memory budgets, power consumption, security, and deployment requirements.

- Provide an architecture that can be optimized for small spaces and have a smaller footprint.

- Focus on devices that can be highly personalized, often used by a single person.

- Provide network connectivity across a varied range of networking capabilities and services. Network connectivity is often vital to devices in the J2ME space and their capabilities range from low bandwidth, wireless, and intermittent connections to high-fidelity, high-bandwidth connections.

- Provide an optimized means for delivering applications and data over a network connection. Often the network is the preferred method of delivering J2ME applications to devices. Applications must have the ability to be installed on the device or loaded directly into memory and discarded after execution.

- Maximize cross-platform capabilities of the Java language while taking advantage of each device's unique capabilities and constraints.

- Maximize flexibility and provide a means to support a rapidly changing marketplace and adapt to existing and unforeseen applications.

- Provide a means for third-party developers to write and deploy applications to J2ME-supported devices independent of the Original Equipment Manufacturer (OEM).

- Provide a means to scale applications across devices with different capabilities, features, and processing abilities.

In the sections that follow we take a closer look at a few of these goals.

### 2.1.1 Support for multiple devices

Support for multiple devices is a goal that has greatly influenced the J2ME architecture. In the J2ME space devices range from cell phones, that may have as little as 160kB of memory and are powered by batteries, all the way up to TV set-top boxes that are nearly as powerful as a desktop computer and plug into the wall. Unlike the J2SE and J2EE architectures, which are designed with desktop and server computers in mind, the J2ME architecture must be flexible and malleable enough to accommodate the constraints and unique features of smaller consumer electronics devices while not imposing unnecessary restrictions on more powerful devices and Internet appliances.

A key goal that comes with supporting multiple device types is allowing for portability between devices. To this end, J2ME identifies core Java features that need to be available on all platforms. These features include classes from `java.lang`, `java.util` and `java.io`. However, it is important to note that in some cases J2ME supports only a subset of the classes and methods of these packages as core functionality found on all J2ME platforms.

### 2.1.2 Support for device-specific functionality

Flexibility is another goal that significantly influences the J2ME architecture. Consumer electronic devices and Internet appliances often cater to specific uses rather than serve as a general-purpose computational machine. For example, a cell phone serves a different purpose than, say a Java-enabled exercise bicycle. An onboard car navigation system may need to use global satellite positioning technology to perform its tasks whereas a Java-enabled TV set-top box would make little use of such capabilities. In addition to performing more specific roles, the devices themselves tend to be very personalized. A cell phone is likely to be used by only one person. PDAs tend to store information specific to the person who owns the device. A TV is typically used by a family or small group of people for specific activities.

The modularity of the J2ME architecture is a good example of how J2ME accommodates flexibility. Unlike J2SE that provides a rich feature set as a single group, J2ME provides a means for partitioning these capabilities into independent units of functionality. Let us examine the use of RMI (Remote Method Invocation) as an example. A cellular phone may be significantly more limited in terms of memory, processing power, and so forth than a communicator class PDA such as an iPaq. Due to the cellular phone limitations, it may not be practical or feasible to use RMI within an application. Furthermore, to reduce the footprint of the J2ME libraries, it is not desirable to require that RMI features be present in the cellular phone's installation of J2ME. However, since a more powerful device would be able to handle the demands of RMI, should an application choose to use such features, there needs to be a way to accommodate this situation as well. For reasons such as this, J2ME has partitioned Java functionality into various groups to allow different devices to require and support different features of Java as they apply to each device. This helps optimize Java for specific devices without restricting capabilities.

### 2.1.3 Maintaining a common architecture

So you may be asking, why maintain a common architecture? Would it not be easier to build a different Java edition to cater to each of these goals?

The answer to this question brings us back to portability and flexibility. A common architecture across different devices provides a foundation that allows applications to be more easily ported, if not directly deployable, across devices. Supporting multiple, device-specific architectures would make porting applications between even the most similar devices difficult and expensive to support.

A single, flexible architecture is more cost-effective to maintain than multiple, special purpose architectures that cater to one or a few devices. A common architecture takes advantage of the similarities between devices and allows reuse across applications. In the case where different devices require different capabilities to be supported, the common architecture can be extended or configured to cater to the specific functionality.

In addition to being portable and maintainable, J2ME needs to be extendible. As new devices come onto the market, J2ME needs to be able to quickly adapt and support these devices.

## 2.2 ACCOMMODATING OPPOSING NEEDS

One of the key problems that the J2ME architecture attempts to solve is how to support a wide range of devices with different constraints, capabilities, features, and intended uses without introducing limitations on any specific device.

One solution might be to create a large, monolithic architecture that includes everything any application would ever need on any given device. However, such an architecture would be too large in terms of memory footprint for some of the smaller devices J2ME is intended to support, such as a two-way pager or a cell phone.

Another solution might be to identify a common denominator of functionality that applies to all devices in the J2ME space. The problem with this approach is that powerful devices then become as limited as the smallest devices. Furthermore, the unique features of devices cannot be adequately supported. In fact, this approach begs the question: does a least common denominator exist between devices such as a Java-enabled dishwasher and a cell phone or between a PDA and an Internet TV set-top box? To a large extent, this is why the J2ME architecture has come to be; it defines a common approach that addresses how to support many devices without limiting their feature sets.

### 2.2.1 Configurations and profiles

J2ME introduces two architectural concepts: configurations and profiles. Configurations make up the set of low-level APIs that define the runtime characteristics of a particular J2ME environment. Specifically, configurations are responsible for defining the following:

- Core Java classes
- Java programming language features
- Virtual machine features

Profiles address the more device-specific and use-specific APIs such as the widgets for the user interface, the data storage mechanisms and other more device-specific features such as the use of IR (infra-red) ports for beaming information between PDAs or accessing telephony features of a cell phone.

Configurations and profiles provide a separation of concern in the J2ME architecture between the need for portability and the need for supporting a wide range of devices and capabilities. Configurations serve to increase portability across many different devices while profiles cater to the features of a specific device or a group of similar devices. For example, configurations include core Java features such as String, System, Thread, and Object, as well as means for dealing with I/O streams and network connectivity. Profiles cater to device characteristics such as user interface widgets, event handling, and data storage. Profiles also provide a means to package specific sets of functionality such as multimedia capabilities or video game features.

An important characteristic of configurations is that they share a nested relationship. This means that configurations can be small or large but they all must fit within the largest J2ME configuration. Their relationship must always be a superset-subset relationship. This concept is illustrated in figure 2.1

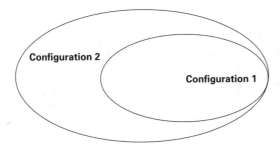

Figure 2.1 Configurations adhere to a nested relationship. This means that all configurations in the J2ME architecture conform to a superset-subset arrangement. This increases portability when moving from a more constrained configuration to a more feature-rich configuration.

The nested relationship of configurations allows for greater portability. Portability is maximized when moving from the more constrained environments to the larger, more feature-rich environments. For example, if an application was developed for a cellular phone using Configuration 1, it may be desirable to make that application available to devices running Configuration 2 as well.

Device manufacturers must adhere to the configuration specification when implementing or porting J2ME virtual machines and configurations to their platform to be J2ME-compliant. This compliance allows for portability across different manufacturer devices as well as between types of devices. This is an example of the Write Once, Run Anywhere (WORA) capabilities of the J2ME architecture. For example, a J2ME cell phone application can be deployed to any J2ME-compliant cell phone with little or no modification. Attempting this with proprietary C libraries or even proprietary Java APIs would mean porting the application to each manufacturer's cell phone since each cell phone is likely to have a different, often proprietary, operating system. Put simply, the WORA capabilities of J2ME begin with the Java programming language and are realized through the J2ME architecture. We'll take a closer look at WORA in section 2.8.

### 2.2.2 A high-level view of J2ME

A complete J2ME environment is composed of one configuration and one or more profiles. Since these two architectural concepts can be mixed around and rearranged given a particular need, the J2ME architecture becomes malleable enough to support the diverse needs of the J2ME space.

J2ME employs different versions of the Java Virtual Machine based on the needs of a particular situation. The configuration specifications define the characteristics of the J2ME virtual machines. In most cases, this involves removing features of the Java Virtual Machine in order to accommodate the needs of a configuration. The removal of features generally has to do with reducing the size of the virtual machine, or with performance and security issues on a particular class of devices.

The virtual machine is the component that sits logically above the host operating system. The configuration and profile APIs access the host operating system APIs through the virtual machine. In a nutshell, these are the components that make up the J2ME architecture. Figure 2.2 illustrates how they fit together.

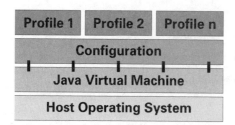

Figure 2.2
The building blocks of J2ME. The J2ME environment consists of a virtual machine, a configuration and one or more profiles. The virtual machine defines the contract between the configuration and the native operating system. Profiles define the contract between an application and the J2ME environment.

## 2.3 CONFIGURATIONS: A CLOSER LOOK

Configurations are specifications within the J2ME architecture that are defined by an expert group using the Java Community Process (JCP). Configuration specifications are created in cooperation with many industry participants.

At present, J2ME defines two configurations:

- Connected Limited Device Configuration (CLDC)
- Connected Device Configuration (CDC)

The CLDC addresses the needs of devices with strict limitations as far as memory, processing power, power consumption, and network connectivity. The CDC addresses the needs of more powerful devices. Figure 2.3 illustrates the relationship between the CDC and the CLDC.

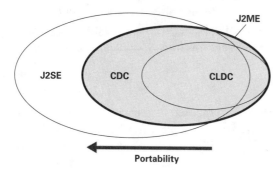

Figure 2.3
Due to the nested relationship between configurations, portability can be greatly enhanced when moving from a more constrained environment to a more feature-rich environment. However, it is important to remember that J2ME defines some APIs that are not present in J2SE.

Configurations define the contract between a profile and the Java Virtual Machine. Recall that profiles provide device- and use-specific APIs. As we mentioned, both the CDC and the CLDC configurations have their own virtual machines. The CDC uses the C-Virtual Machine (CVM) and the CLDC uses what is referred to as the Kilo-byte Virtual Machine (KVM). The implementation of a J2ME virtual machine must adhere to the specifications defined by the configuration. In the case of the KVM, functionality is explicitly removed in order to accommodate the strict memory requirements of the CLDC. Table 2.1 illustrates the relationship between configurations and virtual machines, and provides examples of candidate devices.

**Table 2.1** Configurations, Virtual Machines and some example devices

| Configuration | Virtual Machine | Example devices |
|---|---|---|
| CDC | CVM | Pocket PCs<br>Communicator class devices<br>TV set-top boxes |
| CLDC | KVM | Cellular phones<br>PDAs<br>Two-way pagers |

The next few sections discuss the details of the configurations and their associated virtual machines.

### 2.3.1 Connected Limited Device Configuration (CLDC)

The primary goal of this configuration is to provide a minimum footprint with a lowest common denominator of functionality available to resource-constrained devices. The CLDC specification can be found at java.sun.com/products/cldc.

A resource-constrained device in this case has the following characteristics:

- 160kB to 512kB of total memory available for the Java environment.
- Either a 16-bit or 32-bit processor.
- Low power consumption. Often these devices are battery-powered.
- Supports some type of connectivity to a network. Most likely this is an intermittent, low-bandwidth connection of about 9600 bps and often wireless.

The CLDC is based on J2SE but omits some functionality. The CLDC was created by starting with a clean slate and adding only what is necessary based on the following criteria:

- Is the functionality appropriate for these types of devices?
- Does the functionality require a large amount of binary code space or consume a lot of resources such as memory and CPU cycles?
- Can developers easily recreate the functionality if necessary? This applies to alternate method signatures as well as whole classes.
- Do these devices generally support the functionality?
- Are there security risks regarding the functionality on a constrained device?

To meet the small footprint requirements, the CLDC removes a number of features that are available in the J2SE environment. The following is a concise listing of features that have been removed from or modified for the CLDC environment.

- Java Native Interface (JNI)
- User-defined class loaders
- Reflection

- Thread groups and daemon threads
- Finalization
- Weak references
- Floating point data types (float and double)
- Some security features and APIs
- Class file verification (modified for efficiency)
- Some error handling limitations (not all exceptions are included)

### Reductions in favor of memory and processing power

All of the preceding features fall into this category to some degree since removing them reduces the overall size of the API. However, some of these features have been removed explicitly due to a memory or processing power expense. Floating point data types are such an example. The expert group that defined the CLDC determined floating point arithmetic was too expensive in terms of code size and processing power to implement on the CLDC. This determination is also partly drawn from the fact that many CLDC devices do not support floating point operations to begin with. In these situations, floating point support would need to be implemented entirely within the virtual machine since there are no guarantees that a native API would be available to handle floating point operations.

Class file verification is another example of how the CLDC has been altered from the J2SE environment to more effectively support limited devices. The processing power required to perform class file verification entirely on the device would be substantial. Supporting this feature in the way J2SE does would substantially increase the size of the virtual machine as well. As a result, class file verification takes place in two steps when using the CLDC. The first step is called preverification. This takes place off of the device, on the server or on the developer's workstation before deployment. The second step takes place on the device. Since preverification was performed prior to the class being loaded onto the device, the on-device verification can be much simpler and lightweight. CLDC class file verification is discussed in more detail in a moment.

### Reductions due to security issues

A number of the reductions in the CLDC specification come from the fact that the CLDC does not define the full Java security model. In the absence of a full security model, some features of the J2SE environment become a potential security risk. Security issues are mainly behind the removal of JNI, user-defined class loaders and reflection. However, these features do potentially consume their share of memory and processing power as well.

For example, without a full security model, a user-defined class loader could alter how the classpath is traversed. In doing so, an application could theoretically replace pieces of the core Java libraries and gain access to the device in a way that could harm the device.

### Reductions of convenience classes and methods

The size of the CLDC is further reduced by eliminating classes that developers, if needed, could recreate. `ThreadGroup` is one such example since it is essentially a collection of `Threads`. Developers could create a crude version of `ThreadGroup` using a `Vector`, for example.

Methods were removed in cases where multiple method signatures were introduced for convenience. For example, in J2SE, the `String` class defines the methods `equals(String)` and `equalsIgnoreCase(String)`. This functionality can be accomplished by executing either the `toLowerCase()` or `toUpperCase()` method (which are both present in the CLDC) on each string before performing `equals(String)`.

Furthermore, there are some classes and methods that do not apply to the CLDC. The `java.io.File` class is an example. The CLDC environment does not directly support the concept of a file system. This is because many of the devices that the CLDC targets do not have a file system. Instead, the CLDC relies on the storage facility of the device itself. These storage facilities are highly device-specific and are left for the profiles to define. Often devices in the CLDC space have nothing more than simple byte arrays for persistent storage.

### Other reductions

Features such as finalization and weak references have been removed from the CLDC primarily because these features are not fully utilized or necessary.

Finalization is intended to be used to clean up resources used by a particular object upon garbage collection. In practice, however, relying on finalization to clean up after objects is unreliable and can become dangerous. Finalization is linked to garbage collection. An object's `finalize()` method runs just prior to the object being freed from memory. Garbage collection is non-deterministic. We never know when or if it is going to run. Even when garbage collection is explicitly requested using `System.gc()`, the garbage collector does not immediately run. The call to `System.gc()` simply requests garbage collection as soon as possible. This may never occur if other threads take priority. As a result, a resource such as a database connection or an I/O stream will be tied up as the object that used the resource awaits garbage collection. Furthermore, by default in the J2SE environment, finalization does not occur during the virtual machine shutdown process. Thus, object finalization may never occur for an object. Since this feature is unreliable and should be avoided in the J2SE environment it did not make sense to include it in the CLDC environment.

### 2.3.2  The Kilobyte Virtual Machine (KVM)

The KVM adheres to the Java Virtual Machine Specification (Lindholm and Yellin) as much as possible. However, the capabilities of the KVM are defined by and large by the CLDC specification. The KVM differs from the Java Virtual Machine Specification only when the CLDC requires or allows this to happen for optimization or API support reasons. For example, often float and double are not supported by devices in the CLDC space. As a result, the creators of the CLDC decided that these data types were too expensive to implement on devices that, for the most part, do not support them. As a result, float and double are not supported by the CLDC and are not recognized by the KVM.

The KVM requires a small footprint on the device, between 40kB and 80kB depending on compile options and the target platform. This allows the KVM to run on devices with as little as 128kB of total memory. The KVM was developed from the ground up in C and is designed to be as complete and fast as possible, running at 30% to 80% the speed of the standard JVM, without a JIT (just-in-time compiler).

**NOTE** The KVM reference implementation that is provided with the CLDC is just one implementation of a CLDC-compliant virtual machine. Equipment manufacturers have the option to port the KVM to their devices or to build their own virtual machine that supports the CLDC specification.

### Class file verification

The standard Java virtual machines perform a process at runtime called class file verification. This process occurs before loading any class into memory in order to ensure both that the class is a valid Java class file and that it is considered

to be "well-behaved," in that it does not attempt to access memory outside of its defined namespace, does not replace any of the core java.* and javax.* packages, and so forth. Class file verification plays an important role in the Java security model.

In terms of CLDC devices, class file verification tends to be a rather resource-intensive operation and uses a significant amount of processing power, memory, and binary code space. As a result, the KVM defines class file verification differently than the standard Java Virtual Machines.

In order to reduce the KVM footprint, much of the class file verification process takes place outside the KVM and off of the device. Before the class is deployed to a device the class is modified by a preverify utility. The preverify utility modifies the class file generated by the javac compiler, adding byte codes that identify the class as a valid, verified class file. At runtime the KVM checks for these flags. If the flags are not present or do not contain the correct information, the class loading process is aborted, which results in an exception being thrown.

## 2.3.3 Connected Device Configuration (CDC)

The CDC is the second of the two configurations currently defined within J2ME, and it addresses devices and network appliances with more resources than CLDC devices. The CDC runs on a C-Virtual Machine (CVM) that is fully compliant with the Java Virtual Machine Specification. The CDC profile targets devices with as little as 512kB of memory; however, it is designed for platforms with about 2 MB of available memory. Typically, the devices in this category have substantial processing power, they often can be plugged into the wall, and they support rich networking capabilities such as high-bandwidth connections and high-fidelity Web content.

### 2.3.4 C-Virtual Machine (CVM)

Although the CVM adheres to the Java Virtual Machine Specification (Lindholm and Yellin) completely, its implementation is different than J2SE virtual machines in that it is optimized for devices and network appliances. The garbage collection algorithms are completely separate from the virtual machine allowing different garbage collector algorithms to be plugged into the CVM. The reference implementation employs a generational garbage collector that uses shorter garbage collection periods that do not tie up the virtual machine for long periods of time. Garbage collection runs for shorter periods of time more frequently. The garbage collector is more exact, knowing about all pointers at the time of garbage collecting so there is no need to consume extra processing cycles with conservative scans of the heap.

To increase portability between platforms, the reference implementation defines multithreading completely inside of the virtual machine. Threads that are implemented inside of the virtual machine are called "green threads." Using green threads allows the VM to be more portable since there are no multithreading operating system dependencies. However, the option to employ native threads is possible if a manufacturer or vender chooses to implement this on their target platform.

Class file verification takes place on the device, just as in the J2SE environment. There is no preverification step when using the CDC.

## 2.4 PROFILES: A CLOSER LOOK

Profiles provide APIs that focus on a single device, such as a PDA, or a group of related devices such as cell phones and pagers. The devices supported by a particular profile tend to have much in common in terms of how the device is used, what the user interface capabilities are, how or if the device connects to a network, how the device stores data, and so forth. Profiles are vertical in nature and are designed to meet the needs of a particular industry or market segment. Profiles address the most specific behavior available in the J2ME architecture.

What is a profile, really? Is a profile a conceptual definition defined by a specification or is it software? This is a subtle but important point. Profiles are created by many participants through Sun's Java Community Process (JCP). The output of the JCP in this case is not software so much as it is the specification. Although the JCP expert group often provides reference implementations of the specifications, it is up to the equipment manufacturer to provide a device-specific implementation of the profile that adheres to the specification on the device. The device manufacturer can choose to port the reference implementation provided by Sun or it can create its own implementation that adheres to the specification.

Just as a configuration defines the contract between the profile and the VM, a profile is what defines the contract between the device and your application. For a device manufacturer to support a profile, all APIs and features specified by the profile must be supported completely.

Profile specifications, as well as configuration specifications, may have optional requirements. In these cases, vendors have the option to include or exclude parts of a profile. To ensure maximum portability for a profile it is important to understand what features are mandatory and what features are optional. In general, there are relatively few, if any, optional features in most profile specifications.

Often, profiles are thought to complete a toolkit for development since it is the profile specifications that name the family of devices. Profiles also name a configuration that they base themselves on which indicates the runtime environment characteristics.

Defining profiles helps to ensure compatibility between all devices that support the particular profile. For example, writing a J2ME application using a particular profile means the application should run, without modification, on any device supporting that profile.

## 2.4.1 Two types of profiles

Typically, profiles provide the user interface, input methods, and persistence mechanisms for a given vertical group of devices. These types of profiles are thought to define a complete development environment for a specific set of devices and therefore can be considered device profiles. The profiles discussed so far fall into this category since they support specific device capabilities.

However, profiles can be created to fulfill more specific services or capabilities. Examples of these types of profiles might include a Remote Method Invocation (RMI) profile or a multimedia profile. This type profile could also encapsulate services for a particular market segment, such as uniform bank transactions. These profiles can be thought of as feature-oriented profiles. The advantage to encapsulating specific services and capabilities as profiles is that doing so allows these features to be easily reused across devices. It also provides modularity and flexibility by allowing device manufacturers to choose which features are necessary or most important.

## 2.4.2 Profiles are modular

A device may support more than one profile depending on the needs and capabilities of the device and what the manufacturer chooses to support. Profiles bring modularity into the J2ME architecture, addressing specific needs and functionality. For example, consider three devices: a cell phone, a PDA, and a set-top box. Assume they all support the ability to make credit card purchases over the Internet. Most likely the device-specific APIs would be addressed by three different profiles due to the user interface needs and other device-specific features. However, all three devices could support the same secure credit card transaction profile. Due to the specific nature of profiles and their modularity we can expect to see a large number of profiles created for specific needs as we move into the future.

So how can profiles be modular and support all the necessary device-specific APIs without becoming monolithic or introducing redundancies across the class libraries of different profiles? Quite simply, a single profile or set of profiles does not make a complete J2ME environment. Profiles simply address specific features. Underneath the profiles, providing the core Java support, are configurations and the Java Virtual Machine.

### 2.4.3    J2ME profiles extend J2ME configurations

A configuration is identified in the specification of a profile as this impacts the range of capabilities or devices that the profile intends to support. Once a profile specification names a configuration, the profile implementation must stay within the bounds of the configuration. In the case of figure 2.4, a profile built on top of Configuration 1 cannot use any APIs or functionality defined outside the Configuration 1 circle.

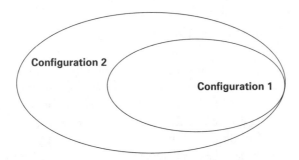

**Figure 2.4**
**The nested relationship of configurations allow for increased compatibility within the J2ME architecture. Since configurations are nested, applications can be moved from a more limited environment, such as Configuration 1, to the more feature-rich environment of Configuration 2 without needing to alter, change or lose functionality.**

However, due to the nested architecture of configurations, profiles that run on Configuration 1 will also run on Configuration 2 (provided there is a device that supports these profile-configuration combinations). In this sense, configurations are upwardly compatible. Downward compatibility requires more architectural thought and technique on the part of the application designer.

## 2.5    *CHOOSING A J2ME PROFILE*

Choosing the correct profile or set of profiles is one of the more important decisions that is made when creating applications using J2ME. This is because, conceptually, the profile is the part of the J2ME architecture that is closest to the devices themselves. Once you have an understanding of the devices that need to be supported, you can choose a profile or set of profiles. Choosing a profile depends on what the target devices support and what you need to do.

There are an increasing number of profiles in development. The Mobile Information Device Profile (MIDP) is one of the better known, since it is the first J2ME profile to have been released through the Java Community Process. In addition to the official J2ME profiles, there is one API that deserves some attention. The API is known as KJava and was developed by Sun Microsystems to test and demonstrate the CLDC. Table 2.2 summarizes the compete set of J2ME profiles, both existing and under development.

**Table 2.2   Profiles currently defined for J2ME**

| Profile | Configuration/VM | Virtual Machine | Target Device Examples |
|---------|-----------------|-----------------|------------------------|
| MIDP | CLDC | KVM | Cellular phones and two-way pagers |
| PDAP | CLDC | KVM | PDAs |
| Foundation | CDC | CVM | Primarily a foundation for Personal Profile |
| Personal | CDC | CVM | Pocket PCs, tablets, communicator class devices |
| RMI | CDC | CVM | Any |
| Personal Basis | CDC | CVM | Any |
| Multimedia | CDC/CLDC | CVM/KVM | Any |
| Gaming | CDC/CLDC | CVM/KVM | Any |
| Telephony (WTCA) | CDC/CLDC | CVM/KVM | Cellular phones |

## 2.5.1 Mobile Information Device Profile (MIDP)

This is the first official profile released by Sun and it targets cellular phones and two-way pagers. This profile has also been implemented to run on the Palm operating system (Palm OS), making it available on devices supporting the Palm operating system. Devices that implement this profile tend to be very personalized. Often the user of the device is the only user. These devices also tend to have very constrained resources such as a small screen for user interface display, limited data entry capability such as a "one-handed" keypad, and limited data storage capabilities usually implemented as byte arrays.

The next version of MIDP (referred to as MIDP Next Generation) will address features such as security and using HTTPS (Hypertext Transfer Protocol over Secure Socket Layer), formal inclusion of over the air provisioning (OTA), push architecture, enhanced user interface capabilities, a small and efficient XML parser, and a sound API.

Part 2 of this book discusses MIDP in great detail and provides examples for building J2ME application using MIDP.

## 2.5.2 PDA Profile (PDAP)

This profile specifically addresses the capabilities and needs of personal digital assistants, particularly in the areas of data storage and user interface capabilities such as PDA-style GUI widgets and touch screen event handling.

## 2.5.3 Foundation Profile

The Foundation Profile serves as a base for additional CDC profiles that provide graphical user interface, data storage, distributed Java networking, and so forth. In addition to its duties as a base profile, the Foundation profile provides rich network support for high-bandwidth, high-fidelity connectivity devices. This profile is intended to be used with other profiles to provide a rich application environment for devices smaller than personal computers.

## 2.5.4 Personal Profile

The Personal Profile is the new home for many of the PersonalJava APIs. The Personal-Java API, which targets pocket PCs, is being rearchitected so that it fits into the design of the J2ME architecture. PersonalJava will be divided into the CDC, the Foundation Profile and the Personal Profile. Extensions of the Personal Profile include JavaPhone and JavaTV APIs.

## 2.5.5 RMI Profile

The RMI Profile provides distributed support to applications in the CDC space. This profile provides the infrastructure to marshal objects as the parameters and return values of remote method calls. Dynamic class loading is utilized to make the marshalled objects available to a particular JVM during a remote call. The wire protocol JRMP (Java Remote Method Protocol) is required to be supported. Implementations of the RMI profile are required to support full RMI semantics as defined by the J2SE 1.3 specification with the following exceptions:

- RMI through firewalls
- RMI multiplexing protocol
- Activation-inactivation model
- Support for the JDK 1.1 stub/skeleton protocol
- Stub-skeleton compiler

The following packages are not part of the RMI Profile specification:

- `java.rmi.server.disableHttp`
- `java.rmi.activation.port`
- `java.rmi.loader.packagePrefix`
- `java.rmi.registry.packagePrefix`
- `java.rmi.server.packagePrefix`

The specific exceptions listed cannot be added to a conforming implementation of the RMI Profile.

## 2.5.6 Personal Basis Profile

This profile will provide a basic level of graphic capabilities to devices running the CDC and Foundation Profile. This profile is intended to provide basic graphical user interface capabilities in environments where the high-fidelity, feature-rich Personal Profile is not fully utilized or necessary. This profile forms the basis for the Personal Profile graphical capabilities.

## 2.5.7 Multimedia Profile

This profile targets the CLDC and CDC configurations to provide basic multimedia support for sound and other media. Many of the ideas from the Java Media Framework are included, but this profile is not compatible with the JMF. This API will provide the means for controlling time-based media such as sound and video along with sampling, streaming and synthetic audio capabilities. The profile is being designed for scalability, providing a set of basic services for more limited devices with a set of optional features for more powerful devices.

The multimedia profile is designed as an optional profile to be used in conjunction with other J2ME profiles.

### 2.5.8    Gaming Profile

This profile will provide gaming support for J2ME devices. The areas of focus include 3D modeling and rendering, 3D physics modeling, 3D character animation, 2D rendering and video buffering, game marshalling and networked communication, streaming media, sound, game controller support, and hardware access. The CDC is the target environment for this profile; however, efforts are being made to provide this profile across a wide range of devices. This profile is intended to be available to the J2SE environments as well.

This is an optional profile designed for use with other J2ME profiles.

### 2.5.9    Wireless Telephony Communications API (WTCA)

This specification will provide J2ME applications with a reusable set of components supporting short message service (SMS), Unstructured Supplementary Service Data (USSD), and Cell Broadcast Service (CBS). The SMS support will include APIs for sending and receiving text messages, a method for sending and receiving data, the ability to push applications to devices and an application trigger. USSD will be used for exchanging data and CBS will allow applications to receive cell broadcast data.

This is an optional profile designed for use with other J2ME profiles.

### 2.5.10    KJava

The KJava API is not an official profile. It is a set of APIs originally provided by Sun as a way of testing the CLDC on the Palm OS. However, some third-party development tools have implemented commercial versions of KJava (such as esmertec's Jbed).

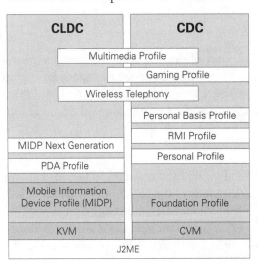

The PDA Profile is the official profile designed to address PDA device needs. The J2ME architecture, as currently planned, is illustrated by figure 2.5.

**Figure 2.5**
**This figure illustrates all of the items currently making up J2ME. The shaded items indicate components that are currently available. The unshaded items are under development.**

## 2.6   WRITE ONCE, RUN ANYWHERE ISSUES

At this point you may be wondering why so much attention is being paid to portability and compatibility issues when the Java mantra is write once, run anywhere. Why should there be any compatibility issues? WORA is not automatic when implementing Java applications on devices. Largely, this is why J2ME came into existence. The J2ME architecture leverages the Java programming language to enhance portability across a wide range of devices with different capabilities and needs.

It is important to note that the Java language itself is not modified, only the Virtual Machine characteristics as described by the CDC and CLDC configurations. The compatibility issues mainly come into play when different device capabilities must be dealt with. Different device capabilities are handled through different profiles in J2ME. As a result, devices that support different profiles may incur compatibility problems. However, WORA problems encountered within the same profile running on different devices are an issue of how a particular profile has been implemented on the devices.

### 2.6.1   Varied device needs

Since device needs vary across device categories it becomes unrealistic to support all features on all devices. This is especially the case on smaller devices that have limitations on memory, processing capabilities, power consumption, network connectivity, and data storage. Manufacturers and developers of cellular phones, for example, are often forced to make difficult decisions on what is essential for developing applications on these devices. Supporting all J2ME features on all devices would require a large amount of memory, processing power that would automatically eliminate many devices from the J2ME picture. Providing the ability to cater to different devices based on device features and constraints requires the Java platform to be rearranged and altered so as to be appropriate and practical for a wide range of devices.

For example, some devices, like PDAs, have touch screen interfaces while other devices, such as two-way pagers, do not. Two-way pagers, on the other hand, often support a full alphanumeric keypad whereas cellular phones have a "one-handed" keypad. Internet screen phones plug into the wall and do not have to be as concerned about power consumption as a pocket PC. Internet TV set-top boxes support high-bandwidth, high-fidelity network connections while wireless devices have more bandwidth limitations. The degree to which WORA can be achieved is largely due to the profile-specific capabilities you choose to support in your application.

These differences in capabilities can prevent an application from porting smoothly across different types of devices where the same profiles are not supported. Therefore, some thought and design is required if an application must run on two different profiles, such as MIDP and PDAP.

### 2.6.2   J2ME architecture increases WORA

The J2ME architecture does not break WORA carelessly. Rather, it is designed to balance compatibility issues between devices and the special needs of each type device. For this reason, it is important to understand the J2ME architecture when creating applications for J2ME devices. Understanding how profiles and configurations relate increases your chances of creating applications that are compatible across many different devices.

## 2.7   *RUNTIME ENVIRONMENT*

So far, we've focused on some fairly basic, yet crucial, J2ME concepts. In chapter 14, we'll discuss the J2ME runtime environment in detail, but to round out this introductory discussion, we'll briefly introduce it here.

There are two basic ways to run J2ME applications on devices. One way is to run them transiently over the network. In this mode of operation the application is loaded into memory by downloading it over the network. Once the application finishes running, the application is discarded. Running applications in this manner requires a network connection. Applications can also be installed onto the device. In this case, an application is available to run with or without a network connection.

Regardless of the method used to run J2ME applications, some device-specific management is involved on the part of the J2ME implementation running on the actual device. The part of the J2ME environment responsible for managing applications on the device is called the Java Application Manager (JAM). Implementation of the JAM is something that is implemented by the device manufacturer. The JAM itself manages activities such as downloading, installing, inspecting, launching, and uninstalling Java applications on the device.

Most devices in the J2ME space will be shipped with the Java environment already on the device. This is good in that the users of the device, and ultimately the application, will not have to deal with loading the Java Runtime Environment. However, this also means there may only be one JRE available on the device. Since different manufacturers will inevitably release versions of their products at different times with different JREs, the code may need to be compatible across a number of different J2ME runtime versions depending on how the device handles this situation.

Chapter 14 discusses concepts such as class file verification, class loading, virtual machine lifecycles and responsibilities, threading, and garbage collecting.

## 2.8   *DESIGNING J2ME APPLICATIONS*

As with any system architecture, there are tradeoffs to consider. This is the art of architecture. Creating an architecture that includes J2ME is no exception. Most likely, there will be a large number of devices involved, possibly different devices types and manufacturers, varying network capabilities, and data storage capabilities. Here are some things to consider when creating J2ME applications. Techniques for addressing some of these issues are discussed in part 4.

The design of J2ME applications should include an understanding of the devices you intend to support. This understanding allows the appropriate profiles to be included in the design and implementation of applications. Additionally, you should have some understanding of the unique capabilities and constraints of each device. This is a good idea even if only one profile is supported. You must remember that a single cell phone application could be used on many different manufacturer's phones. If you plan to support devices with a mixture of capabilities, such as cell phones, pagers, and PDAs, you may want to provide capabilities specific to each device. For example, some pagers have a full keypad where cell phones have a 10-digit keypad. PDAs usually have wider screens than cell phones and pagers. Some PDAs are even powerful enough to run a small-footprint relational database.

Another important consideration is how portability factors into your application requirements, and your organization. As discussed previously, the "write once, run anywhere" promise does not come automatically with J2ME. Is this a necessary requirement for your application? Is it practical?

You will also want to consider how the applications will be delivered to the device and what kind of network capabilities they will need to operate. Different devices may require different network connectivity infrastructures. For example, does your wireless service provider allow the device to connect to the Internet or will you be stuck on their server? How much does it cost per minute to be connected? How much data must be transferred over the network connection? Is this too much for a 19.6 kbps or 9600 bps connection? Will the application run transiently or will it be installed on the device? Will there be a combination of installed and transient applications?

The tradeoff between how much data can be downloaded and how much data can be stored is often a key architectural decision. Some devices must download a fair amount of their "operational" data simply because they do not have the space to store the data locally. Some devices may not even have the ability to store data. Of course, requiring data downloads to operate an application means the device must have a connection. On the other side of the coin, applications that store data locally on the device may have to deal with data synchronization issues between the device and the server.

You will also want to address usability issues with certain devices. For example, what happens when someone is using your stock application on a cell phone and he or she suddenly gets a phone call? Can the user easily suspend the application? Is this automatically done by the device?

## 2.9    SUMMARY

The J2ME architecture defines configurations to address the horizontal needs of the J2ME space. The J2ME Virtual Machines are tightly coupled to the configurations that define them. Profiles fill in the gaps left by configurations and implement specific capabilities for a family of devices. Profiles tend to address vertical aspects of the J2ME space, such as specific device capabilities and limitations, or they encapsulate a set of APIs that address a specific market or technology need. For compatibility between devices, manufacturers must implement the entire profile specification. This allows applications that conform to the profile to run on any device that implements the profile. Finally, it is important to understand that a device may support one or more profiles on a single configuration.

With a solid understanding of how J2ME is put together and what options exist for developing applications, you are ready to try out some of this. The next few chapters cover creating and deploying J2ME applications.

# C H A P T E R   3

# Developing a J2ME application

Throughout the chapters in the next two parts, we investigate the major aspects of J2ME programming through a tutorial application. Why a tutorial application? We find that most people learn by doing. That is why each API introduced in these parts is reinforced with a piece of a working application to demonstrate what the API has to offer. In particular, we will explore the J2ME application user interface, event handling, data storage, networking, and input/output.

As was discussed in the last chapter on architecture, J2ME has several configurations and profiles to address the particular needs of different horizontal and vertical platform and market segments. In other words, J2ME comes in several flavors depending on your platform and application needs. In an attempt to give you a real flavor sampling of J2ME, we examine each of the major application aspects in a couple of devices. We hope that this will not only allow you to learn the J2ME APIs but also provide you with some basis of comparing and contrasting the different features and methods of handling needs across the various environments that make up J2ME. This will not be an exhaustive look at the APIs in any of these areas. Our goal is to cover the basics so that you have the foundational knowledge from which to build your own applications.

The tutorial application will be put together over several chapters. As is good software development practice, we examine the major tiers of the system and build each section so that it is somewhat independent or insulated from the other tiers. We start by developing the application control, and then add the user interface, event handling, data persistences and networking service until the application is complete.

Before getting started, we need to provide a word of warning about the design of the application and code in these next few chapters. To improve instruction, the tutorial focuses on certain aspects and features of J2ME in each chapter. At the end of each chapter, we will have a running application. Since the code in these applications is written with the intention of explaining the APIs, there are cases where good design has been compromised in favor of brevity and/or illustration. In chapter 11, Real-world design, we look at some design and implementation issues and examine how to build better applications.

In this short chapter, we describe the tutorial application and establish some formal requirements. In short, we ask, "What exactly must our application do?" We also do some design work so that we have at least a minimal set of blueprints as we go forward to implement the application in the various APIs for the different platforms. Specifically, we:

- Establish the customer for the tutorial application.
- Define the tutorial application requirements.
- Design the major components of the application based on the requirements.
- Examine the major components and discuss how they may be implemented.

## 3.1 INVESTMENT QUOTE APPLICATION REQUIREMENTS

Every project should have a requirement that it is trying to fulfill. Generally, the better the requirements, the more focused the goal and ultimately the end product developed.

In the case of this tutorial, the application is something of a by-product to the real requirement. Our real goal is to learn some of the J2ME API. Through this tutorial application, we hope to give you (the future J2ME guru) examples of Java in small things and a realistic glimpse at some of the issues and choices associated with developing software for the consumer electronic and embedded device. Although the requesting company and its customers may be fictional, many of the requirements and needs are generic enough to apply to any such application.

### 3.1.1 The investment quote application customer

In this tutorial, we work for a fictitious dot-com online financial planning adviser and commodities broker. This organization has a Web site that has enjoyed considerable success, but they want to expand their client list. The mobile and wireless user base is growing at an incredible rate and they have targeted this audience for new customers.

In the tutorial application, we are going to develop a J2ME investment price service that runs on customers' small and personal devices. This application allows customers to get the latest quoted price for their favorite stocks or mutual funds by providing the stock or mutual fund ticker symbol.

### 3.1.2 Requirements analysis

After meeting with several business and marketing representatives from the company, a short list of requirements has been developed. The prototype application must comply with the general requirements of our tutorial application. The application must:

- be easy to use. Users will only be required to enter a stock or mutual fund symbol for a United States investment and get back a price in United States dollars.
- store the investment symbol, price for the investments viewed. The latest price obtained for one of these commodities can be retrieved out of storage at any time. In order to show how the investment is "trending," a maximum of two prices will be stored for each investment. A current and historical price will allow the system to depict how the price for the investment is changing.
- run on the most ubiquitous small devices of today, which consists of a two-way pager, cellular telephone, and personal digital assistant.
- require the users to be "connected" with their device at the time of retrieving new price quotes.
- store the last quotes retrieved. The user is not required to be "connected" when looking up already stored quotes. The system will allow the user to store up to two prices per symbol.

After analyzing the requirements, it is determined that the prototype will consist of two uses or, more appropriately, use cases. The first use case, ObtainQuote, will provide the user with the ability to obtain a quote and store the quote price and date on the device. A second use case, RetrieveQuote, will allow the customer to pull up the previously retrieved price quotes for any given investment symbol stored in the device. A use case diagram of the system and its "uses" cases is depicted in figure 3.1.

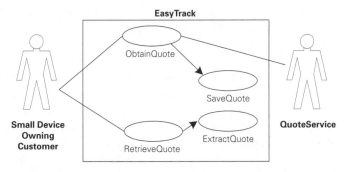

**Figure 3.1** The Investment Quote system is determined to have four use cases. The customer will request to either obtain new investment quotes or retrieve historical quotes. Secondary use cases help in saving or retrieving data from the database. The ObtainQuote use case will also require interaction with an outside QuoteService system.

The ObtainQuote use case will connect to and make use of an outside or third-party quote service to get investment price information. In this system, the third-party quote service is referred to as the QuoteService.

Hidden to the user, the ObtainQuote use case will need to save quote information. The SavePrice use case will be responsible for connecting to the small device's persistent mechanism and storing the investment quote data. Similarly, RetrieveQuote will utilize the same persistent storage service to get back data via the RetrievePrice use case.

## 3.2 DESIGNING THE INVESTMENT QUOTE APPLICATION

In the development of the tutorial application, we examine the implementation of several major components of the system. In particular, we will look at the user interface and event handling, persistent data storage, and networking or input/output means. We design the application around these major components. However, this design will be implemented a couple of times throughout the next two parts of the book. In particular, we will examine the same application implemented under both the MIDP profile and KJava API on top of the CLDC configuration.

### 3.2.1 Application control

We have already determined that there are probably two main uses of the system. One use is to have the customer provide a symbol and have the system obtain a new investment quote while another use is to have a customer provide a symbol and have the system retrieve a historical or already retrieved investment quote from a database that is on the device. To complement the use cases of the system, we decide to set up two general applications.

**WHY TWO APPS?** *Smaller applications*  There are several reasons why you may wish to break apart the required functionality into many smaller applications. Remember, a J2ME application usually runs in a constrained device. A single large application may not be able to run inside of the memory-constrained space of a cell phone or other device. Breaking apart an application allows the required functionally to be delivered within the constraints of a device. In many ways, there is a new application paradigm when working with many of the J2ME devices. The input mechanisms, key pad or stylus input devices do not easily support navigating through a larger multiple-window application, especially when the user's attention is often diverted while using one of these devices (how often have you used a cellular phone while driving?). When developing J2ME applications, consider smaller applications with fewer interactions to get the job done. Finally, there is the issue of deployment. Smaller applications have always been easier to deploy. Since many of the J2ME devices are mobile and wireless, replacing an application with limited connectivity is easier when the applications are smaller.

One application will provide the ObtainQuote functionality while a second application will handle the RetrieveQuote functionality. Each application requires an application control object. An application control object is an instance of a class that forms the contract between the device, and in particular the device's application management software, and the application. The application control object also manages the general action or workflow, such as calling on the appropriate classes or API to display the user interface or make a network connection within the application.

Depending on the J2ME configuration/profile, different classes and method APIs provide application control. For example, an instance of a single type of class handles application control in the MID profile. The CDC is closer to J2SE, using either an applet or any class with a main method used as the application entry point and central class orchestrating actions of other classes (providing general application control).

### 3.2.2    User interface design

The tutorial applications are going to have three general "displays." Whether obtaining a new quote or retrieving an existing quote out of the database, the application must have a way to prompt the customer for an investment type and symbol. The customer enters the symbol for the investment and selects mutual fund or a stock. We expect the first display to look something akin to the sketch in figure 3.2.

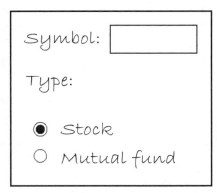

**Figure 3.2**
**The Investment Price Request prototype display anticipates the customer providing an investment symbol and indicates whether the investment is a mutual fund or stock. This type screen can be used to request a new investment quote or to retrieve an existing quote from the database on a device.**

Except for its size, this display does not look that much different from what one would expect to see in a J2SE application. In fact, while the paradigm of text entry fields and radio buttons seems familiar, the actual look and feel of the user interface elements may be quite different when actually implemented for the platform. The profile and/or configuration will help define a common API, but the device constraints (such as screen size, lack of a keyboard, etc.) may require some interesting interface adaptations in order to fulfill the API.

As with any application, we also expect the application to help prevent users from making a mistake. For example, a mutual fund symbol always ends with 'X'. Therefore, the application must check data entry and provide the necessary feedback when a mistake is made.

Once the application obtains the quote from the database or quote service, the investment price is displayed to the customer. The application shows the price on a display that looks something like the sketch in figure 3.3.

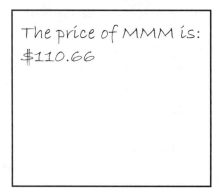

**Figure 3.3**
**Results from a successful request to get a new price quote or to retrieve the price data from the database after providing a valid investment symbol should result in the price data for the investment being displayed in text form.**

Finally, when a previous price for an investment has been obtained, in order to give the user some visual context on which direction the investment price is heading since last checking on the price, the application will provide a third and final display to visually depict the historic and current prices in a graph. This part of the application forces us to examine the drawing capabilities provided by the various APIs. The prototype sketch for this display is provided in figure 3.4.

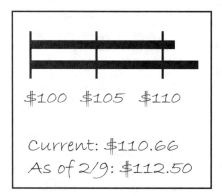

**Figure 3.4**
**If the customer requests price data to be retrieved from the database and the database has at least two prices for the investment stored in the database, then a graphical comparison chart should be depicted, as shown in this Investment Price Comparison prototype.**

Depending on the size of the screen and the graphical capabilities of the device, these displays may be shown on one or multiple screens. User interfaces are defined in profiles built on the J2ME configuration. As will be seen in the various tutorial application implementations, the APIs and set of visual components can be vastly different for each type of platform. The user interface API must adapt to the underlying abilities of the platform.

*CHAPTER 3   DEVELOPING A J2ME APPLICATION*

While not shown on the mock displays, there must be a way for the user to interact with the system and navigate from display to display. Usually, this is done with a series of buttons or similar user interface widgets. Navigating and reacting to user input are the jobs of the event-handling mechanism. Event handling is often associated with the user interface since the user interacting with the graphical user interface (GUI) triggers most events. However, again depending on the configuration and profile, different mechanisms and APIs are provided for catching and reacting to events  In each tutorial section, we examine event handling in combination with the user interface in the various implementations.

### 3.2.3    Persistent storage

Persistent storage means the capability to store data beyond the life of the running application. In other words, persistent storage is a fancy term for a database. In the tutorial application, we expect investment price data to survive the application's start and stop as well as turning the device on and off. Therefore, it is investment data, including both current and historical price information, which must be stored in the database.

On Wall Street, each stock or mutual fund is given an investment symbol. For example, the Janus Growth and Income Fund has a symbol of JAGIX. The tutorial application will use a symbol such as JAGIX as its handle or index to data in the database. A set of price quotes for funds and stocks might look like table 3.2.

**Table 3.1    An example of price data stored in the database is represented in the table below. For two investments, Janus Growth and Income Fund (JAGIX) and IBM, only a current price is stored. For 3M (MMM), both a current price and an historical price have been stored in the database.**

| Symbol | Current Price | Previous or Historical Price |
|--------|---------------|------------------------------|
| JAGIX  | 33.66         |                              |
| MMM    | 117.02        | 116.05                       |
| IBM    | 111.21        |                              |

In this example, we have current prices for the Janus mutual fund as well as 3M and IBM stock. However, we only have a historical or previous price for 3M. We can surmise from this data that the customer has only checked on the JAGIX and IBM price once but has checked the price of 3M at least twice.

We hesitate in using the term "row" in describing the price quote data that is saved in the database. The term row implies that there is some type of tabular or relational database in effect. Even though we have depicted the data this way in the example above, this may be misleading. In reality, many of the implementations do not use any type of relational database structure to make data persistent on the device. Database engines can be expensive in terms of system resources. So in many cases, a simple data structure such as a byte array is used to store data on the device's storage medium.

In the tutorial system, we already have plans for one application to get new price data and put that data into storage (ObtainQuote) and another application to retrieve and display the data (RetrieveQuote), as shown in figure 3.5. This means that the applications will have to share the database. While this may not seem to be much of a hurdle in the design (after all J2SE and J2EE applications share databases all the time), we will see that applications and the database can be more tightly coupled in J2ME. In other words, sharing databases can require certain stipulations of J2ME applications and the deployment of the same.

**Figure 3.5** Both the ObtainQuote and RetrieveQuote applications of the tutorial will share the same "database." One application (ObtainQuote) will use the database to store investment price data it obtains from a QuoteService. The other application (RetrieveQuote) will use the database to retrieve historical price information for display to the customer.

### 3.2.4 Networking and input/output

One of the more device-dependent aspects of writing software for resource-constrained devices is in trafficking and communicating information. Indeed, even the availability of certain familiar input/output paradigms such as a file may not exist in the realm of certain J2ME devices. The developers of the J2ME specifications have recognized this as a potential obstacle to developing highly portable applications across a diverse set of platforms. We have dedicated an entire chapter (chapter 13) to understanding how J2ME configurations and profiles attempt to isolate J2ME applications from device networking and I/O implementation details.

In order to shield the rest of the application from having to deal with any possible network or I/O implementation differences, we design the price quote acquiring service as a stand-alone component answering stock and mutual fund price information when asked. We establish a contract for the quote service, but its implementation details are subject to change based on the changes of the available networking and/or I/O API that is determined by the underlying device.

As we will see, the component fulfilling the quote service need is really just a facade to a financial investment quote service available over the Internet. (Figure 3.6) The application does not get all the stock and mutual fund quotes being published from the trading floor. Instead, the quote service inquires on the current price (or as near to current price as can be obtained through an on-line service) for a stock or mutual fund price via standard networking protocols. Throughout the book we often refer to this external service as the secondary actor depicted in the previous use case diagram (figure 3.1) called the QuoteService.

In the tutorial, the quote service component will connect via the hypertext transfer protocol (HTTP) to this external service. In the real world, our dot-com employer probably provides this external service. As a financial institution, it probably has the price data and merely provides us with a data portal which we can network into in order to get needed price information. However, since our company does not really exist, the application will request price quotes from one of the many popular online stock and mutual fund information web sites. The task is the same; just the location of the data would change in a real world situation. Obviously, for the application to receive price information, it must be able to get connected, in this case to the Web. We will see how J2ME addresses this issue.

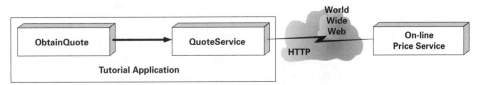

**Figure 3.6   The QuoteService acts as a façade to the "real" Internet quote providing service. Using HTTP and talking through the Internet, the QuoteService will query a real world investment web site for investment quotes and return the resulting prices back to the ObtainQuote application.**

If the fictitious dot-com online financial planning firm that we work for supplied the data, we may have the luxury of getting the price data back in a format we specifically require. The Extensible Markup Language (XML) is popular for this type data exchange and we will look at this possibility in chapter 12. Depending on who else uses the information available through the portal, we may not have this luxury. Furthermore, an unfortunate consequence of dealing with data from a public web site on the World Wide Web is that when we ask for information and we get the data required, we also get a lot of other information we do not need. The world of the Web operates largely in terms of HTML formatted data. We can request a price quote from a third party, but what comes back is an HTML page containing the stock or mutual fund price, historical price information, organization information, and all the banner ads the Web site can sell.

So, the QuoteService will have to locate the actual data amid the mass of HTML tags, investment information and advertising that is returned from any request to get price data. (Figure 3.7) A subcomponent of the QuoteService will parse through HTML provided by the on-line service and extract the price quote.

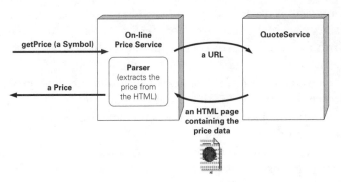

**Figure 3.7**
**Price data returned by the on-line service must be extracted from the HTML before being used by the application. In a real world application, the server should supply the client device with only the data it requires, which in this case is the investment price information.**

In this way, the QuoteService also acts as a filter for the real price information that the application needs and isolates the rest of the application from having to worry about non-price related information. This can be especially important if the on-line price service ever changes the content of its data.

## 3.3 DEVELOPING J2ME APPLICATIONS

So how do we go about building this application we have just documented? As we are about to explore developing J2ME applications, through the remainder of this book we shall see that, in many respects, developing a J2ME application does not differ all that much from developing a J2SE application. The biggest difference associated with developing applications in J2ME is in having to consider the target device(s). While Java is write once and run anywhere, even in J2ME, the available Java API can differ on various target platforms. As we discussed in chapter 2, configurations provide generic Java functionality across a wide range of devices, whereas profiles provide target-specific functionality. Thus, unlike other Java environments, we cannot teach you a single J2ME API and then teach you how to deploy your Java application to many platforms. Instead, with J2ME, one must learn and apply the available API for a given targeted platform. In the next parts of this book we look at developing J2ME applications in two different environments targeted for at least two different devices. In each part, we will demonstrate how to get your development environment set up, how to write the application, and how to run and deploy your application.

### 3.3.1 Obtaining the development environment

Before the first line of code is written, you will need the Java environment required to develop an application for your targeted platform(s). Along with the J2SE JDK (version 1.3 or higher), what other items you will need depends on two things:

- The targeted devices
- The tools you want to use to develop your application

The targeted devices will dictate which configuration, profiles and other APIs you will need in order to create your application. The target device also dictates which emulation environment is needed.

Today's market place also offers several products to assist you in developing your applications. If you are the type that codes with a text editor and the required JDK and class APIs, you are ready to start developing after downloading the necessary APIs and emulators. However, as with J2SE application development, there are several Integrated Development Environments (IDEs) and tools available today to help lighten your load when developing J2ME applications. In some cases, these environments are offered for free as part of the reference implementation.

As we explore each of our environments, we provide you with information on what is required to establish your development environment. Additional information on available IDEs and tools is provided in the appendix of this text.

### 3.3.2    Creating the applications

Writing J2ME applications is similar to how most Java applications are written. The main differences tend to be found in deployment since that is when the actual devices come into the picture. In general, the pattern for creating J2ME applications that we will use throughout this book goes something like the steps listed here:

- Write the code

- Compile the application targeting specific profiles

- Run the preverifier utility to add the necessary preverification flags to the class files. This step may be optional depending on the J2ME environment and vendor implementation of the specifications.

- Package the application. This takes on various forms. For a PDA running Palm OS this may mean creating a PRC file. For a cell phone this may mean creating a JAR file.

- Deploy to a Web server or install on the device

### 3.3.3    Runtime environment

As we shall see in the development of applications throughout the next two parts, there are two basic ways J2ME applications are run on devices. One way is to run them transiently over the network. In this mode of operation the application is loaded into memory by downloading it over the network. Once the application finishes running it is discarded. Running applications in this manner requires a network connection. Alternately, if the device allows, applications can be physically installed onto the device. In this case, the application is available to run with or without a network connection.

In order for J2ME applications to be used on a device some device-specific management is involved. The part of the J2ME runtime environment that does this is called the Java Application Manager (JAM). Implementation of the JAM is something that is done by the device manufacturer. The JAM itself is responsible for activities such as downloading, installing, inspecting, launching and uninstalling Java applications on the device.

Another important peculiarity of the J2ME runtime environment is the absence of a programmer-definable classpath. In J2ME, there is only one class path and it is hidden from the developer. Given the many struggles Java developers have with classpath, this may come as a relief. Of course, there are some hidden issues that come with the absence of a definable classpath. Note that this means there can be only a single set of libraries on a device. When your application starts, the context (-classpath) for loading classes cannot be defined to cater specifically to your application nor can you manipulate the order in which classes are loaded.

Most devices in the J2ME space will be shipped with the Java environment already on the device. This is good in that the users of the device, and ultimately your application, will not have to deal with loading the Java Runtime Environment. However, this also means there may only be one JRE available on the device. Since different manufacturers will inevitably release versions of their products at different times with different JREs, your code may need to be compatible across a number of different J2ME runtime versions.

## 3.4    INVESTMENT QUOTE APPLICATION TOUR GUIDE

In the next two parts of the book (Parts 2 and 3), the tutorial application explained in this section will be implemented. Actually, the application will be implemented twice. Why twice? Again, the targeted platforms dictate the use of various APIs and development environments. In Part 2, we implement the application in the all-J2ME MIDP and CLDC APIs. This development effort will produce an application that runs on a cellular telephone, pager and at least one type of PDA. In the subsequent part, Part 3, we revisit the same application and use the KJava API and CLDC to implement the application for use on Palm OS PDA devices. If you are interested in one type of development over the other, skip the part that least interests you, as these have been written as independent sections of the book.

Throughout both parts we take these same steps toward implementation.

1   Through the small and now almost mandatory step in any programming introduction of HelloWorld we examine the basics of the J2ME environment and API in order to ramp up before building the application.

2   We then examine the application control for each type application. How is the application started and run?

3   Before developing the graphical user interface, we stop to look at the general API for building the user interfaces and then we develop the user interface for the tutorial application.

4   As with almost any user interface, the application must handle the events generated by the user's interactions with the interface in order for the application to do anything. We look at the means by which each environment handles events and triggers response inside the tutorial applications.

5   Each small device provides a means to store data on the device. We inspect the API for data storage and implement a solution to store investment prices on each device using the API.

6   Finally, we will look at what it takes to network these small devices wirelessly using a J2ME networking framework called the Generic Connection Framework. In the process, we will need to deal with information input/output mechanisms available in the environments. We will discover that the networking and input/output service is the same across all environments, so we will not need to reinvent this service for both tutorial implementations. Instead, we will reuse the quote service developed for the MIDP application in the KJava application.

After completing each of the tasks described previously there is a working tutorial application. Therefore, if you would like to skip ahead and look at a particular section of interest, each chapter uses the work from the previous chapter, but it can be worked on and examined as an independent entity without difficulty. The steps of the tutorial application's development are covered in the chapters as outlined in table 3.3.

**Table 3.2  The next two sections of this book are organized around teaching and demonstrating the MIDP and KJava APIs.**

| **Part 2 – Developing for cellular phones and pagers** |
| --- |
| Chapter 4 — A simple MIDP application |
| Chapter 5 — MIDP user interface |
| Chapter 6 — MIDP data storage |
| Chapter 7 — Connecting to the Internet |
| **Part 3 – Developing for PDAs** |
| Chapter 8 — J2ME on a PDA, a KJava introduction |
| Chapter 9 — KJava user interface |
| Chapter 10 — KJava data storage |

\* Note — the networking service is also reused and connected in the KJava version of the application in chapter 10.

## 3.5  SUMMARY

In this chapter, we examined our hypothetical customer and defined the requirements for our tutorial application. Based on the requirements, we established a general system design outlining the major components of the system. With the major features of the application laid out, we are ready to implement our application. As we will see, each API may require certain changes in implementation based on the capabilities of the underlying platform. These will be specifically evident in the user interface and database arenas, as intended by the J2ME configuration/profile architecture. In the end, however, we will have at least two different devices with the same applications outlined in this chapter.

# *Developing for cellular phones and pagers*

In this part, we explore the CLDC and MIDP APIs in some detail. As you may recall from chapter 2, the CLDC and MIDP are guided by J2ME specifications. We will demonstrate the APIs in a tutorial application which was initially described in chapter 3. The tutorial application allows a customer to use a cell phone or two-way pager to get and see stock or mutual fund quotes. This tutorial application will allow us to see the major aspects of a J2ME application, namely user interface, event handling, data storage, input/output and network connectivity.

**C H A P T E R    4**

# A simple MIDP application

This chapter introduces you to the entire process of creating a J2ME application using the Mobile Information Device Profile (MIDP). In order to illustrate this example a simple application will be used. In doing this, we introduce a number of J2ME terms and concepts, and provide a cursory introduction to the J2ME API. It's always a good idea to become familiar with some of the terminology and the paradigm of a new software environment before trying to tackle a big project. This will set the stage for upcoming chapters where each concept will be covered in more detail and we look at using J2ME to build our tutorial application. For now, the goal is to get an application up and running quickly and to introduce you to the MIDP development environment.

All of the examples are described using the Windows operating system. We do not address the particular syntax of other operating system commands, but the general concepts hold. If you are not running Windows, you will need to translate the commands appropriately.

## 4.1 QUESTIONS ABOUT THE MIDP DEVELOPMENT ENVIRONMENT

When starting out in any new application development environment, most people usually have a number of general questions about the environment and tools for doing the job. Let's see if we can head off a few of these before we get started.

### 4.1.1 Can I do this without an actual device?

Absolutely! Many emulators are freely available and allow you to run and test J2ME applications right on your desktop. We will discuss how to obtain and use each type of emulator when the time is right. But first we will concentrate on the code.

### 4.1.2 What device do I start with?

The Mobile Information Device Profile has been designed mainly with cellular phones and pagers in mind. However, MIDP can run on other types of devices, such as PDAs. Sun currently has an implementation of MIDP that runs on Palm OS devices. However, the current MIDP user interface capabilities are rather limiting on a PDA. For this example, a cellular phone will be chosen as the primary target device for the application. Since we are developing to the MIDP, rather than a specific device, the application will run on any MIDP-compliant device. So at this point, all we need to be concerned about is that the desired target devices support MIDP.

### 4.1.3 Do I have to use the command line tools?

No, there are a number of Integrated Development Environments (IDEs) available that take care of the dirty work for you. Sun's Wireless Toolkit is a good example. However, this chapter is intended to give you a detailed, behind-the-scenes example of what goes into creating a J2ME application. Therefore we will use the command line tools provided by Sun's reference implementations. We hope this will give you a better understanding of the technology.

### 4.1.4 The example: what are we going to do?

This chapter uses a variation of the ubiquitous Hello World application. The application is rather simple in functionality; it just displays a string of text to the screen. However, the intent of this chapter is to quickly cover the lifecycle of developing a complete application and deploying it to a device. More sophisticated applications will be built in later chapters.

## 4.2 DEVELOPING MIDP APPLICATIONS

As mentioned previously, this example will work for both a cellular phone and a pager. How does this dual functionality affect the way we write or build the application? As we will see, it does not affect how we create the application at all. The only difference comes at the end when we deploy the application and need to deal with the specific device itself.

Given the range of devices J2ME is designed to support, cellular phones and pagers rank at the low end, being two of the most limited devices in the J2ME spectrum. These limitations are especially noticeable in the areas of the user interface and available memory. Cellular phones, for example, typically have a one-handed keyboard. Entering letters becomes tedious quickly since the user is forced to cycle through three or more alphabetic characters represented on each key. Furthermore, cellular phones may have as little as 40 KB of memory available for your application once the virtual machine and runtime libraries are loaded.

As discussed in chapter 2, in order to deal with these limitations, both cellular phone and pager applications require a configuration and profile combination that addresses these limitations. This is where the Connected Limited Device Configuration (CLDC) and Mobile Information Device Profile (MIDP) come into the picture. The CLDC is designed for devices with limited characteristics. Since configurations address the horizontal needs of a wide variety of devices, an additional architectural piece is needed to support the more device-specific capabilities, most notably user interface and data storage. This is how profiles, or in this case MIDP, fits in.

Another piece that we will need is the virtual machine that supports the CLDC. This is the K virtual machine (KVM), which is also discussed in chapter 2. This is a specially designed reference implementation virtual machine that has a much smaller footprint than the standard Java virtual machine. Because of the small footprint, Java can run on memory-constrained devices such as a cellular phone.

### 4.2.1 Getting started

First we need to get our hands on the MIDP development environment. We will use Sun's reference implementation that is available in a single download from the following URL: http://java.sun.com/products/midp.

DISTRIBUTION NOTE    As of this writing, the current publicly available version of the MIDP from Sun's web site listed above is version 1.0.3. However, depending on when you purchase this text and go to Sun's site, the version of MIDP may have changed. With the 1.0.3 release and using the default installation directories, MIDP installs in a directory called midp1.0.3fcs. This will obviously vary depending on your downloaded version. For this reason, we refer generically to the MIDP directory throughout this text as midp-fcs.

Download and unpack the distribution into the directory from which you want to work. Note that the distribution unpacks into a top-level directory named similar to midp-fcs. For convenience, set up the following system environment variables. These variables are used in this example for convenience and have no effect on the MIDP environment.

```
MIDP=\midp-fcs
MIDPClasses=\midp-fcs\classes
MIDPTools=\midp-fcs\bin
```

With the development environment in place, we are ready to begin developing our first J2ME application. Using MIDP, applications are created by extending the `javax.microedition.midlet.MIDlet` class. This class acts as the interface between the application management software on the device and MIDP applications. It is important to understand that each J2ME profile may define different starting points (classes and methods) for an application. For MIDP the starting point is a MIDlet.

## 4.2.2    What is a MIDlet?

A MIDlet is an abstract class that is subclassed to form the basis of the application. By subclassing the `MIDlet` class, we define an interface between our application and the application management software on the device. A MIDlet is the heart of a MIDP application and allows the device to start, pause and destroy the application.

The `MIDlet` class resides in the package `javax.microedition.midlet`. The code to declare a MIDlet looks something like this:

```
import javax.microedition.midlet.MIDlet;

public class HiSmallWorld extends MIDlet {
}
```

For this example, we need to add a constructor that creates a `TextBox` (a GUI widget that allows us to display a message) and a member variable to hold the `TextBox` instance since we will need to reference it from a couple of places.

```
import javax.microedition.midlet.MIDlet;
import javax.microedition.lcdui.*;

public class HiSmallWorld extends MIDlet {
  private TextBox textbox;
  public HiSmallWorld() {
    textbox = new TextBox("", "Hi Small World!", 20, 0);
  }
}
```

Since `MIDlet` is an abstract class, our `HiSmallWorld` class needs to implement a few methods before it will compile. There are three methods that require attention: `startApp()`, `pauseApp()` and `destroyApp(boolean unconditional)`.

When a device receives a message to start a MIDlet, the MIDlet is instantiated and the application management service on the device calls `startApp()`. At this point, our application takes over and does any initialization that may be required. In our example, we make the textbox the active element. Do not worry about the use of the `Display` class for now, as this will be covered in a subsequent chapter.

> **WARNING**    The `startApp()` method can be called a number of times during the lifecycle of a MIDlet. Therefore, it should not be used to perform initialization. For example, a MIDlet can be placed in a paused state as a result of a call to the `pauseApp()` method. In order to restart, and release it from the paused state, the `startApp()` method is invoked. If you have to do some initialization on the MIDlet, it needs to be carried out in conjunction with the constructor, not the `startApp()` method.

```
public void startApp() {
  Display.getDisplay(this).setCurrent(textbox);
}
```

The pauseApp() method is called by the device when the user, or the device, needs to suspend our application's activity to perform some other task. When the device invokes this method, our application is responsible for placing itself into a paused state.

Since we are only displaying a message to the screen, and there is nothing to do to pause the application, we will implement this as an empty method.

```
public void pauseApp() {
}
```

At the point, if the user chooses to close the application, or for some reason the system requests that the application be closed, the method destroyApp(boolean unconditional) is called. This method is invoked to allow our application to clean up any resources that it may be using, such as a network or database connection. This method takes a single, boolean parameter. This parameter indicates how much say our application has in being destroyed. If the parameter is true, our application will have no choice but to clean up its resources and prepare for being destroyed. If the parameter is false, the application can throw a MIDletStateChange-Exception exception to prevent the destroy method from taking place and to continue running. Again, this exception can only be thrown if the parameter is false. Since there are no resources that need to be cleaned up in this application destroyApp (boolean unconditional) is also implemented as an empty method.

```
public void destroyApp(boolean unconditional) {
}
```

The full source code for our first J2ME application is shown in Listing 4.1.

**Listing 4.1   HiSmallWorld.java**

```java
import javax.microedition.midlet.MIDlet;
import javax.microedition.lcdui.*;

public class HiSmallWorld extends MIDlet {

  private TextBox textbox;
  public HiSmallWorld() {
    textbox = new TextBox("", "Hi Small World!", 20, 0);
  }

  public void startApp() {
    Display.getDisplay(this).setCurrent(textbox);
  }

  public void pauseApp() {
  }

  public void destroyApp(boolean unconditional) {
  }
}
```

This is all the code required to get our application up and running. The next step is to compile the application.

**WIRELESS TOOLKIT** Sun Microsystems provides an IDE for developing MIDP applications. Called the Wireless Toolkit, it is available from Sun's web site at: http://java.sun.com/products/j2mewtoolkit/.We do not use the toolkit throughout our examples and tutorial application for two reasons:

1 We want you to understand what is actually occurring behind the scenes when writing J2ME applications. The compiling, preverifying, jarring and deployment are important parts of the J2ME development process and should be understood.

2 IDEs change or may have bugs. You may switch development tools or you may find an IDE that has a problem or bug. An IDE can do part or most of the work for you when it comes to developing applications, but it is important to understand the work being accomplished by the IDE just in case the IDE has difficulties or you change IDEs.

In appendix D, we demonstrate the use of the Wireless Toolkit for the Hello World example. If you download the Wireless Toolkit from Sun, you should still be able to use the application code in the rest of this text. However, be aware that compiling, preverifying, jarring, and deploying of the applications will require different steps and use a different emulator executable.

## 4.2.3 Compiling the application

This is done using the standard `javac` compiler command. However, since we are compiling an application for the J2ME environment (rather than J2SE) the –bootclasspath option must be used. This option takes advantage of Java's cross-compilation capability. The cross-compilation feature is new in the Java 2 platform and allows the Java compiler to target the class files for an environment other than standard Java. Our target environment is J2ME and by using the –bootclasspath option we can instruct the compiler to use the J2ME libraries. Without this we could accidentally use classes or method signatures not supported by J2ME (such as Double) and as a result, these errors would not be caught until runtime.

Use the following command line to compile the application:

```
>javac -g:none -bootclasspath %MIDPClasses% HiSmallWorld.java
```

The –g:none option is used to prevent debug information from being included in the class files. This is an optional flag, but it helps reduce the size of the class files. The %MIDPClasses% variable is the environment variable we set up earlier. This variable points to the J2ME classes and it is passed as the –bootclasspath parameter.

### 4.2.4 Preverifying the application

For security reasons, the standard Java Runtime Environment verifies each class file before loading it into memory. This is done to ensure that the class file is valid and does not attempt to access memory outside of its boundaries or access disk. Since J2ME must cater to devices that are more limited than a desktop computer, some of the J2ME virtual machines handle class file verification somewhat differently than the standard Java VMs, namely, verification does not entirely take place on the device. Instead, as part of the deployment process, each class file must be preverified using a `preverify` utility provided in the J2ME development environment. This utility verifies each class file and modifies it to include special flags indicating their validity. At runtime, the J2ME virtual machine checks these flags. If the flags are present and indicate a valid class file, the VM assumes the class is OK to run. Without these flags the VM will throw an exception or abort the class loading process.

Preverification is performed using the `preverify.exe` utility found under the bin directory. Run the following command to preverify the application:

```
>%MIDPTools%\preverify -classpath %MIDPClasses%;. HiSmallWorld
```

It is important to note that this utility creates new class files. By default, this command places the output class files in a directory called `\output` off of the current directory. To change the output directory, use the -d option as with other Java utilities. The following version of the command places the class files in a directory named "preverified" nested below the current directory:

```
>%MIDPTools%\preverify -classpath %MIDPClasses%;.
    -d .\preverified HiSmallWorld
```

For each of these commands we specify a `classpath` of only the J2ME classes, and our own classes we have created, to ensure that the class files generated are suitable for the J2ME target environment.

If the `preverify` utility is having trouble loading your class file, which is reported by the message "Error loading class HiSmallWorld", make sure `classpath` is set properly to find the file `HiSmallWorld.class` that was created by `javac`.

### 4.2.5 Running the application

With the classes compiled and preverified, our application is finally ready to run. This is where we need an emulator. If you downloaded the MIDP reference implementation, you already have an emulator and are ready to go. The emulator is an executable named `midp` and is located in the `midp-fcs\bin` directory. We will run our application by typing the following command:

```
>%MIDPTools%\midp -classpath %MIDPClasses%;.\output HiSmallWorld
```

This command runs the `midp` executable, passing the MIDP classes and our application's classes on the -`classpath` parameter. Note that we must direct the `midp` utility to look in the .\output directory (relative to the current directory) for the preverified version of our classes. If we had just specified the current directory ("."), midp would find the original classes generated by javac. Since these classes do not contain the proper preverification flags, the J2ME runtime environment would not be able to load the classes and a runtime exception would abort the class loading process.

If the application runs successfully, your emulator will look like figure 4.1.

**Figure 4.1**
**The HiSmallWorld MIDlet written above is depicted here running in the MIDP emulator. While the MIDP specification dictates common Java functionality across the spectrum of devices, in this case cellular telephones, each device may have a slightly different display. Thus, emulators often provide various "skins" to test applications running in various displays.**

After closing the emulator, the output from the console should look similar to the following text.

```
E:\work\HiWorld>\midp-fcs\bin\midp -classpath \midp-fcs\classes;.\output
HiSmallWorld
Execution completed successfully
8205 bytecodes executed
7 thread switches
204 classes loaded (149 bytes)
220 objects allocated (9572 bytes)
0 garbage collections
0 bytes collected
0 objects deferred in GC
0 (maximum) objects deferred at any one time
0 rescans of heap because of deferral overflow
0 pointer validations requiring heap scans
Current memory usage 9572 bytes
Heap size 300000 bytes
```

### 4.2.6 Troubleshooting

If there are problems running the application here are some debugging tips:

- Make sure the application compiled successfully when you ran javac and make sure the preverify utility ran successfully without errors.

- If an error such as "The name specified is not recognized as an internal or external command, operable program or batch file." occurs, this means Windows was unable to find the midp executable. Adjust the command path to point to midp.exe.

- The most notorious runtime problem in the Java environment is getting the `classpath` set properly so that the correct versions of classes are loaded, and loaded in the proper order. The following two problems are related to `classpath`:

  - If an error such as "One or more `MIDlet` class(es) not found: null" was reported, the `midp` emulator was not able to find your classes. Make sure `classpath` is specified correctly and make certain your class files are where you think they are. Remember, the `classpath` must specify both the J2ME class libraries (`\midp-fcs\classes`) and your application's classes.

  - If an error such as "ALERT: Error verifying class HiSmallWorld" was reported, the `midp` executable was unable to load the class. Most likely the emulator found the unverified version of `HiSmallWorld.class` instead of the preverified version, so make sure `classpath` includes the preverified version of the class. Be certain the unverified version is not included on `classpath` or its path is specified after the preverified path. Try deleting the unverified version of the class file to see if you get a different error or the correct, preverified version is found.

### 4.2.7    JARing MIDlets

The previous example shows the `midp` emulator directly accessing the class file. However, in most cases MIDP applications should be deployed as JAR files. This is done for several reasons. First of all, depending on the network protocol and the client-server software involved, JAR files can be more efficient when downloading multiple applications over protocols such as HTTP since the entire JAR is downloaded with a single connection (rather than a connection for each class file). Furthermore, MIDlets can be deployed as part of a MIDlet suite. The details of creating a MIDlet suite will be covered in a moment, but first we modify the example to use a JAR file for deployment.

Using the existing class files, we can run the following `jar` command to create a JAR file:

```
>jar cf hi.jar -C .\output HiSmallWorld.class
```

The "`cf`" parameters tell the `jar` utility to create a new JAR file named "`hi.jar`". The –C option is used to change to a specified directory and include a specified file. In this case, the –C option is used to switch to the `\output` directory to pick up the `HiSmallWorld.class` file without having the `\output` directory appear in the JAR file as an attribute of the class. (Without using the –C option the runtime environment would think our MIDlet resided in a package named `output`.)

Now let's run `midp` using our newly created JAR file. In order to do this, make a minor adjustment to the `classpath` setting to include the JAR file that now contains the class file.

```
>%MIDPTools%\midp -classpath %MIDPClasses%;.\hi.jar HiSmallWorld
```

This should not change the MIDlet. The only difference is that we are now running the application from a JAR file. If the emulator cannot find the class, then either the JAR file is not valid or there may be something wrong with the `classpath`.

## 4.2.8  Developing MIDlet suites

Multiple MIDlets can be grouped and deployed as a unit using a MIDlet suite. A MIDlet suite is composed of a JAR file containing all the MIDlets and supporting classes and an application descriptor file. The application descriptor file is a text file containing information about the MIDlet suite, such as the names of the MIDlets, the location of the JAR file, vendor information, etc. Application descriptor files have the extension "`jad`" and provide the device, and in some cases a server environment, with information about the MIDlet suite so it can be run over a network or installed physically on the device.

Deploying MIDlets as part of a suite has some advantages over deploying the MIDlets individually. The most significant advantage is that MIDlets in a suite can share resources such as data stored on the device. For example, within an MIDP implementation, records are stored in a device-dependent area that is not directly accessible by the Java APIs. This data storage area is controlled at the MIDlet level. Within a MIDlet suite however, all MIDlets can share record stores and create multiple, uniquely named, record stores. In addition to the ability to share resources, MIDlet suites are deployed using JAR files. As mentioned previously this can allow the client to be more efficient when downloading the application.

To better understand dealing with MIDlet suites, we are going to need more than one MIDlet. For simplicity, make a copy of `HiSmallWorld`, giving it the incredibly innovative name of `HiSmallWorld2` and change the output string to read "Hi Small World2". Once this is done, compile and preverify the new `HiSmallWorld2` class.

```
>javac -g:none -bootclasspath %MIDPClasses% HiSmallWorld2.java

>%MIDPTools%\preverify -classpath %MIDPClasses%;. HiSmallWorld2
```

**NOTE**    *Display limitations*  It is worth pointing out that, on the MIDP cellular phone emulators, a 15-character `String` (give or take a few characters) is about the longest `String` that can be displayed without wrapping. Since the Connected Limited Device Configuration (which is the configuration for MIDP) addresses *limited* device implementations, care should be taken to understand the different limitations of the target devices for which you are writing applications. Different devices have different display limitations even though they all may support MIDP. Pagers, and other cellular phones, for example, may have a wider and narrower screen.

Now we are ready to create our MIDlet suite. There is no real significance to this suite in terms of functionality. The goal is to walk through how MIDlet suites are created.

## The MIDlet suite descriptor file

The first step is to create a descriptor file for the MIDlet suite. A descriptor file is a text file with a `jad` extension. The attribute names are case-sensitive. A list of the attribute names and their purposes is provided in table 4.1. The Java Application Manager (JAM) on the device uses the descriptor to manage the application lifecycle. The JAM is responsible or participates in activities such as downloading, installing, inspecting, executing and uninstalling applications.

**Table 4.1** The Java Application Descriptor is used by the JAM to manage a MIDlet suite's applications on the device. As this table shows, it contains a wealth of information about the suite.

| Attribute Name | Description |
| --- | --- |
| MIDlet-Name | Name of the MIDlet suite. |
| MIDlet-Version | Version of the MIDlet suite. The format must follow the convention Major.Minor.Micro (X.X[.X]) where the micro version is optional (defaults to zero if omitted). Each version number is allowed two digits (0-99). If this tag is missing, the version is assumed to be 0.0.0. Any nonzero version is considered a newer version than 0.0.0. |
| MIDlet-Vendor | Vendor that supplies this MIDlet suite. |
| MIDlet-Description | Text description of the MIDlet suite. (Optional) |
| MIDlet-Info-URL | Location where more information can be found about the suite. (Optional) |
| MIDlet-Jar-Size | Size of the JAR file specified by this descriptor. |
| MIDlet-Jar-URL | The URL indicating from where the JAR can be loaded. |
| MIDlet-Data-Size | The minimum number of bytes of persistent data required by the MIDlet suite. The default is zero. (Optional) |
| MIDlet-Icon | The name of a portable network graphic file (PNG) within the JAR file representing the MIDlet suite. (Optional) |
| Micro Edition-Profile | Profiles used by the application. |
| Micro Edition-Configuration | Configuration used by the application. |
| MIDlet-1 | The first MIDlet in the list of available MIDlets (if this is a MIDlet suite). For each MIDlet specified, the following syntax is observed: *Description, icon name, MIDlet class name.* |
| | The description appears in the menu when the list of MIDlets is displayed. |
| MIDlet-n | Nth MIDlet in the suite |

For our example we define a JAD (Java Application Descriptor) file with the following properties. We do not specify an icon for any of our MIDlets at this point. Create this file in the current directory. If you have been following the examples, this is the same directory where the Java source files you are working with are located.

```
MIDlet-Name: SmallWorldsuite
MIDlet-Version: 1.0.0
MIDlet-Vendor: Catapult Technologies, Inc.
MIDlet-Description: Sample suite of Small World MIDlets
MIDlet-Info-URL: http://www.ctimn.com/
MIDlet-Jar-URL: http://localhost/hi.jar
MIDlet-Jar-Size: 3000
MicroEdition-Profile: MIDP-1.0
```

```
MicroEdition-Configuration: CLDC-1.0
MIDlet-1: Hello1, , HiSmallWorld
MIDlet-2: Hello2, , HiSmallWorld2
```

## JARing the MIDlet suite

The JAR file for a MIDlet suite must contain a manifest. A manifest provides the runtime environment information about how the JAR file is configured, any security information and what the JAR contains. The J2ME runtime environment compares the manifest to the application descriptor as a precaution before loading a MIDlet suite.

The values of `MIDlet-Name`, `MIDlet-Version` and `MIDlet-Vendor` must be the same in both the manifest and the descriptor file. If these values do not match, the MIDlet suite is considered invalid. Developers may define descriptor attributes not beginning with `MIDlet-` to provide property information to the application.

To create a manifest, simply provide the JAD file as input to the `jar` command. Modify the `jar` command used previously to create the JAR for our MIDlet suite.

```
>jar -cfm hi.jar HiMIDletsuite.jad -C ./output HiSmallWorld.class -C
./output HiSmallWorld2.class
```

The `jar` command now contains an "m" option instructing the JAR utility to create a manifest using `HiMIDletsuite.jad`. Note that the `-C` option must be repeated for each class specified in the `jar` operation. If a wildcard is used (e.g., `*.class`) the `-C` option is applied only to the first class file and is ignored for the remaining class files. In this scenario, unverified classes can accidentally be added to the JAR file, causing problems at runtime.

Now we are ready to run our MIDlet suite. Use the `–descriptor` option with the `midp` emulator to run the suite directly.

```
%MIDP%\bin\midp -classpath %MIDPClasses%;.\hi.jar -descriptor HiMIDletsuite.jad
```

The first screen that appears is a list of our MIDlets that make up the MIDlet suite. This list is composed of the MIDlet description specified for each MIDlet in the JAD file. At this point, we do not have an Exit button defined that allows the user to exit the application gracefully. This requires a user interface component and the use of event handling that is beyond the scope of this exercise. Both user interface components and event handling are covered in the next chapter. For now, we have to live with running one MIDlet at a time and exiting the emulator. Figure 4.2 shows the Hello2 MIDlet running.

So now we have managed to build and run MIDlets and MIDlet suites. How are MIDlets intended to be used in the real world? So far we have been running MIDlets directly from the computer on which we develop them, using the `midp` emulator. However, running MIDlets on an actual device is slightly different. First of all, the application must somehow get onto the device. There are basically two ways that MIDlets can find their way onto a device. They can be installed physically to the device or they can be temporarily loaded into memory over a network connection.

**Figure 4.2   HiSmallWorld2 joins HiSmallWorld as part of the HiMIDletsuite running in the MIDP emulator. As the picture on the left shows, when a MIDlet suite is deployed to a device, the device knows to provide an application kick-off screen that allows the user to select MIDlets for execution.**

Fortunately, the midp emulator supports the ability to run MIDlets in both of these ways in addition to running them directly, as we have done so far. To begin, we discuss simulating MIDlet deployment using the midp emulator. This allows us to explore these deployment techniques and get our environment set up correctly. Once these concepts are familiar to us, we will deal with the actual devices.

Accessing MIDlets over the Internet is a very likely scenario so we will begin by accessing our MIDlet suite using a Web server. In this scenario the application is dynamically downloaded to the device each time we run the emulator.

### 4.2.9    Running MIDlet suites from a web server

In order to access a MIDlet using a Web server, you need a Web server that the midp emulator can access. This example uses the Apache web server, which is available at the following URL: http://httpd.apache.org

Once the Web server is installed, the MIME type configuration needs to be modified to handle the jad extension. MIME stands for Multipurpose Internet Mail Extension and allows the Web server to know what types of content the client supports.

For Apache, adding the following line to the mime.types file specifies the JAD MIME type.

```
text/vnd.sun.j2me.app-descriptor       jad
```

Deploying a MIDlet suite to a web environment is simply a matter of placing the JAR and JAD files in an area visible to the Web server. For Apache, this is the htdocs directory. Copy the files hi.jar and HiMIDletSuite.jad into this directory and start the web server. Make sure the Web server starts without errors. Then invoke midp.exe using the –transient option.

```
>%MIDP%\bin\midp -transient http://localhost/HiMIDletSuite.jad
```

There should not be any differences in the application itself. The only difference is that we are now accessing the application over http.

### 4.2.10    Installing MIDlet suites locally

The midp emulator supports the ability to emulate installing a MIDlet suite from a location, either a file or URL, so we can run it locally on the "device." The following command simulates installing a MIDlet suite locally on a device via a Web server.

This command assumes the Web server is up and running and the application has been deployed to an area visible to the Web server. (See the previous example to understand how to set this up.)

```
>%MIDP%\bin\midp -install http://localhost/HiMIDletSuite.jad
```

Before we run the installed suite, let us make sure our application is installed. This can be done using the –list option:

```
>%MIDP%\bin\midp -list
```

The output should be something like the following:

```
E:\_book\work\HiWorld>\_book\midp-fcs\bin\midp -list
JamMode = LIST
 SmallWorldSuite
   Hello1
   Hello2
```

Once a MIDlet suite is installed, the Web server is no longer necessary. The application can run as if physically installed on the device using the –run option:

```
>%MIDP%\bin\midp -run SmallWorldSuite
```

Note that the –run option requires the name of the suite specified in the JAD file, not the name of the JAD file.

To remove an installed MIDlet suite use the –remove option followed by the name of the suite to remove:

```
>%MIDP%\bin\midp -remove SmallWorldSuite
```

To obtain profile and configuration information for an installed suite, use the –version option followed by the name of the suite:

```
>%MIDP%\bin\midp -version SmallWorldSuite
```

## 4.3  SUMMARY

In this chapter, we have looked at setting up a J2ME development environment, specifically a MIDP environment. We also examined a little of the CLDC and MIDP API while developing the simplest of applications. With the development environment in place and a fundamental understanding of how J2ME applications are built and deployed using MIDP, you are ready to get into some of the more powerful capabilities of this J2ME environment.

# MIDP user interface

We start our exploration of the J2ME API with a look at the Mobile Information Device Profile on the Connected Limited Device Configuration. The CLDC was designed for very resource-constrained devices (those with less than 512 KB of memory). On top of that, the MIDP was designed for devices on the lowest end of this low-range configuration. Specifically, the MIDP was designed primarily for cellular telephones and pagers. These devices have restrictive memory, screen real estate and input devices, which are just some of the qualities that make building applications at this end of the spectrum more challenging.

In this chapter, we look primarily at the graphical user interface of the MIDP. Because most of the events that must be handled are generated from the interactions with the user interface, we also examine MIDP's event handling. Although touched on in the Hello World example of chapter 4, the MIDP's application control is unique and requires additional explanation. Therefore, we also take a more in-depth look at the MIDP's MIDlet class. As is the case in all the tutorial chapters, we will bring to life the API reviewed in this chapter by implementing the appropriate piece of the tutorial application with what was learned in the chapter.

In summary, we will:

- revisit the MIDP Application Control
- assess the general state and constraints of UI development for MIDP devices
- examine the MIDP graphical user interface high-level and low-level APIs
- look at general event handling in MIDP
- examine the high-level and low-level event models and event handling API in the MIDP
- implement the tutorial application control and user interface in the MIDP by:
  - developing the tutorial application control using MIDP MIDlets
  - implementing the tutorial application's user interface displays using the MIDP high-level and low-level APIs
  - developing the tutorial application's MIDP event handling mechanism

## 5.1  MIDP APPLICATION CONTROL

Before we examine the user interface API in MIDP, we will take a closer look at application control and infrastructure. As we discussed in chapter 4, application control is provided by extending the `javax.microedition.midlet.MIDlet` class. Therefore, the application controllers on cell phone and pager applications will extend the MIDP abstract `javax.microedition.midlet.MIDlet` class. As we also saw in the last chapter, MIDlets must implement three abstract, protected methods specified by `MIDlet`. Namely, our applications will have to override `destroyApp(boolean unconditional)`, `startApp()` and `pauseApp()`. MIDlets can exist in one of three states: Active, Paused and Destroyed. These abstract methods allow the application to conduct work in the transition between the states (figure 5.1).

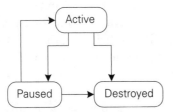

**Figure 5.1**
**MIDlets exist in one of three states as depicted in this state diagram. When started, the MIDlet is in the Active state. Once active, the MIDlet can be destroyed or paused. From the paused state, the application can be reactivated.**

When a MIDlet is started with a call to `startApp()`, the MIDlet enters the Active state. In an Active state, a MIDlet can utilize any resources it has available. In the Paused state, a MIDlet must release all resources and become inactive. A MIDlet enters the paused state through a call to the `pauseApp()` method. A MIDlet application can go back and forth between the Active and Paused state. From either the Active or Paused state, the MIDlet can enter the Destroyed state by invoking the `destroyApp(boolean unconditional)` method. Once in the Destroyed state, a MIDlet cannot return to either the Active or Paused state. All resources must be released and persistent data must be saved. Any failure to enter a desired state is met with a `MIDletStateChangeException`. This exception is only valid during a call to `destroyApp(boolean unconditional)` when the unconditional flag is set to false. Otherwise, the MIDlet will still enter the Destroyed state no matter what is returned from a `destroyApp(true)` call.

## 5.2  THE INVESTMENT QUOTE APPLICATION CONTROL IN MIDP

As a first step in implementing the tutorial application in the MIDP, two application control classes are created. The `ObtainQuoteMIDlet` will handle the ObtainQuote features from our use case requirements while the `RetrieveQuoteMIDlet` will manage the other identified use, namely RetrieveQuote. The structure for the controllers looks like the class diagram depicted in figure 5.2.

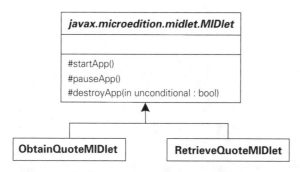

**Figure 5.2**
**ObtainQuoteMIDlet and RetrieveQuoteMIDlet serve as application controllers for the Investment Quote system. Both classes extend MIDlet as depicted in this class diagram.**

Given the required three MIDlet abstract methods, the general construct to implement `ObtainQuoteMIDlet` starts off looking something like the code in listing 5.1.

**Listing 5.1  ObtainQuoteMIDlet.java**

```
import javax.microedition.midlet.*;

public class ObtainQuoteMIDlet extends MIDlet{

  public ObtainQuoteMIDlet () {
  }

  protected void startApp() {
  }

  protected void pauseApp() {
  }

  protected void destroyApp(boolean unconditional) {
  }
}
```

❶ **The required MIDlet methods**

Along with the required methods, we have also provided the MIDlet with a single constructor method. At this time, these methods do nothing. We will fill in the details as we need them. Likewise, the code to implement `RetrieveQuoteMIDlet` begins with that in listing 5.2.

```
import javax.microedition.midlet.*;

public class RetrieveQuoteMIDlet extends MIDlet{

  public RetrieveQuoteMIDlet () {
  }

  protected void startApp() {
  }

  protected void pauseApp() {
  }

  protected void destroyApp(boolean unconditional) {
  }
}
```

❶ Again, the required MIDlet methods

We will want to JAR the two MIDlets and create a MIDlet suite called QuoteMIDletSuite. To do this, we need a Java Application Descriptor (JAD) file. For our tutorial application we define a JAD file as shown in listing 5.3. We will not specify an icon for any of our MIDlets at this point. Create this JAD file in the directory containing the MIDlet Java files.

```
MIDlet-Name: QuoteMIDletSuite
MIDlet-Version: 1.0
MIDlet-Vendor: Catapult Technologies, Inc.
MIDlet-Description: Obtain and Retrieve Quote Tutorial MIDlets
MIDlet-Info-URL: http://www.ctimn.com/
MIDlet-Jar-URL: http://localhost/quote.jar
MIDlet-Jar-Size: 3000
MicroEdition-Profile: MIDP-1.0
MicroEdition-Configuration: CLDC-1.0
MIDlet-1: ObtainQuote, , ObtainQuoteMIDlet
MIDlet-2: RetrieveQuote, , RetrieveQuoteMIDlet
```

**WHY A MIDLET SUITE?** Nothing in the requirements of the tutorial application necessitates the creation of a MIDlet suite here. However, the need for a suite will become more evident in the next chapter when we look at persistent storage for the application. Given the fact that the two applications are related to each other and are likely to share common classes at some point in the future, having a suite is a good idea.

To compile, preverify, JAR, and run our MIDlets, invoke the commands listed below. As we did in chapter 4, we assume that environment variables have been conveniently set up to help in the compile, preverify and execute commands. The `MIDP` environment variable should be set to the location of your MIDP directory (\midp-fcs in our case), the `MIDPClasses` environment variable should be set to the location of your MIDP classes (\midp-fcs\classes in our case), and finally, the `MIDPTools` variable should be set to the location of the MIDP tool set (\midp-fcs\bin on our system).

### Compile

```
>javac -g:none -bootclasspath %MIDPClasses% ObtainQuoteMIDlet.java
>javac -g:none -bootclasspath %MIDPClasses% RetrieveQuoteMIDlet.java
```

### Preverify

```
>%MIDPTools%\preverify -classpath %MIDPClasses%;. ObtainQuoteMIDlet
>%MIDPTools%\preverify -classpath %MIDPClasses%;. RetrieveQuoteMIDlet
```

### JAR

```
>jar -cfm quote.jar QuoteMIDletSuite.jad -C .
/output ObtainQuoteMIDlet.class -C ./output RetrieveQuoteMIDlet.class
```

### Run

```
>%MIDPTools%\midp -classpath %MIDPClasses%;.\quote.jar -descriptor
QuoteMIDletSuite.jad
```

Congratulations! If you were successful in implementing the first phase of the tutorial application in MIDP, then the results of executing this last line should look something like the picture in figure 5.3.

**Figure 5.3**
**Even though the two MIDlets of the Investment Quote system do little at this point, the MIDlet selection menu provides the ObtainQuote and RetrieveQuote after successfully writing, compiling, preverifying and deploying the MIDlets. The names displayed in the selection menu are obtained from the JAD file.**

Pressing either selection in the MIDlet suite choice list will activate that MIDlet. However, since neither MIDlet currently performs any action, nothing will occur and the customer must exit the system (the emulator) to leave the application. We now have the basic structure for the MIDP applications, and while the applications are not very exciting yet, we will begin to hang functionality off of this basic structure. We will start with a simple means to interact with the user.

**OPERATING
A KEYPAD**

If you have been programming desktops and servers for years but never pro-grammed a device that does not have a keyboard, you may be surprised to find out that operating the input mechanism associated with a cell phone is unique. In the previous example, you may have executed the run com-mand without knowing how to select any menu option or operate the em-ulator on the screen.

Operating a keypad on a device such as a cellular telephone can vary from device to device. However, each device has at least one button on the keypad associated with "selection." Pushing this button on the keypad is analogous to hitting the Enter key on a desktop computer with a keyboard. On the default emulator provided with the J2ME reference implementa-tions, the Select button is the button at the center of the directional buttons (see figure 5.4). Again, while the Select button must exist, its implementa-tion is device-specific.

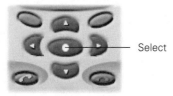

**Figure 5.4**
**The keypad select button on the MIDP
emulator and several cell phones is
located at the center of the arrow keys.**

Each device must also provide some means of navigating the different menu choices and text displayed on a screen. In the default phone emula-tor, menu navigation, character entry, and other user interface widgets that are displayed on the screen are accessed using the arrow keys. In the exam-ple provided, only the up and down arrow keys are needed to navigate be-tween the MIDlet application choices. (figure 5.5)

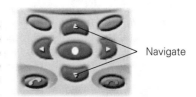

**Figure 5.5**
**The up and down arrow keys on the
keypad allow the users to navigate
through menu choices such as the
menu choice for choosing which
MIDlet to run in a suite.**

The power button on a cell phone will end execution of an application. In the emulator, pressing the simulated power button will also cause the em-ulator to close. (figure 5.6)

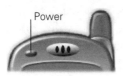

**Figure 5.6**
**You can also exit an application by
pushing the power off button.**

*CHAPTER 5   MIDP USER INTERFACE*

"Typing" with the keypad in a text entry field can be a cumbersome activity. The keys of a keypad each represent up to four characters. For example, the number '9' key on the keypad also represents the characters 'W', 'X', 'Y' and 'Z'. In user interface widgets where text entry is required, in order to type a 'W', hit the '9' key once. To generate an 'X', the '9' key must be pressed twice. However, do not take too long when pushing the keys on the keypad to get the desired character. Pausing between pushes of the key indicates that you wish to enter a second 'W', not an 'X'. To get the integer character associated with each key in the keypad, you must press the key once for each associated character and then press the key once again to get the integer. For example, to type the character '9', one must press the number '9' key five times without pause. On the emulator, the '0' key provides the 'Space'. This is, however, a non-standard implementation across various cellular phone keypads.

In the emulator, the '#' and '*' keys also provide some additional functionality. Again, functionality on these keys does not represent standard practice across all devices. Each vendor is provided some latitude in the mapping of functionality to the keypad keys. On the emulator, the '#' key can be used as a backspace key when editing text. The '*' key provides a kind of shift key. It toggles the rest of the keys between the upper case character set, lower case character set and numbers (allowing a user to be able to circumnavigate the problem of having to hit the '9' key five times to get a '9').

Some keys on the device can be programmed to represent certain actions on the part of the user. These are known as soft buttons. These will be discussed in the event handling portion of this chapter.

Take some time to play with the emulator and the target device and discover the mappings and functionality they offer. Unlike the now fairly standard keyboards that come with desktop computers, not all emulators and devices have the same keypad or the same keypad functionality.

---

## 5.3 TWO TYPES OF MIDP USER INTERFACE AND EVENT HANDLING

Developing user interfaces for J2ME devices can be quite challenging. A J2ME device is not even required to have a user interface and the size, shape and interactive capabilities of the device's interface can vary quite a bit. The unique display characteristics for devices are a large part of what J2ME profiles address. Recall that J2ME profiles provide focused support for devices and thus, specifically address user interface characteristics.

Developing user interfaces for small devices such as cell phones, pagers, PDAs, and so forth presents much more of a challenge. These devices have an even more restrictive user interface. The display capabilities of these devices may be restricted to a screen that is only an inch or two wide. Often, these devices are utilized with one hand and without the full attention of the user. Therefore, even simple pointing devices may not be available for user input.

Those familiar with J2SE are probably well acquainted with the Abstract Windowing Toolkit (AWT) and Java Foundation Classes (JFC). These packages provide the rich graphical user interface API for larger Java systems. However, the features of the AWT were considered to be too much for many of the J2ME resource-constrained environments, including the MIDP. Specifically, the AWT's event model is too big and expensive in its memory usage for constrained devices. Secondly, the screen size of a MIDP device is too small to support multiple and possibly overlapping windows, which the AWT provides. Finally, the AWT assumes a pointer (mouse or pen) input device that the MIDP is not required to have. For this reason, the MIDP has its own unique GUI API.

The MID Profile assumes only a 96×54 pixel, one-bit depth display and input from either a keypad or a touch screen. While the MIDP specification allows for user input via a one or two-handed keyboard or touch screen, most of the devices in the MIDP space operate with a simple keypad.

There are actually two types of GUI APIs provided for in the MIDP. A high-level API is intended for business applications and provides abstraction from low-level graphics management and placement of graphical elements. The high-level API allows the application to be highly portable from one MIDP device to the other, but at the cost of giving up fine-grained control of the application's look and feel.

## 5.3.1 High-level API

The high-level API provides a series of widgets or predefined graphical elements that can be added to and used on a display. With the high-level GUI API, the device, and not the application, handles the layout, scrolling, navigation, and visual characteristics such as color, shape, font and painting of the elements on the display. Along with the high-level GUI API, the MIDP has a high-level input event model, which will be covered later in this chapter.

## 5.3.2 Low-level API

Alternatively, in the low-level GUI API, the application has much more control over the display. This API was developed for applications such as games where the precise control and placement of graphical elements is required. In the low-level GUI API, a series of drawing methods allow the applications to create the display, shape by shape, if necessary, and paint it to the screen. This API also has a corresponding low-level event handling mechanism that will also be covered later in this chapter.

Applications that use the non-abstracted low-level API may not be portable to another platform since the application may be allowed to access system resources that may not be available on all devices. For example, an application could be written to draw in a pixel range that is outside of the display size of another device. To keep an application portable, the low-level API provides convenience methods for checking on the availability of non-portable resources. For instance, the application should check on the available display size before drawing to unavailable pixel ranges.

In the tutorial application, we take advantage of the high-level API to capture the customer's investment request information and display the results. However, in order to display the comparison chart depicting the price change in a bar graph, we utilize the low-level API.

## 5.4    THE MIDP USER INTERFACE API

The MIDP GUI API, from user interface widgets to event handling mechanisms, is wholly contained in the `javax.microedition.lcdui` package. Again, the user interface is broken out into two API levels:  high and low. We will first explore the high-level API that provides a set of predefined user interface elements used in building more business-oriented applications. Afterwards, we will examine the low-level API that provides the application developer with a great deal of freedom to draw shapes on the screen but at a cost of more acutely managing the display.

### 5.4.1    MIDP display control

Before the display of any widgets or shapes, we need access to the device screen. In MIDP, the device display is accessed through a manager called the `Display` object.

### The Display object

You may recall the use of the `Display` object in the `startApp()` method of our simple HelloWorld MIDlet in chapter 4.

```
Display.getDisplay(this).setCurrent(textbox);
```

In the MIDP, the `Display` object represents the manager of the device's screen or display. We see later that it also manages the system input devices. There is only one `Display` object for every MIDlet. The `Display` object provides methods to draw and display graphical user interface elements on the screen (if the device has a screen), regardless of whether the high-level or low-level GUI API is used. The `Display` instance also provides methods to get properties from the display device such as whether the device supports color and what object is currently displayed on the device.

We obtain the instance of `Display` by calling the static `getDisplay(MIDlet)` method on the `Display` class. A valid `Display` instance can be obtained any time after the beginning of the `startApp()` method and until the `destroyApp(boolean unconditional)` call returns.

### Displayable objects

We now have the capability through the `Display` manager instance to put something on the cell phone or pager's screen, yet we have nothing to display. We want to start adding graphical elements to the display. However, we cannot add graphical elements, whether high or low-level graphical elements, directly to the display. Instead, all user interface objects that are to be shown on a device screen must be contained inside of a `Displayable` object. `Displayable` is an abstract class from which all

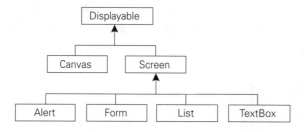

**Figure 5.7**
**This UML class diagram shows the hierarchical relationship among the available `Displayable` classes in MIDP. Screen and its descendents are used to develop high-level user interfaces. whereas `Canvas` is used to create low-level user interfaces.**

of the UI display classes derive (see figure 5.7). `Screen`, and its many subclasses, are the display classes for high-level GUIs. Alternatively, `Canvas` is used as the `Displayable` class for all low-level GUIs.

**NOTE** *Screen versus screen* The MIDP specification refers to the central abstraction of the MIDP UI as a "screen" (with a lowercase 's'). The abstract class of `Displayable` represents the implementation of this "screen" abstraction. We find this naming convention to be rather confusing since there is a `Displayable` subclass "Screen" (with an uppercase 'S'). In order to avoid confusion, we do not refer to the abstract idea of a MIDP display as a screen, but be aware of this terminology when reading MIDP documentation. Instead, we choose to use the class `Displayable` or the more generic "display" term to refer the abstract idea of an MIDP device screen.

Only one `Displayable` object can be shown at a time. The `Displayable` object that is shown is called the current `Displayable`. The `Display` object allows for getting and setting the current `Displayable` object with two complementary methods: `getCurrent()` and `setCurrent(Displayable nextDisplayable)`.

Why have an abstract class encapsulating all display objects? The `Displayable` object helps to isolate MIDP applications from having to deal with component layout, screen scrolling, widget focus, and so forth. For those familiar with either AWT or Swing in J2SE, the `Displayable` object does the job of the Layout Manager and then some. Given the diversity among MIDP devices, an application would be overwhelmed in trying to handle these tasks for all devices. The single, simple display also helps to keep the GUI easy to use and learn.

## 5.4.2 MIDP high-level user interface API

`Screen` is the superclass for all high-level GUI `Displayable` objects. The `Screen` provides subclasses with an optional title that can be displayed at the top of the display area. The high-level MIDP GUI has two kinds of `Screen` subclasses that can be used to display graphical elements. The first type completely encapsulates the user interface components and has a predefined structure for displaying information to the user. Most `Screen` components do not allow the application to add or remove other user interface components. `List`, `TextBox`, and `Alert` are subclasses of `Screen` that fall under this type.

The second kind of Screen allows for the applications to add and remove other graphical elements from the display. This second type is handled by the Form subclass of Screen. Constrained only by the limits of the display size and memory, a Form allows developers to create arbitrary displays of specific graphical user elements called items. Thus, forms do not completely encapsulate their elements as other Screen subclasses.

## Form

A form can be thought of as a data entry page. It contains an arbitrary mixture of images, text fields, data fields, choice selections, and other common graphical user interface widgets called items. Items are graphical elements that subclass from Item. Item classes include: ImageItem, StringItem, TextField, DateField, Choice-Group, and Gauge (see the "Items" section on page 80).

As with all high-level Displayable objects, the system handles layout, traversal or focus, and scrolling. Scrolling may occur if all the graphical components do not fit on the display. Depending on the implementation for a given device, some components may either pop up into a new display screen or expand only when the user edits the item.

Changes made to a form while it is displayed take effect immediately without the need for refresh action on the part of the application. However, it is recommended that applications change the contents of a Displayable object only while it is not visible. In other words, changes should be made to the Displayable object while it is not considered the current displayable object by the Display object. Depending on the device, changing the contents of a Displayable object when it is visible can result in poor performance. Also, the way in which the device may handle the refresh of the display may cause the user to get confused while interacting with the device.

The following MIDlet code in listing 5.4 creates and displays a simple Form object without any items. Using the Display object for the MIDlet, the form is also made the current Displayable for the MIDlet.

### Listing 5.4    FormDemo MIDlet

```
import javax.microedition.midlet.*;
import javax.microedition.lcdui.*;

public class FormDemo extends MIDlet{

  Display d;
  Form aForm;

  public FormDemo () {
    aForm = new Form("Demo Form");
  }

  protected void startApp() {
    d = Display.getDisplay(this);
    d.setCurrent(aForm);
  }
```

**1** Creates Form object with title "Demo Form" and no items

**2** Using the Display object for the MIDlet, sets the current displayable to the new Form

```
protected void pauseApp() {
}

protected void destroyApp(boolean unconditional) {
}
}
```

## Items

Item is the superclass for the interactive graphical elements that can be added to a Form object. Methods are provided on the form to add, append, delete, insert, or set items. An item can only be placed on one Screen object. Attempts to place the same Item object on the same or another Screen object will cause an IllegalState-Exception to be thrown.

**Table 5.1  Items serve as the principal means for users of an MIDP application to enter data. This list outlines the item subclasses and how and when to use the item in a high-level GUI.**

| Item Subclass | Description |
|---|---|
| ChoiceGroup | A ChoiceGroup object is a group of selectable choices or elements similar to the List discussed later in this section. The ChoiceGroup must implement the Choice interface (see Choice interface in the description that follows). The group can require a single choice or multiple choices. While the system is responsible for graphically displaying an instance of ChoiceGroup, the device is required to provide some visual differences in the way single versus multiple select choices are displayed. A single choice group is usually depicted as a set of radio buttons, whereas a multiple choice group is depicted as a set of check boxes. |
| DateField | A DateField instance provides the means to get and display calendar date and time information in a Form object. |
| Gauge | A Gauge object is a slide bar graph depicting a range of possible small integer values and a current value. A gauge may be interactive (allowing the user to modify the current value) or non-interactive (prohibiting the user from setting the current value). The system may change the appearance of a Gauge instance based on whether it is interactive or non-interactive. A non-interactive gauge will likely be used for progress indicators whereas interactive gauges can be used for visual data entry. |
| ImageItem | An ImageItem is an Item instance wrapper for images (see page 89). Each ImageItem object contains a reference to an immutable Image object. The ImageItem provides layout control over the Image when added to a Form. If the Image instance's size is larger than can be displayed, alternative text can be specified and displayed in the image's place. |
| StringItem | A display-only item that shows textual information to the user. |
| TextField | A TextField is a text editor for Form objects. Like TextBox (see page 83), the amount of text and the type of text (for example, only numeric text or text in the format of a telephone number) that can be entered into a text field by a user can be specified by the application. The device determines the number of characters displayed and their arrangement into rows and columns. |

Item instances have a text string label field that is displayed near the element when displayed on the Screen. The system will usually display the label on the same horizontal row or just above the item, and will attempt to keep the item and label visible at the same time during any necessary scrolling of the Screen object.

Again, depending on the implementation for a given device, some items may force a system-generated popup into a new display or expand the current display when the user interacts with the component. In these cases, the label should be displayed with the popup or expanded view in order to allow the user to continually identify the graphical element. Table 5.1 is a list of the subclasses of Item and their usage.

Each item in Listing 5.5 is created and added to the form inside of the FormDemo constructor. The following code extends the simple form example a little farther by creating a single instance of each of these items:

**Listing 5.5  FormDemo Constructor**

```
Display d;
Form aForm;
ChoiceGroup aChoiceGroup;
DateField aDateField;
Gauge aGauge;
StringItem aStringItem;
TextField aTextField;
ImageItem anImageItem;
Image anImage;

public FormDemo () {
  aForm = new Form("Demo Form");
  String choices[] = {"This", "That"};
  aStringItem = new StringItem(null,"Demo Items");
  aChoiceGroup = new ChoiceGroup("Choose",Choice.EXCLUSIVE,choices,null);
  aDateField = new DateField(null,DateField.TIME);
  aGauge = new Gauge("Score",true,10,1);
  aTextField = new TextField("Comments","Your comments here",20,0);
  try {
    anImage = Image.createImage("/star.png");
  } catch (java.io.IOException ioE) {
    System.out.println("Problem reading image");
  }
  anImageItem = new ImageItem("Demo Image",
    anImage,ImageItem.LAYOUT_CENTER,"No image");
  aForm.append(aStringItem);
  aForm.append(aChoiceGroup);
  aForm.append(aDateField);
  aForm.append(aGauge);
  aForm.append(aTextField);
  aForm.append(anImageItem);
}
```

**❶** Creating single instances of various Items

**❷** Add the items to the form

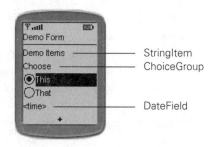

**Figure 5.8**
**Example StringItem, ChoiceGroup and DateField items displayed as part of the FormDemo MIDlet. The StringItem is static, non-editable text. The <time> label serves as a marker for bringing up the DateField display (see figure 5.9) for time entry.**

Because the display size of the MIDP device, in this case our MIDP cell phone emulator, is so small, the form automatically provides a scroll mechanism to allow the user to be able to see all the items on the form. When the MIDlet executes and displays the form, it should look something like the picture in figure 5.8.

Notice that the time in the DateField instance does not actually display a time. Instead, when selected, another display is shown on the device to allow the user to enter the time. In this case, when used with the emulator, interaction with the date field in time input mode (versus date input or both date and time input mode) causes the display to switch to the display shown in figure 5.9.

**Figure 5.9**
**Upon entering the DateField component when in time input mode, this nice display tool allows users to easily enter a time in hours and minutes. Alternate displays are used for entering dates or both date and time.**

As was mentioned previously, when interacting with the various items in a display, the system may force the user into system-generated displays such as this one in order to allow the user to interact with the component. The additional items of the form are displayed by scrolling down. (figure 5.10)

**Figure 5.10**
**Gauge, TextField and ImageItem displayed as part of the FormDemo MIDlet. Selecting the TextField for editing the text in the field will likely cause the field to expand into a full screen text editor that must be dismissed to return to the MIDlet Form.**

## List

As its name implies, a list displays a set of choices to the user and allows the user to select from the choices. The choices are called elements. An element consists of a text string and, optionally, an image. The List and ChoiceGroup (see Items above) must implement the Choice interface (see Choice Interface in the description that follows). A list allows the user to traverse or scroll through the elements before finally making a selection. A list can allow for multiple or single (called exclusive) selection of elements.

How an element is selected is device-dependent. Soft-buttons are application programmable buttons on the device and, in some cases, these may be used to register selection. However, selection functionality is usually not done by soft-button and is instead accomplished by a key that is not programmably labeled. For example, in the emulator, the selection button is the non-programmable key at the center of the navigation keys. (figure 5.11)

**Figure 5.11**
**On the emulator, the List selection key is at the center of the navigational buttons. However, the location of this non-programmable key is device-dependent.**

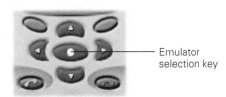

Emulator selection key

While we will not explicitly build a list in our tutorial application, the device application manager will build one for us to allow our customers to choose which application to run. Once we have deployed our MIDlets to the device, the device will show us a choice to run either the ObtainQuote or RetrieveQuote applications (see figure 5.3 earlier in the chapter).

## TextBox

A TextBox object provides a means for the user to enter and edit text. Along with the text field item (see page 80), the amount of text that can be entered and the type of text entered by a user (for example only numeric text or text in the format of a telephone number) can be set and constrained by the application.

The device determines the number of text rows and columns displayed for a text box at any one time. Furthermore, the device must also provide a means to scroll when the amount of text to be displayed is larger than the number of characters that can be displayed at any one time.

In chapter 4, The HiSmallWorld MIDlet utilized TextBox for its Screen object.

```
textbox = new TextBox("", "Hi Small World!", 20, 0);
```

In the example, the text box was given an empty string title (the first parameter) and initial contents of "Hi Small World!". The third parameter specified the maximum number of characters that can be contained in the text box. The final parameter allows for input constraints on TextBox objects. An application can use constraints to restrict user inputs in a text box or text field (see TextField item under Items above). For example, a constraint can be set up to allow only numbers to be entered. In our example, no constraints on the text box were set. In other words, this text box allows for any characters to be entered by the user. Other text box constraints could include allowing only an email address, an integer value, a phone number, or a URL. Additionally, a constraint is available to hide the true characters typed by showing a mask character such as '*' instead of the actual character. This is important when entering specific data or passwords.

## Alert

Alert is a kind of message Screen that shows text and images to the user. It is used to inform users of errors or exceptional conditions. An alert's single image is set with a call to setImage(Image img) (see the "Images" section in 5.4.3), while an alert's text is set with a call to setString(String str). Like a Form, changes made to an alert while it is displayed take effect immediately without the need for refresh action on the part of the application. Again, as a Displayable object, changes to the Alert object should only be made while it is not visible to avoid potential performance or user confusion issues.

By default, an alert is displayed for a period of time that is determined by the device, or can be set in milliseconds by the application. In fact, the application can set the display time to be indefinite with a call to the setTimeout(Alert.FOREVER) method. In this case, the alert becomes a modal Displayable object meaning that the user must dismiss it before something else is displayed. The system must provide a feature that allows the user to dismiss the alert. An Alert instance may also become modal if the application provides too much text and/or images to be displayed forcing the display to provide automatic scrolling.

An instance of the AlertType class is usually associated with the alert to indicate the nature of the alert and provide more information to the user of the device. This is done by calling an alert's setType(AlertType type) method with the appropriate AlertType. When the device has the capability of playing sound, the Alert- Type object can be used to provide audible information. The predefined types of alerts are listed in table 5.2.

**Table 5.2  Alert Types, listed in this table, help provide visual and sometime audible context to alerts presented to the user.**

| Alert Type | Description |
| --- | --- |
| ALARM | Alerts the user about some event based on a prearranged condition. |
| CONFIRMATION | Prompts the user to confirm a user action. |
| ERROR | Indicates an erroneous operation has occurred. |
| INFO | Provides non-threatening information to the user. |
| WARNING | Warns the user of potentially harmful or dangerous operations. |

Demonstrating the use of an alert type, the following code snippet creates a modal INFO Alert object:

```
Alert testAlert = new Alert("News Flash", "Man bites dog.", null,
  AlertType.INFO);
testAlert.setTimeout(Alert.FOREVER);
```

In order to display this, the display manager is used to set the current display to the alert. Unlike forms and lists, however, the next Displayable object must be specified so that when the alert is dismissed, the display manager knows what to display next. Therefore, the setCurrent(Alert alert, Displayable nextDisplayable) method is used with the display manager object as opposed to the setCurrent(Displayable nextDisplayable) method used with other Displayable objects. The Alert object created in the preceding code should look like the picture in figure 5.12. When executed inside the emulator, it is likely that you will also hear a sound based on the alert type used.

**Figure 5.12**
**An alert works as a kind of message box**
**in MIDP. Alerts can be used to provide**
**warnings, information, error messages, etc.**

The "Done" text shown on the alert is the label associated with a key on the keypad, which allows the user to dismiss this alert display. Recall that the alert was created as a modal display with the setTimeout(Alert.FOREVER) method call. When the user presses the key associated with the Done label, the display manager shows the next displayable.

### Ticker

Along with the title string associated with each Screen object, a Ticker object can be associated with Screen subclass objects. A Ticker instance mimics a ticker tape. In a ticker tape, a text string repeatedly runs in an animated fashion across the display. The speed and direction of the Ticker are set by the system, and the application cannot start or stop the ticker. The system may pause the scrolling to reduce power consumption when the user has not interacted with the system for some time. A single simple constructor method is provided to create a Ticker object. A Screen method, setTicker(Ticker ticker), allows the Ticker instance to be associated with the Screen instance. After being associated with a Screen object, the ticker displays with the Screen object when displayed. For example, the following code builds a Ticker object and associates it to the form built previously in this section.

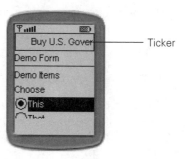

Ticker

**Figure 5.13**
Like the ticker tape machines of old Wall Street,
a `Ticker` instance displays a message atop the
MIDP emulator. A ticker can be shared by many
`Screen` instances thus providing the illusion
that the ticker is part of the device display
as opposed to the application.

```
Ticker aTicker = new Ticker ("Buy U.S. Government Savings Bonds today!");
aForm.setTicker(aTicker);
```

Figure 5.13 depicts the results of the display manager setting the current displayable to aForm.

Unlike other display items, multiple `Screen` objects may share a `Ticker` instance. Each `Screen` object can use the `setTicker(Ticker ticker)` method to set its display ticker. In order to promote an illusion that the `Ticker` instance is really part of the display instead of each `Screen`, the `Ticker` is supposed to be displayed in the same position and continue scrolling its last displayed characters when moving between screens that share it.

### Choice interface

An interface has been provided as part of the MIDP's high-level user interface API for components that provide selection from a set of predefined choices. This includes the `List` (`Screen` subclass) and `ChoiceGroup` (`Item` subclass) classes.

A text string, and, optionally, an image represent a `Choice`. The image will be displayed next to the text string unless it exceeds the size limits allowed by the device. In this case, the image will be ignored. A choice's text string will wrap onto multiple lines if its length is too wide for the display.

There are three different choice types supported by the `Choice` interface. An `EXCLUSIVE` choice represents a selection of elements where only one element can be selected. A `MULTIPLE` choice represents a selection of elements where more than one element can be selected. Finally, an `IMPLICIT` choice is a selection of the element that has focus when a `Command` object is initiated. We will explore commands later in this chapter.

### Screen layout

Screen layout is handled by the device and is not something the application controls. Nevertheless, there is a layout policy by which the device does abide: items that are appended or inserted to a form or an Alert are placed on the same line as the previous item unless the item does not fit on the line. In this case, a new line is started with the new item. A new line will also be started with a new item if the previous item was a string ending with a `newline` character or a layout directive (such as those available to items of the `ImageItem` class), which indicates a non-default layout is desired.

### 5.4.3 MIDP low-level user interface API

While there are fewer classes and instances to deal with in MIDP's low-level graphical user interface API, the developer must deal with many low-level details such as pixel coordinate systems, fonts, geometric shapes for drawing and screen refresh.

#### Canvas

Unlike the high-level API, there is only one `Displayable` subclass to use when creating low-level graphical user interfaces. It is the `Canvas` class. However, the `Canvas` class is abstract and requires applications to subclass it in order to use it. Two-dimensional geometric shapes and/or text are displayed on a `Canvas` object through a drawing mechanism called a `Graphics` object. An instance of a `Canvas` subclass is passed a `Graphics` object through the device's call to the `paint(Graphics g)` method of a canvas. Each `Canvas` subclass must implement this abstracted method, and only during the duration of the `paint(Graphics g)` method can applications draw low-level graphics to the display. However, the application never invokes the `paint(Graphics g)` method directly. This job is left up to the device.

Repainting of the display is done automatically for all `Screen` objects in the high-level API. Instances of the `Canvas` subclasses, however, are responsible for their own repainting. An application requests the display to be repainted by calling the `Canvas'` `repaint()` method, which eventually calls on the `paint(Graphics g)` method provided by the `Canvas` superclass. Repainting of a canvas is an asynchronous event, so several calls to the `repaint()` method can be made before the actual `paint(Graphics g)` takes place. This allows the display to be optimally refreshed, which is very important for applications such as games. Repaint requests can be forced by calling the `serviceRepaints()` method. For further optimization, the application can request to repaint only a portion of the display using the `repaint(int x, int y, int width, int height)` method, which targets a specific region of the display to be repainted.

#### Graphics

An instance of the `Graphics` object does all of the drawing for MIDP's low-level GUI API. It provides several draw methods to display characters or strings, images, lines rectangles, rounded-corner rectangles, and arcs. Rectangles, rounded-corner rectangles and arcs can be either filled or unfilled. The `Graphics` object does not have to be created. Rather, a new instance of a `Graphics` object is created and passed to a `Canvas` object through the `Canvas` object's `paint(Graphics g)` method. This allows graphics to be displayed directly the next time the `Canvas` object's `paint(Graphics g)` method is invoked by the system. Alternatively, a `Graphics` object can be obtained from an off-screen buffered image by making a call to `getGraphics()` on the preferred `Image` instance. This allows draw commands to be issued to the off-screen image for later display.

All drawing operations do a pixel replacement. In other words, any drawing operation specified in the Graphics object that sets a pixel value replaces the previous value. There is no capability for combining or blending pixel values as is provided in more sophisticated drawing systems.

The Graphics object does support 24-bit color. The red, green and blue color components are each allotted 8 bits. However, not all devices support 24-bit color. In these cases, the system will attempt to map available colors as close as possible to the colors requested by the application. The Display class provides methods for obtaining device capabilities, such as the support for color, which can be used by the application to provide better looking displays that are not washed out by automatic color mapping. This also helps the application to remain portable and not dependent on the features of a specific device.

All geometric drawing methods in the Graphics object make use of a coordinate system. The default coordinate system assumes that the upper left-hand corner of the device's display is the coordinate (0, 0). The coordinate system actually represents the location between each pixel. For example, the following coordinates bound the first pixel in the upper left-hand side of the display: (0,0), (1,0), (0,1), (1,1). Each increment of the X and Y coordinates represents moving one pixel in the display. The X coordinate moves in a positive direction to the right and the Y coordinate moves in a positive direction downward or toward the bottom of the display. Applications are allowed to assume that pixels are square. In other words, the horizontal and vertical distances in the coordinate system represent equal distances. Drawing operations performed by the Graphics object are done with a one-pixel wide pen that fills the pixel immediately below and to the right of the specified coordinate and includes both endpoints.

Text drawing makes use of an "anchor point" to minimize the computation required when placing text on the display. When drawing a string or character, the application must specify both an (x, y) anchor point coordinate and a horizontal and vertical constant for positioning the string on the display. A horizontal constant (LEFT, HCENTER, RIGHT) is combined with a vertical constant (TOP, BASELINE, BOTTOM) in a logical OR operation. This provides the direction from the (x, y) anchor that the string is drawn. For example, a method call of drawString("Hi there", 15, 20, TOP|LEFT) has the effect of drawing a "Hi there" string below and to the right of the (15,20) coordinate, as shown in figure 5.14.

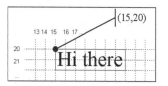

**Figure 5.14**
**Text must be anchored to the display via a combination of horizontal (LEFT, HCENTER, RIGHT) and vertical constants (TOP, BASELINE, BOTTOM). In this example, the "Hi there" text is anchored in the MIDP's graphical coordinate system by a TOP and LEFT anchor point.**

The horizontal and vertical values are static constants provided by the Graphics class. Both a horizontal and vertical constant must be supplied or unpredictable consequences (such as application failure) can result.

As discussed earlier in this section, recall that the Canvas class is abstract and so must be subclassed in order to develop a low-level graphical user interface displayable. A simple example of a Canvas class is shown in listing 5.6.

**Listing 5.6   CanvasDemo**

```
import javax.microedition.lcdui.*;                          Displaying a string  ❶
                                                              at position I,I
class CanvasDemo extends Canvas {

  protected void paint(Graphics g){
    g.drawString("Canvas Demo",1,1,Graphics.TOP|Graphics.LEFT);
    g.fillRect (20,30,30,20);        ❷  Drawing a filled rectangle
    g.drawLine(50,50,75,50);
    g.drawLine(75,50,75,75);
    g.drawLine(75,75,50,75);
    g.drawLine(50,75,50,50);         ❸  Drawing a rectangle
  }                                       using four lines
}
```

In the preceding code, paint() method should never be called directly by the application. Instead, the system calls on paint(Graphics g) to render the display as needed. In this method, a string is drawn at coordinate position 1,1, and a filled rectangle is drawn starting a coordinate position 20,30 with a width of 30 and height of 20. Finally, a second rectangle is drawn, but this rectangle is created by drawing four separate lines.

Notice that the only method that must be implemented is the paint(Graphics g) method. Inside of the paint method, specific draw commands are issued to display strings and shapes. However, the device will control when this method gets called. Inside of the MIDlet, as shown below, all that is required in an application is to create the Canvas object and set it to the current Displayable object, much as we did for the Form object in the high-level user interface. The results of running the MIDlet in listing 5.7 with the code in listing 5.6 appear in figure 5.15.

### Images

An Image instance holds graphical image data. This data exists in off-screen memory and is independent of any display device. An Image object can only be painted on the display when explicitly instructed by the application. An application instructs an image to display in one of two fashions. In the high-level API, the application can add an image directly to an alert, choice, form, or image item. Alternatively, in the low-level API, an Image object can be displayed to a canvas using the drawImage(Image img, int x, int y, int anchor) method on a Graphics object. In the low-level API, images can also be created in off-screen memory using a Graphics object. A Graphics object is created and then the application paints to the Image where it can later be displayed (see the previous Graphics section).

There are two types of images. The type image is dependent on how it was created. Immutable images are usually created by loading image data from a resource such as a file.

**Listing 5.7   CanvasMidlet using CanvasDemo from above**

```
import javax.microedition.midlet.*;
import javax.microedition.lcdui.*;

public class CanvasMidlet extends MIDlet{

  Display d;
  Canvas c;

  protected void startApp() {                    ❶ Creating an instance
    d = Display.getDisplay(this);                   of the Canvas object
    c = new CanvasDemo();
    d.setCurrent(c);
  }
                                                 ❷ Setting the current
  protected void pauseApp() {                       Displayable to the
  }                                                 Canvas object

  protected void destroyApp(boolean unconditional) {
  }
}
```

As the name implies, these types of images cannot be changed. Only immutable images can be used with the high-level API. That is, only immutable `Image` objects can be placed within an `Alert`, `Choice`, `Form` or `ImageItem` object. Because the high-level graphical display's refresh is determined by the system, having only immutable images associated with these components allows the system to update the display without notifying the application. Mutable `Image` objects are created in off-screen memory and are generally used in low-level GUI applications.

There are several static `createImage()` methods on the `Image` class that can create immutable images from mutable images and vice-versa.

**Figure 5.15**
The `CanvasDemo` class and CanvasMIDlet produce this image when successfully deployed and run on a device or emulator. The size of the device's screen may cause clipping of the shapes drawn if they extend beyond the dimensions of the screen.

## Fonts

A `Font` is used in the low-level API to set the font of any text that is drawn to the screen. The application does not have control of the font when using the high-level API. Unlike in larger systems, fonts cannot be created by the application. The application can only query for a font based on a set of predefined attributes. Fonts have attributes dealing with style, face and size with symbolic static constants provided to represent the choices for each attribute. Table 5.3 lists examples of attribute constants from which the application can choose.

**Table 5.3  These static fields, defined in the Font class, are used to specify the font when drawing text to the screen in an MIDP application.**

| STYLE | FACE | SIZE |
|-------|------|------|
| STYLE_BOLD | FACE_MONOSPACED | SIZE_LARGE |
| STYLE_ITALIC | FACE_PROPORTIONAL | SIZE_SMALL |
| STYLE_UNDERLINED | FACE_SYSTEM | SIZE_MEDIUM |
| STYLE_PLAIN | | |

Some attribute constants such as STYLE_BOLD and STYLE_ITALIC can be combined and used on the same string. Other attribute constants like SIZE_SMALL and SIZE_LARGE are contradictory and thus cannot be used simultaneously. By default, the font for any string is STYLE_PLAIN, SIZE_MEDIUM, and FACE_SYSTEM.

The system will attempt to provide a font that matches the requested attributes, but this is not guaranteed. The system may only have a small subset of fonts that an application can use. A Font instance is obtained through a call to the static get-Font(int face, int style, int size) method on the Font class. A Graphics object then uses the Font object to set the current font for all subsequent drawings of strings or individual characters. The setFont(Font font) method is used on a Graphics instance to set the current font.

### 5.4.4  The investment quote application's user interface in MIDP

Given an understanding of both the high-level and low-level graphical user interface, we can now develop the user interface for the tutorial application. Earlier in this chapter, we developed the application control for the tutorial application by implementing two MIDlets. The next step in our development effort is to implement the user interface for our application.

#### Using the Display class

The Display class, along with the other user interface classes that we use, resides in the javax.microedition.lcdui package. Therefore, MIDlets with a user interface must include this package in the import statement at the top of the .java files.

```
import javax.microedition.lcdui.*;
```

Because we are going to utilize the Display object often in the tutorial application, we set up a local variable to hold onto the instance throughout our application's lifecycle. Thus, in both the ObtainQuoteMIDlet and RetrieveQuoteMIDlet, we add the following variable declaration.

```
private Display displayMngr = null;
```

Since our application will be straightforward, we immediately get the `Display` instance and put its reference into the `displayMngr` variable from inside of the `startApp()` method.

```
protected void startApp() {
  displayMngr = Display.getDisplay(this);
}
```

### Data entry using forms

Given an understanding of forms and their associated items, we are ready to build the investment price request display (see figure 3.2 in section 3.2.2). In this display, the customer is requested to enter an investment symbol and investment type in order for the system to obtain investment price information. To begin, we create a new class called `EntryForm` that extends the current `Form` class. We did not have to create a new subclass of `Form` in order to create a `Form` object. However, this will help us in two ways. First of all, the new `EntryForm` class can be used by both our ObtainQuote and RetrieveQuote MIDlets to get the symbol of concern from the customer. Secondly, this class will also help keep our MIDlet code tidy. Our new form subclass extends `Form` so we must import the `javax.microedition.lcdui` package. The `Form` class also provides two constructor methods. At least one of the constructor methods must be overridden in the new class. This is all we need to start our new `EntryForm` class.

```
import javax.microedition.lcdui.*;

public class EntryForm extends Form {

  public EntryForm(String title) {
    super(title);
  }
}
```

Next we want to add some items to the new `Form` object to make it look similar to our design sketch (again, see figure 3.2 in section 3.2.2). In particular, we want to add a text field to allow the customer to enter the investment symbol and we want to add a choice group to allow the user to indicate what type investment has been specified by the symbol. Two variables are defined for the class to retain references on the two items we create.

```
private TextField symbolField = null;
private ChoiceGroup investmentChoice = null;
```

In order to allow the application that uses this form to get access to the items, two getter methods are provided to return these items.

```
public TextField getSymbolField() {
  return symbolField;
}

public ChoiceGroup getInvestmentChoice() {
  return investmentChoice;
}
```

On construction of the form, the various items must also be created and added to the new Form object. Therefore, inside of the EntryForm class constructor, we create each of the items, set the appropriate reference variable to the item and add the item to the form.

```
public EntryForm(String title) {
  super(title);
  symbolField = new TextField("Investment Symbol", "", 5, TextField.ANY);
  String choices[] = {"Stock", "Fund"};
  investmentChoice = new ChoiceGroup("Type", Choice.EXCLUSIVE, choices, null);
  append(symbolField);
  append(investmentChoice);
}
```

Using the TextField constructor, TextField(String label, String text, int maxSize, int constraints), we create a TextField object to capture the investment symbol. The field has a label but no initial text contents. We have limited the maximum number of characters that the customer can enter to 5 (this should be sufficient for common stock and mutual fund exchanges), but we do not put any input constraints on the entry. Similarly, we create a new ChoiceGroup object to allow the customer to specify the type investment to be researched. It can be either a stock or mutual fund. There are two ChoiceGroup constructors from which to choose. We use the ChoiceGroup(String label, int choiceType, String[] string-Elements, Image[] imageElements) constructor. The ChoiceGroup is given a label and choice strings. We do not assign any icons for the choices at this time. The choice type is set to EXCLUSIVE indicating that exactly one selection can be selected at any given time. Exactly one choice must be selected, but since we just created the choice group, no item has been physically selected. In other words, there is no default selection. In this case, the choice of which element is selected is left to the device. A condition where the choice group may not have a selected item could also occur if an element is added to an empty list or if the selected choice is deleted. Whenever the selected item cannot be determined, the system is left to select an element. In order to avoid having the system make an arbitrary selection on any choice, use setSelected-Index(int elementNum, boolean selected). Finally, the text field and choice group items are appended to the instance of EntryForm and automatically display when their associated form is displayed.

In its own EntryForm.java file, the code for the new Form class should appear similar to listing 5.8.

**Listing 5.8 EntryForm**

```
import javax.microedition.lcdui.*;

public class EntryForm extends Form {                    ❶ The class defining the
                                                             investment request form
  private TextField symbolField = null;
  private ChoiceGroup investmentChoice = null;

  public EntryForm(String title) {
    super(title);
    symbolField = new TextField("Investment Symbol",
      "", 5, TextField.ANY);              ❷ TextField for entering a symbol
    String choices[] = {"Stock", "Fund"};
    investmentChoice = new ChoiceGroup("Type", Choice.EXCLUSIVE,
      choices, null);
    append(symbolField);
    append(investmentChoice);             ❸ ChoiceGroup for
  }                                           selecting Stock
                                              or Fund type
  public TextField getSymbolField() {
    return symbolField;
  }

  public ChoiceGroup getInvestmentChoice() {
    return investmentChoice;
  }
}
```

To establish an instance of the newly created EntryForm class, we first add a variable and a method to the MIDlets. The variable keeps a reference to an instance of the form.

```
private EntryForm entryForm = null;
```

The method checks to see if an instance of the entry form has already been created. If not, a new instance of the form will be created and its reference will be stored in the variable. With the reference to the entry form (whether existing or newly created), the application makes the form visible by invoking the Display class's method set-Current(Displayable nextDisplayable).

```
private void displayEntryForm () {
  if (entryForm == null) {
    entryForm = new EntryForm("ObtainQuote");
  }
  displayMngr.setCurrent(entryForm);
}
```

Finally, a line is added to the startApp() method of the ObtainQuoteMIDlet that calls our displayEntryForm() method.

```
protected void startApp() {
  displayMngr  = Display.getDisplay(this);
  displayEntryForm();
}
```

The results of running the ObtainQuoteMIDlet application, after successfully compiling, preverifying, and JARing the MIDlet suite with the following commands, should resemble those shown in figure 5.16.

Compile

```
>javac -g:none -bootclasspath %MIDPClasses%;. EntryForm.java
>javac -g:none -bootclasspath %MIDPClasses%;. ObtainQuoteMIDlet.java
>javac -g:none -bootclasspath %MIDPClasses%;. RetrieveQuoteMIDlet.java
```

Preverify

```
>%MIDPTools%\preverify -classpath %MIDPClasses%;. ObtainQuoteMIDlet
>%MIDPTools%\preverify -classpath %MIDPClasses%;. RetrieveQuoteMIDlet
>%MIDPTools%\preverify -classpath %MIDPClasses%;. EntryForm
```

JAR

```
>jar -cfm quote.jar QuoteMIDletSuite.jad -C ./output ObtainQuoteMIDlet.class
-C ./output RetrieveQuoteMIDlet.class -C ./output EntryForm.class
```

Run

```
>%MIDPTools%\midp -classpath %MIDPClasses%;.\quote.jar -descriptor
QuoteMIDletSuite.jad
```

The JAD file (QuoteMIDletSuite.jad) for this application will look something like the following:

```
MIDlet-1: ObtainQuote, ,   ObtainQuoteMIDlet
MIDlet-2: RetrieveQuote, ,  RetrieveQuoteMIDlet
MIDlet-Name: EasyTrack
MIDlet-Vendor: Catapult Technologies
MIDlet-Version: 1.0
MicroEdition-Configuration: CLDC-1.0
MicroEdition-Profile: MIDP-1.0
```

**Figure 5.16**
**This form fulfills the prototype screen design for capturing the customer's investment symbol of interest. It provides the means to enter an investment symbol and investment type in the Investment Quote EntryForm. The form utilizes a `TextField` and `ChoiceGroup` object.**

Notice that the entry form's display is too large for the device. However, as is expected in the high-level GUI API of MIDP, the customer is automatically presented with a scroll option in order to be able to view the entire form. This gives us a good opportunity to advocate some restraint in user interface design. While the resources of the device limit the number of items that can be added to a form, it is highly recommended that a form contain as small a number of items as possible. Only those items that are important and closely related to the given interaction should be displayed on a single form. Remember that these devices will be operated by one hand and can be used by people while busy doing other activities. The more a user must scroll, the more they must fully concentrate solely on the device.

When text is entered into the `TextField`, you will also notice that the display changes and opens up an entire new data entry area (figure 5.17). Did we ask for this in our user interface development? In a way, we did. Remember, the device may switch to a system-generated display when user input or interaction takes place. In this case, the device implemented a new display for text entry.

**Figure 5.17**
**For user convenience, when text fields are selected or "entered" by the user, the device may offer a system-generated display for easier text entry. In the emulator, entering the symbol in the text field results in a system-generated display for capturing the symbol as shown here.**

## Messages, using alerts

In the tutorial application, we are going to use an alert for showing the price of the investment. The price may either have been obtained from the quote service or retrieved from the system's data storage. To do this, we must first set up a reference variable that keeps a reference to an `Alert` object.

```
private Alert resultsAlert = null;
```

Next, we create a method to display the quote via the alert whenever it is called. We call this method `displayPrice` and pass in a text string providing the customer with the investment price information found. When this method is called, it first determines whether an `Alert` instance has ever been created. If not, it first creates a new `Alert` object and puts its reference in the alert reference.

```
private void displayPrice(String quoteString) {
  if (resultsAlert == null) {
    resultsAlert = new Alert("Quote Price", null, null, AlertType.CONFIRMATION);
    resultsAlert.setTimeout(Alert.FOREVER);
  }
  resultsAlert.setString(quoteString);
  displayMngr.setCurrent(resultsAlert, entryForm );
}
```

**Creating an ❶ Alert instance**

**❷ Displaying the alert on the device**

To create the Alert object, we use the Alert (String title, String alert-Text, Image alertImage, AlertType alertType) constructor. In creation, we set its alert type to CONFIRMATION and provide it the title of "Quote Price." The marketing department of the company we work for should also be happy since we have provided an advertising marquee ticker to be displayed with the quoted price on the alert display (see the subsequent "Using tickers" section).

In creating our alert, we did not set either the string or image. We left the alert text to be set later in the method with a setString(String str) method call. This allows the price string to be displayed to an existing alert that has already been set up and referenced via the resultsAlert variable. In this particular example, we did not need an image to be displayed.

After ensuring that the Alert object is properly created and its string text set, we need to have it displayed. To do this, we call on the Display manager object, whose reference was previously stored in the displayMngr variable to set the current Displayable object to the alert. Remember, a Displayable object must be shown after an alert is dismissed. In this case, we make sure that the Displayable object shown after the price quote alert is the investment price request entry form created earlier. This allows the user to enter another symbol and get another quote. We put the reference of this Displayable object into the entryForm variable. Thus, in order to display the Alert, we simply call on the Display manager's setCurrent(Alert alert, Displayable nextDisplayable) method with our resultsAlert and entryForm variables.

Notice that we have set up our alert to be modal by setting the timeout to Alert.FOREVER. This forces the customer to dismiss the alert before changing the display. Again, the dismissal of an alert is dependent on the system implementation. In the MIDP emulator, dismissal is accomplished by pressing a soft button, which has been labeled "Done" by the system. This dismisses the Alert object and returns display to the entry form Displayable object.

Right now, we don't have a means to launch the alert. Later in this chapter, we add events that allow the system to do something based on the user's actions. To test the alert display for now, add a single line to the ObtainQuoteMIDlet's startApp() method.

```
protected void startApp() {
    displayMngr  = Display.getDisplay(this);
    displayEntryForm();
    displayPrice("The price of MMM is 111.19");
}
```

The code shown here displays the entry form and immediately calls to display the alert. When we learn how to handle events, this last line can and will be removed. Then the alert display will be shown after the user has requested a price for a given investment symbol.

To recompile, preverify, re-JAR, and run the MIDlet suite issue via the following commands:

## Compile

```
>javac -g:none -bootclasspath %MIDPClasses%;. EntryForm.java
>javac -g:none -bootclasspath %MIDPClasses%;. ObtainQuoteMIDlet.java
>javac -g:none -bootclasspath %MIDPClasses%;. RetrieveQuoteMIDlet.java
```

   or

```
>javac -g:none -bootclasspath %MIDPClasses%;. *.java
```

## Preverify

```
>%MIDPTools%\preverify -classpath %MIDPClasses%;.   ObtainQuoteMIDlet
>%MIDPTools%\preverify -classpath %MIDPClasses%;.   RetrieveQuoteMIDlet
>%MIDPTools%\preverify -classpath %MIDPClasses%;.   EntryForm
```

   or

```
>%MIDPTools%\preverify -classpath %MIDPClasses%;.   "."
```

## JAR

```
>jar -cfm quote.jar QuoteMIDletSuite.jad -C ./output ObtainQuoteMIDlet.class
-C ./output RetrieveQuoteMIDlet.class -C ./output EntryForm.class
```

   or

```
>jar -cfm quote.jar QuoteMIDletSuite.jad -C ./output .
```

## Run

```
>%MIDPTools%\midp -classpath %MIDPClasses%;.\quote.jar -descriptor
QuoteMIDletSuite.jad
```

This time, when the MIDlet suite's ObtainQuote choice is selected, the alert should display itself and look something like the picture in figure 5.18.

**Figure 5.18**
**Alerts can be used in a variety of ways. They can be used to display an error or warning message. In the ObtainQuoteMIDlet, an alert is used to inform the customer of the price for an investment of interest.**

### Using tickers

While we are at it, let's add a little promotional advertising to our application. To do this, we use a ticker. We create an advertisement `Ticker` instance and assign it to a reference variable. The declaration for this object would look something like the following:

```
private Ticker adTicker = new Ticker("Track your investments with " +
   "Easy Track");
```

Later, we can use the reference variable and set the ticker for any `Screen` object. For now, we simply set the ticker for the alert we just created. To do this, we add a line to set the ticker of the `Alert` object created in the `displayPrice()` method:

```
private void displayPrice(String quoteString) {
  if (resultsAlert == null) {
    resultsAlert = new Alert("Quote Price", null, null,
      AlertType.CONFIRMATION);
    resultsAlert.setTicker(adTicker);
    resultsAlert.setTimeout(Alert.FOREVER);
  }
  resultsAlert.setString(quoteString);
  displayMngr.setCurrent(resultsAlert, entryForm);
}
```

**❶ Setting the ticker on the results alert**

Now if we rerun the same compile, preverify, JAR, and execution steps, the alert not only displays the price quote, but also the advertisement inside of the ticker at the top of the display, as shown in figure 5.19.

### Drawing, using Canvas

We are now ready to develop the third and final user interface display in the MIDP version of the tutorial application. Given an investment, like a stock or mutual fund, we want to provide the customers with a picture of how the investment is doing on the market. Remember, users of MIDP devices may not be able to give their full attention to the device. Therefore, we want to give them a picture of how the stock has done recently. Per the requirements, the application tracks the last two prices (current and historical) for each investment requested by the user. If a quote for an investment has been retrieved before, we want to provide a bar graph depicting the current and previous prices in relationship to each other (see figure 3.4 in chapter 3). To do this, we draw geometric shapes directly to the screen. This is done using the low-level graphical user interface API.

The only `Displayable` class available to encapsulate graphical elements in the low-level API is `Canvas`. Unlike the `Displayable` class counterparts (`Form`, `Alert`, `List`, or `TextBox`) in the high-level API, the `Canvas` class is abstract requiring the developer to create his or her own concrete `Canvas` subclass. We name our `Canvas` subclass `ChartCanvas` and put it in its own ChartCanvas.java file. The `Canvas` class has one abstract method, `paint(Graphics)`, which requires implementation.

**Figure 5.19**
**The addition of a ticker can spice up any application. Here, a ticker located at the top of the display is used with the ObtainQuoteMIDlet to display advertisements to the customers.**

Therefore, our `ChartCanvas` class begins with:

```
import javax.microedition.lcdui.*;

class ChartCanvas extends Canvas {

  protected void paint(Graphics g){
  }
}
```

Notice that the low-level UI API also comes from the `javax.microedi-tion.lcdui` package and therefore we must also import this package. Next, we want to draw the bar graphs and investment information to the `ChartCanvas`. Inside of the `paint(Graphics g)` method, we paint shapes and strings to the display. Draw operations on the `Graphics` object allow for displaying text, images, lines, rectangles, and arcs. However, it is important to note that drawing to the display using the `Graph-ics` object can only occur during the duration of the canvas `paint()` method.

> **WARNING** A sometimes frustrating aspect of using the `Graphics` and `Canvas` object is forgetting that the drawing using a `Graphics` object can only occur during the `paint(Graphics g)` method of an instance of a `Canvas` subclass. Neither the compiler nor the runtime environment informs you when you attempt to draw outside of this method. Instead, you are left wondering why perfectly compiled and running code is not displaying all of your draw commands.

The draw commands issued to the `Graphics` object are straightforward and require use of the pixel coordinate system to specify the location and size of many of the shapes drawn on the display. Drawing strings to the display requires sending the text to be displayed, the x and y pixel anchor point position, and a `Graphics` static integer value to indicate the positioning of the text around the anchor point to the `drawString(String str, int x, int y, int anchor)` method. In the example, all of our text is anchored from the top, left-hand point of the text string. A corresponding `drawChar(char character, int x, int y, int anchor)` method is available for drawing single characters to the screen if desired.

```
g.drawString(symbol + " Performance",1,1,Graphics.TOP|Graphics.LEFT);
g.drawString("current vs. historic ", 1, 12, Graphics.TOP|Graphics.LEFT);
g.drawString("$" + currentPrice, 1, 24, Graphics.TOP|Graphics.LEFT);
g.drawString("$" + historicPrice, 1, 36, Graphics.TOP|Graphics.LEFT);
```

In the tutorial application, we display the title of the display that includes the investment symbol obtained through a variable symbol that will be set before we start drawing. We also display the current and historical prices. The graphical bars depicting the price for an investment are displayed by drawing filled rectangles on the screen. A starting (x, y) pixel coordinate and width and height of the rectangle are required to draw a rectangle. Separate `Graphics` object methods exist for drawing filled versus unfilled rectangles as well as rounded-corner versus nonrounded-corner rectangles. Before drawing our bar chart, the tutorial application will need some information in order to draw the rectangles.

```
private final static int MAX_BAR_SIZE = 65;
private final static int START_X_POSITION = 30;
private final static int START_Y_CURRENT = 27;
private final static int START_Y_HISTORIC = 39;
private final static int BAR_HEIGHT = 10;
private int currentPrice;
private int historicPrice;
```

In the tutorial, the prices will be displayed as horizontal bars drawn starting from the left of the display to a position on the right that is dependent on the price of the investment. The START_X_POSITION is the unchanging x pixel position coordinate for each rectangle or bar in the graph. Correspondingly, the START_Y_CURRENT and START_Y_HISTORIC values provide the static starting y pixel locations for our two rectangles depicting the current and historical price bars. The BAR_WIDTH variable provides the static height of all bars. The actual investment prices will be sent to the ChartCanvas object and stored in the two integer variables labeled current-Price and historicPrice. Notice that the prices are integers. In reality, investment prices are floating-point numbers such as $110.55. The floating point type is not supported in the CLDC. However, given the size of most MIDP device displays (not more than 96 pixels in width), it is unlikely that the cents could accurately be displayed in the bar graph. Therefore, in this part of the tutorial application, the comparison chart will show current and historical prices to the nearest whole dollar.

To display the current price depicted as a rectangle or bar over the historical price depicted by a second rectangle or bar, two separate fillRect (int x, int y, int width, int height) method calls are made.

```
int[] prices = {currentPrice, historicPrice};
int[] lengths = determineLengths(prices);
g.fillRect (START_X_POSITION, START_Y_CURRENT, lengths[0], BAR_HEIGHT);
g.fillRect (START_X_POSITION, START_Y_HISTORIC, lengths[1], BAR_HEIGHT);
```

The determineLengths(int[] prices) method is developed, as we show subsequently, to determine the length of the rectangle bars depicting the price of each investment. This method returns an integer array containing two widths. The first element in the array will contain the width of the rectangle depicting the current price and the second element in the array will contain the width of the rectangle depicting the historical price. Static variables declared above provide the remaining rectangle dimensions.

To give the bar graph some dimension in order to assist the customer in comparing the prices, we add three "tick" lines to our display that are drawn at even positions across the screen. Lines are drawn by simply providing the starting and ending (x, y) coordinates of the line.

```
g.drawLine(30,26,30,50);
g.drawLine(50,26,50,50);
g.drawLine(70,26,70,50);
g.drawLine(90,26,90,50);
```

The only thing left to implement the simple graphical display of the investment prices is a method for kicking of the low-level API display and a method for determining the length of each price bar. The method to kick off the display, called displayChart is passed the investment symbol and two investment prices (current and historic).

```
public void displayChart(String sym, int amtCur, int amtHist) {
  symbol = sym;
  currentPrice = amtCur;
  historicPrice = amtHist;
  serviceRepaints();                    ❶ Force a call to repaint the canvas
}
```

There are many ways to depict the price of an investment. The determine-Lengths(int[] prices) method as coded in listing 5.9 is provided as an example. In this listing, the length of a bar is determined by finding the higher of the two prices and using a ratio of the two to find a proportional length for each price that accurately depicts the difference in price and will fit on the maximum display. Other length calculating formulas could easily replace this method.

**Listing 5.9   The ChartCanvas' determineLengths method**

```
private int[] determineLengths (int[] prices) {

  int ratio, higherPrice, lowerPrice;
  boolean currentHigher;

  if (prices[0] < prices[1]) {
    higherPrice = prices[1];          ❶ Determine the
    lowerPrice = prices[0];              highest price
    currentHigher=false;
  } else {
    higherPrice = prices[0];
    lowerPrice = prices[1];
    currentHigher=true;
  }

  ratio = higherPrice/MAX_BAR_SIZE + 1;
  while (ratio > 1) {                 ❷ Calculate the bar length
    higherPrice = higherPrice/ratio;    based on the highest price
    lowerPrice = lowerPrice/ratio;
    ratio = higherPrice/MAX_BAR_SIZE + 1;
  }
  if (currentHigher) {
    int[] ends = {higherPrice, lowerPrice};
    return ends;
  } else {
    int [] ends = {lowerPrice, higherPrice};
    return ends;
  }
}
```

*CHAPTER  5   MIDP USER INTERFACE*

All the pieces of the ChartCanvas class are assembled in one file in listing 5.10.

**Listing 5.10   ChartCanvas**

```
import javax.microedition.lcdui.*;
import java.util.*;

class ChartCanvas extends Canvas {

  static final int MAX_BAR_SIZE = 65;
  static final int START_X_POSITION = 30;
  static final int START_Y_CURRENT = 27;
  static final int START_Y_HISTORIC = 39;
  static final int BAR_HEIGHT = 10;

  private int currentPrice;
  private int historicPrice;
  private String symbol = null;

  public ChartCanvas() {
  }

  protected void paint(Graphics g){
    int currentColor = g.getColor();
    g.setColor(255,255,255);
    g.fillRect(0,0,getWidth(),getHeight());
    g.setColor(currentColor);
    g.drawString(symbol + " Performance",1,1, Graphics.TOP|Graphics.LEFT);
    g.drawString("current vs. historic ", 1, 12, Graphics.TOP|Graphics.LEFT);
    g.drawString("$" + currentPrice, 1, 24, Graphics.TOP|Graphics.LEFT);
    g.drawString("$" + historicPrice, 1, 36, Graphics.TOP|Graphics.LEFT);
    int[] prices = {currentPrice, historicPrice};
    int[] lengths = determineLengths(prices);
    g.fillRect (START_X_POSITION, START_Y_CURRENT, lengths[0], BAR_HEIGHT);
    g.fillRect (START_X_POSITION, START_Y_HISTORIC, lengths[1], BAR_HEIGHT);
    g.drawLine(30,26,30,50);
    g.drawLine(50,26,50,50);
    g.drawLine(70,26,70,50);
    g.drawLine(90,26,90,50);
  }

  public void displayChart(String sym, int amtCur, int amtHist) {
    symbol = sym;
    currentPrice = amtCur;
    historicPrice = amtHist;
    serviceRepaints();
  }
  private int[] determineLengths (int[] prices) {
    int ratio, higherPrice, lowerPrice;
    boolean currentHigher;

    if (prices[0] < prices[1]) {
      higherPrice = prices[1];
      lowerPrice = prices[0];
      currentHigher=false;
    } else {
```

**①** Static constants to create bars of graph

**②** Display title, current price next to price bars

**③** Draw bars depicting prices

**④** Draw graph grid or "tick" lines

**⑤** Force canvas to paint

**⑥** Method to determine length of price bar

```
        higherPrice = prices[0];
        lowerPrice = prices[1];
        currentHigher=true;
      }
    ratio = higherPrice/MAX_BAR_SIZE + 1;
    while (ratio > 1) {
      higherPrice = higherPrice/ratio;
      lowerPrice = lowerPrice/ratio;
      ratio = higherPrice/MAX_BAR_SIZE + 1;
    }
    if (currentHigher) {
      int[] ends = {higherPrice, lowerPrice};
      return ends;
    } else {
      int [] ends = {lowerPrice, higherPrice};
      return ends;
    }
  }
}
```

**6** **Method to determine
length of price bar**

As a test, we used the ObtainQuoteMIDlet to kick of the high-level API displays. Here, we take advantage of the RetrieveQuoteMIDlet to initiate and test the low-level API display. Just as in the ObtainQuoteMIDlet, a variable is added to the RetrieveQuoteMIDlet in order to keep a reference to an instance of the ChartCanvas that is created.

```
private ChartCanvas chartCanvas = null;
```

Next, a method is added to the MIDlet to create a new ChartCanvas object when it has not yet been instantiated, or use the existing object when it has already been created. This method will also kick off the test of the canvas display by setting the current display to the new Canvas object and then calling the displayChart (String symbol, int current, int historic) method that was created earlier.

```
private void displayChartCanvas() {
  if (chartCanvas == null) {
    chartCanvas = new ChartCanvas();
  }
  displayMngr.setCurrent(chartCanvas);
  chartCanvas.displayChart("MMM",75,110);
}
```

Finally, the startApp() method to the RetrieveQuoteMIDlet is modified to call on the display manager with a call to the displayChartCanvas() method.

```
protected void startApp() {
  displayMngr  = Display.getDisplay(this);
  displayChartCanvas();
}
```

After successfully compiling, preverifying, JARing and running of the application, the low-level API display should reflect that depicted in figure 5.20.

**Figure 5.20**
**Investment prices depicted as bars in a bar graph are made possible with the low-level API and canvas. Each bar in the graph is just a filled rectangle drawn to the canvas. Unlike the StringItem used in the high-level API, even the text for the title and prices must be drawn to the canvas.**

### Compile

```
>javac -g:none -bootclasspath %MIDPClasses%;. EntryForm.java
>javac -g:none -bootclasspath %MIDPClasses%;. ChartCanvas.java
>javac -g:none -bootclasspath %MIDPClasses%;. ObtainQuoteMIDlet.java
>javac -g:none -bootclasspath %MIDPClasses%;. RetrieveQuoteMIDlet.java
```

or

```
>javac -g:none -bootclasspath %MIDPClasses%;. *.java
```

### Preverify

```
>%MIDPTools%\preverify -classpath %MIDPClasses%;.  ObtainQuoteMIDlet
>%MIDPTools%\preverify -classpath %MIDPClasses%;.  RetrieveQuoteMIDlet
>%MIDPTools%\preverify -classpath %MIDPClasses%;.  EntryForm
>%MIDPTools%\preverify -classpath %MIDPClasses%;.  ChartCanvas
```

or

```
>%MIDPTools%\preverify -classpath %MIDPClasses%;.  "."
```

### JAR

```
>jar -cfm quote.jar QuoteMIDletSuite.jad -C ./output ObtainQuoteMIDlet.class
-C ./output RetrieveQuoteMIDlet.class -C ./output EntryForm.class -C ./out-
put ChartCanvas.class
```

or

```
>jar -cfm quote.jar QuoteMIDletSuite.jad -C ./output .
```

### Run

```
>%MIDPTools%\midp -classpath %MIDPClasses%;.\quote.jar -descriptor
QuoteMIDletSuite.jad
```

## 5.5  HANDLING USER INTERACTIONS IN MIDP

When a user interacts with an application, we expect the application to respond and take appropriate action. A user interaction, such as the push of a button, selection from a list of choices, or entry of data into a field, is known as an event. An event is a notice generated at runtime each time the user interacts with the device. In response, an application is constructed to wait or "listen" for the events and take action depending on the particular event. For example, entry of data in a field may require the application to listen for text entry and then validate the data entered. An application is constructed to listen for events by implementing a listener interface and realizing methods known as callbacks. Callback methods are special methods that are not usually invoked by the application code directly, but are invoked by the system for a specified event. In the case of the MIDP user interface, a device automatically invokes callback methods each time the user has triggered a particular event for which an application listens.

As part of the tutorial application in this chapter, we developed a user interface without reacting to any user interactions other than the selection and starting of the application. In fact, the user interface did not even let the users exit the application gracefully. Users had to turn the device off in order to leave the application. This is probably not the type of functionality customers enjoy. In this section, we correct this problem and provide a more graceful means to exit the application as well as handle other customer interactions with the application.

Under the MID profile there are two means of event handling. Corresponding to the MIDP's high-level and low-level user interface, there is both a high-level and low-level event API. The high-level events and event handling mechanisms are more abstract and are meant to address the general needs of more traditional business applications. Low-level events and event handling, on the other hand, are provided to capture and handle primitive events from specific keys being pressed and released or from a pointer being pressed or dragged (provided the device has a pointer). As with the high-level and low-level UI APIs, the high-level events are considered more portable to different devices running the MID profile. Alternately, the low-level event API allows for capturing and handling of very specific events, which makes activity in gaming applications possible, but these events may be more specific to a particular device and thus less portable.

Using the term "low-level" in describing the MIDP's alternate event handling mechanism is also a little misleading. In fact, the MIDP UI is relatively abstract in that it does not allow applications to have access to very low-level user interactions such as traversing a form from item to item or form scrolling.

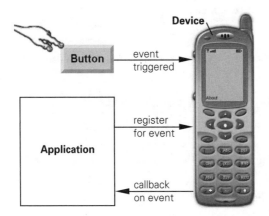

**Figure 5.21**
**Each time the user pushes a button or key on the keypad of the device, the potential exists for an event to be triggered inside of the application. The user's push of a button causes an application method, termed a callback, to be invoked based on an earlier application registration of the event to that method.**

The user interface events handled via callbacks are serialized, which means that handling of events never occurs in parallel. A user interface callback is invoked as soon as an earlier callback returns. Timer events are not user interface events and so their callback methods do not adhere to the same serialized rule. A `Timer` object, in MIDP, is a means for scheduling tasks for future execution in a background thread. Timer callback methods can run concurrently with UI event callbacks.

## 5.5.1 High-level event handling

In the high-level API, events come from two types of user interactions. A user can initiate a high-level event by changing the value or internal state of an item within a `Form` instance or a user can initiate a `Command`. Commands are a kind of user interface selector and event launcher construct rolled into one object. Correspondingly, handling high-level events requires two types of listeners. There are listeners for command events and listeners for item state change events.

### ItemStateListener

The user initiates an item state change event when he performs any of the following actions on an `Item` object contained in a form:

- adjusts the value of an interactive `Gauge`
- enters or modifies the value of a `TextField`
- enters a new date or time in a `DateField`
- changes (sets or unsets) the selected values in a `ChoiceGroup`

**GAUGE STATE CHANGE** A `Gauge` item can be created in a noninteractive mode. In this case the `Gauge` item serves as a progress bar or indicator and any change to the value is made by the application through a call to the `setValue(int value)` method. Calls by the application to `setValue(int setValue)` should not then trigger an item state change.

To capture and handle item state events, an object in the application must implement the `ItemStateListener` interface and it must notify the form that it is listening for item state events. The `ItemStateListener` interface comes from the `javax.microedition.lcdui` package and it has only one method that must be implemented by implementing classes. The `itemStateChanged(Item item)` method is the callback method invoked by the device when the state of an item has changed.

A form is notified that a listener's `itemStateChanged(Item item)` method should be invoked on item state changes by calling on the form's `setItemState-Listener(ItemStateListener iListener)` method with the listener object. This act of tying a specific `ItemStateListener` implementer object to a specific `Form` object is called registration. An `ItemStateListener` is registered for events coming from a form. A `Form` object can have only one `ItemStateListener` and subsequent calls to the `setItemStateListener(ItemStateListener iListener)` method will cause the previous listener to be replaced.

Per the MIDP specification,[1] it has been left up to the device implementation to determine exactly what constitutes a change and when the change occurs in the value of an item. For example, a text field could be considered changed after the entry or modification of a character in the field. The specification only requires that the Item-StateListener implementer be called before it is called for a change on another Item, and before a command is delivered to the Form object's CommandListener (see the CommandListener section on page 109). If a device provides for the concept of input focus, the specification suggests that the ItemStateListener itemStateChanged(Item item) method be called no later than when an affected item that has been changed loses focus. It further suggests that the listener should only be invoked if an item's value has actually been changed.

### Commands

In the previous examples both in this chapter and chapter 4, the user interface was built lacking a critical component. Namely, there was no way for the customer to initiate any action, not even the action to leave the application. In most desktop applications, basic actions are provided through the push of a "button" or selection of an option from a menu. In MIDP, the equivalent user interface object is called a Command.

Due to the diversity of MIDP devices, a command may be implemented as a soft button, menu selection, or other appropriate mechanism that activates a single action. Remember, a J2ME, MIDP device is not even required to have a user interface. Therefore, a command could be implemented as a voice tag in a non-graphical speech interface.

The Command class, like all user interface classes, is defined in the javax.micro-edition.lcdui package. A command encapsulates the meaning or purpose of a user's action; however it does not handle the actual action. That is, a Command object encapsulates the semantic information of an action but not its behavior. Another event listener, a CommandListener, which is described later in this chapter, provides the behavior.

A Command object is displayed or more precisely "presented" in the user interface based on the information contained within the object, the device presenting the Command, as well as the number of commands being displayed. For example, a device may choose to display a string next to a device button on the device screen.

Alternatively, if the number of commands to be displayed exceeds the number of physical buttons a device has, then the device may display the commands in a menu. Again, the implementation and presentation of commands is left up to the device implementer.

A command has three parts: a label, type, and priority. A command's label is the string used by the device to represent the command in the user interface. The device may override the label of a command with a device-assigned label if the command's type is other than SCREEN. This allows devices to specify a consistent and appropriate label for common functions. Each Command object also has a priority value that the

---

[1]  Mobile Information Device Profile Specification, Version 1.0, Final Candidate for Shipment, September 15, 2000, Sun Microsystems, Inc.

**Figure 5.22**
Commands, such as `Get` and `Exit` here, can be associated with keys (buttons) on the device. The type and priority of a command determine how and where the command is presented to the user.

application uses to determine the importance of one command relative to another command on the same user interface. Priority values must be integers and a lower number indicates greater importance. A command type specifies the intent of a command. There are several statically available types already defined for `Command` objects. These include `BACK`, `CANCEL`, `HELP`, `OK`, `SCREEN`, and `STOP` types.

A device's implementation will utilize type and priority to help determine the presentation of commands on the user interface. The implementation will first use type in determining the placement of a command and then it will place similar commands in order of priority. This allows, for example, a device to establish a standard placement of operations such as "help" on the appropriate soft-button. Usually, higher priority commands are placed so that they can be directly initiated by the push of a soft button while lower priority commands are arranged in a menu. It is legal to have several commands on the same screen with the same type and priority. In this case, the device will choose how commands are displayed and adjust the type and/or priority accordingly.

The `Command` class provides a single constructor, `Command(String label, int commandType, int priority)`, for creating a `Command` object. The developer must supply the label, type and priority at the time of creation. The `Command` object has get methods to retrieve the label, type and priority information, but has no methods to set these values after the object has been created.

Like other user interface objects, `Command` objects cannot be displayed on a screen by themselves. They must be added to an encapsulating `Displayable` object. Unlike other graphical elements, `Commands` can be added to any `Displayable` object, which includes both `Screen` and `Canvas` objects. The `Displayable` methods `addCommand(Command cmd)` and `removeCommand(Command cmd)` allow for adding and removing commands from these display objects.

We indicated that commands are a kind of user interface selector or button and event-launcher construct rolled into one object. Each command triggers a command event. Like item state changes, these events must be captured and acted on by another object. This is done through another high-level event listener.

### CommandListener

To capture and handle command events, an object in the application must implement the `CommandListener` interface and it must notify the `Displayable` object that it is listening for command events. Customarily, a nested or an inner class is created in an application to implement the listener. The `CommandListener` interface comes from the `javax.microedition.lcdui` package and, like the other high-level event `ItemStateListener` interface, it has only one method, `commandAction(Command c, Displayable d)` that must be implemented by the implementing listener class.

How does the `commandAction()` method get called? Like with the `ItemState-Listener`, a `CommandListener` must first register with the `Displayable` object (either `Screen` or `Canvas`) holding the `Command` object whose event is of interest. A command listener is registered by utilizing the `setCommandListener(CommandListener cmdlist)` method on the `Displayable` object. A `Displayable` object can have only one command listener at any one time. Therefore, subsequent calls to the `setCommandListener(CommandListener cmdlist)` method on the same `Displayable` object can cause any previous listener to be replaced. After registering, the `commandAction(Command c, Displayable d)` method will be triggered by the device each time a command event is initiated by the user on the `Displayable` object.

The two parameters provided the `commandAction(Command c, Displayable d)` callback specify the `Command` object selected by the user, and the possessing or owning `Displayable` object. This allows the `commandAction(Command c, Displayable d)` method to handle many command events from various `Screen` and `Canvas` objects. However, typically, a nested class or inner class inside of a canvas or screen is set up to receive the high-level events for that single `Displayable` object.

It is important to note again that event handling callbacks are serialized. The device does not create threads for event delivery. If a listener's event handling method does not return or takes a long time to return, the entire system may be blocked. Therefore, the listener methods should return as quickly as possible.

## 5.5.2 Low-level event handling

The high-level event API is meant to abstract as much of the event and event handling detail away from the application as possible. However, if your application uses an object instantiated from a subclass of `Canvas` (recall that the `Canvas` class is abstract in nature) to draw low-level graphical elements, you may want or need to handle low-level events. Game applications are the proverbial example of where low-level graphics are likely used to provide more precise and fine-grained drawings. Likewise, the low-level event API is used in gaming applications to provide the user with more game control through handling of specific game action, key and pointer events.

The `Canvas` class, which is abstract and must be extended by the implementing application, provides methods to handle the low-level events. The `Canvas` class also provides a number of convenience methods to help developers discover the device's event capabilities and event-to-keyboard mappings.

### Key codes and low-level API Events

In the low-level event API, key pressed or released events that emanate from the application are reported with respect to a key code. Key codes are static variables assigned to constant integer values that represent the concrete keys of the device. A key code is assigned to every key that reports events to an MIDP application. The key code value is unique to each device key unless two keys are synonyms for each other. The key code values are equal to the Unicode encoding of the keypad character they represent. In the `Canvas` class, the following key codes are defined:

- KEY_NUM0
- KEY_NUM1
- KEY_NUM2
- KEY_NUM3
- KEY_NUM4
- KEY_NUM5
- KEY_NUM6
- KEY_NUM7
- KEY_NUM8
- KEY_NUM9
- KEY_STAR
- KEY_POUND

The MIDP low-level event API requires that standard key codes be assigned to the ITU-T keypad. This keypad includes the '0' through '9' keys as well as the '*' and '#' keys that are on cellular telephones. Device implementers are allowed to assign additional key codes to additional device keys, but these are considered non-standard key code mappings. Applications that utilize non-standard key codes are considered not portable to other devices.

A method on the `Canvas` object, `getKeyName(int keyCode)` will provide the key string or name for any key code passed as the parameter. This string should resemble the text physically printed on the key on the device. If the key code given to the `getKeyName (int keyCode)` method is not valid an `IllegalArgumentException` is thrown.

### Game actions

Game actions are static final variables assigned to constant integer values that represent arrow key and gaming action key events. In order to keep an application portable, an application that uses arrow key or gaming related events should use game actions over key codes since the key codes associated with the event representing an arrow key or game action key press may be nonstandard. The `Canvas` class defines the following game actions:

- UP
- DOWN
- LEFT
- RIGHT
- FIRE
- GAME A
- GAME B
- GAME C
- GAME D

Key codes can be mapped to at most one game action, but game actions may be associated to more than one key code. For example, all of the key codes associated with keys usually found on the left side of a key pad (`KEY_NUM1`, `KEY_NUM4`, `KEY_NUM7`) could be mapped to the `LEFT` game action, but no other game actions could then be

**Figure 5.23**
**Game actions are typically assigned to the directional or navigational (arrow) keys, if these are available.**

mapped to these key codes. The getKeyCode(int gameAction) and getGame-Action(int keyCode) methods on the Canvas class offer translation between key codes and game actions.

Devices differ greatly on how game actions are mapped to the physical keys. Some devices have navigational arrow keys. In these devices, it is apt for the LEFT, RIGHT, UP, and DOWN game actions to be mapped to these physical keys.
In other devices where navigational arrow keys do not exist, the '2', '4', '6' and '8' keys on the key pad may be used for LEFT, RIGHT, UP, and DOWN game actions. (Figure 5.24)

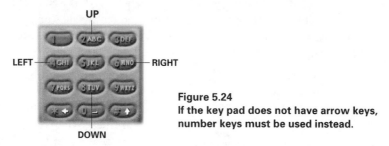

**Figure 5.24**
**If the key pad does not have arrow keys, number keys must be used instead.**

Key codes could be used to determine if a key event came from a navigational arrow key. However, this would require checking for a non-standard key code on the part of the application. In order to keep an application portable across devices, key events should be translated to a game action with the getGameAction(int keyCode) method. In this way, whether the key assigned to the game action has a standard key code (as with the 2 key) or nonstandard key code (as with the up arrow key), the application is portable to either type of device.

### Event delivery methods

Key codes and game actions represent the events in the low-level API, but how are these events handled? In the high-level API, a listener object is created to handle events generated from the high-level user interface objects (either items or commands). The listener's callback method is called whenever the event is triggered. In the low-level API, there are no listener objects. Instead, the event callback methods are contained within the Canvas object. The device calls the following canvas methods when a low-level event occurs:

```
keyPressed(int keyCode)
keyReleased(int keyCode)
keyRepeated(int keyCode)
```

```
pointerPressed(int x, int y)
pointerDragged(int x, int y)
pointerReleased(int x, int y)
```

The Canvas class is abstract and so it requires the application to subclass it in order to use these methods. The default implementation for the callback methods or event delivery methods, as they are called in the MIDP API documentation, is empty. This means that the application, by default, takes no action when the low-level key events fire and these methods are called. The application must override these methods in the implementation subclass of Canvas in order for the application to handle the low-level events.

You probably noticed the pointer methods at the bottom of the event handling methods above. A pointing device or input mechanism is considered optional for MIDP devices. Some devices do not support a pointer input device. In this case, the pointer methods will never be called. The Canvas class does have two methods, hasPointerEvents() and hasPointerMotionEvents(), for checking whether a pointer is available. Likewise, not all devices allow for repeated key presses. A has-RepeatEvents() method is available to check for this option's availability on the device.

The Canvas class also has other event delivery methods that are not associated with the key or pointer related events. These include:

```
showNotify()
hideNotify()
paint(Graphics g)
```

The showNotify() method is called prior to a canvas actually being displayed. Alternately, the hideNotify() method is called after a canvas has been removed from display. The key and pointer event handling, paint and command callback methods can only be called if the Canvas object is actually being displayed.

Like the high-level event callback methods, the event delivery methods are also called serially. Therefore, the device will never call any two event delivery methods in parallel. An event delivery method is invoked only after an earlier event delivery method returns.

### Commands with the Canvas

A Canvas object is also a Displayable object and so can have Command objects attached to it. Therefore, a Canvas object can participate in high-level and low-level event handling. Commands are particularly useful for navigating to and from the different displays. However, the Canvas object was meant to provide an encapsulating drawing object for low-level user interfaces such as those required in games and geographical display systems. Some devices may not provide high-level command events when the Canvas and low-level user interface graphical elements are displayed. In this case, the device may provide a means to switch in and out of the command mode with the use of a hot key on the device. The Canvas object's showNotify() and hideNotify() methods are called during these transitions.

### 5.5.3 Handling the events of the Investment Quote Application

In the first part of this chapter, we were able to draw some very nice user interfaces with both high-level and low-level user interface APIs. The problem with these interfaces, as already indicated, is that there is no way for the user to indicate what he wants done on any display. Once the user has entered the symbol for the investment, he cannot tell the system to retrieve the quote. Once he has seen the prices for an investment, he cannot tell the system to stop and leave the application. In this portion of the tutorial, we will add Commands to the user interface and allow the application to react to user interactions causing events triggered by commands as well as other items shown on the display.

#### Using ItemStateListener

In the tutorial application, the customer is requested to enter the symbol for an investment for which they would like price information. Except for unusual circumstances, common stocks are given three, four or five letter symbols. Thus, the text field in our entry form was given a maximum size of 5 characters. Mutual funds are also up to five letters in length, but a mutual fund symbol ends in the letter X. To help insure that the customers have entered an appropriate string of characters when requesting a price quote for a mutual fund, the tutorial application is retrofitted to check the customer's input on the entry form's symbolField when the "Fund" choice is selected from the form's choice group. This is accomplished by outfitting the MIDlets with an ItemStateListener to listen for item state changes to the choice group item called investmentChoice (see chapter 3 for a review of the tutorial application user interface). A single method is added to our MIDlet that establishes the ItemStateListener and registers it with the EntryForm.

**Listing 5.11    Adding ItemStateListeners to the MIDlets**

```
private void initListener () {
  ItemStateListener itemListener = new ItemStateListener () {      ❶
    public void itemStateChanged (Item item) {
      if ((item == entryForm.getInvestmentChoice()) &&
          (entryForm.getInvestmentChoice().getSelectedIndex() == 1) &&
          !(entryForm.getSymbolField().getString().
          toUpperCase().endsWith("X"))) {
          Alert symbolAlert = new Alert("Check Symbol",
            "Mutual Funds end in 'X'",null, AlertType.WARNING);    ❷
          symbolAlert.setTimeout(Alert.FOREVER);
          displayMngr.setCurrent(symbolAlert, entryForm);
      }
    }
  };
  entryForm.setItemStateListener(itemListener);      ❸
}
```

**❶** ItemState Listener defined by inner class

**❷** Use an alert to indicate to the user a discrepancy with the symbol and the investment type

**❸** Assign or register listener with the entry form

In this example, an anonymous inner class is used to implement the `ItemState-Listener`. If the customer makes any change in state to any item on the entry form, the listener checks to see if the item changed is the `investmentChoice` item. If it is, the listener also makes certain that the choice selected was the "Fund" choice (the "Fund" choice has an index of 1 in the list of choices) and that the symbol entered does not end in 'X'. When these conditions have been met, the customer is prompted with a warning alert displayed over the entry form indicating the symbol for a mutual fund may not be correct since it should end in 'X'. All that is left to do is to initialize the listener when the entry form is created inside of the `displayEntryForm()` method.

```
private void displayEntryForm () {
  if (entryForm == null) {
    entryForm = new EntryForm("ObtainQuote");
  }
  initListener();
  displayMngr.setCurrent(entryForm);
}
```

After compiling, preverifying, and JARing the MIDlet suite in the usual manner, the application should look like the display captured in figure 5.25.

## Compile

```
>javac -g:none -bootclasspath %MIDPClasses%;. EntryForm.java
>javac -g:none -bootclasspath %MIDPClasses%;. ChartCanvas.java
>javac -g:none -bootclasspath %MIDPClasses%;. ObtainQuoteMIDlet.java
>javac -g:none -bootclasspath %MIDPClasses%;. RetrieveQuoteMIDlet.java
```

or

```
>javac -g:none -bootclasspath %MIDPClasses%;. *.java
```

## Preverify

```
>%MIDPTools%\preverify -classpath %MIDPClasses%;.  ObtainQuoteMIDlet
>%MIDPTools%\preverify -classpath %MIDPClasses%;.  RetrieveQuoteMIDlet
>%MIDPTools%\preverify -classpath %MIDPClasses%;.  EntryForm
>%MIDPTools%\preverify -classpath %MIDPClasses%;.  ChartCanvas
>%MIDPTools%\preverify -classpath %MIDPClasses%;.  ObtainQuoteMIDlet$1
```

or

```
>%MIDPTools%\preverify -classpath %MIDPClasses%;.  "."
```

## JAR

```
>jar -cfm quote.jar QuoteMIDletSuite.jad -C ./output ObtainQuoteMIDlet.class
-C ./output RetrieveQuoteMIDlet.class -C ./output EntryForm.class
-C ./output ChartCanvas.class -C ./output ObtainQuoteMIDlet$1.class
```

or

```
>jar -cfm quote.jar QuoteMIDletSuite.jad -C ./output .
```

Run

```
>%MIDPTools%\midp -classpath %MIDPClasses%;.\quote.jar -descriptor
QuoteMIDletSuite.jad
```

If the symbol entered in the symbolField does not end in an "X", then the item state listener triggers an alert whenever the InvestmentChoice experiences a state change.

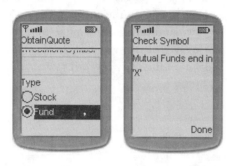

**Figure 5.25**
**Mutual fund symbols end in 'X'. If the investment type signified by the last character in the symbol does not match the type selected in the ChoiceGroup, then the customer needs to be warned. Appropriately, our application uses an Alert, as shown here, to indicate text entry errors as triggered via an ItemStateChange.**

## Using Commands and CommandListeners

There are several places in the tutorial application that require use of a Command, not the least of which is the tutorial application's MIDlets, which require a means to exit the application gracefully—that is, without turning off the device. Secondly, each MIDlet in the tutorial application requires the customer to enter a symbol. Presumably the customer indicates when the symbol has been entered with some action and the ObtainQuoteMIDlet then requests the price from the quote service. Similarly, the RetrieveQuoteMIDlet, when provided a symbol, attempts to retrieve the historical price from the persistent storage on the device. The problem is, the MIDlets currently have no way for the customer to indicate when the symbol has been entered. Instead, the MIDlets are simulating the customer's entry of a symbol in the first form and simply calling on the subsequent Displayable object to show the new or retrieved price. Commands provide the perfect solution for allowing the user to signal when a symbol has been entered and for the MIDlet to take over and complete some action. Let's fix the MIDlets to provide real customer interaction and behavior more appropriately to those actions.

First, we modify the EntryForm and ChartCanvas Displayable classes to contain exit commands. This will allow these displays, and in some cases the entire application, to be exited gracefully. In both Displayable objects, a private variable is added to contain the exit command.

```
private Command exitCommand;= null;
```

Next, two lines are added to the constructor of each of the `Displayable` objects to create the exit command object and add it to the display.

```
exitCommand = new Command("Exit", Command.EXIT, 1);
addCommand(exitCommand);
```

The exit command has been given an "Exit" label. More importantly, it has been given the `EXIT` type and a high priority value of 1. This serves to give the command a prominent place in the display. In the cell phone emulator, the high priority of the exit command serves to get it assigned to upper-left soft button. Finally, in order for the MIDlet applications to have access to the exit `Command` objects, a getter method is added to both the `EntryForm` and `ChartCanvas` objects.

```
public Command getExitCommand() {
  return exitCommand;
}
```

Now, when either the `EntryForm` or `ChartCanvas` are displayed, the new exit commands are displayed. Based on the command type and priority, and depending on how the device presents commands, the `Displayable` objects should look similar to the emulator depiction in figure 5.26.

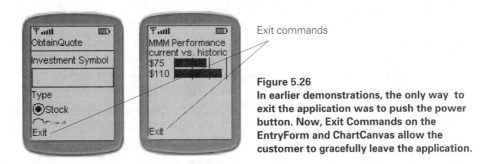

Exit commands

**Figure 5.26**
**In earlier demonstrations, the only way to exit the application was to push the power button. Now, Exit Commands on the EntryForm and ChartCanvas allow the customer to gracefully leave the application.**

An exit `Command` on the chart canvas is all that is needed to allow the customer to leave the price graph when he or she is done viewing it. On the entry form, however, we need a mechanism to allow the customer to signify when the investment symbol has been entered. To provide for this user interaction, an additional "Get" `Command` is added to the entry form. Similar to the exit commands, a private variable is added to contain the get `Command`.

```
private Command getCommand = null;
```

Lines are added to the `EntryForm` class constructor to create and add the new command to the `Form` object.

```
getCommand = new Command("Get", Command.SCREEN, 2);
addCommand(getCommand);
```

The second command is given a lower priority and SCREEN type that results in a presumably less predominant spot on the user interface than the exit command was given. Additionally a getter method is provided for public access to the get Command object.

```
public Command getGetCommand() {
  return getCommand;
}
```

Now the entry form should have two commands when displayed.

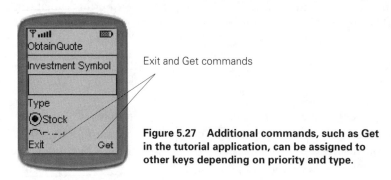

Figure 5.27   Additional commands, such as Get in the tutorial application, can be assigned to other keys depending on priority and type.

This work puts commands on the displays, but it does not allow the application to handle the events generated when the customer initiates other actions. To handle other events, other listeners must be established and registered with the appropriate Displayable object.

What actions should occur when the customer triggers the various events associated with each command? Earlier in this chapter, we simply put together the various user interfaces but did not provide customer triggered navigation. Now that we have the ability to allow the user to trigger actions through commands, we will want to reconfigure our user interface displays. Figure 5.28 depicts what navigation we expect to occur when the user presses the various commands.

Both the ObtainQuote and RetrieveQuote MIDlets can make use of the Entry-Form class to get the investment symbol from the user. In the case of the ObtainQuote MIDlet, we expect the application to use the symbol to obtain a new quote from the quote service and display the results in the results alert we developed earlier. In the case of the RetrieveQuote MIDlet, the symbol will be used to obtain the last prices from persistent storage to be displayed graphically in the ChartCanvas display. The exit command on the entry form used by either the ObtainQuote or RetrieveQuote MIDlets, should close down the MIDlet gracefully, allowing the customer to return to the application menu. The exit command on the chart canvas returns application control back to the EntryForm object of the RetrieveQuote MIDlet. This allows the customer to retrieve other historical quotes.

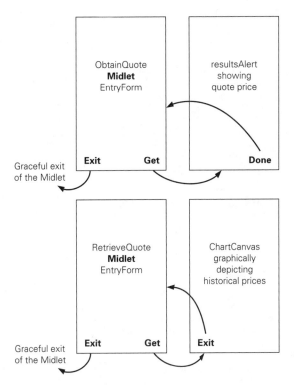

**Figure 5.28**
**This diagram shows how the various commands and event handling of those commands on the ObtainQuote and RetrieveQuote MIDlets invoke displays.**

To handle the event launched by the exit and get commands on either MIDlet's `EntryForm` object, we take advantage of the `initListener()` method set up earlier for handling changes to the choice group item. Inside of the `initListener()` method, another anonymous inner class is used to implement the `CommandListener` and handle the exit and get command events. The code for both listeners is shown in listing 5.12.

```
private void initListener () {
  ItemStateListener itemListener = new ItemStateListener () {
    public void itemStateChanged (Item item) {
      if ((item == entryForm.getInvestmentChoice()) &&
          (entryForm.getInvestmentChoice().getSelectedIndex() == 1) &&
          !(entryForm.getSymbolField().getString().
            toUpperCase().endsWith("X"))) {
        Alert symbolAlert = new Alert("Check Symbol",
          "Mutual Funds end in 'X'",null, AlertType.WARNING);
        symbolAlert.setTimeout(Alert.FOREVER);
        displayMngr.setCurrent(symbolAlert, entryForm);
      }
    }
  };
```

**❶**

```
CommandListener commandListener = new CommandListener() {
  public void commandAction(Command c, Displayable d) {
    if (c == entryForm.getExitCommand()) {
      destroyApp(true);
    } else if (c == entryForm.getGetCommand()) {
      if ((entryForm.getInvestmentChoice().getSelectedIndex() == 1) &&
          !(entryForm.getSymbolField().getString().
          toUpperCase().endsWith("X"))){
        Alert symbolAlert = new Alert("Check Symbol",
          "Mutual Funds end in 'X'", null, AlertType.WARNING);
        symbolAlert.setTimeout(Alert.FOREVER);
        displayMngr.setCurrent(symbolAlert, entryForm);
      } else {
        if (entryForm.getSymbolField().getString().length() > 0) {
          String sym = entryForm.getSymbolField().getString();
          displayPrice("The price of " + sym + " is $111.19");
        }
      }
    }
  }
};

entryForm.setItemStateListener(itemListener);
entryForm.setCommandListener(commandListener);
}
```

❷

❸

❹

❺

❶ The anonymous inner class defining the item state listener

❷ An anonymous inner class defining the command listener

❸ "Exit" command event, destroy the MIDlet

❹ "Get" command event, display the price

❺ Assign or register the listeners with the form

In this code, two anonymous inner classes are used. The first inner class defines the previously mentioned item state listener and how the MIDlet will react to item events. The second anonymous inner class defines the command listener and how the MIDlet will react to command events. The new command listener must react to two commands. On an Exit command, the listener requests to destroy the MIDlet. On a Get command, the listener either displays the price for the investment or launches an alert if there is a type or symbol discrepancy. Along with defining the listeners, the init-Listener() method also registers the item and command listeners with the EntryForm.

Both MIDlets handle the exit command in the same way, namely, they call on the destroyApp(true) method in the MIDlet to force the MIDlet into the destroyed state. Both MIDlets also handle the get command events, but each handles the event a little differently. The ObtainQuote MIDlet calls on the alert to display the new price for the investment symbol provided by the customer. As shown in listing 5.13, the RetrieveQuote MIDlet, on the other hand, calls to display the canvas to show the historical price information for the investment symbol provided by the customer.

Listing 5.13   The initListener method for the RetrieveQuoteMIDlet

```
private void initListener () {
  ItemStateListener itemListener = new ItemStateListener () {
    public void itemStateChanged (Item item) {
      if ((item == entryForm.getInvestmentChoice()) &&
          (entryForm.getInvestmentChoice().getSelectedIndex() == 1) &&
          !(entryForm.getSymbolField().getString().
          toUpperCase().endsWith("X"))) {
            Alert symbolAlert = new Alert("Check Symbol",
              "Mutual Funds end in 'X'",null, AlertType.WARNING);
            symbolAlert.setTimeout(Alert.FOREVER);
            displayMngr.setCurrent(symbolAlert, entryForm);
          }
      }
  };
  CommandListener commandListener = new CommandListener() {
    public void commandAction(Command c, Displayable d) {
      if (c == entryForm.getExitCommand()) {
        destroyApp(true);
      } else if (c == entryForm.getGetCommand()) { {          ❶
          if ((entryForm.getInvestmentChoice().getSelectedIndex() == 1) &&
              !(entryForm.getSymbolField().getString().
              toUpperCase().endsWith("X"))){ {          ❶
            Alert symbolAlert = new Alert("Check Symbol",
              "Mutual Funds end in 'X'", null, AlertType.WARNING); {     ❶
            symbolAlert.setTimeout(Alert.FOREVER);
            displayMngr.setCurrent(symbolAlert, entryForm);
          } else
            if (entryForm.getSymbolField().getString().length() > 0)
              displayChartCanvas();
        }
      }
  };
  entryForm.setItemStateListener(itemListener);
  entryForm.setCommandListener(commandListener);
}
```

❶ On a "Get" command event, display the chart canvas depicting the current and historical prices or alert on error

Notice that the listeners (listings 5.12 and 5.13) are all registered with the Entry-Form object at the end of the method. These are important lines in the code that should not be forgotten. Without registration, the events would fire and code would be ready to handle the responses, but no part of the application would actually catch and handle the events.

The RetrieveQuote MIDlet must also be set up as a listener for the exit command event on the ChartCanvas class. For this, a second CommandListener class is created. Like the listener for the exit and get commands originating from the entry form, this listener is established through an anonymous inner class in an initialization method within the RetrieveQuote MIDlet.

```
private void initCanvasListener() {
  CommandListener commandListener = new CommandListener() {
    public void commandAction(Command c, Displayable d) {
      if (c == chartCanvas.getExitCommand())
        displayMngr.setCurrent(entryForm);
    }
  };
  chartCanvas.setCommandListener(commandListener);
}
```

Notice, again, that the listener is registered with the canvas object at the end of the method. When the exit command on the canvas is triggered, this commandAction() method in this listener calls on the display manager to set the current Displayable back to the EntryForm object. The displayChartCanvas() method in the RetrieveQuote MIDlet must be modified to call this initialization method when a ChartCanvas object is displayed.

```
private void displayChartCanvas() {
  if (chartCanvas == null) {
    chartCanvas = new ChartCanvas();
  }
  initCanvasListener();
  displayMngr.setCurrent(chartCanvas);
  String currentSymbol = entryForm.getSymbolField().getString();
  chartCanvas.displayChart(currentSymbol,75,110);
}
```

The user interface and event handling on our MIDlets are now complete. Listings 5.14–5.17 show the four completed .java files. The code over the last few pages replaces or augments much of the code from previous listings. Some example code that was introduced earlier to explore features has been replaced with code that gets us closer to our completed application. Check your code against the following listings, especially if you have difficulties in compiling, preverifying or running your applications.

### Listing 5.14   EntryForm.java

```
import javax.microedition.lcdui.*;

public class EntryForm extends Form {

  private TextField symbolField = null;
  private Command exitCommand = null;
  private Command getCommand = null;
  private ChoiceGroup investmentChoice = null;

  public EntryForm(String title) {
    super(title);
    symbolField = new TextField("Investment Symbol", "", 6, TextField.ANY);
    String choices[] = {"Stock", "Fund"};
    investmentChoice = new ChoiceGroup("Type", Choice.EXCLUSIVE,
      choices, null);
    exitCommand = new Command("Exit", Command.EXIT, 1);
```

**❶ Reference variable declaration for the exit and get commands**

```
    getCommand = new Command("Get", Command.SCREEN, 2);
    append(symbolField);
    append(investmentChoice);
    addCommand(exitCommand);           ③ Add commands to form
    addCommand(getCommand);
  }

  public TextField getSymbolField() {
    return symbolField;
  }

  public ChoiceGroup getInvestmentChoice() {
    return investmentChoice;
  }

  public Command getExitCommand() {
    return exitCommand;
  }

  public Command getGetCommand() {
    return getCommand;
  }
}
```

② Creating the exit and get commands, giving the exit command highest priority

④ Provide getter methods to access commands for use by the MIDlets

Listing 5.15   ChartCanvas.java

```
import javax.microedition.lcdui.*;
import java.util.*;

class ChartCanvas extends Canvas {

  static final int MAX_BAR_SIZE = 65;
  static final int START_X_POSITION = 30;
  static final int START_Y_CURRENT = 27;
  static final int START_Y_HISTORIC = 39;
  static final int BAR_HEIGHT = 10;

  private int currentPrice;
  private int historicPrice;              Reference variable
  private String symbol = null;           declaration for the
  private Command exitCommand;         ① exit command

  public void displayChart(String sym, int amtCur, int amtHist) {
    symbol = sym;
    currentPrice = amtCur;
    historicPrice = amtHist;
    serviceRepaints();
  }

  public ChartCanvas() {
    exitCommand = new Command("Exit", Command.EXIT, 1);    ② Create exit
    addCommand(exitCommand);      ③ Add commands              command
  }                                  to Canvas

  public Command getExitCommand() {
```

```
    return exitCommand;
  }
  protected void paint(Graphics g){
    int currentColor = g.getColor();
    g.setColor(255,255,255);
    g.fillRect(0,0,getWidth(),getHeight());
    g.setColor(currentColor);
    g.drawString(symbol + " Performance",1,1,Graphics.TOP|Graphics.LEFT);
    g.drawString("current vs. historic ", 1, 12, Graphics.TOP|Graphics.LEFT);
    g.drawString("$" + currentPrice, 1, 24, Graphics.TOP|Graphics.LEFT);
    g.drawString("$" + historicPrice, 1, 36, Graphics.TOP|Graphics.LEFT);

    int[] prices = {currentPrice, historicPrice};
    int[] lengths = determineLengths(prices);
    g.fillRect (START_X_POSITION, START_Y_CURRENT, lengths[0], BAR_HEIGHT);
    g.fillRect (START_X_POSITION, START_Y_HISTORIC, lengths[1], BAR_HEIGHT);

    g.drawLine(30,26,30,50);
    g.drawLine(50,26,50,50);
    g.drawLine(70,26,70,50);
    g.drawLine(90,26,90,50);
  }

  private int[] determineLengths (int[] prices) {

    int ratio, higherPrice, lowerPrice;
    boolean currentHigher;

    if (prices[0] < prices[1]) {
      higherPrice = prices[1];
      lowerPrice = prices[0];
      currentHigher=false;
    } else {
      higherPrice = prices[0];
      lowerPrice = prices[1];
      currentHigher=true;
    }

    ratio = higherPrice/MAX_BAR_SIZE + 1;
    while (ratio > 1) {
      higherPrice = higherPrice/ratio;
      lowerPrice = lowerPrice/ratio;
      ratio = higherPrice/MAX_BAR_SIZE + 1;
    }

    if (currentHigher) {
      int[] ends = {higherPrice, lowerPrice};
      return ends;
    } else {
      int [] ends = {lowerPrice, higherPrice};
      return ends;
    }
  }
}
```

**Listing 5.16    ObtainQuoteMIDlet.java**

```java
import javax.microedition.midlet.*;
import javax.microedition.lcdui.*;

public class ObtainQuoteMIDlet extends MIDlet {

  private Display displayMngr  = null;
  private EntryForm entryForm = null;
  private Alert resultsAlert = null;
  private Ticker adTicker =
    new Ticker("Track your investments with Investment Tracker");

  public ObtainQuoteMIDlet () {
  }

  private void initListener () {
    ItemStateListener itemListener = new ItemStateListener () {
      public void itemStateChanged (Item item) {
        if ((item == entryForm.getInvestmentChoice()) &&
            (entryForm.getInvestmentChoice().getSelectedIndex() == 1) &&
            !(entryForm.getSymbolField().getString().
            toUpperCase().endsWith("X"))) {
          Alert symbolAlert = new Alert("Check Symbol",
            "Mutual Funds end in 'X'", null, AlertType.WARNING);
          symbolAlert.setTimeout(Alert.FOREVER);
          displayMngr.setCurrent(symbolAlert, entryForm);
        }
      }
    };
    CommandListener commandListener = new CommandListener() {
      public void commandAction (Command c, Displayable d) {
        if (c == entryForm.getExitCommand()) {
          destroyApp(true);
        } else if (c == entryForm.getGetCommand()) {
          if ((entryForm.getInvestmentChoice().getSelectedIndex() == 1) &&
              !(entryForm.getSymbolField().getString().
              toUpperCase().endsWith("X"))){
            Alert symbolAlert = new Alert("Check Symbol",
              "Mutual Funds end in 'X'", null, AlertType.WARNING);
            symbolAlert.setTimeout(Alert.FOREVER);
            displayMngr.setCurrent(symbolAlert, entryForm);
          } else {
            if (entryForm.getSymbolField().getString().length() > 0) {
              String sym = entryForm.getSymbolField().getString();
              displayPrice("The price of " + sym + " is $111.19");
            }
          }
        }
      }
    };
    entryForm.setItemStateListener(itemListener);
    entryForm.setCommandListener(commandListener);
  }
```

**❶** Inner class used to listen and react to command event

**❷** Registering the event listener with the Form

```java
    private void displayEntryForm () {
      if (entryForm == null) {
        entryForm = new EntryForm("ObtainQuote");
      }
      initListener();
      displayMngr.setCurrent(entryForm);
    }

    private void displayPrice(String quoteString) {
      if (resultsAlert == null) {
        resultsAlert = new Alert("Quote Price", null, null,
          AlertType.CONFIRMATION);
        resultsAlert.setTicker(adTicker);
        resultsAlert.setTimeout(Alert.FOREVER);
      }
      resultsAlert.setString(quoteString);
      displayMngr.setCurrent(resultsAlert, entryForm);
    }

    protected void startApp() {
      displayMngr  = Display.getDisplay(this);
      displayEntryForm();
    }

    protected void pauseApp() {
    }

    protected void destroyApp(boolean unconditional) {
      notifyDestroyed();
    }

    public void commandAction(Command c, Displayable s) {
    }
}
```

```java
import javax.microedition.midlet.*;
import javax.microedition.lcdui.*;

public class RetrieveQuoteMIDlet extends MIDlet {

  private Display displayMngr  = null;
  private EntryForm entryForm = null;
  private ChartCanvas chartCanvas = null;

  public RetrieveQuoteMIDlet () {
  }

  private void initListener () {
    ItemStateListener itemListener = new ItemStateListener () {
      public void itemStateChanged (Item item) {
        if ((item == entryForm.getInvestmentChoice()) &&
```

```
                    (entryForm.getInvestmentChoice().getSelectedIndex() == 1) &&
                    !(entryForm.getSymbolField().getString().
                    toUpperCase().endsWith("X"))) {
                Alert symbolAlert = new Alert("Check Symbol",
                    "Mutual Funds end in 'X'", null, AlertType.WARNING);
                symbolAlert.setTimeout(Alert.FOREVER);
                displayMngr.setCurrent(symbolAlert, entryForm);
            }
        }
    };
    CommandListener commandListener = new CommandListener() {     ❶
        public void commandAction(Command c, Displayable d) {
            if (c == entryForm.getExitCommand()) {
                destroyApp(true);
            } else if (c == entryForm.getGetCommand()) {
                if ((entryForm.getInvestmentChoice().getSelectedIndex() == 1) &&
                    !(entryForm.getSymbolField().getString().
                    toUpperCase().endsWith("X"))){    ❶
                Alert symbolAlert = new Alert("Check Symbol",
                    "Mutual Funds end in 'X'", null, AlertType.WARNING);
                symbolAlert.setTimeout(Alert.FOREVER);
                displayMngr.setCurrent(symbolAlert, entryForm);     ❶
                } else
                if (entryForm.getSymbolField().getString().length() > 0) |
                    displayChartCanvas();
            }
        }
    };

    entryForm.setItemStateListener(itemListener);        ❷
    entryForm.setCommandListener(commandListener);
}
private void initCanvasListener() {
    CommandListener commandListener = new CommandListener() {     ❸
        public void commandAction(Command c, Displayable d) {
            if (c == chartCanvas.getExitCommand())
                displayMngr.setCurrent(entryForm);
        }
    };
    chartCanvas.setCommandListener(commandListener);     ❹
}
private void displayEntryForm () {
    if (entryForm == null) {
        entryForm = new EntryForm("RetrieveQuote");
    }
    initListener();
    displayMngr.setCurrent(entryForm);
}
private void displayChartCanvas() {
    if (chartCanvas == null) {
        chartCanvas = new ChartCanvas();
    }
    initCanvasListener();
    displayMngr.setCurrent(chartCanvas);
```

```
    String currentSymbol = entryForm.getSymbolField().getString();
    chartCanvas.displayChart(currentSymbol,75,110);
  }
  protected void startApp() {
    displayMngr  = Display.getDisplay(this);
    displayEntryForm();
  }

  protected void pauseApp() {
  }

  protected void destroyApp(boolean unconditional) {
    notifyDestroyed();
  }
}
```

❶ Anonymous event listener inner class used to listen and react to command events coming from the EntryForm

❷ Registering the event listener with the Form

❸ Anonymous event listener inner class used to listen and react to command events coming from the ChartCanvas

❹ Registering the event listener with the Canvas

After compiling, preverifying, and JARing these files of the MIDlet suite with the following commands, the tutorial application should look and behave as the pictures depicted in the series of displays in figure 5.29.

Compile

```
>javac -g:none -bootclasspath %MIDPClasses%;. EntryForm.java
>javac -g:none -bootclasspath %MIDPClasses%;. ChartCanvas.java
>javac -g:none -bootclasspath %MIDPClasses%;. ObtainQuoteMIDlet.java
>javac -g:none -bootclasspath %MIDPClasses%;. RetrieveQuoteMIDlet.java
```

    or

```
>javac -g:none -bootclasspath %MIDPClasses%;. *.java
```

Preverify

```
>%MIDPTools%\preverify -classpath %MIDPClasses%;.  ObtainQuoteMIDlet
>%MIDPTools%\preverify -classpath %MIDPClasses%;.  RetrieveQuoteMIDlet
>%MIDPTools%\preverify -classpath %MIDPClasses%;.  EntryForm
>%MIDPTools%\preverify -classpath %MIDPClasses%;.  ChartCanvas
>%MIDPTools%\preverify -classpath %MIDPClasses%;.  ObtainQuoteMIDlet$1
>%MIDPTools%\preverify -classpath %MIDPClasses%;.  ObtainQuoteMIDlet$2
>%MIDPTools%\preverify -classpath %MIDPClasses%;.  RetrieveQuoteMIDlet$1
>%MIDPTools%\preverify -classpath %MIDPClasses%;.  RetrieveQuoteMIDlet$2
>%MIDPTools%\preverify -classpath %MIDPClasses%;.  RetrieveQuoteMIDlet$3
```

    or

```
>%MIDPTools%\preverify -classpath %MIDPClasses%;.  "."
```

## JAR

```
>jar -cfm quote.jar QuoteMIDletSuite.jad -C ./output ObtainQuoteMIDlet.class -C
./output RetrieveQuoteMIDlet.class -C ./output EntryForm.class -C
./output ChartCanvas.class -C ./output ObtainQuoteMIDlet$1.class -C
./output ObtainQuoteMIDlet$2.class -C ./output RetrieveQuoteMIDlet$1.class -C
./output RetrieveQuoteMIDlet$2.class -C ./output RetrieveQuoteMIDlet$3.class
```

   or

```
>jar -cfm quote.jar QuoteMIDletSuite.jad -C ./output .
```

## Run

```
>%MIDPTools%\midp -classpath %MIDPClasses%;.\quote.jar -descriptor
QuoteMIDletSuite.jad
```

**Figure 5.29  Having completed the implementation of event handling in the MIDlets, the many faces of the ObtainQuoteMIDlet are shown above. The customer enters a symbol in the TextField of the EntryForm and the investment price is displayed in an alert.**

A question might arise as to why we do not have to add a Command object (and associated listeners) to the alert displays in the tutorial application. In fact, when an Alert object is displayed in a FOREVER mode, the Alert objects have built commands (usually labeled "Done"), which are displayed on the alert. When the default command is triggered, the resulting action is to return control of the application to the next Displayable setup when the setCurrent(Alert alert, Displayable nextDisplayable) method was invoked to show the alert.

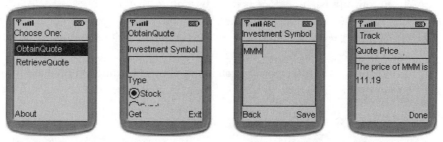

**Figure 5.30  Similar in appearance to the ObtainQuoteMIDlet, the implementation of the RetrieveQuoteMIDlet is shown in the set of screen shots above. The same EntryForm is used in the RetrieveQuoteMIDlet to get the investment symbol, but the current and historical price data is displayed on a canvas.**

### Using the low-level event API

Since our tutorial application is not a game or similar application requiring a lot of user key pad interaction, we will demonstrate how the low-level event handling works with the ChartCanvas object through simple output stream print lines (System.out.println). This will not add any real customer functionality to our application, but it should give you a feel for how the low-level event handling is accomplished. All we need to do to see low-level key events in action is to add a single method to the ChartCanvas class.

```
protected void keyReleased(int keyCode) {
  System.out.println("Key released is ->:" + getKeyName(keyCode));
  if (keyCode == KEY_NUM1) {
    System.out.println("#1 Key released.");
  }
}
```

This method simply sends a message indicating what key has been released to the system's output stream. It checks for when the '1' key has been released and prints a special message to the same stream. Notice that no code is required to register anything with the Canvas object. In fact, these are callback methods that come with the Canvas class. The preceding code overrides the default and empty implementation callback methods in the Canvas class. When the Canvas object is displayed and keys are pressed while it is displayed, the output in the designated system output stream should look like the following:

```
Key released is ->:4
Key released is ->:5
Key released is ->:6
Key released is ->:3
Key released is ->:2
Key released is ->:1
#1 Key released.
Key released is ->:7
Key released is ->:8
Key released is ->:9
```

While our application does not really require that we react specially to these keys when the chart is displayed in the canvas, they most certainly could be used to provide a more dynamic display. For example, certain actions such as zoom in and zoom out, or requesting to see the next stored quote in the database could all be assigned to different keys on the key pad. Then the application would simply have to provide the appropriate event handling if one of these keys gets pressed.

## 5.6    MIDLETS ON OTHER DEVICES

So our MIDP application works on a cell phone. But what happened to our requirement that said it must also work on a two-way pager? In our design of the applications, we said that our MIDlets should work on the cell phone, two-way pager, and some

PDAs. How much work is left to get this application working for a pager? The answer is zero! By using MIDP, we have simultaneously developed an application that will also run on any MIDP-compliant two-way pager or other device. Because of the device's latitude in MIDP implementation, the user interface may look and behave a little differently. Otherwise, the MIDlets should operate identically as they do in our cell phone.

After successfully deploying our MIDlets to the two-way pager, we should see results that look similar to the pictures running in our pager emulator in figure 5.31.

**Figure 5.31**
**The same ObtainQuoteMIDlet as seen on a pager emulator. Because the screen is of different dimensions, the layout of the various high-level user interface elements may be a little different. However these elements still behave as they did on the cell phone.**

"Great!" you say, but what about the PDA? There is a profile, namely the PDA Profile, dedicated to providing user interface and persistent storage to PDAs much in the way MIDP has brought this functionality to the cell phones and pagers. This profile is not yet available. In chapters 8-10, we look at the KJava API for delivering Java applications in the CLDC and special API built for the Palm OS. However, Sun has also taken the MIDP and extended it for use in certain PDA devices. Currently, there is an implementation available for devices running the Palm OS. This extension is called MIDP for Palm OS and it is available from Sun at: http://java.sun.com/products/midp4palm.

This implementation includes a J2ME virtual machine for the Palm OS device in a single Palm PRC files, namely MIDP.prc. The PRC file can be loaded to the device with a synchronization program (see chapter 8). With the PRC VM loaded on the device running Palm OS, the device is ready to run MIDP applications.

In the release of MIDP for Palm devices, Sun has provided a desktop tool to convert a MIDlet .jar file associated with the MIDP development into a PRC file that runs on a Palm device. The tool is called the PRC Converter Tool and it is a Java application. A batch file, converter.bat, has been provided to start the converter tool with Java. The tool should look similar to the picture in figure 5.31. The Converter Tool .jar file and converter.bat are installed in a \Converter directory off of the directory where the MIDP for Palm OS download was installed.

The tool makes use of the current MIDlet JAD file. To convert a MIDlet suite into a Palm OS PRC, simply open the QuoteMIDletSuite.jad file and request that the tool convert the application (see figure 5.32).

Click on the [icon] icon to find the JAD/JAR file pair to convert to a PRC.

**Figure 5.32**
**Running converter.bat starts Sun's MIDP for the Palm OS Converter Tool. This tool allows a MIDlet suite to be converted to a PRC file which can be executed on a Palm OS device.**

The tool should indicate if there was success or a problem during the conversion. The MIDlet suite PRC must also be loaded onto the device with a synchronization program. You will learn more about where to get an emulator and how to deploy PRCs to a Palm OS device in chapters 8 and 9. When the MIDlet suite PRC is moved to the device, an icon representing the application should appear on the device as depicted in figure 5.33. The JavaHQ is the virtual machine PRC.

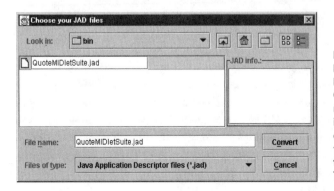

**Figure 5.33**
**In order to generate a Palm OS PRC file, the QuoteMIDletSuite's jad file must be found and chosen in this screen. This JAD chooser is displayed when you request to open a file from the PRC Converter Tool as shown.**

When the QuoteMIDlet icon is selected (or tapped as is the term used when selecting a user interface item with the device pointer), the familiar ObtainQuote and RetrieveQuote options are presented, albeit in a different format. While the arrangement and presentation of the displays and items may look a little different, all the pieces and functionality from the original MIDlets are there, right down to the advertising ticker in our alert.

**Figure 5.34**
The MIDP Investment Quote MIDlet suite is represented by the QuoteMID... icon displayed on the Palm after completing conversion and deploying. The JavaHQ icon displayed in this screen is the virtual machine PRC on the Palm OS device.

As we see, the goal of write once, run anywhere applies to these devices. However, as we look at other APIs, we are not as lucky when moving across profiles.

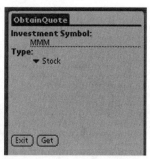

**Figure 5.35** Running the ObtainQuote MIDlet in the Palm OS looks similar to running the MIDlet on the phone emulator. After selecting the QuoteMID... icon as seen in figure 5.34, a selection list allows the customer to select which MIDlet in the suite to run. The other two screens depict the EntryForm for entering the investment symbol and type and the Alert for displaying the investment price.

## 5.7    SUMMARY

In this chapter, we examined MIDP's graphical user interface and event handling mechanisms. We also looked deeper at MIDP's application control object, namely the MIDlet. We found the UI and event handling mechanisms are divided into high-level and low-level APIs. The high-level API is more portable and is provided for traditional business applications. The low-level API provides more control over the interface and reaction to events, but is less portable. The low-level API was designed for games and similar graphically intensive applications. Finally, through some simple examples and the tutorial application, we demonstrated many of the common user interface elements.

# MIDP data storage

There was a time when a large mainframe platform was required to accommodate a database. However, all the data in the world bottled up on a mainframe cannot help a mobile and/or disconnected user out in the field on business. The need for transportable data at remote locations has encouraged the development of smaller and more mobile database systems. Today, relatively extensive databases can be found on a laptop. If for no other reason, these databases exist to transport a subset of a much larger database.

J2ME platforms, and the MID profile in particular, are the next step in a natural progression to even smaller and more mobile devices. It is fitting, therefore, that these devices also be outfitted with some type of persistent data storage. The databases that now fit on a laptop can be fairly sophisticated. These databases even rival the relational database management systems (RDBMS) of thirty or even twenty years ago. While the current physical limits of the MIDP platform make employing a full RDBMS difficult, the MIDP API has at least provided for some limited data storage in very mobile devices. Now, literally, small subsets of a database can be put into the pockets of their users.

In this chapter, we look at the persistent data storage mechanism in MIDP, which is called the Record Management System (RMS). In particular, we examine:

- the implementation of the RMS
- features of an RMS
- the API for accessing and storing data

Lastly, in this chapter, we retrofit our tutorial application to allow quotes received by the system to be stored in a local RMS for later use. Storing this quote data is important because the data can be retrieved later to provide the customer with a historical or trend perspective to any new quote received.

## 6.1   *JDBC* PARALLEL

In applications written with the other Java editions, namely J2SE and J2EE, third party vendors usually provide the data storage mechanisms. In these editions, a Java API is provided to allow common access and processing of data across various vendor provided databases. Typically the API provides access to an RDBMS. This API is called JDBC. In many ways, the MIDP RMS API provides the standard means to access and process data on MIDP devices such as JDBC does in other Java edition applications. (figure 6.1)

Whereas the JDBC API provides a common access means to various vendors' databases, the MIDP RMS API provides a common access protocol to the platform implementer's simple byte array storage mechanisms.

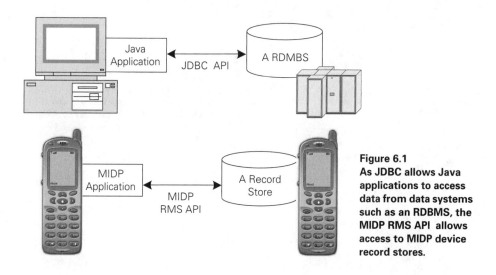

**Figure 6.1**
**As JDBC allows Java applications to access data from data systems such as an RDBMS, the MIDP RMS API allows access to MIDP device record stores.**

## 6.2 STORAGE STRUCTURE

The wonderful thing about Java APIs is that the API establishes the contract to which both sides, the user and the provider, abide without telling either side how to implement their part of the application. Like JDBC, the MIDP RMS API provides an instruction set, in this case for cellular telephone and pager applications to store data, albeit for small amounts of data. At the same time, RMS allows the cell phone and pager manufacturers some freedom on how and where to store this data. Because the platform implementer is instrumentally involved in providing the persistent data mechanism, there is no database driver or other third party software required to allow applications to access data. Furthermore, given the simplicity of these databases and the lack of query languages, heavy-duty concurrency provisions, result set handling, and so forth, present in higher-end database systems, RMS requires only one main class, `RecordStore`, to store or retrieve data on an MIDP platform.

### 6.2.1 Record store

At the heart of the Record Management System is a record store. A record store is a collection of records, and a record is an array of bytes. The platform implementer, and thus RMS implementer, determines the location of a record store on a device. However, no matter where a record store is physically located on the device, it is not directly accessible to a MIDlet. MIDP applications access the RMS only through the provided API as depicted in figure 6.2.

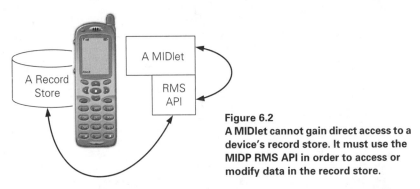

**Figure 6.2**
**A MIDlet cannot gain direct access to a device's record store. It must use the MIDP RMS API in order to access or modify data in the record store.**

It is also the platform provider's job to make sure the record store survives "normal" operations of the device. This includes operations such as shutdowns, reboots and battery changes.

Record stores are associated with a MIDlet suite. That is, the data in a record store may be shared and utilized by any number of MIDlets in a suite. In fact, when two different MIDlets request access to the same record store, each is given an object reference to the same record store on the system. When the MIDlet suite is removed from the device, all record stores associated with the suite must also be removed from the device. Each record store must have a unique name as it pertains to the MIDlet suite.

Record store names can be up to 32 characters (Unicode characters) long and are case-sensitive. Record stores that are not part of the same MIDlet suite may have the same name. If a MIDlet is not part of a suite, in essence it is a virtual suite containing that single MIDlet. In this case, the MIDlet owns the record store. When the MIDlet is removed from the platform, so too should the record store be removed.

Each time the record store is modified, the platform stamps the database with a date and time stamp in the form of a long integer. Specifically, the record store is stamped with a long integer returned from a call to System.currentTime-Millis(). This method call returns the number of milliseconds since January 1, 1970 at 12:00 a.m. The platform is also required to stamp the record store with a version number each time the database is modified. The version number gets incremented with each modification. The RMS implementer determines the initial version number, but it must be greater than 0. Both the date/time and version stamps assist the platform in synchronizing the database, as discussed subsequently, but they can also be accessed and used by the application.

As with most implementation aspects of the RMS, the platform implementer must provide atomic, synchronous, and serialized access to the record store, guaranteeing no corruption of the database even across multiple accesses. The MIDP applications are not provided a means to lock individual records or the entire record store through the RMS API. And while the platform implementer ensures the integrity of the data, an MIDP application that uses multiple threads must take special care when updating the record store to avoid overwriting data provided by a previous thread. For example, if two threads, A and B, are processing data and both attempt to update record X, the record store implementation guarantees that both A and B safely be allowed to update X without data corruption or system failure. In fact, calls to the record store are serialized to avoid simultaneous access. In this example, A is allowed to update record X and then B is allowed to update record X. However, the MIDP application has the responsibility to prevent or resolve issues surrounding the fact that thread B has overwritten thread A's update. With no locking of the record or record store, undesired consequences can result. In this example, thread A may behave incorrectly if it continues to operate on the assumption that data in the record store is data it updated. An MIDP application updating a record store with multiple threads can and should make use of the record store timestamp and version number to check on previous updates.

## 6.2.2   Records in the record store

Again, a record is a simple byte array. Each record within the record store has a unique integer identifier called a recordId. The first record created in a record store has a recordId of 1. The recordId is incremented for each record added to the record store. Using the analogy of a spreadsheet to represent a record store, a byte is represented by a cell and each byte array can be thought of as a series of cells within the record store that is identified by the recordId, as shown in figure 6.3.

| Record ID | | | | | |
|---|---|---|---|---|---|
| 1 | byte 0 | byte 1 | byte 2 | ... | byte n |
| 2 | byte 0 | byte 1 | byte 2 | ... | byte n |
| 3 | byte 0 | byte 1 | byte 2 | ... | byte n |
| . | . | . | . | . | . |
| . | . | . | . | . | . |
| . | . | . | . | . | . |
| n | byte 0 | byte 1 | byte 2 | ... | byte n |

**Figure 6.3   The record store, as shown here, comprises a number of indexed byte arrays. The index or the "recordId" of the first byte array is 1. Within the resource limits of the device, each record store can have any number of arrays and each array can have any number of bytes.**

It is tempting to view the recordId as a kind of index to the various byte arrays in the record store. However, recordIds are not reused when a record is deleted from the record store. Therefore, it is neither safe nor appropriate to view the recordId as an actual index.

The recordId is used to access or get a handle on a particular record within the record store. However, as we will examine in section 6.3, the recordId is not the only way to get a handle on records. We can develop an enumerator that provides a means to bidirectionally access records within the record store without using the recordId directly.

# 6.3   RMS API

Given an understanding of the record store and its general structure, we can now explore the API that controls the record store. Most importantly, we can explore the API that allows MIDlet applications to store and retrieve data on the devices.

The `javax.microedition.rms` package contains the entire API for the MIDP Record Management System. Because a record is just a byte array, there is only one concrete class in the entire package, namely, `RecordStore` is the class that implements the RMS record store.

## 6.3.1   Record store construction and access

The API for the `RecordStore` is very straightforward. It contains a single static method for creating a record store and instance methods for adding, removing and updating records in the store. Other than methods for destroying the record store and obtaining ancillary information out of the record store, such as the number of records contained within the record store, there is not a lot to the API.

### Record store lifecycle

A record store is created or opened with the same method, namely the `open-RecordStore(String recordStoreName, boolean createIfNecessary)` static `RecordStore` method attempts to open an existing record store in the MIDlet suite associated with the running MIDlet. The system creates a new record store if a store by the same name is determined not to already exist in the suite and if the `createIfNecessary` boolean is set to true. So, for example, to open an existing record store named "Customers" and to create the new database if it does not exist, the following lines of code would be executed.

```
try {
  RecordStore anRMS = RecordStore.openRecordStore("Customers" , true);
} catch (RecordStoreFullException fullStore) {
  //handle a full record store problem
} catch (RecordStoreNotFoundException notFoundException) {
  //handle store not found which should not happen with the
  //createIfNecessary tag set to true
} catch (RecordStoreException recordStoreException) {
  //handling record store problems
}
```

The method `closeRecordStore()` is used to close an instance of the record store. Interestingly, the record store does not actually close until the close method is called as many times as the open method was called. The number of MIDlet calls to open and close the record store is tracked over an entire suite and the number of closes must match the number of opens before the record store is really closed. Again, the reason for this is that the record store is shared by MIDlets within a suite. Before the record store is considered closed, it must be closed with regard to every single MIDlet application that has access to it. When finally closed, all listeners to the record store are removed. We discuss record store listeners below. Figure 6.4 depicts the various states of the record store's life and how they are achieved.

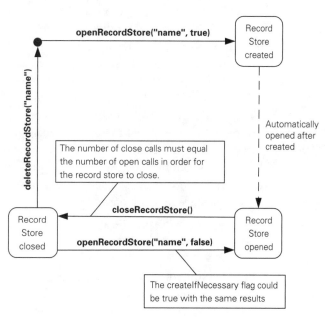

**Figure 6.4**
**The lifecycle of a record store begins with its creation using the `openRecordStore` (`String,Boolean`) method. It is automatically opened after creation. Once created, it can be opened and closed any number of times. In order to close the record store, however, an equal number of `closeRecordStore()` to `openRecordStore()` methods must be called. Finally, when no longer needed, the life of a record store ends with a call to `deleteRecordStore()`.**

A list of the available record stores can be obtained for a MIDlet suite. From inside a MIDlet application, a static method call to `listRecordStores()` returns an array of Strings. This array contains a list of record store names for the suite to which the MIDlet is associated. If the MIDlet suite has no record stores, the method returns null.

A static method on the `RecordStore` class also allows a record store to be destroyed. The `deleteRecordStore(String recordStoreName)` method deletes the record store of the given name for the suite, provided the record store exists and it is not currently open by any MIDlet within the suite. These last two conditions, if false, cause a `RecordStoreException` to be thrown by the delete method.

### Record access

A record store instance must be opened before record operations can be performed on it. Otherwise, a `RecordStoreNotOpen` exception gets thrown when trying to access a closed record store. To retrieve an existing record, or byte array, from the database one needs a recordId. With a recordId and the `getRecord(int recordId)` method, the byte array stored under the provided id is returned. For example, to get the record at recordId 2, the following method would be called on the open record store referenced by anRMS.

```
byte[] b = anRMS.getRecord(2);
```

In the event that a record does not exist with the provided recordId, then an `InvalidRecordIDException` exception is thrown. An alternate `getRecord` method allows a record to be read directly into an existing byte array at an offset specified. The `getRecord(int recordId, byte[] buffer, int offset)` method reads the contents of the record at the specified `recordId` into the byte array passed in as the `buffer` at the offset specified. Additionally, this method can throw one more type of exception, namely the `ArrayIndexOutOfBoundsException`, if the byte array pulled from the record is larger than the buffer can accept.

A record store has several methods for inserting, removing, and updating individual records within the store. Each of these methods requires the recordId of the record being managed. To add a record to a record store instance, the method `addRecord (byte [] data, int offset, int numBytes)` is used. The byte array passed as the first parameter is the data to be inserted in the record store. An offset index and number of bytes count can be used to insert just part of the byte array. For example, executing the following lines of code results in storing the string "a test" in a new record in the referenced record store.

```
String test = "This is a test";
byte[] b = test.getBytes();
anRMS.addRecord(b, 8, 6);
```

On successful completion, the `addRecord(byte [] data, int offset, int numBytes)` method returns the recordId of the newly inserted record.

Deleting a record from the record store is done by calling on `deleteRecord (int id)` with the recordId of the to-be-removed record. Again, the removed record's identifier is retired and not reused with subsequent inserts into the record store.

Updating is accomplished through the `setRecord(int id, byte [] data, int offset, int numBytes)` method. Updating a record in a record store amounts to replacing the entire byte array stored at the particular recordId. Therefore, the same arguments used in insert are used. The offset index and number of bytes can be used on the new byte array to replace the existing record with all or part of the new byte array.

There are several convenient methods for pulling additional information from the record store. Table 6.1 lists them.

**Table 6.1** Convenience methods on a record store instance provide ancillary information about the record store such as its name, size, capacity, next recordId, version, etc. These methods can be especially useful when performing maintenance on the stores.

| Method | Purpose |
| --- | --- |
| getLastModified() | Returns the last time the record store was modified. |
| getName() | Returns the name of the record store instance. |
| getNextRecordId() | Returns the integer value of the next record identifier used for the next add record operation. |
| getNumRecords() | Returns the number of records in the record store instance. |
| getRecordSize(int recordId) | Returns the size, in bytes, of the record specified by the recordID. |
| getSize() | Returns the size of the record store, in bytes. |
| getSizeAvailable() | Returns the maximum number of bytes the record store is allowed to grow. |
| getVersion() | Returns the last version stamp for the record store. |

Again, the API used to create and remove record stores or to manipulate the data inside of a record store is straightforward. As we shall see, there is also a set of helper classes to help locate and compare data in this very simple database as well as means to react to changes in the record store.

### 6.3.2 Record store exceptions

Use of the `RecordStore` class and manipulation of the data in a record store can result in certain exceptions. The general exception thrown for any unknown problem that occurs when dealing with the `RecordStore` class or instance of the same is `RecordStoreException`.

More specific subclasses that are descendents of `RecordStoreException` are listed in table 6.2 along with a description of the circumstances on when they are thrown.

All of these exceptions are checked exceptions requiring the developer to either catch and handle the exception or rethrow the exception to calling methods.

**Table 6.2** These are the exceptions defined in the `javax.microedition.rms` package that can be encountered when dealing with a record store. All descend from the generic `RecordStore-Exception`.

| Exception | Description |
|---|---|
| InvalidRecordIDException | Thrown any time a referenced recordId does not exist. |
| RecordStoreFullException | Encountered only when attempting to insert a new or update an existing record when the store is already at capacity. This exception can also be thrown when trying to open an already full record store. |
| RecordStoreNotFoundException | Occurs when trying to open or remove a record store that does not exist. |
| RecordStoreNotOpenException | Thrown anytime information is sought from a record store instance without its being open. This can also be thrown if an attempt is made to close a non-open record store instance. |

### 6.3.3 Record store listener

Remember, a record store can be accessed by any MIDlet within the same suite. In order to allow applications to coordinate and react to changes in record store data, a set of record store event handling interfaces have been provided. Any object can be set up as a listener for modifications made to any record store in a MIDlet suite (see figure 6.5). The object only has to implement the `RecordListener` interface and be registered with a record store instance as a listener for modification events.

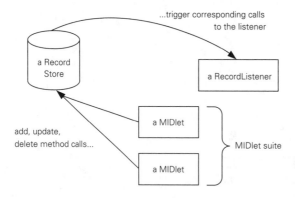

**Figure 6.5**
**An object, set up as a record listener to a record store, is notified of any record addition, modification or deletion made from any MIDlet in the suite.**

To establish the object as a valid listener for modifications taking place on a record store, it must first be registered with the record store. Two methods are provided for registering and unregistering a listener.

- addRecordListener(RecordListener listener)
- removeRecordListener(RecordListener listener)

Registering a listener with a record store has no effect on the store and when a record store is closed, all listeners are removed.

The RecordListener interface requires that the event handling object have three methods, namely:

- recordAdded (RecordStore recordStore, int recordId),
- recordChanged (RecordStore recordStore, int recordId) and
- recordDeleted (RecordStore recordStore, int recordId).

Each callback method is called with the specific record store that was modified and the recordId of the record that was changed, added or removed. These methods are called after a new record is inserted into the record store (recordAdd), an existing record is modified (recordChanged), or a record is removed from the store (recordDeleted).

A simple example listener that merely reports when records in a record store have been added, changed or removed is shown in listing 6.1.

**Listing 6.1   Example RecordListener**

```
import javax.microedition.rms.*;

public class TestListener implements RecordListener {

  public void recordAdded(RecordStore rs, int id) {
    try {
      System.out.println(rs.getName() + " added record " + id);
    } catch (RecordStoreNotOpenException e) {
      //exception handling procedures
    }
  }
```
Triggered when a MIDlet adds **❶**
a record to the record store

```
  public void recordChanged(RecordStore rs, int id) {
    try {
      System.out.println(rs.getName() + " changed record " + id);
    } catch (RecordStoreNotOpenException e) {
      //exception handling procedures
    }
  }
```
Triggered when a MIDlet changes **❷**
a record in the record store

```
  public void recordDeleted(RecordStore rs, int id) {
    try {
      System.out.println(rs.getName() + " removed record " + id);
    } catch (RecordStoreNotOpenException e) {
      //exception handling procedures
    }
  }
}
```
Triggered when a MIDlet removes **❸**
a record from the record store

In order to register this listener with an instance of record store, programming code like the following would be required.

```
RecordStore anRMS = RecordStore.openRecordStore("TestRMS" , true);
anRMS.addRecordListener(new TestListener());
```

The first line opens the record store named TestRMS. Given the true boolean passed as createIfNecessary parameter to the method, the record store is created and then opened if it does not already exist. The second line registers an instance of TestListener, (code provided in Listing 6.1), to react to any record changes from any MIDlet within the MIDlet suite.

Given the simplistic nature of RMS record stores, record listeners allow MIDlets to more easily implement data validation mechanisms, trigger warnings such as out of space messages, and other data related activities that are usually automatically handled by more sophisticated databases.

### 6.3.4 Comparing records

In J2SE, the Comparable interface provides a means to define a comparison operator that allows any two like objects to be evaluated or compared. The result of a comparison operation results in finding one object is equal to, greater than or less than the other object. This interface allows developers to establish order on objects even when the order is less than obvious. So, for example, ordering customer numbers could be by last name or social security number.

While the Comparable interface is not available in J2ME, inside the Record Management System an equivalent interface has been provided to allow records of a record store to be compared. The RecordComparator interface allows any object to be established as a comparing facility for any two RMS records given to it. Actually, a RecordComparator implementer compares two byte arrays. Because it has been built generically to accept and compare two byte arrays, it could be set up for use outside of comparing record store records. In general, however, a record comparator is useful for sorting or sequencing the record store records for enumeration purposes.

The RecordComparator interface requires the implementation of a single compare(byte[] rec1, byte[] rec2) method that examines the two passed-in records and evaluates to either 0, 1 or −1. The value 0 indicates that the records are equivalent or equal in terms of search or sort order. 1 indicates that the first record follows the second record in search or sort order. Finally, a compare() return value of −1 indicates that the first supplied record precedes the second in search or sort order. Table 6.3 lists the static fields that have been established on the interface to provide meaningful names to the compare results.

Table 6.3   These static fields have been provided to name integer return values for comparison operation. When used, these fields make code using the comparator easier to read and understand.

| Static Field | Assigned Value |
|---|---|
| RecordComparator.EQUIVALENT | 0 |
| RecordComparator.FOLLOWS | 1 |
| RecordComparator.PRECEDES | −1 |

For example, suppose records added to a record store contained simple strings and a record comparator implementation looked like the following code.

```
import javax.microedition.rms.*;

public class TestComparator implements RecordComparator {

  public int compare(byte[] rec1, byte[] rec2) {
    String r1 = new String(rec1);
    String r2 = new String(rec2);                    (1)
    if (r1.compareTo(r2) > 0)                                  (2)
      return (RecordComparator.FOLLOWS);
    else if (r1.compareTo(r2) < 0)
      return (RecordComparator.PRECEDES);
    else return (RecordComparator.EQUIVALENT);
  }
}
```

(1) Extract simple Strings from records

(2) Use the standard String compareTo operator

In that case, executing the lines below in an MIDP application should produce results that read: "Comparator found —> -1" since the comparator would be comparing the String "a test" to "is". Indeed "a test" does precede "is" in a string comparison.

```
anRMS = RecordStore.openRecordStore("TestRMS" , true);
String test = "This is a test";
byte[] b = test.getBytes();                         (1)

anRMS.addRecord(b, 8, 6);
anRMS.addRecord(b, 5, 2);
RecordComparator rc = new TestComparator();     (2)
byte[] r1 = anRMS.getRecord(1);
byte[] r2 = anRMS.getRecord(2);                  (3)
System.out.println("Comparator found --> " + rc.compare(r1,r2));   (4)
```

(1) Open/create the record store and store string records

(2) Create an instance of the record comparator

(3) Get the records from the record store

(4) Use the comparator to compare the two records retrieved

While the comparator may be useful by itself in comparing records in a record store, it becomes an even more powerful tool when combined with a record filter and record enumeration as described in the next section. Objects that implement these three RMS interfaces can be utilized on a record store to intelligently access and work on specific data in a record store.

## 6.3.5    Filtering records

In a similar fashion to the RecordComparator, the RMS API provides a record filtering interface that allows any object to serve as a strainer for records in a record store. The RecordFilter interface requires its implementing object to implement a single method. This method, `matches(byte[] candidate)`, checks the passed byte array to determine if its data meets the filtering criteria. This method returns a simple boolean indicating whether the passed-in record meets the filter criteria. A record filter could, for instance, be set up to determine if a record in a record store begins with the letter 'A' (either small or capital). The code for such a filter would resemble the following:

```
import javax.microedition.rms.*;

public class TestFilter implements RecordFilter {

  public boolean matches(byte[] rec) {
    String r = new String(rec);
    return ((r.charAt(0) == 'a') || (r.charAt(0) == 'A'));
  }
}
```

The filter could then be used, as shown below, to determine if a record does match the criteria. Using this filter, as below, would produce the system output "The first record starts with 'A'."

```
anRMS = RecordStore.openRecordStore("TestRMS" , true);     ❶
String test = "A test";
byte[] b = test.getBytes();                                ❷
anRMS.addRecord(b, 0, b.length);
RecordFilter rf = new TestFilter();                        ❸
if (rf.matches(anRMS.getRecord(1)))                        ❹
  System.out.println("The first record starts with 'A'");
else
  System.out.println("The first record does not start with 'A'");
```

❶ Open/create the record store

❷ Store a record containing a string

❸ Create an instance of the record filter above

❹ Use the filter to get all matching records

### 6.3.6    Enumerating through records

Both record filtering and comparing are two features of RMS that assist in intelligently enumerating through record store records. Enumerations are used throughout Java to cycle through all sorts of data structure objects, such as vectors, in order to perform a set of operations on each element in the structure. An enumeration prepares a sequence of the data elements and provides a series of access methods to retrieve elements from the sequence. Likewise, MIDP's RMS has provided a `RecordEnumeration` interface that allows for enumerating through the records in a record store. Even better, a record comparator and/or record filter can be used in conjunction with the record enumeration to loop through the various records in some sort order and act on only certain filtered records.

A record enumeration can be obtained for any record store instance by calling the `enumerateRecords(RecordFilter filter, RecordComparator comparator,` boolean keepUpdated) method on the instance. The filter supplied, if not null, determines what subset of records to include in the enumeration. The filter or comparator could be null.

- If the record filter is null, all records in the record store are included in the enumeration.
- If the record comparator is not null, the records in the enumeration are sorted per the comparator.
- If the comparator is null, the records in the enumeration are not sorted and records included in the enumeration are traversed in an undetermined way. The recordId does not serve as any kind of default order.

The last parameter to the record store's enumeratRecords() method is a boolean indicating whether to keep the enumeration up to date with regard to changes being made to the record store. In other words, the enumeration's sequence of records can be automatically synchronized with underlying changes being made to the record store from other threads on the device. Consider possible performance penalties when setting this parameter to true. Alternatively, a record listener could be used to re-establish the enumeration when a change in the record store is discovered. Both of these options have the potential of creating a performance problem since every modification would cause the enumeration index to be rebuilt. If the keepUpdated parameter is not set to true, then the enumeration may reference records that are no longer valid. This can occur, for example, when another thread deletes a record on the underlying database that happens to also be a record in an enumeration's sequence. Furthermore, inserts or changes to the data in the underlying records may cause the sort order to be inaccurate with regard to the new data. These risks must be weighed against the possible performance effects when looking at means to keep the enumeration accurate with regard to underlying database changes.

A record enumeration comes with a set of access methods that get records (i.e. byte arrays) or recordIds from the enumeration. An enumeration has a kind of cursor or pointer that references a particular record or element in the sequence. Unlike other Java enumeration APIs that are usually forward only, the RMS RecordEnumeration is bi-directional, meaning elements can be obtained in either direction from the current record. A call to the nextRecord() method returns the next element or record in the sequence from wherever the element pointer is located. Likewise, a call to the previousRecord() method gets the previous byte array in the sequence. Where a MIDlet is only interested in getting the recordId instead of the actual record or byte array, nextRecordId() and previousRecordId() methods are also available. Two methods, hasNextElement() and hasPreviousElement(), both return a boolean indicating whether there are next records in either a forward or backward direction in the sequence. A call to numRecords() returns the total number of records in the enumeration's sequence set.

Again, the enumeration may be set to keep updated with the updated contents of the record store. The rebuild() method allows for the enumeration to be rebuilt or constructed based on the new record store contents. Alternately, the reset() method resets the enumeration to the state right after its initial creation. Finally, an enumeration uses a fair number of resources to accomplish its job. The MIDlet application is required to trigger the destroy() method when finished with any record enumeration in order to release the resources it uses.

To demonstrate the use of RecordEnumeration, we make use of the Record-Comparator and RecordFilter from our previous examples. Listing 6.2 shows code that populates a small record store with several names. Then it calls on a RecordEnumeration instance to iterate through the records and display the list of names beginning with the letter 'A' in alphabetical order.

**Listing 6.2 Finding specific records using RMS interfaces**

```
anRMS = RecordStore.openRecordStore("TestRMS" , true);          ❶
byte[] george = "George".getBytes();
byte[] bob = "Bob".getBytes();
byte[] andy = "Andy".getBytes();
byte[] harry = "Harry".getBytes();
byte[] adam = "Adam".getBytes();
byte[] amos = "Amos".getBytes();
byte[] fred = "Fred".getBytes();                                ❷
anRMS.addRecord(george, 0, george.length);
anRMS.addRecord(bob, 0, bob.length);
anRMS.addRecord(andy, 0, andy.length);
anRMS.addRecord(harry, 0, harry.length);
anRMS.addRecord(adam, 0, adam.length);
anRMS.addRecord(amos, 0, amos.length);
anRMS.addRecord(fred, 0, fred.length);
RecordComparator rc = new TestComparator();          ❸
RecordFilter rf = new TestFilter();          ❹
RecordEnumeration rEnum = anRMS.enumerateRecords(rf,rc,false);
while (rEnum.hasNextElement()) {                                ❺
  byte[] nextRec = rEnum.nextRecord();
  String nextName = new String(nextRec);
  System.out.println(nextName);
}
rEnum.destroy();          ❻
```

❶ Open/create the record store

❷ Create several records containing first names

❸ Using the comparator from above

❹ Using the filter from above

❺ Use comparator and filter to create an enumeration to find select records

❻ Close the enumeration to free resources

After running this code as part of a MIDlet application, the system output should produce the following results:

Adam
Amos
Andy

As seen through this last example, the RecordComparator, RecordFilter and Record-Enumeration RMS interfaces combined to provide a powerful mechanism to reach inside a record store, filter, sort and extract specific data for use in an MIDP application. While this type of search, sorting and extracting could be done without the use of these interfaces, these interfaces help reduce the time and effort it takes to do this common work and they provide a consistent pattern which helps in later maintenance of the code.

## 6.4 PERSISTENT STORAGE IN THE INVESTMENT QUOTE APPLICATION

With an understanding of the MIDP Record Management System, we can apply that knowledge to the tutorial application. In the previous chapter, we created the basic MIDP application structure (the MIDlet), the user interface and event handling mechanisms for a stock and mutual fund quote system. Remember, the purpose of this system was to get current stock and mutual fund prices and store them for later retrieval. Up to this point, no data has actually been stored or retrieved by the application. Instead, we stubbed out the user interface to respond as if data were being retrieved when, in reality, it was just phony data remanufactured for each user interface request.

In the design of the application, recall that ObtainQuote and RetrieveQuote use cases made use of two other use cases, namely SavePrice and RetrievePrice. These use cases stored and fetched investment price information in and out of the persistent mechanism. We create the code that implements these use cases in sections 6.4.2 and 6.4.3.

### 6.4.1 Defining the stock/mutual fund record

In this section, we retrofit our application to actually store and retrieve investment quote data in a record store. As was learned in this chapter, a record is nothing more than a byte array. In this tutorial, a record consists of a converted string containing the stock or mutual fund symbol along with the current and historical price.

As mentioned previously, the CLDC on which MIDP relies, does not support floating-point numbers. Therefore the use of Java's double or float base types cannot be used to represent dollar/cent prices of most stock and mutual fund quotes. Instead, we use two integers to represent one price. For example, if the stock price was $120.55, then the price must be stored as two integers, 120 and 55. One integer represents the dollars associated with the price, while the second represents the cents of the price.

Remember that the application must be able to store a current and a historical price for each stock or mutual fund. Therefore, along with a symbol to identify the stock or mutual fund, two sets of dollar and cent integer values must be stored.

In order to store all this data in a single string, a marker or delimiter is needed to indicate where one value stops and the next data value begins. For this tutorial, we choose the semicolon as a data delimiter.

So, the string representing a current price of $120.55 and a historical price of $113.45 for 3M (a Fortune 500 manufacturing company based in St. Paul, Minnesota with a symbol of MMM) would look like the following:

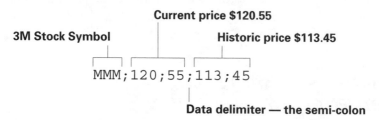

**Figure 6.6**  Each investment price quote (both current and historical) can be represented by a single string. In this example, the current price and historical per share of 3M are $120.55 and $113.45.

In the case where only one price has been obtained for the stock or mutual fund, the last two trailing integers are omitted. So, using our previous example, when the first price of $113.45 was obtained for 3M, the original record string would have been represented as:

MMM;113;45

The string record that contains the stock or mutual fund price quotes and investment symbol needs to be converted to a byte array before being stored as a record in the record store. Recall that the record store contains byte array records. This can easily be accomplished using the method `getBytes()` on any string object.

## 6.4.2  Storing quotes

The ObtainQuoteMIDlet controls all aspects of getting and storing stock or mutual fund quotes. Since this class will now be using RMS, it must import the RMS package. Therefore, the RMS import statement must be included at the top of this class file.

```
import javax.microedition.rms.*;
```

In the previous chapter, a command listener was created in the `initListener()` method in ObtainQuoteMIDlet to wait for the user to push the "Get" command. When the user triggers this command, the command listener would determine what command button was pushed and then trigger the right system response. From the previous chapter, when the "Get" command was pressed, the command listener first checked to insure that symbol was valid. In other words, it checked to see that some symbol was entered and that if the symbol entered was for a mutual fund symbol, the symbol was checked to insure that it ended in 'X'. Otherwise, the listener simply called to display a fake price for the given investment symbol. The old command listener from the previous chapter is provided in listing 6.3.

```
CommandListener commandListener = new CommandListener() {
  public void commandAction(Command c, Displayable d) {
    if (c == entryForm.getExitCommand())
      destroyApp(true);
    else if (c == entryForm.getGetCommand()) {
      if ((entryForm.getInvestmentChoice().getSelectedIndex() == 1) &&
          !(entryForm.getSymbolField().getString().
          toUpperCase().endsWith("X"))) {
        Alert symbolAlert = new Alert("Check Symbol",
          "Mutual Funds end in 'X'", null, AlertType.WARNING);
        symbolAlert.setTimeout(Alert.FOREVER);
        displayMngr.setCurrent(symbolAlert, entryForm);
      } else
        if (entryForm.getSymbolField().getString().length() > 0)
          displayPrice("The price of " +
            entryForm.getSymbolField().getString() + " is $111.19");
    }
  }
};
```

From previous work, the price ❶
found was always $111.19

In fact, the same fake price of $111.19 was always returned for each symbol. The price was not really retrieved from an investment or quote service and the data was never stored in a database for later retrieval. In the next chapter, we will see how the real price can be obtained from an investment service using standard communications protocols and a connection framework. However, given the RMS, now we can at least store and retrieve price quotes in a record store. To improve upon the idea of a quote service and in order to demonstrate that new data is really being added to the record store, we will also improve on the fake quote service to at least provide a random price to the MIDlet as opposed to the same fake price.

### Retrofitting the command listener

Since the command listener responds to the customer's push of the "Get" command, the listener must be updated to allow it to capture quote data and send the data off to be stored in the record store. Thus, to store quotes for any symbol, we replace the last part of the ObtainQuoteMIDlet's command listener as depicted in listing 6.4.

Now, when a proper investment symbol is entered, the MIDlet calls on a quote service class to obtain a price. This service is implemented in temporary form in the code shown here. In the next chapter, we rebuild the service to capture real investment information. Provided the string passed to this service is a valid investment symbol, it returns an integer array containing two integers. The first int represents the current dollars for the stock or mutual fund and the second int represents the current cents

**Listing 6.4  ObtainQuoteMIDlet's New Get Command Listener**

```
CommandListener commandListener = new CommandListener() {  ❶
  public void commandAction(Command c, Displayable d) {
    if (c == entryForm.getExitCommand()) {
      destroyApp(true);
    } else if (c == entryForm.getGetCommand()) {
      if ((entryForm.getInvestmentChoice().getSelectedIndex() == 1) &&
          !(entryForm.getSymbolField().getString().
          toUpperCase().endsWith("X"))){
        Alert symbolAlert = new Alert("Check Symbol",
          "Mutual Funds end in 'X'", null, AlertType.WARNING);
        symbolAlert.setTimeout(Alert.FOREVER);
        displayMngr.setCurrent(symbolAlert, entryForm);
      } else if (entryForm.getSymbolField().getString().length() > 0) {
        String sym = entryForm.getSymbolField().getString();
        int type = entryForm.getInvestmentChoice().getSelectedIndex();
        int[] price = QuoteService.getPrice(sym, type);
        storePrice(sym, price);  ❷
        displayPrice("The price of " + sym + " is $" + price[0] +
                    "." + price[1]);  ❸
      }
    }
  }
};
```

❶ The command listener replacement

❷ A call to store the price obtained in a record store

❸ Now display the symbol and prices obtained via the quote service

for the same investment. Thus, if 3M has a price of $115.45 a share, the array returned from `QuoteService.getPrice("MMM", 0)` would be {115, 45}.

Given that our MIDlets still have no connection to the outside world, the quote service must still return a fake price. However, to provide data that starts to look a little more like that which would actually be received by a quote service, the CLDC's Random class is used in a new `QuoteService` class to help generate two integer values between 0 and 99.

```
import java.util.Random;        ❶ Import the Random
                                   class from the CLDC

public class QuoteService {

  public static int[] getPrice(String symbol, int type) {
    Random generator = new Random();
    Random generator = new Random();
    int dollars = Math.abs(generator.nextInt()) %100;     ❷ Randomly generate
    int cents = Math.abs(generator.nextInt()) %100;          two numbers
    int[] priceParts = {dollars, cents};                     between 0 and 99
    return priceParts;        ❸ Return the new dollar/cent
  }                              price for the investment
}
```

Now the MIDlet and its command listener are properly outfitted to shuffle data between a temporary quote service and the display. Next we look at implementing the means to store quotes obtained from the service for later retrieval.

### Creating and saving investment price data

While the QuoteService returns the dollars and cents price, in the integer array, the MIDlet calling on the `QuoteService` still needs to store the price and associated symbol in a record store. This is accomplished in an ObtainQuoteMIDlet method called `storePrice(sym, price)` as shown in listing 6.5.

**Listing 6.5   The storePrice method of ObtainQuoteMIDlet**

```java
private void storePrice(String symbol, int[] price) {
  String newRecord = symbol + ";" + price[0] + ";" + price[1];      ❶
  byte[] byteRec;

  try {
    RecordStore anRMS = RecordStore.openRecordStore("Quotes" , true);   ❷
    RecordFilter rf = new QuoteFilter(symbol);
    RecordEnumeration rEnum = anRMS.enumerateRecords(rf,null,false);
    if (rEnum.hasNextElement()) {
      int recId = rEnum.nextRecordId();
      newRecord += ';' + getLastPrice(anRMS.getRecord(recId));
      byteRec = newRecord.getBytes();                                   ❸
      anRMS.setRecord(recId,byteRec,0,byteRec.length);
    } else {
      byteRec = newRecord.getBytes();
      anRMS.addRecord(byteRec,0,byteRec.length);
    }
    rEnum.destroy();                                    ❹
    anRMS.closeRecordStore();
  } catch (RecordStoreFullException fullStore) {
    //handle a full record store problem
  } catch (RecordStoreNotFoundException notFoundException) {
    //handle store not found which should not happen with the
    //createIfNecessary tag set to true
  } catch (RecordStoreException recordStoreException) {
    //handling record store problems
  }
}
```

❶ Prepare the record string

❷ Open the record store named "Quotes"

❸ Locate and update an existing record, or add a new record

❹ Destroy the enumerator and close the record store

This method is the `insert` and `update` method for the investment quote database, basically implementing the `SavePrice` use case in our tutorial application design. Its first job is to open the RMS record store on the device named "Quotes." Then, using a record filter called `QuoteFilter` and a record enumeration, the `storePrice()` method attempts to locate the record for the investment with the symbol provided. As suggested previously, a common use of both filters and comparators is demonstrated here as it is used in conjunction with an enumerator. If the record is found via the enumerator, then a previous price has been obtained for the investment. In this case, the record must be updated to have a new current price and the old price stored in the record is made to be the investment's historical price. To update the investment's record in the record store, simply create the record's new data string and use `setRecord(int recordId, byte[] newData, int offset, int numBytes)` to overwrite the existing record. When updating an existing record, the last current price becomes the new historical price, as shown in figure 6.7.

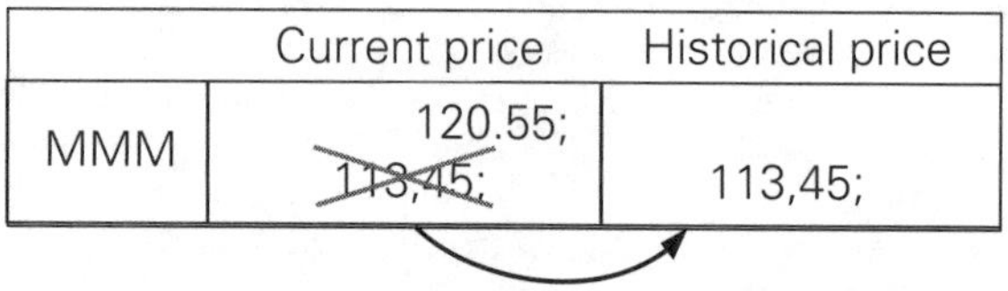

| | Current price | Historical price |
|---|---|---|
| MMM | 120.55;<br>~~113,45;~~ | 113,45; |

**Figure 6.7** When the `storePrice()` method gets called, the record store is checked for an existing price for the symbol provided. If an there is an existing price, then the existing or current price becomes the historical price and the new price becomes the current price.

In the case where no investment record is found for the symbol provided, a new record is added to the record store. This is accomplished using the `addRecord(byte[] data, int offset, int numBytes)` method and passing this method the symbol and price information stored in a byte array.

To assist in getting price data from the byte array record, another method is used to convert the byte array back to a string and to extract the last price from the string.

```
private String getLastPrice(byte[] rec) {
  String recString = new String(rec);

  int dollarPos = recString.indexOf(';');
  int centPos = recString.indexOf(';',dollarPos+1);
  int centEnd = recString.indexOf(';',centPos + 1);

  if (centEnd > 0) //had a historical price
    return recString.substring(dollarPos+1,centEnd);
  else     //no previous historical price
    return recString.substring(dollarPos+1);
}
```

**1** Get the position of the last price within the string

**2**

**2** Return the current price string, regardless of a historical price

The getLastPrice() method is a byte array to string converter with some string manipulation to find the appropriate dollar and cent values stored in between the appropriate ';' character delimiters.

The record filter used with the enumerator helps extract the right investment record for any given symbol provided by the user. Only one record for each symbol requested will ever exist in the database. As seen in the following code, the filter's constructor can be used to provide filter information, such as the symbol string in our example.

```java
import javax.microedition.rms.*;

public class QuoteFilter implements RecordFilter {

    private String symbol;

    public QuoteFilter(String sym) {          ❶ Method to specify the
        symbol = sym;                             investment symbol
    }

    public boolean matches(byte[] rec) {
        String r = new String(rec);
        return (r.startsWith(symbol + ';'));   ❷ Match records based on the
    }                                             symbol and delimiter mark
}
```

When called upon by the enumerator, only those records matching the symbol string will be included in the enumerator's sequence.

As seen in figure 6.7, when compiled, preverified and executed, the Obtain-QuoteMIDlet will look no different than it did in the previous chapters. However, now all data being obtained for each investment is stored in the record store. In section 6.4.3 we see how this information can be retrieved from the persistent storage provided by the platform.

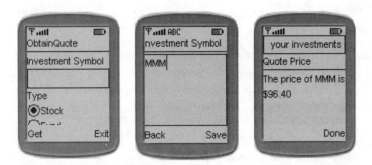

**Figure 6.8  The user interface does not change after adding persistent storage to the ObtainQuoteMIDlet. The screens to get the investment symbol and display the price are the same. Now, however, behind the screens of this MIDlet, quote service data is stored in the record store on the device.**

### 6.4.3     Retrieving quotes

Having the data stored in a database does no good unless it is saved for later retrieval. In this part of the tutorial, the stock and mutual fund quotes are retrieved to display the current and historical prices of a given investment. Recall that in the exploration of the MIDP user interface (in chapter 5), we even developed a means to graphically depict the current and historical prices in a comparison bar chart using the low level MIDP user interface API.

As with the ObtainQuoteMIDlet, the RetrieveQuoteMIDlet was written in chapter 5 to demonstrate the user interface capabilities and so the actual investment symbol and quote were simply passed as fake parameters to the display methods. From earlier in our tutorial, the `displayChartCanvas()` method of RetrieveQuoteMIDlet called on a `ChartCanvas` object to display the quote chart with the same "MMM" symbol and current and historical prices ($75 and $110) respectively.

```
private void displayChartCanvas() {
  if (chartCanvas == null) {
    chartCanvas = new ChartCanvas();
  }
  displayMngr .setCurrent(chartCanvas);
  chartCanvas.displayChart("MMM",75,110);      ❶ Fake $75 and $110 price
}                                                 quotes for 3M
```

Based on work earlier in this chapter, the ObtainQuoteMIDlet now stores price quotes for investment symbols and with the ability to extract information from the record store, our application does not have to pass phony data to the display anymore. Because ObtainQuoteMIDlet and RetrieveQuoteMIDlet are part of the same MIDlet suite, the "Quotes" record store can be shared and utilized by both applications.

### *Extracting price data*

Getting investment price quote data back out of the record store is even easier than saving it. First, like in the ObtainQuoteMIDlet, the RetrieveQuoteMIDlet must import the RMS package.

```
import javax.microedition.rms.*;
```

Then, because we do not want the chart canvas to continually receive the same two prices ($75 and $110), but rather the stored price quotes, the initial `display-ChartCanvas()` method needs some updating. The method is altered to call first on the record store to retrieve price information for the given user-entered symbol.

```
private void displayChartCanvas() {
  if (chartCanvas == null) {
    chartCanvas = new ChartCanvas();
  }
  String currentSymbol = entryForm.getSymbolField().getString();
  int[] prices = retrievePrices(currentSymbol);      ❶ Call to retrieve the current
  ...                                                  and historical prices
```

At first glance, the retrievePrices(currentSymbol) method (listing 6.6) looks a lot like the storePrice() method from the ObtainQuoteMIDlet. In fact, they both use the same record enumeration and record filter to locate a record. However this time, instead of updating or adding the record, the retrievePrices() method simply extracts the current and historical dollar prices from any matching record found. This method serves as the implementation of the RetrievePrice use case in our tutorial application design.

**Listing 6.6  RetrieveQuoteMIDlet's retrievePrices method**

```
private int[] retrievePrices(String symbol) {

  int[] dollars = null;

  try {                                                                    ❶
    RecordStore anRMS = RecordStore.openRecordStore("Quotes" , true);
    RecordFilter rf = new QuoteFilter(symbol);
    RecordEnumeration rEnum = anRMS.enumerateRecords(rf,null,false);
    if (rEnum.hasNextElement()) {
      byte[] rec = rEnum.nextRecord();
      dollars = parsePrices(rec);          ❷
    } else
      dollars = null;  ·  ❸
    rEnum.destroy();
    anRMS.closeRecordStore();
  } catch (RecordStoreFullException fullStore) {
    //handle a full record store problem
  } catch (RecordStoreNotFoundException notFoundException) {
    //handle store not found which should not happen with the
    //createIfNecessary tag set to true
  } catch (RecordStoreException recordStoreException) {
    //handling record store problems
  }
  return dollars;    ❹
}
```

❶ Open the "Quotes" record store

❷ Parse out the current and historical prices from the record.

❸ Return null signifying no prices and no record

❹ Return array containing the prices

Extracting the dollar prices from a record is again a matter of string manipulation and character matching. It is handled by the parsePrices(byte[] quoteRec) method which is shown in listing 6.7.

```
private int[] parsePrices(byte[] quoteRec) {
  String rec = new String(quoteRec);
  int dollar1Pos = rec.indexOf(';');
  int cent1Pos = rec.indexOf(';',dollar1Pos+1);
  int dollar2Pos = rec.indexOf(';',cent1Pos + 1);

  if (dollar2Pos > 0) { //had a historical price
    int cent2Pos = rec.indexOf(';',dollar2Pos + 1);
    int currentDollars = Integer.parseInt(rec.substring(dollar1Pos + 1,
      cent1Pos));
    int currentCents = Integer.parseInt(rec.substring(cent1Pos + 1,
      dollar2Pos));
    int historicalDollars = Integer.parseInt(rec.substring(dollar2Pos + 1,
      cent2Pos));
    int historicalCents = Integer.parseInt(rec.substring(cent2Pos + 1));
    int[] returnPrices = {currentDollars, currentCents, historicalDollars,
      historicalCents};
    return returnPrices;
  } else {    //no previous historical price
    int currentDollars = Integer.parseInt(rec.substring(dollar1Pos + 1,
      cent1Pos));
    int currentCents = Integer.parseInt(rec.substring(cent1Pos + 1));
    int[] returnPrices = {currentDollars, currentCents};
    return returnPrices;
  }
}
```

Each record contains the symbol for the investment and up to two sets of integers for the dollars and cents of each price quote (current and possibly historical price). The current and historical prices are extracted from the record and returned in an integer array. If the investment has only one price stored for it, then the array returned contains two integers; the dollar and cents of the currently known price for the investment. If a historical price is also known for the investment, the integer array will have four numbers representing the current dollars and cents price as well as the historical dollars and cents price respectively.

### Retrofitting the canvas display

The RetrieveQuoteMIDlet and its canvas display object currently only depict the dollar value portion of the investment prices. So after the prices are retrieved, the array is checked for two (indicating only a current investment price is available) or four integers have been obtained from the record store. While the retrieve-Prices() method returns dollars and cents, the size of the graphical user interface is limited and so only the dollar parts of the price are depicted in the comparison bar charts. Both current and historical dollar prices are required in order to display the graphical bar chart showing the price changes. With only a current price and no historical price available, the user is given the current price via an informational alert window. This is also true if no record for the requested symbol exists in the record store. The `retrievePrices()` method would have returned null. In this case, an alert is used to inform the user that no data exists for the symbol provided. The updated `displayChartCanvas()` method, shown in listing 6.8, performs the check for available price information and calls to display the appropriate information to the customer.

**Listing 6.8    The new displayChartCanvas of RetrieveQuoteMIDlet**

```
private void displayChartCanvas() {
  if (chartCanvas == null) {
    chartCanvas = new ChartCanvas();
  }
  String currentSymbol = entryForm.getSymbolField().getString();
  int[] prices = retrievePrices(currentSymbol);
  if (prices != null) {
    if (prices.length > 2) {        ❶
      initCanvasListener();
      displayMngr.setCurrent(chartCanvas);
      chartCanvas.displayChart(currentSymbol,prices[0],prices[2]);
    } else {        ❷
      Alert noDataAlert = new Alert("Recorded Price","Recorded price for "
        + currentSymbol + " is:  $" + prices[0] + "." + prices[1] +
        ". No historical data exists.", null, AlertType.INFO);
      noDataAlert.setTimeout(Alert.FOREVER);
      displayMngr.setCurrent(noDataAlert, entryForm);
    }
  } else {        ❸
    Alert noDataAlert = new Alert("No prices", "No price data exists
      for " + currentSymbol, null, AlertType.INFO);
    noDataAlert.setTimeout(Alert.FOREVER);
    displayMngr.setCurrent(noDataAlert, entryForm);
  }
s}
```

❶ If current and historical price exists, display the comparison bar charts

❷ If current price exists, display price in an Alert

❸ If no price information exists, use Alert to indicate no price

As with the ObtainQuoteMIDlet, most of the RetrieveQuoteMIDlet will not look different when running. As shown in figure 6.8, after compiling, preverifying and executing, the only change seen on the part of the user comes when there is only a current price stored in the database. In this case, the new Information alert will provide the user with the current, but no historical, price information. But the information displayed in the RetrieveQuoteMIDlet now comes directly from the record store as a result of quotes obtained by the other MIDlet in the suite, namely ObtainQuoteMIDlet.

**Figure 6.9  Like the ObtainQuoteMIDlet, no change is seen in the RetrieveQuoteMIDlet user interface after adding an RMS. The screens to get the investment symbol and display the price for saved price quotes are the same. Again, behind the screens of this MIDlet, quote service data is retrieved from the record store on the device.**

Before we depart this chapter, we want to give you a complete listing of the code for our MIDlet applications. Listings 6.9 and 6.10 are the Java files for our MIDP applications. The EntryForm and ChartCanvas.java files from chapter 5 are unchanged so please refer to the code listing at the end of that chapter if you need those class files. Full source code for QuoteService.java and QuoteFilter.java were provided earlier in this chapter.

**Listing 6.9    The full ObtainQuoteMIDlet**

```java
import javax.microedition.midlet.*;
import javax.microedition.lcdui.*;
import javax.microedition.rms.*;

public class ObtainQuoteMIDlet extends MIDlet {
  private Display displayMngr = null;
  private EntryForm entryForm = null;
  private Alert resultsAlert = null;
  private Ticker adTicker =
  new Ticker("Track your investments with Investment Tracker");

  public ObtainQuoteMIDlet () {
  }

  private void initListener () {
    ItemStateListener itemListener = new ItemStateListener () {
      public void itemStateChanged (Item item) {
        if ((item == entryForm.getInvestmentChoice()) &&
      (entryForm.getInvestmentChoice().getSelectedIndex() == 1) &&
            !(entryForm.getSymbolField().getString().toUpperCase().
            endsWith("X"))) {
          Alert symbolAlert = new Alert("Check Symbol",
            "Mutual Funds end in 'X'", null, AlertType.WARNING);
          symbolAlert.setTimeout(Alert.FOREVER);
          displayMngr.setCurrent(symbolAlert, entryForm);
        }
      }
    };
```

```
        CommandListener commandListener = new CommandListener() {
          public void commandAction(Command c, Displayable d) {
            if (c == entryForm.getExitCommand()) {
              destroyApp(true);
            } else if (c == entryForm.getGetCommand()) {
              if ((entryForm.getInvestmentChoice().getSelectedIndex() == 1) &&
                  !(entryForm.getSymbolField().getString().toUpperCase().
                  endsWith("X"))){
                Alert symbolAlert = new Alert("Check Symbol",
                  "Mutual Funds end in 'X'", null, AlertType.WARNING);
                symbolAlert.setTimeout(Alert.FOREVER);
                displayMngr.setCurrent(symbolAlert, entryForm);
              } else if (entryForm.getSymbolField().getString().length() > 0) {
                String sym = entryForm.getSymbolField().getString();
                int type = entryForm.getInvestmentChoice().getSelectedIndex();
                int[] price = QuoteService.getPrice(sym, type);
                storePrice(sym, price);
                displayPrice("The price of " + sym + " is $" + price[0] +
                  "." + price[1]);
              }
            }
          }
        };
        entryForm.setItemStateListener(itemListener);
        entryForm.setCommandListener(commandListener);
      }

      private void displayEntryForm () {
        if (entryForm == null) {
          entryForm = new EntryForm("ObtainQuote");
        }
        initListener();
        displayMngr.setCurrent(entryForm);
      }

      private void displayPrice(String quoteString) {
        if (resultsAlert == null) {
          resultsAlert = new Alert("Quote Price", null, null,
          AlertType.CONFIRMATION);
          resultsAlert.setTicker(adTicker);
          resultsAlert.setTimeout(Alert.FOREVER);
        }
        resultsAlert.setString(quoteString);
        displayMngr.setCurrent(resultsAlert, entryForm);
      }

      private void storePrice(String symbol, int[] price) {
        String newRecord = symbol + ";" + price[0] + ";" + price[1];
        byte[] byteRec;
        try {
          RecordStore anRMS = RecordStore.openRecordStore("Quotes" , true);
          RecordFilter rf = new QuoteFilter(symbol);
          RecordEnumeration rEnum = anRMS.enumerateRecords(rf,null,false);
          if (rEnum.hasNextElement()) {
```

```
      int recId = rEnum.nextRecordId();
      newRecord += ';' + getLastPrice(anRMS.getRecord(recId));
      byteRec = newRecord.getBytes();
      anRMS.setRecord(recId,byteRec,0,byteRec.length);
    } else {
      byteRec = newRecord.getBytes();
      anRMS.addRecord(byteRec,0,byteRec.length);
    }
    rEnum.destroy();
    anRMS.closeRecordStore();
  } catch (RecordStoreFullException fullStore) {
    //handle a full record store problem
  } catch (RecordStoreNotFoundException notFoundException) {
    //handle store not found which should not happen with the
  } catch (RecordStoreException recordStoreException) {
    //handling record store problems
  }
}

private int[] parsePrices(byte[] quoteRec) {
  String rec = new String(quoteRec);
  int dollar1Pos = rec.indexOf(';');
  int cent1Pos = rec.indexOf(';',dollar1Pos+1);
  int dollar2Pos = rec.indexOf(';',cent1Pos + 1);
  if (dollar2Pos > 0) { //had a historical price
    int cent2Pos = rec.indexOf(';',dollar2Pos + 1);
    int currentDollars = Integer.parseInt(rec.substring(dollar1Pos +
      1,cent1Pos));
    int currentCents = Integer.parseInt(rec.substring(cent1Pos +
      1,dollar2Pos));
    int historicalDollars = Integer.parseInt(rec.substring(dollar2Pos +
      1,cent2Pos));
    int historicalCents = Integer.parseInt(rec.substring(cent2Pos + 1));
    int[] returnPrices = {currentDollars, currentCents, historicalDollars,
      historicalCents};
    return returnPrices;
  } else { //no previous historical price
    int currentDollars = Integer.parseInt(rec.substring(dollar1Pos + 1,
      cent1Pos));
    int currentCents = Integer.parseInt(rec.substring(cent1Pos + 1));
    int[] returnPrices = {currentDollars, currentCents};
    return returnPrices;
  }
}

private String getLastPrice(byte[] rec) {
  String recString = new String(rec);
  int dollarPos = recString.indexOf(';');
  int centPos = recString.indexOf(';',dollarPos+1);
  int centEnd = recString.indexOf(';',centPos + 1);
  if (centEnd > 0) //had a historical price
    return recString.substring(dollarPos+1,centEnd);
  else //no previous historical price
    return recString.substring(dollarPos+1);
}
```

```java
  protected void startApp() {
    displayMngr = Display.getDisplay(this);
    displayEntryForm();
  }

  protected void pauseApp() {
  }

  protected void destroyApp(boolean unconditional) {
    notifyDestroyed();
  }

  public void commandAction(Command c, Displayable s) {
  }
}
```

**Listing 6.10    The full RetrieveQuoteMIDlet**

```java
import javax.microedition.midlet.*;
import javax.microedition.lcdui.*;
import javax.microedition.rms.*;

public class RetrieveQuoteMIDlet extends MIDlet {
  private Display displayMngr = null;
  private EntryForm entryForm = null;
  private ChartCanvas chartCanvas = null;

  public RetrieveQuoteMIDlet () {
  }

  private void initListener () {
    ItemStateListener itemListener = new ItemStateListener () {
      public void itemStateChanged (Item item) {
        if ((item == entryForm.getInvestmentChoice()) &&
            (entryForm.getInvestmentChoice().getSelectedIndex() == 1) &&
            !(entryForm.getSymbolField().getString().toUpperCase().
            endsWith("X"))) {
          Alert symbolAlert = new Alert("Check Symbol",
            "Mutual Funds end in 'X'", null, AlertType.WARNING);
          symbolAlert.setTimeout(Alert.FOREVER);
          displayMngr.setCurrent(symbolAlert, entryForm);
        }
      }
    };
    CommandListener commandListener = new CommandListener() {
      public void commandAction(Command c, Displayable d) {
        if (c == entryForm.getExitCommand()) {
          destroyApp(true);
        } else if (c == entryForm.getGetCommand()) {
          if ((entryForm.getInvestmentChoice().getSelectedIndex() == 1) &&
              !(entryForm.getSymbolField().getString().toUpperCase().
              endsWith("X"))){
            Alert symbolAlert = new Alert("Check Symbol",
              "Mutual Funds end in 'X'", null, AlertType.WARNING);
```

```
              symbolAlert.setTimeout(Alert.FOREVER);
              displayMngr.setCurrent(symbolAlert, entryForm);
            } else
            if (entryForm.getSymbolField().getString().length() > 0)
              displayChartCanvas();
          }
        }
      };
      entryForm.setItemStateListener(itemListener);
      entryForm.setCommandListener(commandListener);
  }

  private void initCanvasListener() {
      CommandListener commandListener = new CommandListener() {
        public void commandAction(Command c, Displayable d) {
          if (c == chartCanvas.getExitCommand())
            displayMngr.setCurrent(entryForm);
        }
      };
      chartCanvas.setCommandListener(commandListener);
  }

  private void displayEntryForm () {
      if (entryForm == null) {
        entryForm = new EntryForm("RetrieveQuote");
      }
      initListener();
      displayMngr.setCurrent(entryForm);
  }

  private void displayChartCanvas() {
      if (chartCanvas == null) {
        chartCanvas = new ChartCanvas();
      }
      String currentSymbol = entryForm.getSymbolField().getString();
      int[] prices = retrievePrices(currentSymbol);
      if (prices != null) {
        if (prices.length > 2) {
          initCanvasListener();
          displayMngr.setCurrent(chartCanvas);
          chartCanvas.displayChart(currentSymbol,prices[0],prices[2]);
        } else {
         Alert noDataAlert = new Alert("Recorded Price","Recorded price for " +
            currentSymbol + " is: $" + prices[0] + "." + prices[1] +
            ". No historical data exists.", null, AlertType.INFO);
          noDataAlert.setTimeout(Alert.FOREVER);
          displayMngr.setCurrent(noDataAlert, entryForm);
        }
      } else {
       Alert noDataAlert = new Alert("No prices", "No price exists data for "
          + currentSymbol, null, AlertType.INFO);
        noDataAlert.setTimeout(Alert.FOREVER);
        displayMngr.setCurrent(noDataAlert, entryForm);
      }
  }
```

```java
    private int[] retrievePrices(String symbol) {
      int[] dollars = null;
      try {
        RecordStore anRMS = RecordStore.openRecordStore("Quotes" , true);
        RecordFilter rf = new QuoteFilter(symbol);
        RecordEnumeration rEnum = anRMS.enumerateRecords(rf,null,false);
        if (rEnum.hasNextElement()) {
          byte[] rec = rEnum.nextRecord();
          dollars = parsePrices(rec);
        } else
          dollars = null;
          rEnum.destroy();
          anRMS.closeRecordStore();
        } catch (RecordStoreFullException fullStore) {
          //handle a full record store problem
        } catch (RecordStoreNotFoundException notFoundException) {
          //handle store not found which should not happen with the
          //createIfNecessary
      } catch (RecordStoreException recordStoreException) {
        //handling record store problems
      }
      return dollars;
    }

    private int[] parsePrices(byte[] quoteRec) {
      String rec = new String(quoteRec);
      int dollar1Pos = rec.indexOf(';');
      int cent1Pos = rec.indexOf(';',dollar1Pos+1);
      int dollar2Pos = rec.indexOf(';',cent1Pos + 1);
      if (dollar2Pos > 0) { //had a historical price
        int cent2Pos = rec.indexOf(';',dollar2Pos + 1);
        int currentDollars = Integer.parseInt(rec.substring(dollar1Pos +
          1,cent1Pos));
        int currentCents = Integer.parseInt(rec.substring(cent1Pos +
          1,dollar2Pos));
        int historicalDollars = Integer.parseInt(rec.substring(dollar2Pos +
          1,cent2Pos));
        int historicalCents = Integer.parseInt(rec.substring(cent2Pos + 1));
        int[] returnPrices = {currentDollars, currentCents, historicalDollars,
        historicalCents};
        return returnPrices;
      } else { //no previous historical price
        int currentDollars = Integer.parseInt(rec.substring(dollar1Pos +
          1,cent1Pos));
        int currentCents = Integer.parseInt(rec.substring(cent1Pos + 1));
        int[] returnPrices = {currentDollars, currentCents};
        return returnPrices;
      }
    }

    protected void startApp() {
      displayMngr = Display.getDisplay(this);
      displayEntryForm();
    }
```

```
  protected void pauseApp() {
  }

  protected void destroyApp(boolean unconditional) {
    notifyDestroyed();
  }
}
```

## 6.5  SUMMARY

In this chapter, we explored the MIDP Record Management System. Specifically, we examined the MDIP RMS API and what device manufacturers are required to support. At the center of data storage on an MIDP device is the record store. A record store can be utilized and shared by many MIDlet applications that are part of the same MIDlet suite. Through examples and the tutorial application, we examined how to store, update, and retrieve information in the record store.

The tutorial application is already behaving as expected. We have a user interface that allows customers to specify investment symbols and the application can store and retrieve price quote data for those investments. The only thing our application lacks is connectivity to the outside world and real price quote data. We explore how to add this connectivity in the next chapter.

**C H A P T E R   7**

# Connecting to the Internet

Our first tutorial application implementation is almost complete. We have a user interface that interacts with the customer to get an investment symbol and type. We also have a means to store and retrieve data on an investment in a database on the device. What is missing is the application's communication with the outside world to get the investment data.

In essence, we now have a mobile application, but it is not wireless. To make our MIDP application wireless, it is going to need to communicate with the World Wide Web or other source of electronically available investment data for stock and fund prices. In this tutorial, we use the hypertext transfer protocol (HTTP) to request quote data from a popular financial Internet web site to pull back a hypertext markup language (HTML) page containing an investment price. We then parse the page to extract the price for storage in our MIDP RMS database.

In J2ME, connecting to the Internet, a socket, a file, or any other networked data resource occurs via a standard framework called the Generic Connection Framework (GCF). In chapter 13, we are going to cover the GCF in detail. The Generic Connection Framework provides the foundation for all network communications within the J2ME architecture. The Generic Connection Framework interface is defined within the configuration layer (in this case the CLDC) yet it provides no protocol implementations. The profiles themselves, or more specifically, the vendors supplying the devices or profile implementations must support the necessary Generic Connection Framework interface implementations.

In this chapter, we will look at MIDP's support of the GCF, and we examine its use in connecting our tutorial application to a source of investment price information. We will also look at the `java.io` package in light of J2ME and connecting to the outside world.

## 7.1 MICRO EDITION PACKAGE CONNECTIVITY

The Generic Connection Framework resides in the `javax.microedition.io` package and consists of one class called `Connector`, one exception called `ConnectionNotFoundException`, and many "Connection" interfaces, depending on the profile's implementation. In the case of the MIDP, there are currently nine defined interfaces.

The `Connector` class is used to create instances of a connection protocol using one of the `Connector` class's static methods. The object returned from the static connection methods is either a stream or an implementation supporting the generic `Connection` interface (or one of its descendents). In chapter 13, we cover the various connection interfaces in more detail. For the purposes of this chapter, we are concerned with obtaining a simple input stream from the Internet via HTTP. To do this, we will use the generic `Connector` class provided in the GCF in combination with an `InputStreamReader` object available from the `java.io` package.

### 7.1.1 Using the Connector class to open a channel

The `Connector` class is not designed to be instantiated. It is used to create instances of a connection through various protocols and connection types such as a socket, HTTP, file, datagram, and so forth. All of the methods `Connector` defines are static and serve this purpose. The `Connector` defines three variations of `open()` that each return a `Connection` instance. The `Connector` class also defines methods that return input and output streams.

The stream methods, `openInputStream(String name)`, `openOutputStream(String name)`, `openDataInputStream(String name)`, and `openDataOutputStream(String name)` are convenient methods for creating different types of input and output streams at the same time the connection is established. In most cases, applications are not concerned with the `Connection` instance itself, but rather the stream that can be read from or written to. By using one of these four methods, the application can obtain the stream directly, without needing to be concerned about the connection instance. The following example illustrates how to get a stream using the Connector class.

```
try {
  InputStream is = Connector.openInputStream("socket://127.0.0.1:8888");
  is.close();
} catch (IOException x) {
    //Handle Exception
}
```

The string provided to the open stream methods is a Uniform Resource Identifier (URI). It is composed of three parts: a scheme, an address, and a parameter list. The general form of the name parameter is as follows:

```
<scheme>:<address>;<parameters>
```

The scheme identifies how the connection is made (socket, HTTP, file, datagram, etc.). The address identifies what to connect to (for example, www.ctimn.com, myfile.txt, and so forth) and the parameters identify other information that is required by the protocol to establish a connection such as a connection speed. The parameters, when needed, are specified as name=value pairs. Some examples of URIs are listed in table 7.1. Note that in some cases the parameter is not necessary and thus the ";" is not always present.

**Table 7.1   These example strings specify how an application should connect to various information sources. They specify various protocols, addresses, and parameter data. All are Uniform Resource Identifier formatted.**

| Example URI |
| --- |
| http://www.ctimn.com:8080 |
| socket://localhost:8080 |
| file:c:/myfile.txt (Windows only) |
| file:/myfile.txt (Unix) |
| datagram://127.0.0.1:8099 |
| comm:0;baudrate=9600 |

There is a lot more to the `Connector` class and the entire GCF that we will leave for later (see chapter 13). For now, this is enough to get connected wirelessly to our financial quote source.

## 7.2   *SIMILAR BUT SMALLER I/O PACKAGE*

The `java.io` package in J2ME is, for the most part, a subset of the `java.io` package in J2SE. In general, the `java.io` package has been reduced to a few input and output stream subclasses and a single concrete reader and writer class to work with the streams. Because of the much-reduced size of the `java.io` package, J2SE users familiar with the standard package probably recognize that some methods seem out of place and are not associated with the normal J2SE classes. This is because some of the subclasses in the J2SE `java.io` hierarchy are missing.

Take the `DataInputStream` class, for example. In the standard `java.io` package, this class descends from `FilteredInputStream`. In J2ME, `Filtered-InputStream` does not exist. Instead, `DataInputStream` descends directly from the abstract `InputStream`. In standard `java.io`, the `FilteredInputStream`'s `close()` method closes the input stream and releases any system resources associated with the stream. With the J2SE `FilteredInputStream` class not available, this method is housed in the `DataInputStream` class.

## 7.2.1     Streams

`InputStream` and `OutputStream` are the abstract superclasses of all byte streams in J2ME, just as in J2SE. J2ME has only three subclasses of streams, unlike the rich set of input and output stream subclasses in J2SE that allow for handling stream data in a multitude of fashions. The subclasses of InputStream and OutputStream in J2ME are listed in table 7.2.

**Table 7.2   J2ME has only a limited number of stream classes, unlike the rich set of stream subclasses available in J2SE. In J2ME, developers must use ByteArray, Data, or Print streams for input/output.**

| Stream Class | Description |
| --- | --- |
| ByteArrayInput/OutputStream | Contains an internal buffer that holds bytes that may be read/written to and from the stream. |
| DataInput/OutputStream | Provides applications with the means to read/write primitive Java data types from an underlying input/output stream in a machine-independent fashion. |
| PrintStream | Extends OutputStream and provides convenience methods for printing or displaying various objects and data values. |

To demonstrate the use of streams in conjunction with the `Connector` class we expand on the earlier example. This code reads characters from the opened stream obtained with the help of the GCF `Connector`.

```
try {
  InputStream is = Connector.openInputStream("socket://127.0.0.1:8888");
  int ch;
  while ((ch = in.read()) > 0) {
    //do something with the data read
  }
  is.close();
} catch (IOException x) {
    //Handle Exception
}
```

The stream serves to capture the information coming from the open connection, in this case a socket connection, so that the application can read characters from it as need be.

## 7.2.2     Readers/Writers

The `Reader` and `Writer` abstract super classes for reading and writing character streams are the same as they are in J2SE. However, as with streams, the number of concrete subclasses is severely reduced. In the case of readers and writers, there is only one concrete subclass of each, namely `InputStreamReader` and `OutputStreamWriter`. Instances of these classes are used in conjunction with streams and serve as translators from bytes to characters (`InputStreamReader`) and from characters to bytes (`OutputStreamWriter`) just as their J2SE counterparts.

We will return to look at the java.io classes again in a later chapter. For now, this is enough to allow us to get a real QuoteService up and running.

## 7.3 IMPLEMENTING THE INTERNET INVESTMENT QUOTE SERVICE

In the last chapter, we implemented a fake quote service that handed out phony price quotes from a random number generator. In this chapter, we implement the Quote-Service described in the tutorial application design. You may recall from our tutorial application design discussion in chapter 3, that the price quote acquiring service should be developed as a stand-alone component. As a service, it simply answers stock and mutual fund price information when provided the symbol and type of the investment. This allows it to be reused by several platform implementations in the future. In particular, the service is used later when we rebuild our tutorial application for a PDA device in KJava (chapters 8–10). A separate service also makes for good design since this can also isolate the application from changes required in the service, and transversely isolate the application from changes in the service.

In this tutorial example, we keep our connection and communications very simple, opting to use simple streams to get data. In fact, through the MIDP implementation of the GCF, we could use more specific `Connection` interfaces such as the `Http-Connection` (discussed in chapter 13). The `HttpConnection` provides a convenient HTTP protocol connection to MIDP applications without having to worry about how the communication/networking details.

There are two reasons why this is not done in the tutorial. First, the `HttpConnection` is an MIDP implementation interface of the GCF. While it is mandatory for all MIDP vendor implementations, other profiles, or applications that do not use a profile may not have this type of interface availability. In order to maximize the portability of our QuoteService, we want to shy away from using a profile-specific implementation. Secondly, we are going to communicate with the Internet and ask for standard web pages. The great part about the World Wide Web is that it freely provides so much information to its users. Unfortunately, this information is not always free from the standpoint that many web pages today contain a deluge of advertisements and uninteresting data. If we were to use something like the `HttpConnection` and pull off an entire investment web page into the device at one time, it could overflow the device's available memory. For example, we found a typical investment center web page like those available from Yahoo or NASDAQ to contain as much as 35K of text. Therefore, the tutorial application must weed out the portions of the page needed as it reads the HTML in from a stream while ignoring the extra data in the page. In a real world implementation, quote data might be made available over a corporate server and served up as convenient XML data or, at least, very streamlined price data. Without this luxury, we want to be careful not to choke our small device with the amount of data coming from a single web page.

**WARNING** The code in this portion of the chapter is meant to demonstrate how to connect to and get information from a network resource (like the Internet) in a wireless fashion using the GCF and MIDP/CLDC API. In a real world situation, a company building an application like the tutorial application we are about to demonstrate would likely have data available on its own Internet or intranet site.

## 7.3.1　Getting a quote service connection

From the last chapter, recall that the QuoteService was provided by the Quote-Service class. We retain the same class and signature in order to avoid any significant changes to our application. However, the contents of the class will change significantly.

### *Preparing for a connection*

To begin, the new implementation of the class uses both the GCF, located in the javax.microedition.io package, and the J2ME, CLDC java.io package. Therefore, both of these packages should be imported at the top of our QuoteService.java file.

```
import javax.microedition.io.*;
import java.io.*;
```

Per our tutorial application design, the all-important service that this class provides is that of getting and returning stock and mutual fund price quotes. QuoteService offers this service through a single public method, getPrice(String symbol-String, int type). Because this class exists only to provide a service, creating instances of this class is not necessary. Therefore, the getPrice() method remains a static method returning an array of integers. When the service is successful in finding a quote for a given investment, the array will contain two integers representing the price. One integer is for price dollars, and the other is for the price cents. Remember, floating-point numbers are not available in many J2ME environments such as the CLDC/MIDP.

The getPrice() must be passed two parameters. The first, the investment symbol, is the symbol representing the stock or mutual fund in which the customer has expressed interest. This parameter must be a string. Given the customer could have mistyped the symbol or not know the exact characters used in the symbol, the string may not be a valid symbol for a stock or mutual fund. Regardless, the service attempts to find a price for a stock or mutual fund using this string and assuming that it is valid. As will be seen, the getPrice() method must handle the possible condition that the symbol is not valid and return appropriate results. The second parameter passed to the getPrice() method is an integer representing the investment type. The value 0 (the index of the Stock radio button in the choice group) will signify that the customer desires a quote on a stock. Alternately, a value of 1 sent as the type parameter signifies a search for a mutual fund is desired. In our implementation, this is an important piece of information to the QuoteService because we may need to use a different Internet site, or more precisely a different URI, to get stock prices versus mutual fund prices.

An implementation of the getPrice() method is provided as follows:

```
public static int[] getPrice(String symbolString, int type) {
  String quotePage = getQuotePage(symbolString, type);

  if (quotePage.length() > 0)
    return parseQuote(quotePage, type);
  else
    return null;
}
```

The getQuotePage() method is covered below, but its duty is to return to get-Price() an HTML page, or portion of an HTML page, containing the investment price in String format. If the Internet quote service is not available or the symbol provided by the application to the QuoteService is not a valid investment symbol for the type of investment specified, then the getQuotePage() method simply returns an empty string. No matter what the problem, if a page containing the price is not available, the get-Price() method and the QuoteService then returns null to the calling application.

**IMPROVING THE QUOTE SERVICE** In a more robust service, the application may want to know more about why a price is not available. Is the service down? Is the symbol not valid? A lot can go wrong when dealing with external agencies over a network, wired or wireless. Feel free to augment this implementation to provide different responses depending on the circumstances of a failure.

If a page or portion of a page containing the price quote is found, then the price must be extracted from the page and returned to the application in the form of the int array discussed before. This task is performed by the parseQuote(String quotePage, int type) method.

The really interesting part of QuoteService, then, occurs in the getQuote-Page() method. This method takes the same two symbol and investment type arguments passed to getPrice(). Its job is to open an HTTP connection to the Internet, contact a financial quote web site, pass the web site information on the desired investment, and capture the sites response.

Before we charge off and construct this page fetching method, let's think a little about where this method is going to be running and what it might encounter. When successfully built and deployed, this method is going to be operating in a small J2ME device. These devices have very limited resources to include available memory. Today's web sites, especially like those that provide stock and mutual fund quotes are very "electric" and filled with a lot of information (figure 7.1).

While informative to us, the charts, additional information, advertisements, links to other web sites, and so forth mean nothing to the application or device. This is all clutter around the information the application is really going after on behalf of the customer. Unfortunately, there is a lot of clutter. A typical financial quote web page may contain nearly 35,000 characters. Of this, the application needs around six or seven characters. If the QuoteService attempts to read in and hold all 35,000 characters (35K), a lot of the very finite resources on the device will have just been taken up by clutter. Therefore, the getQuotePage() method must be a little wise and memory miserly as it talks to the Internet and pulls down data. Instead of getting the entire web page, the getQuotePage() method finds and retains the portion of the page containing the price and drops the rest of the document avoiding potential memory problems.

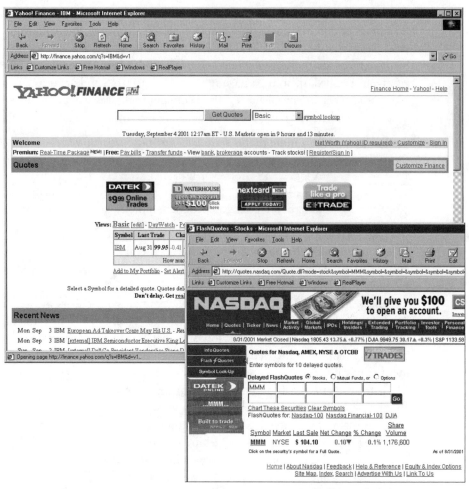

**Figure 7.1   Finance.Yahoo.com and Quotes.NASDAQ.com are two popular investment quote web sites shown here. As can be seen, there is a lot of exciting material on your typical financial quote web site, but not all of it is useful or desired by the J2ME application.**

The portion of the web page that does contain the price quote is assembled and stored in a `StringBuffer`. A new instance is defined at the top of the method. The string buffer is returned at the end of the method.

```
StringBuffer quotePage = new StringBuffer();
```

### *Opening an HTTP connection*

Next we want to open a connection to the Internet. Some web sites offer mutual fund quotes while other sites offer stock quotes. In this example, we call on two different URLs (both owned by the same popular organization) in order to demonstrate how to open an HTTP connection using the GCF. However, implement your getQuotePage() method by choosing your favorite financial quote web site and substituting its URL in the following code. In a real world situation, the company developing the application would likely have its own web site. Furthermore, it is likely that data from this site would be available in a format more amenable to the application we are developing and we would not have to parse the data out of a public web page. To open a connection, the GCF's Connector class from the javax.micro-edition.io package and an InputStreamReader from the java.io package are used.

```
String protocol = "http://";
String stockURL = "quotes.nasdaq.com/Quote.dll?" +
                  "page=multi&page=++&mode=stock&symbol=";
String fundURL = "www.nasdaq.com/asp/quotes_mutual.asp?" +
                  "page=++&mode=fund&symbol=";
InputStream in;
if (type == 0) {
  in = Connector.openInputStream(protocol + stockURL + symbolString);
} else {
  in = Connector.openInputStream(protocol + fundURL + symbolString);
}

String protocol = "http://";
String stockURL = "quotes.nasdaq.com/Quote.dll?" +
                  "page=multi&page=++&mode=stock&symbol=";
String fundURL = "www.nasdaq.com/asp/quotes_mutual.asp?" +
                  "page=++&mode=fund&symbol=";
InputStreamReader in;
if (type == 0) {
  in = new InputStreamReader(Connector.openInputStream(protocol +
                             stockURL + symbolString));
} else {
  in = new InputStreamReader(Connector.openInputStream(protocol +
                             fundURL + symbolString));
}
```

Having an open connection to a web site server and an input stream on an investment quote HTML page, we can read the page and extract the price data.

### Reading HTML data

The openInputStream() method call makes an InputStream available, but no data has come across the line yet. The read() method is used to read data from the input stream, and it returns a byte of data in the form of an int. If the end of the stream has been reached, it will return −1. Therefore, all that is required to read the HTML page all the way to the end is a while loop checking on the return value of the read() call.

```
int ch;
while ((ch = in.read()) > 0 ) {
}
```

Inside this loop, the method must find and extract the portion of the HTML containing the price. It so happens that the web sites we have chosen to get price quotes from provide a very natural marker for indicating the price among all the data in their web pages. The price is placed on the web page preceded by a '$' character. Luckily for us, when a valid symbol has been used to get the page, it also happens to be the first '$' character used on the page. Therefore, inside of the read loop, in this implementation of getQuotePage(), we simply read until the character '$' is encountered. Depending on the price and extra information around the price, we extract about 20 characters and return this portion of the HTML page to the getPrice() method for parsing. Again, individual results may vary depending on choice of quote service supplier, but an implementation of the getQuotePrice() read loop might look something like the following code.:

```
while ((ch = in.read()) > 0 ) {
  if (((char) ch) == marker) {
    char[] end = new char[readLength];
    in.read(end,0,readLength);
    quotePage.append(new String(end));
    break;
  }         }
}
```

On completion of the read, the input stream must be closed. Furthermore, when dealing with most any class and operation from the java.io or javax.micro-edition.io packages, IOExceptions must be caught and handled. Finally, at the end of the method, the portion of the page containing the quote is returned. Of course, if no price is found in the page (possibly because the symbol was not valid) then the StringBuffer used to capture the page would be empty and a null string is returned. The complete getQuotePage() method is shown in listing 7.1.

Listing 7.1   The getQuotePage() method in QuoteService

```
private static String getQuotePage(String symbolString, int type) {
  char marker = '$';
  int readLength = 20;

  StringBuffer quotePage = new StringBuffer();              ❶
  try {
    String protocol = "http://";
    String stockURL = "quotes.nasdaq.com/Quote.dll?" +
                      "page=multi&page=++&mode=stock&symbol=";
    String fundURL = "www.nasdaq.com/asp/quotes_mutual.asp?" +    ❷
                     "page=++&mode=fund&symbol=";
    InputStream in;
    if (type == 0) {
      in = new InputStreamReader(Connector.openInputStream(protocol +
                                 stockURL + symbolString));
    } else {
      in = new InputStreamReader(Connector.openInputStream(protocol +
                                 fundURL + symbolString));
    }
```

```
    int ch;
    while ((ch = in.read()) > 0 ) {
      if (((char) ch) == marker) {
        char[] end = new char[readLength];
        in.read(end,0,readLength);
        quotePage.append(new String(end));
        break;
      }            }
    in.close();                    ❹
  } catch (IOException ex) {
    System.out.println("Exception reading quote from HTTP Connection "
                          + ex.getMessage());
  }
  return quotePage.toString();
}
```

❶ Create a StringBuffer to hold part of the page

❷ Open a stream to the appropriate Web site

❸ Read characters until the price has been found

❹ Don't forget to close the input stream

Again, because there is no real need for an instance of QuoteService, the get-QuotePage() method is declared static. It is also private since its only caller is getPrice() from within the class.

### 7.3.2    Extracting the price quote from the HTML

In the section above, we opened an HTTP connection and pulled down an HTML document. We do not know the contents of the page or even if it contains the price quote in which we are interested. If a price quote is found in the string of the portion of the HTML page, the actual price must be extracted from the string. The contents of a price extracting method vary greatly depending on the content of the HTML page used to get the quote. An implementation has been provided here in listing 7.2 as an example for completeness.

**Listing 7.2   The parseQuote() method in QuoteService**

```
private static int[] parseQuote(String aQuotePage, int type){

  String skip;
  String dollarsEnd;
  String quoteEnd;
  String quoteDollars = null;
  String quoteCents = null;
  int[] dollarsCents = new int[2];

  if (type == 0) {
    skip = "$ ";
    dollarsEnd = ".";
    quoteEnd = "</b>";
```

```
  } else {
    skip = "$";
    dollarsEnd = ".";
    quoteEnd = "</b>";
  }

  try {
    int generalPos = aQuotePage.indexOf(skip);
    int dollarStop = aQuotePage.indexOf(dollarsEnd, generalPos);
    int quoteStop = aQuotePage.indexOf(quoteEnd, dollarStop);
    quoteDollars = aQuotePage.substring(generalPos + (skip.length()),
      dollarStop);
    dollarsCents[0] = Integer.parseInt(quoteDollars);
    quoteCents = aQuotePage.substring(dollarStop + 1, quoteStop);
    dollarsCents[1] = Integer.parseInt(quoteCents);
    return dollarsCents;
  } catch (Exception e){
      System.out.println("Error attempting to parse quote from " +
      "source page. Improper Symbol?");
      return null;
  }
}
```

The `parseQuote()` method returns the int array containing the dollars and cents of the price parsed from the HTML or null if no price was found or could not be extracted. An implementation of the full and complete `QuoteService` class is provided in listing 7.3. Modify the URLs, read loop in `getQuotePage()`, and parse methods to allow your MIDlets to incorporate investment price quotes from your favorite web site.

### Listing 7.3   The complete QuoteService.java

```
import javax.microedition.io.*;
import java.io.*;

public class QuoteService {

  public static int[] getPrice(String symbolString, int type) {
    String quotePage = getQuotePage(symbolString, type);

    if (quotePage.length() > 0)
      return parseQuote(quotePage, type);
    else
      return null;
  }

  private static int[] parseQuote(String aQuotePage, int type){

    String skip;
    String dollarsEnd;
    String quoteEnd;
    String quoteDollars = null;
    String quoteCents = null;
    int[] dollarsCents = new int[2];
```

*CHAPTER 7   CONNECTING TO THE INTERNET*

```
if (type == 0) {
  skip = "$ ";
  dollarsEnd = ".";
  quoteEnd = "</b>";
} else {
  skip = "$";
  dollarsEnd = ".";
  quoteEnd = "</b>";
}

try {
  int generalPos = aQuotePage.indexOf(skip);
  int dollarStop = aQuotePage.indexOf(dollarsEnd, generalPos);
  int quoteStop = aQuotePage.indexOf(quoteEnd, dollarStop);
  quoteDollars = aQuotePage.substring(generalPos + (skip.length()),
    dollarStop);
  dollarsCents[0] = Integer.parseInt(quoteDollars);
  quoteCents = aQuotePage.substring(dollarStop + 1, quoteStop);
  dollarsCents[1] = Integer.parseInt(quoteCents);
  return dollarsCents;
} catch (Exception e){
    System.out.println("Error attempting to parse quote from " +
    "source page.  Improper Symbol?");
  return null;
}
}

private static String getQuotePage(String symbolString, int type) {
  char marker = '$';
  int readLength = 20;

  StringBuffer quotePage = new StringBuffer();
  try {
    String protocol = "http://";
    String stockURL = "quotes.nasdaq.com/Quote.dll?" +
                      "page=multi&page=++&mode=stock&symbol=";
    String fundURL = "www.nasdaq.com/asp/quotes_mutual.asp?" +
                     "page=++&mode=fund&symbol=";
    InputStream in;
    if (type == 0) {
      in = Connector.openInputStream(protocol + stockURL +
          symbolString);
    } else {
      in = Connector.openInputStream(protocol + fundURL +
          symbolString);
    }
    int ch;
    while ((ch = in.read()) > 0 ) {

      if (((char) ch) == marker) {
        int cnt = 0;
        while (cnt < readLength) {
          ch = in.read();
          quotePage.append((char)ch);
```

```
        cnt++;
      }
      break;
    }
  }
  in.close();
} catch (IOException ex) {
  System.out.println("Exception reading quote from HTTP Connection " +
    ex.getMessage());
}
return quotePage.toString();
  }
}
```

The QuoteService now provides real investment price data via an integer array, back to the calling application. In our case, this application is our ObtainQuoteMIDlet.

### 7.3.3 The MIDlet's handling of quote data

No additional work should be needed to hook the QuoteService into the tutorial application since the QuoteService API did not change with this new implementation. Namely, the ObtainQuoteMIDlet's CommandListener continues to call on getPrice(symbolString, type). However, since the service may not find a price and would return null in this instance, a little error handling and an appropriate message to the customer are in order. Listing 7.4 shows the new CommandListener.

**Listing 7.4   Modified ObtainQuoteMIDlet's CommandListener**

```
CommandListener commandListener = new CommandListener() {
  public void commandAction(Command c, Displayable d) {
    if (c == entryForm.getExitCommand()) {
      destroyApp(true);
    } else if (c == entryForm.getGetCommand()) {
      if ((entryForm.getInvestmentChoice().getSelectedIndex() == 1)
          && !(entryForm.getSymbolField().getString()
            .toUpperCase().endsWith("X"))){
        Alert symbolAlert = new Alert("Check Symbol",
          "Mutual Funds end in 'X'", null, AlertType.WARNING);
        symbolAlert.setTimeout(Alert.FOREVER);
        displayMngr.setCurrent(symbolAlert, entryForm);
      } else if (entryForm.getSymbolField().getString().length() > 0) {
        String sym = entryForm.getSymbolField().getString();
        int type = entryForm.getInvestmentChoice().getSelectedIndex();
        int[] price = QuoteService.getPrice(sym, type);
        if (price != null) {  ❶
          storePrice(sym, price);
          displayPrice("The price of " + sym + " is $" + price[0] + "."
                    + price[1]);
        } else {
          Alert symbolAlert = new Alert("Check Symbol/Type",
            "No quote found.", null, AlertType.WARNING);
```

```
            symbolAlert.setTimeout(Alert.FOREVER);
            displayMngr.setCurrent(symbolAlert, entryForm);
          }
        }
      }
    }
  }
};
```

❶ New error check added

❷ Alert added if no data is available

From a user interface perspective, the ObtainQuoteMIDlet will not appear any differently than it did after the last chapter, with a single exception. When the customer now enters characters in the symbol entry field that do not represent a valid stock or mutual fund, an Alert will display suggesting the customer should check the symbol and type.

**Figure 7.2**
**What happens if the customer makes a mistake in entering the investment symbol, or enters a symbol that does not exist?**
The MIDlet requesting the QuoteService to provide a price quote for the investment will get back an HTML page containing some sort of error but no price data. Therefore a new Alert display, shown above, is added to the MIDlet to inform the customer of the error when attempting to gain the price of an invalid or non-existent investment symbol.

The first implementation of the tutorial application in MIDP is complete! Having developed a complete mobile and wireless Java application running in the cellular telephone or pager, the boss is probably happy, but there is still work left to do. In the next section, we port this same application to a personal digital assistant.

The complete ObtainQuoteMIDlet.java and QuoteService.java files are provided in Listings 7.5 and 7.6. The RetrieveQuoteMIDlet and QuoteFilter did not change. The Java code for these classes can be found in chapter 6. Also, the code in Entry-Form.java and CanvasChart.java did not change and the complete listing for these files can be found in chapter 5.

| Listing 7.5    ObtainQuoteMIDlet.java |

```
import javax.microedition.midlet.*;
import javax.microedition.lcdui.*;
import javax.microedition.rms.*;

public class ObtainQuoteMIDlet extends MIDlet {
```

```java
private Display displayMngr = null;
private EntryForm entryForm = null;
private Alert resultsAlert = null;
private Ticker adTicker =
new Ticker("Track your investments with Investment Tracker");

public ObtainQuoteMIDlet () {
}

private void initListener () {
  ItemStateListener itemListener = new ItemStateListener () {
    public void itemStateChanged (Item item) {
      if ((item == entryForm.getInvestmentChoice()) &&
          (entryForm.getInvestmentChoice().getSelectedIndex() == 1) &&
          !(entryForm.getSymbolField().getString().toUpperCase().
          endsWith("X"))) {
        Alert symbolAlert = new Alert("Check Symbol",
          "Mutual Funds end in 'X'", null, AlertType.WARNING);
        symbolAlert.setTimeout(Alert.FOREVER);
        displayMngr.setCurrent(symbolAlert, entryForm);
      }
    }
  };
  CommandListener commandListener = new CommandListener() {
    public void commandAction(Command c, Displayable d) {
      if (c == entryForm.getExitCommand()) {
        destroyApp(true);
      } else if (c == entryForm.getGetCommand()) {
        if ((entryForm.getInvestmentChoice().getSelectedIndex() == 1) &&
            !(entryForm.getSymbolField().getString().toUpperCase().
            endsWith("X"))){
          Alert symbolAlert = new Alert("Check Symbol",
            "Mutual Funds end in 'X'", null, AlertType.WARNING);
          symbolAlert.setTimeout(Alert.FOREVER);
          displayMngr.setCurrent(symbolAlert, entryForm);
        } else if (entryForm.getSymbolField().getString().length() > 0) {
          String sym = entryForm.getSymbolField().getString();
          int type = entryForm.getInvestmentChoice().getSelectedIndex();
          int[] price = QuoteService.getPrice(sym, type);
          if (price != null) {
            storePrice(sym, price);
            displayPrice("The price of " + sym + " is $" + price[0] +
              "." + price[1]);
          } else {
            Alert symbolAlert = new Alert("Check Symbol/Type",
              "No quote found.", null, AlertType.WARNING);
            symbolAlert.setTimeout(Alert.FOREVER);
            displayMngr.setCurrent(symbolAlert, entryForm);
          }
        }
      }
    }
  };
  entryForm.setItemStateListener(itemListener);
```

```java
        entryForm.setCommandListener(commandListener);
    }

    private void displayEntryForm () {
        if (entryForm == null) {
            entryForm = new EntryForm("ObtainQuote");
        }
        initListener();
        displayMngr.setCurrent(entryForm);
    }

    private void displayPrice(String quoteString) {
        if (resultsAlert == null) {
            resultsAlert = new Alert("Quote Price", null, null,
            AlertType.CONFIRMATION);
            resultsAlert.setTicker(adTicker);
            resultsAlert.setTimeout(Alert.FOREVER);
        }
        resultsAlert.setString(quoteString);
        displayMngr.setCurrent(resultsAlert, entryForm);
    }


    private void storePrice(String symbol, int[] price) {
        String newRecord = symbol + ";" + price[0] + ";" + price[1];
        byte[] byteRec;
        try {
            RecordStore anRMS = RecordStore.openRecordStore("Quotes" , true);
            RecordFilter rf = new QuoteFilter(symbol);
            RecordEnumeration rEnum = anRMS.enumerateRecords(rf,null,false);
            if (rEnum.hasNextElement()) {
                int recId = rEnum.nextRecordId();
                newRecord += ';' + getLastPrice(anRMS.getRecord(recId));
                byteRec = newRecord.getBytes();
                anRMS.setRecord(recId,byteRec,0,byteRec.length);
            } else {
                byteRec = newRecord.getBytes();
                anRMS.addRecord(byteRec,0,byteRec.length);
            }
            rEnum.destroy();
            anRMS.closeRecordStore();
        } catch (RecordStoreFullException fullStore) {
            //handle a full record store problem
        } catch (RecordStoreNotFoundException notFoundException) {
            //handle store not found which should not happen with the
        } catch (RecordStoreException recordStoreException) {
            //handling record store problems
        }
    }

    private int[] parsePrices(byte[] quoteRec) {
        String rec = new String(quoteRec);
        int dollar1Pos = rec.indexOf(';');
        int cent1Pos = rec.indexOf(';',dollar1Pos+1);
```

```
            int dollar2Pos = rec.indexOf(';',cent1Pos + 1);
            if (dollar2Pos > 0) { //had a historical price
              int cent2Pos = rec.indexOf(';',dollar2Pos + 1);
              int currentDollars = Integer.parseInt(rec.substring(dollar1Pos +
                1,cent1Pos));
              int currentCents = Integer.parseInt(rec.substring(cent1Pos +
                1,dollar2Pos));
              int historicalDollars = Integer.parseInt(rec.substring(dollar2Pos +
                1,cent2Pos));
              int historicalCents = Integer.parseInt(rec.substring(cent2Pos + 1));
             int[] returnPrices = {currentDollars, currentCents, historicalDollars,
                historicalCents};
              return returnPrices;
            } else { //no previous historical price
              int currentDollars = Integer.parseInt(rec.substring(dollar1Pos + 1,
                cent1Pos));
              int currentCents = Integer.parseInt(rec.substring(cent1Pos + 1));
              int[] returnPrices = {currentDollars, currentCents};
              return returnPrices;
            }
        }
    private String getLastPrice(byte[] rec) {
        String recString = new String(rec);
        int dollarPos = recString.indexOf(';');
        int centPos = recString.indexOf(';',dollarPos+1);
        int centEnd = recString.indexOf(';',centPos + 1);
        if (centEnd > 0) //had a historical price
          return recString.substring(dollarPos+1,centEnd);
        else //no previous historical price
          return recString.substring(dollarPos+1);
    }

    protected void startApp() {
        displayMngr = Display.getDisplay(this);
        displayEntryForm();
    }

    protected void pauseApp() {
    }

    protected void destroyApp(boolean unconditional) {
        notifyDestroyed();
    }

    public void commandAction(Command c, Displayable s) {
    }
}
```

**Listing 7.6  QuoteService.java**

```java
import javax.microedition.io.*;
import java.io.*;

public class QuoteService {
  public static int[] getPrice(String symbolString, int type) {
    String quotePage = getQuotePage(symbolString, type);
    if (quotePage.length() > 0)
      return parseQuote(quotePage, type);
    else
      return null;
  }

  private static int[] parseQuote(String aQuotePage, int type){
    String skip;
    String dollarsEnd;
    String quoteEnd;
    String quoteDollars = null;
    String quoteCents = null;
    int[] dollarsCents = new int[2];

    if (type == 0) {
      skip = "$ ";
      dollarsEnd = ".";
      quoteEnd = "</b>";
    } else {
      skip = "$";
      dollarsEnd = ".";
      quoteEnd = "</b>";
    }
    try {
      int generalPos = aQuotePage.indexOf(skip);
      int dollarStop = aQuotePage.indexOf(dollarsEnd, generalPos);
      int quoteStop = aQuotePage.indexOf(quoteEnd, dollarStop);
      quoteDollars = aQuotePage.substring(generalPos + (skip.length()),
      dollarStop);
      dollarsCents[0] = Integer.parseInt(quoteDollars);
      quoteCents = aQuotePage.substring(dollarStop + 1, quoteStop);
      dollarsCents[1] = Integer.parseInt(quoteCents);
      return dollarsCents;
    } catch (Exception e){
      System.out.println("Error attempting to parse quote from " +
        "source page. Improper Symbol?");
      return null;
    }
  }

  private static String getQuotePage(String symbolString, int type) {
    char marker = '$';
    int readLength = 20;
    StringBuffer quotePage = new StringBuffer();
    try {
      String protocol = "http://";
```

```
        String stockURL = "quotes.nasdaq.com/Quote.dll?" +
            "page=multi&page=++&mode=stock&symbol=";
        String fundURL = "www.nasdaq.com/asp/quotes_mutual.asp?" +
            "page=++&mode=fund&symbol=";
        InputStreamReader in;
        if (type == 0) {
          in = new InputStreamReader(Connector.openInputStream(protocol +
            stockURL + symbolString));
        } else {
          in = new InputStreamReader(Connector.openInputStream(protocol +
            fundURL + symbolString));
        }
        int ch;
        while ((ch = in.read()) > 0 ) {
          if (((char) ch) == marker) {
            char[] end = new char[readLength];
            in.read(end,0,readLength);
            quotePage.append(new String(end));
            break;
          }
        }
        in.close();
      } catch (IOException ex) {
        System.out.println("Exception reading quote from HTTP Connection " +
          ex.getMessage());
      }
      return quotePage.toString();
    }
}
```

## 7.4 SUMMARY

In this chapter, we have taken a short glance at the Generic Connection Framework and networking with the `javax.microedition.io` API. More details on GCF and networking are forthcoming in chapter 13. We also examine the greatly reduced but still recognizable version of `java.io` in J2ME. Together, we used the tools available in these two J2ME packages to connect our MIDP application to the Internet, completing our MIDP tutorial application.

**P A R T** **3**

# Developing for PDAs

In this part, we explore the CLDC API in use with the KJava API. KJava is a test and demonstration API initially developed by Sun for demonstrating the CLDC and KVM on Palm OS devices. Lacking a profile for PDA devices, companies such as esmertec have provided IDEs for developing Palm OS applications with this API. Having implemented the tutorial application once in the CLDC and MIDP APIs, this part will allow us to reimplement the tutorial application in KJava so that we can deploy the application to a Palm OS PDA device. Again, the tutorial application will allow us to see the major aspects of a building a KJava application; namely user interface, event handling, data storage, input/output and network connectivity.

# CHAPTER 8

# J2ME on a PDA,
# a KJava introduction

J2ME was first demonstrated at JavaOne in 1999. At that time, the most ubiquitous personal digital assistant (PDA) platform was the Palm device. It seemed logical to show the power and future of Java on all sizes and shapes of platforms by targeting this small but very popular platform. To demonstrate the lightweight virtual machine, already called the KVM, at that conference Sun developed a minimal set of Java packages along with a set of classes that provided user interface and database classes for the Palm. This last set of classes was bundled into a package named com.sun.kjava. Thus, it came to be known as the KJava API.

In this chapter, we focus on how to build and deploy a simple J2ME application for Palm OS devices using KJava. In addition, Sun has provided a way to allow MIDP applications to run on Palm OS devices as well. Thus we also show you how an MIDP application can be moved to the Palm OS PDA using something known as MIDP for Palm OS.

## 8.1  *PDA* PROFILE ALTERNATIVES

If a set of classes that provide user interface, persistent storage and other features for a specific device or set of devices sounds familiar to you, then you have been paying attention in earlier chapters. It should sound like the start of a profile! In fact, in 1999, the idea of Java throughout the enterprise, from server to small device, was being sold and was starting to explode. The concept of three Java editions was just getting started. Likewise, J2ME was still evolving. The idea of profiles and configurations was not formalized until after the 1999 conference.

Sun and others involved in J2ME evolution recognized that the programming needs across the wide spectrum of devices were going to be enormous and diverse. Each device, or set of devices, was going to require some of its own APIs. From this realization sprang profiles (as well as configurations to address more general needs).

Today, while a request for the specification for a PDA profile exists (as discussed in chapter 2), the actual specification, let alone an implementation, is still forthcoming from within the JCP. Without a valid J2ME profile to address the development of Java applications on PDAs, you will need to find an alternative development environment. KJava is one of the alternatives. One of the benefits of the KJava alternative is that it allows the developer to use a J2ME configuration, namely the CLDC, as the basis for the application.

### 8.1.1  Java PDA development environments

As the Romans said, "natura adhorret vacuum"—nature abhors a vacuum, and so luckily there are options. Palm and other PDA providers have always provided non-Java development kits and tools for building applications, but there are Java PDA development environments as well. In fact, some third-party vendors are attempting to live and abide by the CLDC configuration already in place and hope to implement the PDA profile after it is specified. So what are the alternatives in building Java applications for PDA devices today? Current Java PDA development environments include:

- *KJava*  Some vendors provide a supported version of the KJava API for use with their implementation of CLDC and the KVM.

- *Proprietary solutions*  Still other vendors are providing non-J2ME Java development environments. IBM, for example, provides the Visual Age Micro Edition and its J9 virtual machine that runs on a host of PDA processors.

- *PersonalJava*  A whole host of companies provide Java virtual machines and Java for slightly larger PDAs like Compaq's iPaq. These fall under the realm of PersonalJava discussed in chapter 2 (we present some of the PersonalJava environments in chapter 15).

- *MIDP for Palm OS*  Finally, Sun has also produced a reference implementation of the MID Profile for use with the Palm device. This profile provides a minimal user interface and database interface to Palm OS systems.

In this chapter, we explore the KJava API used in combination with the CLDC provided by a third party IDE vendor. We will also take another brief look at MIDP for Palm OS, as this is the only Sun-supported and fully J2ME implementation for PDA devices (and specifically only Palm OS PDA devices) available as of this writing.

## 8.1.2 What is KJava?

KJava is a package containing classes and interfaces that provide four functions:

1 Application Control

2 Graphical User Interface

3 Persistent Storage, specifically an interface to the Palm OS Data Manager

4 Additional collections.

It was initially distributed with the CLDC reference implementation available from Sun. The "K" in KJava corresponds to the "K" in Sun's KVM and unofficially stands for "kilobyte." Today, Sun considers KJava an add-on package and provides it only for backward compatibility. In fact, getting a copy of this package can be tricky. Sun no longer supplies it with part of the CLDC download as of release 1.0.2. Instead, some vendors provide an implementation of KJava API through their IDE products. In looking at the KJava, we show you one such IDE.

Like profiles, the KJava classes and interface do not stand alone. They must be used on top of a configuration and virtual machine. The KJava API was designed to extend the generic functionality provided via the CLDC for applications living in a KVM that run on Palm OS devices (most notably Palm, Handspring, and SONY handheld devices). Because it was used as a proof-of-concept API for CLDC and the KVM running exclusively on a Palm OS device, it is also called the "CLDC Palm Overlay."

Some of the API is completely transportable to other Java environments. The additional collections are simply wrapped arrays, for example. Other classes, such as the database and user interface classes in the KJava API provide Palm OS specific functionality.

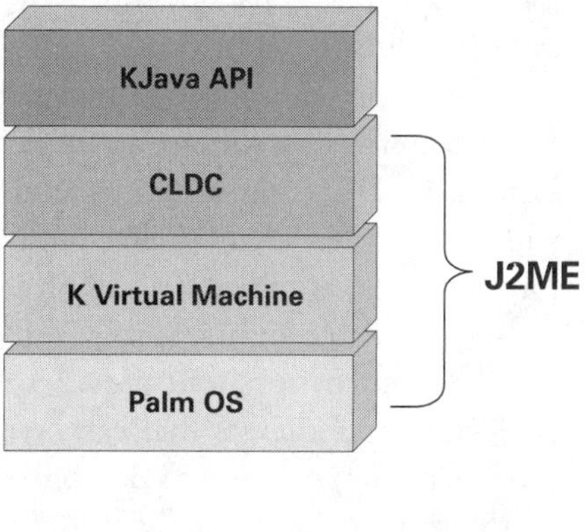

**Figure 8.1
The KJava environment adds user interface and database classes to the CLDC environment for the Palm OS.**

### 8.1.3     What is MIDP for Palm OS?

While the Palm device has lost some market share to other PDA devices, it is still the leading PDA on the market. Without a PDA specification in sight, and with only the KJava "demonstration only" API, Sun had a bit of a support problem. So, in the spring of 2001, they produced a reference implementation of the MID Profile for use on Palm OS devices. "But...," you may be thinking, "...the MIDP was for cellular phones and pagers!?" Yes, and for the time, it can also be used with at least one type of PDA device, namely a PDA running the Palm OS.

The API for the MIDP for Palm OS is the same as the MIDP for cell phones and pagers (the focus of Part 2 of this book). Therefore, MIDP for Palm OS is a runtime environment for MIDP on Palm OS devices. Essentially, MIDP for Palm OS has two items in addition to the standard reference implementation:

- a custom virtual machine for use on the Palm OS
- a tool to convert a MIDlet Suite into an application that can run on the MIDP Palm OS virtual machine.

We will explore MIDP for Palm OS at the end of this chapter.

## 8.2     *HiSmallWorld in KJava*

As we did with the MIDP development environment, we explore the KJava environment with a simple application to look at the development tools as well as an introduction to the basic API. We do this by revisiting the ubiquitous "Hello World" in KJava and CLDC.

### 8.2.1     Getting Started

To develop applications in the CLDC and KJava classes, an implementation of the CLDC and KVM for the Palm device is needed. The reference implementation of the CLDC is available from Sun at the following URL: http://java.sun.com/products/cldc As mentioned previously, KJava and the required Palm deployment tools formerly came with the CLDC provided by Sun. However, this environment is no longer available directly from Sun. Copies exist throughout the J2ME community, but obtaining one requires some research and cooperation from your fellow developers. For this exercise we will use an implementation provided by a third party. Jbed Micro Edition CLDC is produced by esmertec (no typo here, the company's name starts with a lowercase "e") in Switzerland and provides one of the fastest virtual machines for resource constrained devices on the market today. Information and downloads on Jbed are available at: http://www.esmertec.com

The Jbed environment provides the CLDC, KJava API and the complete means to develop applications that can be deployed to the Palm OS devices. This will also provide the opportunity to demonstrate one of the various micro Java IDEs available on the market today (see figure 8.2).

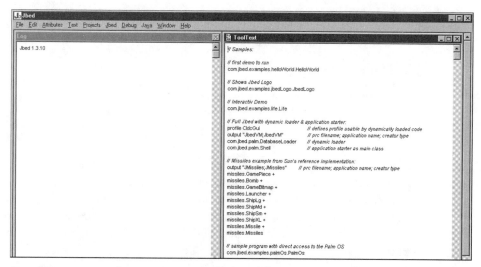

**Figure 8.2   Jbed, by esmertec Inc., provides an integrated development environment (IDE) for CLDC and KJava application development. Jbed has been integrated into use with the Palm OS Emulator (POSE) to test applications before deploying them to a Palm OS device.**

## 8.2.2   What is a Spotlet?

The base or central component of a KJava application is a Spotlet. `Spotlet` is the KJava class that provides application control and handles application events through a set of callback methods. While an application can be made up of several Spotlets, only one Spotlet can have "focus" at any one time. In other words, at any given instance in the K virtual machine, only one Spotlet can receive events that trigger its callback methods (see figure 8.3). This Spotlet is said to have the current focus. There will be more on this in the next chapter.

In order to create a simple KJava application, extend the `Spotlet` class and provide a static `main` method that serves as the application's startup method when

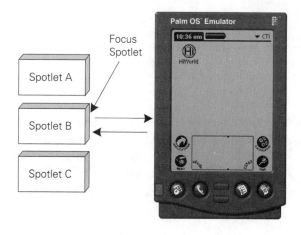

**Figure 8.3**
**A Spotlet is a KJava application. Only one Spotlet can have "focus" at any given time. When Spotlet has focus, as Spotlet B does in this picture, it is the only Spotlet getting and handling events from the Palm OS device.**

invoked by the virtual machine. Therefore, the simplest of all KJava applications might resemble the following program.

```
import com.sun.kjava.*;
public class VerySimpleApp extends Spotlet {
  public static void main(String[] args) {
    System.out.println("Hello very small world");
  }
}
```

To do something a little more exciting with the Spotlet, we need access to what is known as the graphics context. In KJava, and the corresponding KVM there is a single global `Graphics` context object. This object manages the display of all items on the screen, including text, geometric shapes, and user interface widgets. To get the `Graphics` context object, call the `getGraphics()` method on the KJava `Graphics` class. This is a static method and will always return the single global instance of the `Graphics` object. To draw anything to the display, use the various draw methods provided on the `Graphics` object. Actually, all the graphics methods are static methods on `Graphics` so we could draw to the display by just calling the draw methods on the `Graphics` class directly. So, to spice up our HiSmallWorld application a little bit, we call on the `Graphics` object to draw some text on the display.

**Listing 8.1   HiSmallWorld.java**

```
import com.sun.kjava.*;

public class HiSmallWorld extends Spotlet {

    private Graphics g = Graphics.getGraphics();

    public static void main(String[] args) {
        HiSmallWorld app = new HiSmallWorld();
    }

    public HiSmallWorld() {
        g.clearScreen();
        g.drawString("Hi Small World!", 45, 80);
    }
}
```

This is all the code we need for our first Spotlet. The next step is to compile the application.

### 8.2.3   Compiling HiSmallWorld

Compiling the HiSmallWorld application requires having access to the appropriate classes. Specifically, compiling requires both the CLDC and the KJava classes to be accessible to the Java development environment. If you have access to the KJava classes, then you can use the command line to compile the HiSmallWorld application. If KJava is part of your IDE, then you will need to compile through that IDE.

## Command line

Compiling the KJava application can be done with the standard `javac` compiler that comes with the J2SE environment. When using `javac`, remember to include the right base J2ME classes appropriate for J2ME development and to not use the base J2SE classes. As with MIDP development, this can be done by using the appropriate `-bootclasspath` option with `javac` to inform the compiler where J2ME classes can be found. The command line entry to compile the HiSmallWorld application would look like the following:

```
>javac -g:none -d . -bootclasspath %CLDCClasses% *.java
```

In this command line, it is assumed that the `CLDCClasses` environment variable has been set up to point to the CLDC and KJava classes and that the command is executed from inside the directory containing the HiSmallWorld.java file.

## Via IDE

Alternatively, most IDEs provide the means to compile the application. With an IDE, compiling is usually menu or button-triggered. However, depending on the IDE, some assistance is also required to indicate where the various classes and possibly the standard Java SDK (and compiler in particular) can be found. In Jbed, for example, a project is defined and the various classpath and bootclasspath property options must be established in the project's file. First, in order to quickly and simply create a project in Jbed and to edit its associated properties, a Projects menu with project action options is provided from the main menu bar of the IDE window (see figure 8.4).

To create the HiSmallWorld project, copy an existing Jbed example project and then edit the properties file to suit the new projects needs. Jbed comes with a set of example projects. We recommend copying the Palm Hello World project. This is accomplished by selecting the Copy Project option from the Projects menu of Jbed.

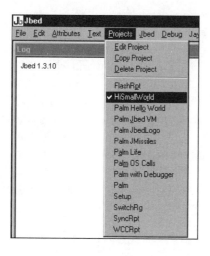

**Figure 8.4**
**Applications are organized by Project in Jbed. In this picture the HiSmallWorld project is currently active. Set up a new HiSmallWorld project in Jbed by copying an existing project such as Palm Hello World. Select the Palm Hello World project in the Projects menu and then select Copy Project from the same Projects menu.**

Select Palm Hello World from the project list and then select the Copy Project menu option. An editor should appear that allows you to create and modify the new project. In the Name field on the editor, enter the name of the new project to HiSmallWorld. Figure 8.5 depicts the project file in the editor with its various settings for the HiSmallWorld application.

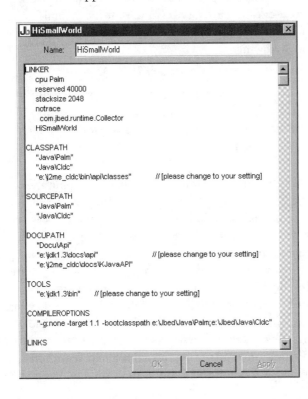

**Figure 8.5**
**After creating the HiSmallWorld project, add the application classes to the Linker section and update the various paths in Jbed Project editor, as depicted in this picture. In particular, make sure the required classes and source code directories are listed in the CLASSPATH and SOURCEPATH sections.**

We will discuss the project file editor in more detail later and in the next chapter. For now, there are just a few changes that we need to make. In the LINKER section of the editor are a number of properties as well as classes that are used to create the application. At the bottom of the list should be the HiSmallWorld class as depicted in figure 8.5.

Notice the area for making CLASSPATH and TOOLS settings. The Jbed IDE makes use of the installed Java SDK and J2ME CLDC on the development machine. The compiler is associated with the IDE through the TOOLS option. The local CLDC is referred to in the CLASSPATH option. Make sure settings in these parts of the properties file point appropriately to the J2ME CLDC and Java paths in your environment. After adjusting the settings, press the OK button to close the properties file editor.

With a project established, we can now enter the HiSmallWorld code as described above into a .java file through the Jbed's IDE file editor. Inside of Jbed, select the File menu and the New menu option, or press Ctrl+N (see figure 8.6).

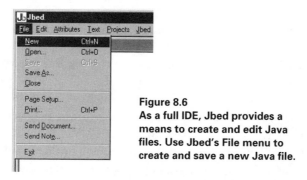

Figure 8.6
As a full IDE, Jbed provides a
means to create and edit Java
files. Use Jbed's File menu to
create and save a new Java file.

In the new file editor provided (probably labeled untitled1 if it is your first newly opened file), type in the HiSmallWorld code shown previously. Save the code in a file named HiSmallWorld.java. Save the code by selecting the Save or Save As... options in the File menu. By default installation, Jbed locates the code in the \Java\Palm directory within Jbed's directory structure. However, source code can be located anywhere by adding the project folder to the SOURCEPATH section of the Jbed project file.

After establishing the project with the appropriate settings and creating the HiSmallWorld.java file in the editor, compiling a .java file in Jbed is as easy as selecting the Compile option from the IDE's Java menu (see figure 8.7) with the target source code file open.

Figure 8.7
Once you have entered your Java
code in the file editor, you can use
Jbed's built-in Java compiler.
Jbed's Java file compiler can be
found under the Java option in
the menu bar.

This triggers the IDE to kick off javac with the appropriate parameters. With the right properties settings, the compile is able to accomplish the same task as when called upon directly by the developer via the command line, namely to create the byte code .class files. Instead, results of the compile operation will be displayed in the Log file.

## 8.2.4    Preverifying KJava applications

As with compiling, preverifying your KJava application will depend on the development environment. In fact, preverification may not be a required step in the development process with some IDEs and virtual machine environments.

### Preverify utility

As was discussed in development of MIDP applications, verification of class files is a standard part of the Java runtime environment. Again, verification is too much of a task for the limited resources of the target devices, namely a Palm OS or similar PDA device. Therefore, verification takes place both on and off the device. The part of the verification that occurs off the device is called preverification.

If you find or have a copy of an early CLDC release (prior to 1.0.2) that includes the KJava API along with the KVM virtual machine for the Palm OS, all class files are required to be preverified before they can be packaged and used by the virtual machine on the Palm device. Not unlike the preverifying that was demonstrated with the MIDP applications, this was accomplished with a preverify utility. The preverify utility verifies each class file and modifies it to include special flags indicating their validity. At runtime, the J2ME virtual machine checks these flags. If the flags were present and indicate a valid class file, the KVM assumes the class is OK to run. Without these flags the VM throws an exception and aborts the class loading process.

### No preverification required

As we will see in the next section, the application and virtual machine functionality may be in one or multiple application files. In some cases, the vendor assumes that application file(s) need no verification. For example, Jbed assumes the source is considered trusted and no verification is done.

Thus, while preverification is a step provided for in many J2ME development environments, some vendors do not make this a required step in application development.

## 8.2.5 Creating the Palm OS application

Java class files, as byte code files, are not deployed as they exist to be used by the KVM on a Palm OS system. Instead, to run an application on the Palm OS, the class files must be converted to a file form the Palm OS can utilize.

### What's a PRC (Palm Resource File)?

With the compiled application classes, we must perform one more step before our code is ready to deliver to the Palm OS device. Applications for Palm OS devices must be specially formatted. Any application for a Palm OS device is packed into something known as a Palm resource file. To get a Java application and the Java virtual machine (remember, the virtual machine is an application too) into this required form, they must be converted and loaded into a file that has a .PRC file extension. Depending on the virtual machine implementation, parts of an application may also reside in a Palm database file. Palm database files have a .PDB file extension. Along with general application data, PDB files may contain certain classes that can be loaded by the virtual machine.

There are two general means to converting the application and virtual machine into PRC and PDB files. The first involves having a virtual machine in PRC format and then converting our application into PRC and/or PDB files to be used by the virtual machine. The other is to compile the virtual machine functionality and the application to native machine code in a single PRC.

### Single PRC approach

Java programmers have become accustomed to writing applications that become byte codes, which then get deployed and run on a virtual machine. The benefits of this technology, that is to be able to write an application once and then run it anywhere, have become the anthem of the industry. However, this strategy does not produce the best performing application nor does it make the job of deployment easy given the number of files that must be loaded on the device. This last item can be especially important when the target platform is mobile and with only limited connectivity.

Jbed provides the means to deploy an application in a couple of different fashions. Along with the more traditional deployment of a virtual machine in one (or more) PRCs and classes loaded via other PDB or PRC files, they also provide the means to create a single PRC that contains both the virtual machine and the application's byte codes. In Jbed, the process of building the PRC file is called linking. Linking to a single file makes for a very convenient delivery mechanism, as only one PRC file is created and thus only one PRC file needs to be deployed onto the device.

### Generating the PRC file

To generate, or more appropriately "link," the application class files and virtual machine functionality into a PRC file, Jbed provides a menu driven utility that again uses the project properties file to do its job. From the IDE, the developer simply requests the tool to generate the PRC by selecting the appropriate project and then selecting to Link the project from the IDE's Java menu (see figure 8.8). Barring any errors in the link process, the IDE notifies the developer via the IDE Log that the PRC was successfully written to disk along with the size of the new PRC.

### Multiple PRC approach

When all is said and done, we have produced a HiSmallWorld PRC file ready for deployment to the Palm OS device that is approximately 32K in size. To contrast this

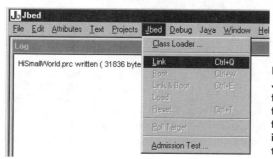

**Figure 8.8**
**Java class files and the virtual machine functionality are combined into a PRC file using Jbed's Linker. To link the class files and virtual machine functionality into a Jbed application, select Link from the Jbed menu options.**

approach, we develop a similar application using MIDP for Palm OS a little later in this chapter. In that example, creating the MIDP-over-Palm OS version of the HiSmallWorld application produces a single 4K PRC file containing just the application class files. Remember, however, class files need a virtual machine. The accompanying virtual machine, MIDP.PRC, required to run this version of the HiSmallWorld application is a whopping 586K. By linking the virtual machine and the application, only the bytes codes required are linked into the PRC. This has the effect of reducing the entire footprint of the application on the Palm device to over 1/10th of the multiple PRC application + virtual machine.

Of course, with a single PRC, if a future bug fix or enhancement is isolated to a single class file, we cannot send out a minute PRC file containing the new class and leave the virtual machine unchanged. In this case, we must replace the entire PRC. Furthermore, if we have more than one Java application running on the same device, we need to replicate some parts of the virtual machine functionality in each PRC.

### Application icon and name

Each application (PRC to be exact) that is deployed and run on a Palm OS device has an associated set of icons and application name. These are displayed on the PDA device screen and serve as the activating elements much like an icon is used to start an application on a Windows desktop system. In most cases, the icons and name associated with the Java application PRC are associated to the PRC at the time the application is converted to a PRC file.

There can be two icons associated with each application. Small and large icons represent the application when displayed in different application views that the Palm OS provides. The user of the device can either see the applications in a list view or in an iconic view. In an iconic view, the large icon and a short application name are displayed to represent each application. In a list view, the small icon and the full application name are displayed. For example, using Jbed's default icons, the HiSmallWorld application available on a Palm OS device would look similar to the pictures in figure 8.9.

**Figure 8.9**
**Applications, such as the HiSmall-World, can be displayed in either an application list or as a set of icons in the Palm OS. An application list is displayed on the device on the left. Applications listed by Icon are displayed on the device on the right.**

*CHAPTER 8   J2ME ON A PDA, A KJAVA INTRODUCTION*

Jbed provides a means to set both the displayed name and large icon. In order to set the icon of the application, first create an icon using your favorite drawing tool. The icon must be in Windows bitmap form and should not exceed 22×22 pixels in size. Icons up to 32×32 pixels will work, but the name of the application will display over the top of the bottom portion of the icon. Additionally, the icons are restricted to a one-bit color depth. In other words, the icons have only two colors: black and white. In some development environments, the developer can also provide the small icon. In these cases, the small icon must not exceed 9 pixels high and 15 pixels wide.

After creating a bitmap to be used as the large icon for an application, place the bitmap in the appropriate icon directory. For Jbed version 1.3, the icon is to be placed in either the Jbed home directory or Palm subdirectory within Jbed's home directory. Name the bitmap file the same as the anticipated PRC file but with a .bmp file extension. Now, when the application is linked, Jbed adds the bitmap to the PRC and associates the new bitmap with the application for display on the Palm device.

The name of the application can also be set through Jbed. As can be seen from figure 8.9, the name of our application, HiSmallWorld, is a bit too big for display in the icon list. The operating system truncates the name for display purposes and lists it as "HiSmallWo...". Therefore, to have an application that displays better in this listing, we shorten the displayed name of our HiSmallWorld application to "HiWorld." We set the name of the application by providing a setting in the LINKER section of the project properties file. Next to the output tag in the LINKER section, put the desired name of the application, in this case "HiWorld," as shown in figure 8.10.

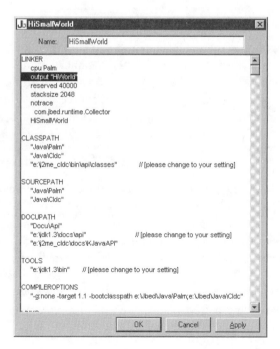

**Figure 8.10**
**The default name of an application is the name of the Spotlet class. To change the name of the application as it is displayed on the device, change the "output" name in the project properties editor as shown above. The new name of the HiSmallWorld Spotlet is HiWorld.**

Now when the application is linked, the new name and new large icon display (see figure 8.11) when the application is finally deployed to the device. If you get the error "wrong format in HiWorld.bmp" displayed in the Jbed Log when linking the application, check your bitmap image and make sure that it is no larger than 32×32 bits and that it has only 1 bit of color depth (i.e. black and white).

**Figure 8.11**
**The same HiSmallWorld application shown earlier is displayed here with new application name and icon.**

### 8.2.6    Running the application

Whew! So we have a Java application in the form of a PRC file ready to load onto our Palm OS device. Not so fast. Just as with the MIDP application developed in chapter 4, it is probably a good idea to test the application on an emulator first before we accidentally toast any device with our application. After successfully running the new application on the Palm Emulator, then it is safe to try to run the application on the actual device.

#### *Palm Emulator*

The Palm OS Emulator, known as the POSE, is available from Palm's Developer Site at the following address: http://www.palmos.com/dev.

The emulator and associated files come in ZIP file format. Simply unzip the contents of this file into a directory on your system. However, the emulator alone is not enough to test the application. The POSE emulates the Palm device hardware, but it requires something known as a ROM image to emulate the entire device environment. The ROM ("read only memory") image contains the Palm OS. A ROM image can be obtained either by downloading it from Palm's web site, or extracting it from a Palm OS device.

### ROM from the Palm web site

Obtaining a ROM image from Palm requires joining Palm's Alliance Program. To join this program, go to the Palm's Resource Pavilion at: http://www.palmos.com/alliance/resources.

Getting established as a member of the Alliance Program usually takes about a day. Once a member of this program, and if you are a developer located in the United States, you can obtain a ROM image directly from the Palm web site. Developers from outside the US are required to sign and return a license agreement before they are allowed to download ROM images.

The site has ROM images for the different types of devices and device features, such as color screens, as well as images that support debugging. Furthermore, there are ROM images for each of the various major and minor Palm OS releases. When downloading a ROM from the Palm site, be sure to obtain the ROM image for your target platform. Jbed supports Palm OS version 3.3 or greater operating on the Dragonball EZ and VZ processors. Palm V, Vx, and IIIx devices usually have this "EZ" processor.

After downloading the ROM image, save it in the POSE directory for the sake of convenience. When you launch the emulator for the first time, you are presented with several choice buttons (see figure 8.12). To start the emulator with the downloaded ROM image, select New to signify that you want to start a new emulator session.

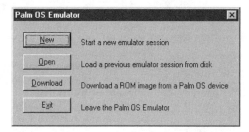

**Figure 8.12**
**When starting the Palm OS Emulator (POSE) on the development system for the first time, this window is displayed. The POSE remembers the ROM file, device type, skin, and RAM size of the last session. However, on the first invocation of the POSE, without a prior session, the user is left to press New and select the new session information.**

When starting a new emulator session, you are asked to pick the ROM image, device, skin, and RAM size for the device you are emulating as displayed in figure 8.13. Pick your recently downloaded ROM image and set the settings appropriate for your target device, and the emulator should display.

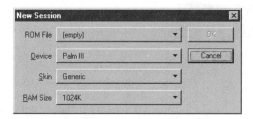

**Figure 8.13**
**On a new session, the ROM file and target device settings must be selected. Select the ROM file, device, skin and RAM size for the targeted device.**

If the emulator does not start or if an error message is displayed, check the new session settings to make sure that the settings are compatible with the actual device.

## ROM from your Palm

As an alternate approach (and recommended approach from esmertec) to downloading an image from Palm, if you have the target Palm OS device, you can extract its ROM image to your development computer. When you downloaded the POSE, a ROM transfer application came in the zip file. If you go into the directory where the POSE zip file contents were extracted, you will find a ROM Transfer.prc file. When run on the Palm OS device, this application allows the device to deliver the device's ROM image while it is cradled and connected to a computer. "Cradled" is the term used with many PDA devices to indicate when the device is physically connected to another computer usually by a cup or "cradlelike" looking attachment.

First, to transfer the "ROM Transfer.prc" to the Palm OS device, launch the Palm Desktop Software's Install tool that came with the device. Pick the correct user of the device and then push the Add... button on the tool (see figure 8.14).

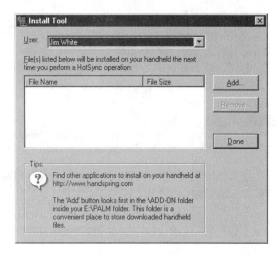

**Figure 8.14**
**The Palm Desktop Software Install Tool is used to select files, both applications and data, to add or remove from the Palm OS device. The applications and data listed in the center section of the Install Tool are transferred to the device on the next HotSync operation. Use this tool to move or "deploy" PRC files to the Palm OS device.**

From the file selection window that opens like that displayed in figure 8.15, browse to the directory containing the transfer PRC file, select the file and then press the Open button.

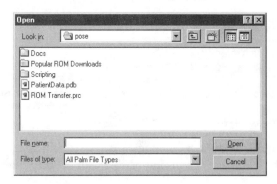

**Figure 8.15**
**This window is displayed when the Add... button is pressed on the Palm OS Desktop Install Tool (figure 8.14). Move the ROM Transfer.prc located in the POSE directory to the device by selecting the ROM Transfer.prc file and pressing the Open button.**

This act prepares the PRC file for delivery to the Palm OS device the next time the HotSync operation is performed (see figure 8.16). Exit the Install tool.

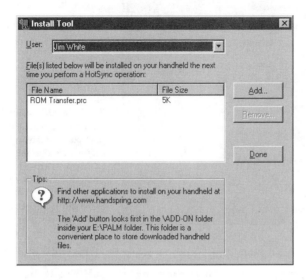

**Figure 8.16**
**The ROM Transfer.prc is shown here ready to be installed to the device via the Install Tool.**

To HotSync the device and install the transfer application to the device, place the device in the cradle and push the HotSync button. The HotSync button is the only button on the cradle for Palm devices. When the hot sync has finished and the PRC file has transferred successfully to the Palm OS device, run the ROM Transfer application on the device, with the device still cradled. On your computer, run the Emulator.exe and pick the Download option as depicted on figure 8.17 in order to receive the ROM.

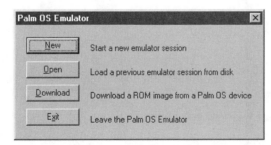

**Figure 8.17**
**After successfully deploying the ROM Transfer PRC to the Palm OS, run the application on the device with the device still cradled. This will cause the window above to be displayed on the desktop. Select Download on this window to receive the ROM image from the Palm OS device.**

A window appears providing instructions on how to transfer the ROM from the Palm OS device that is cradled. Make sure the emulator is listening to the appropriate COM port (the COM port to which the cradle for the device is attached) in the Transfer ROM window that is provided and then press the Begin button (see figure 8.18).

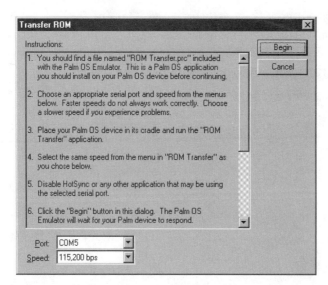

**Figure 8.18**
**The Palm OS device has a cradle that is attached to a particular desktop COM port. Make sure the appropriate COM port and speed are set in this window before attempting to transfer the device's ROM during execution of the ROM Transfer.prc application.**

On the actual Palm OS device, after selecting the ROM Transfer icon, push the Begin Transfer button to begin the process of transferring the ROM image to your computer (see figure 8.19). It takes about five minutes to transfer the file.

When the transfer is complete, save your ROM image under the POSE directory. Now the emulator environment is set up and we are ready to deploy the HiSmall-World application to the emulator for testing.

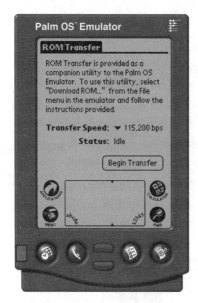

**Figure 8.19**
**When the desktop has been set up appropriately to receive the ROM image from the device via the cradle, push the Begin Transfer button, as seen in this picture, to send the ROM image of the device to the emulator on the computer.**

## Deploying and running HiSmallWorld on the POSE

Assuming the emulator already has a working ROM, deploying a PRC file to the emulator is very easy. First of all, you need to configure the emulator to work with PRC files generated by Jbed. The default emulator configuration settings cause the emulator to generate many warning messages when running Jbed PRCs. To disable these warning messages, find the Palm OS Emulator.ini file on your desktop. The file is most likely located in the Windows directory for Windows 98/2000 systems or in the Winnt director for WindowsNT systems. Open the Palm OS Emulator.ini in any text editor and change the following parameters to the values listed:

```
ReportHardwareRegisterAccess=0
ReportLowMemoryAccess=0
ReportStackAlmostOverflow=0
ReportStackOverflow=0
```

The details of configuring the emulator for Jbed files are available in the documentation from esmertec. You can also visit their web site at www.esmertec.com/pose for more information. After saving the configuration file with the modifications made, start the emulator and right click on the POSE screen. This displays a menu to appear over the emulator as depicted in figure 8.20.

**POSE ISSUE**  According to esmertec, an unresolved issue with Palm OS Emulator versions 3.2 and 3.3 does not allow Jbed-produced PRC files to run on it. Version 3.0a7 of the POSE will run these files without incident. As an alternative to running the old version of the emulator, esmertec provides a modified POSE on their web site at www.esmertec.com/POSE.

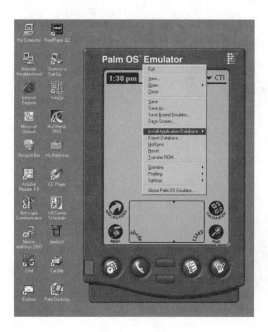

**Figure 8.20
Right-click anywhere on the emulator application to get the emulator's menu. This menu provides the options to load applications and databases among other options.**

Select the Install Application/Database menu option and pick the Other... option from the pursuing menu. Then simply pick the PRC file created by the development tool. In this case, browse to and select the HiWorld.prc file generated by Jbed and press the Open button as depicted in figure 8.25 to load the application to the Palm OS emulator.

**PALM OS CATEGORIES** Palm device's applications are organized into a series of "Categories." A category is analogous to a folder in a Windows system. The categories for any given Palm OS device are listed in the dropdown list located in the upper right-hand corner of the display (see figure 8.21). Tapping on this list displays all the categories.

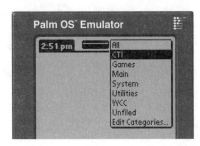

**Figure 8.21**
**A Palm device's applications are organized into a series of categories. The list of categories on a Palm OS device or emulator can be found by tapping on the arrow icon and current category name in the upper right-hand corner of the display. As seen in this picture, tapping on the icon/category name produces the Palm OS Categories List.**

When a category is selected, just the applications associated with that category have their icon and application name displayed on the screen. This serves as a convenient way to organize applications. There is also an "All" category that includes all the applications on the device.

To add a category to the set of categories on the device, select the Edit Categories... option at the bottom of the categories list. Categories can be added, renamed, or removed from this screen.

**Figure 8.22**
**Selecting the "Edit Categories..." option in the Categories List displays the Category Editor shown here. This display allows the user to add or remove a category or to rename an existing category.**

By default, when an application is first loaded onto the emulator or the actual device, it is associated with the "Unfiled" category. It can be assigned to a Palm OS or user defined category. An application that is not assigned a category will only display under the "Unfiled" and "All" category. To move the HiSmallWorld application to a different category, push the Menu button on the device and select the Category... menu option (see figure 8.23).

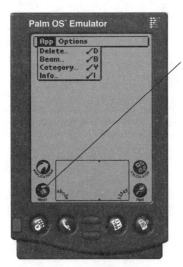

Menu button

**Figure 8.23**
**Push the Menu button, labeled in this picture, to activate the Application Menu in the Palm OS. This menu offers options to get information about an application or database, delete an application or database as well as an option to view/modify the applications assigned to any category through the Category editor. The Category... option opens the Category editor as seen in figure 8.24.**

From the Category screen that follows, the HiSmallWorld application (recall we changed the display name of the application to HiWorld which is what displays in the application listing) can be associated with a new category by finding the application and selecting its associated category from the dropdown list provided (figure 8.24).

**Figure 8.24**
**The category of any application, like HiSmallWorld, can be changed in the Category editor. Each application or database loaded on the device (or emulator) is displayed in a scrollable list. Next to each application is a dropdown list of categories. To change the category of an application, simply select another category from the dropdown list.**

Now whenever the category assigned to the application is selected from the Palm OS category list, the HiSmallWorld application icon is included in the display.

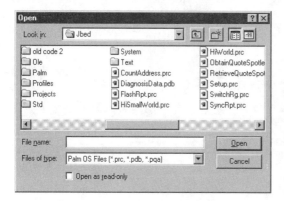

**Figure 8.25**
**After selecting the Install Application/Database option from the emulator menu (right-click on the emulator screen to display this menu), the Open dialog box shown here is displayed. In the Open dialog box, browse to the correct directory and select the PRC application to load onto the emulator.**

With the application successfully loaded to the emulator, find the HiWorld icon on the Palm desktop and tap on it. If the application has been compiled, converted (linked), and loaded correctly, the emulator's screen should look like the image shown in figure 8.26:

**Figure 8.26**
**The HiSmallWorld application running on the emulator after successfully compiling, linking and deploying the HiSmallWorld.prc file to the emulator and tapping on the HiSmallWorld application icon.**

In our Jbed example application, the virtual machine functionality and application are all in one PRC file. Don't forget to also load the virtual machine PRC(s) or other class files in a case where the application, auxiliary classes or virtual machine are located in multiple PRCs.

### Troubleshooting

If you have difficulty in getting your application running, here are a few items to check:

- If using Jbed or other IDE, make certain that the application compiled and linked successfully. Errors will be displayed in the Log window.

- If not using an IDE, make sure the application compiled successfully when you ran `javac` and certify that the preverify utility ran successfully without errors.

- The most notorious runtime problem in the Java environment is getting the `classpath` set properly so that the correct versions of classes are loaded, and loaded in the proper order. If you are using Jbed and classes cannot be found when compiling your application, check the CLASSPATH and CLASSPATH-OPTIONS setting in the Jbed Project properties editor.

- When using Jbed, if you attempt to link the application and get the following error: "no 'void main (String[])' present in com.jbed.runtime.Collector," check to ensure your application's classes are listed in the LINKER section of the project properties and that the class containing the main method (in this case HiSmallWorld Spotlet) is listed at the bottom of that list of classes.

- If you are able to successfully compile and deploy your application, but get a Palm OS Emulator error like "'Setup' (unknown version) has just written directly to low memory" when running the application in the Emulator, check the Palm OS Emulator settings in the Palm OS Emulator.ini file as specified in this section. This error will not manifest itself in the actual device, as the error results from certain emulator-only execution settings.

## 8.3  DEPLOYING TO THE ACTUAL DEVICE

With the application successfully tested on the POSE, we can deploy it to an actual Palm OS device with the relative assurance that it runs correctly and without adverse affects to the device. Deploying a Java application to the device is not unlike deploying any application to the device.

First, locate the Install Tool that came with the Palm Desktop Software. Start this application and select the user whose device is to receive the new HiSmallWorld application. Alternatively, you can start the Palm Desktop application and then press the Install button (see figure 8.27) located on the main window. This has the same effect as starting the Install Tool. Again, don't forget to select the appropriate user. If the Palm Desktop has never been used, you will have to set up a user or hot sync your Palm device with the desktop before proceeding to the next steps. See your Palm OS manual for guidelines on these operations.

Push the Add... button on the Install Tool and pick the application PRCs to load onto the Palm OS device. In this case, locate the HiSmallWorld application (HiWorld.prc) that should be located in the Jbed root directory. Remember to load all the application PRCs as well as the virtual machine PRCs depending on the struc-

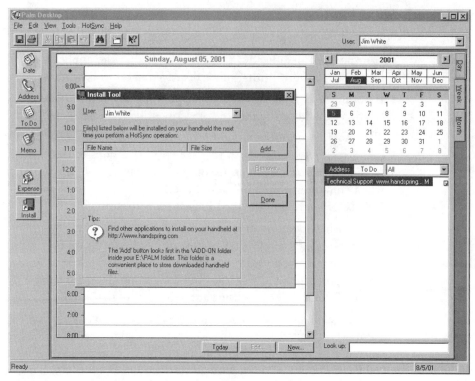

**Figure 8.27** **The Palm Desktop, along with the Install Tool, help coordinate and synchronize applications and data between the device and the desktop.**

ture and organization of the application. Also check that the VM functionality and application have been linked together. Press the Done button when finished adding the appropriate files (see figure 8.28).

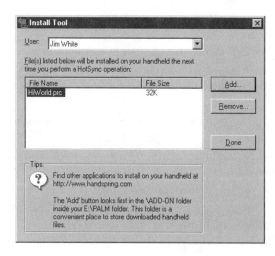

**Figure 8.28**
**The Install tool allows users to designate files to load onto the Palm OS devices during the next sync operation. To load a Java application created by Jbed onto the device, push the Add... button and select the PRC file to be installed.**

On the next HotSync operation, those PRCs, PDBs and other associated files will be loaded onto the device. HotSync is the operation of physically moving files from the desktop to the device and vice versa (the Palm OS device can be set up to be backed up with each HotSync operation). A HotSync occurs when the device is cradled and the HotSync button is pushed on the device cradle.

To run the application once deployed, simply tap on the HiWorld icon on the device. The results should be the same as when the application ran on the emulator. The application can also be placed in a category, as describe earlier, for more convenient locating on the device.

## 8.4  *HiSmallWorld revisited using MIDP for Palm OS*

As indicated earlier in this chapter, there are several options for developing Java applications for PDAs, and specifically Palm OS devices. Many of these solutions are not guided by J2ME specifications. Even KJava, which was born out of a need to demonstrate and test J2ME applications, is not a profile and is not guided by any part of the J2ME specification set.

Today, there is only one all-J2ME environment for developing and deploying a J2ME application for Palm OS PDA devices. This entails using the MIDP for Palm OS development environment. The MIDP Palm OS J2ME environment is the standard MIDP environment with the addition of an extra conversion tool and another implementation of the KVM that runs of the Palm OS device.

Is an all-J2ME application better than one that is not guided by the J2ME specifications? The advantage of having a set of specifications is in the isolation the specification gives to the developer. The developer of a J2ME application should be able to port his or her application to a variety of specification implementations without the need to rewrite the application. Remember, however, that MIDP was created for cell phones and pagers. The user interface of these types of devices is far more restrictive than the user interface on a device such as Palm OS device. Therefore, while guided by a specification, the MIDP for Palm OS may offer a rather limited GUI in comparison to other non-J2ME environments. The specification allows for potential implementation by several vendors. Thus, you, the developer, need to weigh portability against functionality.

To obtain the reference implementation of MIDP for Palm OS runtime environment, go to Sun's MIDP for the Palm OS web page at: http://java.sun.com/products/midp4palm.

The download provided from this site will not include either the base MIDP or CLDC environments required to build MIDP for Palm OS applications. These must be installed and available per instructions already covered in this and previous chapters. Download and unpack the MIDP for Palm OS files into a directory of your choice. Note that the distribution unpacks into a top-level directory named midp4palm1.0. It should be noted that esmertec, and a number of other tool and virtual machine providers also support MIDP and provide tools to build MIDP for Palm OS applications.

## 8.4.1    MIDP application code

In chapter 4, you were introduced to the MIDP through the HiSmallWorld Midlet. We are going to reuse the same MIDlet code here to demonstrate MIDP for Palm OS. Recall also, that for convenience, the following variables were set up to more easily compile and preverify the application.

```
MIDP=\midp-fcs
MIDPClasses=\midp-fcs\classes
MIDPTools=\midp-fcs\bin
```

Listing 8.2 once again lists the code for the MIDlet from chapter 4.

**Listing 8.2    HiSmallWorld MIDlet**

```java
import javax.microedition.midlet.MIDlet;
import javax.microedition.lcdui.*;

public class HiSmallWorld extends MIDlet {

 private TextBox textbox;
 public HiSmallWorld() {

  textbox = new TextBox("", "Hi Small World!", 20, 0);
 }

 public void startApp() {

  Display.getDisplay(this).setCurrent(textbox);
 }

 public void pauseApp() {
 }

 public void destroyApp(boolean unconditional) {
 }
}
```

As a refresher, to compile, preverify and JAR the application, run the following commands:

Compile

```
>javac -g:none -bootclasspath %MIDPClasses% HiSmallWorld.java
```

Preverify

```
>%MIDPTools%\preverify -classpath %MIDPClasses%;. HiSmallWorld
```

JAR

```
>jar cf hi.jar -C .\output HiSmallWorld.class
```

We will also need the descriptor (JAD) file similar to the file created in chapter 3. The contents of the HiSmallWorld.jad file should resemble the following:

```
MIDlet-Name: HiSmallWorldSuite
MIDlet-Version: 1.0.0
MIDlet-Vendor: Catapult Technologies, Inc.
MIDlet-Description: Sample Suite of Small World MIDlets
MIDlet-Info-URL: http://www.ctimn.com/
MIDlet-Jar-URL: hi.jar
MIDlet-Jar-Size: 3000
MicroEdition-Profile: MIDP-1.0
MicroEdition-Configuration: CLDC-1.0
MIDlet-1: Hello, , HiSmallWorld
```

Notice that in MIDP for Palm OS, we are required to preverify once again. Up to this point, not one line of code or development action differs from the development of the initial MIDP HiSmallWorld application developed in chapter 4.

## 8.4.2    Converting the JAR file to PRC

Recall in the development of the KJava HiSmallWorld application that it was necessary to convert the various byte code class files and the virtual machine into a form that could be used by the Palm OS device. The same step must occur here to convert the MIDP class or jar file into a PRC file that can be used by the device. The virtual machine would also need to be converted, but Sun, in its reference implementation, has already taken care of this step for us. The downloaded and unpacked files contained a MIDP.prc file. This is the virtual machine used by the Palm OS device to run the applications we develop. We will see how this and our MIDP for Palm OS HiSmallWorld application gets loaded to the device in a bit.

In order to convert the HiSmallWorld jar file into something the device can use, the MIDP for Palm OS reference implementation provides a converter tool. The converter tool is itself a Java application and requires the use of the Java Runtime Environment on your desktop to run. An environment variable, JAVA_PATH, is also required to be set in order for the converter tool to run. Set this appropriately to the Java SDK in your environment.

With the Java path set, the converter tool can now be run. You will find the converter tool, converter.bat, in the /Converter subdirectory off the /midp4palm1.0 directory. When you execute converter.bat, the converter tool user interface should display as shown in figure 8.29.

**Figure 8.29**
**The MIDP for Palm OS PRC Converter tool allows MIDP JAD/JAR files to be converted to Palm OS PRC files. Running converter.bat starts Sun's MIDP for the Palm OS Converter Tool. Use the File menu to locate and open a MIDlet Suite JAD file for conversion.**

From the File menu, select the Convert menu option and then select the JAD file describing the HiSmallWorld Midlet Suite, HiSmallWorld.jad. If everything is successful, results of the conversion should look similar to those pictured in figure 8.30. Then, the HiSmallWorld.prc is ready for deployment to the emulator and the Palm OS device.

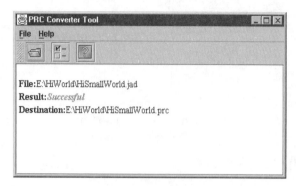

**Figure 8.30**
**Results of attempting to convert a MIDP JAR/JAD file to a PRC file are displayed in the text area of the Convert Tool window.**

## 8.4.3 Deploying the MIDP for Palm OS applications

Deploying the Midlet in HiSmallWorld.prc to either the POSE or the actual device is accomplished in the same manner as deploying any PRC file to the emulator or device. However, it is important to remember that the MIDP for the Palm OS PRC file will not run without the corresponding virtual machine. Therefore, remember to load both the application PRC as well as the MIDP.prc file if it is not already on the device. Because the MIDP virtual machine is a shared virtual machine, only the one VM (MIDP.prc) is required on each device to run any MIDP for Palm OS application. The MIDP.prc file can be found in the /PRCfiles subdirectory off the /midp4palm1.0 directory.

When successfully deployed, the MIDP virtual machine and HiSmallWorld MIDlet suite should look similar to the picture in figure 8.31. The MIDP for Palm OS virtual machine shows up under the name JavaHQ on the Palm OS device.

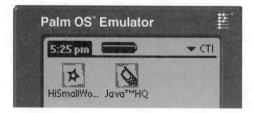

**Figure 8.31**
**Unlike the Jbed applications, MIDP for Palm OS applications requires an underlying virtual machine. The virtual machine is in a PRC file and can be loaded independently of the MIDlet Suite PRCs. In this picture, the HiSmallWorld MIDlet Suite and MIDP for Palm OS VM are depicted on the device.**

And does the application look and behave the same way as the HiSmallWorld Midlet on the cell phone or pager in chapter 4? As can be seen from figure 8.32, the behavior is the same, while the display is slightly different based on the implementation of TextBox for Palm devices. Consider too that the MIDP was initially designed for cell phones and pagers. This then is considered one of the shortcomings of the MIDP, that its capabilities are limited to the lowest common denominator, which in terms of display, are cell phones and pagers.

**Figure 8.32   Running the HiSmallWorld MIDlet on the Palm OS device results in similar behavior as seen in the HiSmallWorld Spotlet developed with Jbed earlier. However, the user interface does have a little different look (see figure 8.26 for comparison).**

## 8.5   SUMMARY

In this chapter, we explored some of the options available to Java and J2ME developers targeting PDA devices. Specifically, we have looked at two means to develop and deploy J2ME applications for the most popular PDA devices, those running Palm OS. KJava is a user interface and database API designed initially by Sun as a means to demonstrate and test the first CLDC and KVM implementations. The KJava API is not a J2ME Profile, but some vendors provide a supported implementation of this API for developing applications targeted for the Palm OS device. KJava offers a rich set of user interface and database capabilities to the CLDC for applications destined for Palm OS devices. In the next few chapters, we will explore the details of KJava in more detail. Specifically, we will examine KJava's user interface and the KJava Database class which wrappers the Palm OS database.

An alternate approach must be sought if one is looking for an all J2ME environment. Therefore, we felt it important to at least introduce you to the MIDP for Palm OS. MIDP for Palm OS is a fully supported J2ME environment, although somewhat limited, for developing and deploying J2ME applications to the Palm OS. While both of these environments might suffice for application development in the short term, the J2ME community awaits a fully supported and rich environment, namely the PDA Profile, for developing PDA applications.

# KJava user interface

In the last chapter we introduced the KJava API. Because there is not yet a PDA Profile to be used with PDA devices, J2ME developers today are left with the choice of using MIDP for Palm OS or the KJava API. In this chapter, the KJava user interface and event handling mechanisms are covered in more depth. While not a valid J2ME profile, this API does at least extend the J2ME's CLDC and offers a basic set of user interface components and graphical drawing tools that allow for custom widgets to be developed if required. One thing to consider is that both KJava and MIDP for Palm OS only address one type of PDA device, those handhelds running the Palm OS.

If you are already familiar with Java's Swing classes for developing stylish user interfaces in J2SE, you will probably not complain that KJava or any J2ME user interface API is too thorough an API. As you will see, KJava offers a very basic set of user interface components and a simple event handling mechanism. Nonetheless, it does offer a means to develop fairly sophisticated applications for the Palm OS device in Java. In particular, we hope to demonstrate some of its capabilities as we look to re-implement the tutorial application in KJava, starting with the user interface and event handling in this chapter.

So, in this chapter we will

- revisit Spotlet application control
- explore the user interface widget set
- look at Spotlet event handling
- implement the tutorial application control and user interface in KJava by:
  - developing the tutorial application control using KJava Spotlets.
  - implementing the tutorial application's user interface displays using the Graphics object and KJava widget set
  - developing the tutorial application's KJava event handling mechanism.

As we did in chapter 8, we use Jbed to develop the KJava applications demonstrated in this chapter.

## 9.1  KJAVA APPLICATION CONTROL

A Spotlet serves as the central, controlling object in a KJava application. Its main purpose is to listen to events and provide relevant event processing methods. In most applications, the `Spotlet` class is extended and this extending class usually houses the static `main` method that serves as the entry or startup point for a KJava application.

An application, however, can have multiple Spotlets, but only one Spotlet can have control to listen and react to events via event-handling methods at any given time. When a Spotlet is actively responding to events, it is said to have "focus." Focus is obtained and released by a Spotlet through the methods `register(int eventOptions)` and `unregister()`. When a Spotlet is to gain focus, the `register(int eventOptions)` method is called. The eventOptions parameter can be one of two Spotlet static int values: `NO_EVENT_OPTIONS` or `WANT_SYSTEM_KEYS`. `WANT_SYSTEM_KEYS` signifies that the Spotlet should be notified and intends to handle system key selections. System keys on a Palm OS device include the four hard buttons at the bottom of the device which trigger the Calendar, Address Book, To Do List and Memo applications, as well as the Home, Menu, Calculator and Find soft keys around the Graffiti area of the device (see figure 9.1). System keys also include the device's power button as well as the HotSync button (which is located on the device's cradle). When registered with `NO_EVENT_KEYS`, the application only captures and reacts to page up and down keys as well as Graffiti input.

**Figure 9.1**
**The Soft and Hard Keys on a Palm OS device allow for a user to quickly launch a Palm OS application such as the Calculator or Address Book. A Spotlet can be set up to be notified when one of these system keys is pushed.**

Because only one Spotlet is allowed to have focus at any one time, this method has the consequence of unregistering any Spotlet that currently has focus. Unregistering can be done explicitly with a call to `unregister()`.

A Spotlet has one non-event-related method, the `getFlashID()` method. This method, when called on an instance of a Spotlet, returns the Flash ID of the device. The Flash ID is the serial number of the device followed by a hyphen followed by the serial number checksum.

## 9.2 THE INVESTMENT QUOTE APPLICATION CONTROL IN KJAVA

As with the MIDP application, we will implement the investment quote application in KJava and the CLDC with two major application control elements in the form of Spotlets. Fulfilling the needs of the ObtainQuote use case from our tutorial design will be ObtainQuoteSpotlet. In general, this Spotlet controls the getting of investment price information from an outside source and storing it persistently in a Palm database. The other Spotlet, RetrieveQuoteSpotlet, guides a user through the process of retrieving and displaying historical prices.

Unlike MIDlets, Spotlets have no lifecycle methods or other abstract methods that must be overridden. However, since these Spotlets serve as the entry point for our applications on the device, they both require a static `main` method. We cover the user interface and event handling mechanisms of Spotlets a little later, so for now, in order to establish application control, our two applications are very simple.

Before we write the code, we need to set up our two Jbed projects, each of which will contain one of the two Spotlets. Just as was done in chapter 8, copy an existing project and edit the project's property file for the new project. To do this, select the Copy Project option in the Projects menu of Jbed. When installed, Jbed comes with some example projects and programs. You may want to take one of these existing simple projects, such as esmertec's Palm Hello World project to use as the template for your project. Select Palm Hello World from the project list and then select the Copy Project menu option (figure 9.2).

**Figure 9.2**
**In this chapter, we create two new applications; namely KJava Spotlet applications. To create a new project in Jbed, select an existing project, such as Palm Hello World from the Projects menu and then execute Copy Project in the same Projects menu.**

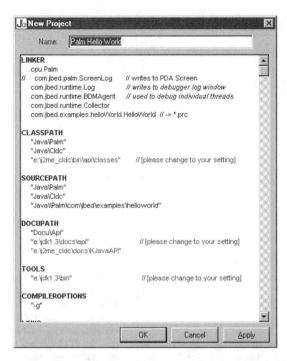

**Figure 9.3**
**After copying a project file, update the project name and LINKER options to include the project's classes. This is accomplished in the New Project editor shown here.**

On copying the project, the New Project editor displays as in figure 9.3.

Put the name of the project in the Name entry field at the top of the window. In the example shown in figure 9.4, the project is named ObtainQuote. Edit the LINKER, CLASSPATH, SOURCEPATH, TOOLS, COMPILEROPTIONS and LINKS options as required based on your installation and setup of Jbed, CLDC, and your application. However, we found it minimally necessary to do the following:

- add the classes of your project to the list of classes in LINKER section.
- modify the CLASSPATH section to find your J2ME CLDC API classes.
- modify the DOCUPATH section to refer to the JDK and J2ME docs as required. This is an optional step depending on your need for the help documents.
- modify the TOOLS section to point to the location of the binaries for the tools on your system. In particular, Jbed needs access to the JDK bin directory.

The last class in the LINKER class list must contain a `main()` method. As both the ObtainQuote and RetrieveQuote examples have only one class at this time, they necessarily must be at the bottom of this list. Your project should look something like the project depicted in figure 9.4 before you press the OK or Apply button and save the new project.

Use the copy process again to create the second project RetrieveQuote. At the bottom of the LINKER options, instead of putting the ObtainQuoteSpotlet, put the RetrieveQuoteSpotlet.

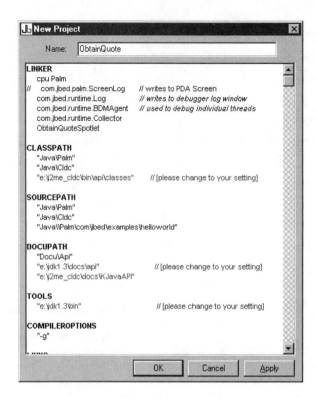

**Figure 9.4**
**The ObtainQuote Project should look similar to the project depicted here. The paths in the CLASSPATH, SOURCEPATH, TOOLS, and DOCUPATH areas may be different based on the location of files used by the application.**

With the projects created, we can now write the code that creates our two Spotlets. In the ObtainQuote project, open a new file. Inside of Jbed, select the File menu and then the New menu option. If you prefer to use short-cut key combinations, press Ctrl+N. (figure 9.5)

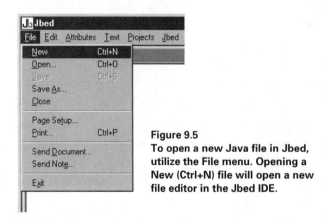

**Figure 9.5**
**To open a new Java file in Jbed, utilize the File menu. Opening a New (Ctrl+N) file will open a new file editor in the Jbed IDE.**

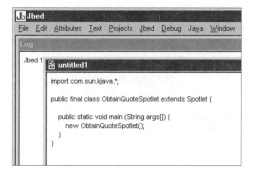

**Figure 9.6**
**Upon opening a New Java file, an "untitled1" editing window will open in the Jbed IDE. Enter the ObtainQuoteSpotlet code in the editor provided.**

In the new file editor provided (probably labeled untitled1 if it is your first new file — see figure 9.6), type the following code.

```java
import com.sun.kjava.*;

public class ObtainQuoteSpotlet extends Spotlet {

    public static void main (String args[]) {
        new ObtainQuoteSpotlet();
    }
}
```

Save the code in a file named ObtainQuoteSpotlet.java. Save the code by selecting the Save or Save As… options in the File menu. By default installation, Jbed locates the code in the \Java\Palm directory within Jbed's directory structure. However, source code can be located anywhere by adding the project folder to the SOURCEPATH section of the Jbed project properties file. So for example, if we had created a package, say com.ctimn.example for our Spotlet code, then the ObtainQuoteSpotlet.java will be stored in the directory \Java\Palm\com\ctimn\example\ObtainQuoteSpotlet.java.

To compile the program ObtainQuoteSpotlet.java and insure the code was entered correctly, either select the Java menu and pick the Compile option or press Ctrl+L.

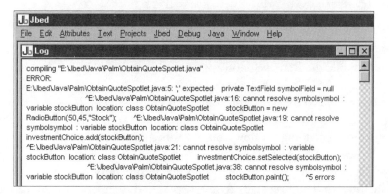

**Figure 9.7    After entering and saving the Java program in the text editor, compile the application by selecting the Compile option from the Java menu of the IDE. Compiler errors, if you have any in your Java files associated with the project, are displayed in Jbed's Log window.**

If you have errors in your code, they will be depicted in the log window. (figure 9.7) When you have successfully compiled, Jbed prints "ok" in the lower left-hand corner of the IDE's window.

At this time, there is no other code or files to our application, so we can link it. To link the ObtainQuote project, select the Jbed menu option from the Jbed menu bar and select the Link option (or press Ctrl+Q). When finished with either a compile or link operation, it's a good idea to check the Log window. If this is not displayed in Jbed, open it by selecting the Open Log option in the Java menu. If successful in compiling and linking the ObtainQuoteSpotlet file and project respectively, the results in the Jbed log should look similar to those depicted in figure 9.8.

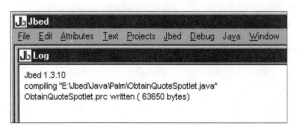

**Figure 9.8   Use the Link menu option in the Jbed menu to create the PRC that can be deployed to Palm OS devices. Results of compiling and linking activity also get displayed in the Log window. On a successful link operation, the size of the PRC file is displayed with the indication that the link is complete and the file was written.**

After completing the development of the ObtainQuoteSpotlet, take similar actions to create the RetrieveQuote application. To start, open the RetrieveQuote project and open another new file. In this file, enter the RetrieveQuoteSpotlet code.

```
import com.sun.kjava.*;

public class RetrieveQuoteSpotlet extends Spotlet {

    public static void main (String args[]) {
        new RetrieveQuoteSpotlet();
    }
}
```

Save and compile the RetrieveQuoteSpotlet and then link the RetrieveQuote project as was done for the ObtainQuote case.

Having completed the successful compiling and linking of the projects, take a peek at the Jbed directory on your system. You should see two new .PRC files in this directory structure (depending on how you have Jbed configured, the PRC files may be deposited elsewhere on your hard drive. See the Jbed documentation for more information). The PRC files are the application files destined for our device.

Ordinarily, we would get ready to test, deploy and run these PRC files on the emulator and subsequently on the actual application. However, with no interface or action occurring in our Spotlets to this point, we will save this exercise for a little later.

CHAPTER 9   *KJAVA USER INTERFACE*

## 9.3 KJAVA USER INTERFACE

As Dickens wrote in A Tale of Two Cities, "it was the best of times, it was the worst of times." This line could be used to describe developing user interfaces on resource-constrained platforms. The good news is that the API is usually small compared to other GUI APIs and so it is easy to learn. The bad news is that developers are constantly challenged as to how to put together an aesthetically pleasing and user-friendly application with such a small set of user interface components.

The screen size and capabilities of many PDA platforms is very limited. The Palm device is limited to 160 pixels in height and width. While PDAs with color screens are showing up on the market, the predominant display is still only 1-bit color.

Those familiar with the Java Swing set or its predecessor, the Abstract Windows Toolkit (AWT), should prepare to be disappointed and left wanting for a richer set of GUI components when looking at J2ME application development, and KJava is no exception. In the next sections, we explore the user interface environment and widget set provided by KJava. It is limited and in many cases you may need to extend the GUI to meet your application needs. In chapter 11, we explore some design ideas and issues to think about when developing your applications. Furthermore, third party vendors are starting to provide add-in components to augment the CLDC and other J2ME environments. These are discussed in chapter 15. One such group, the kAWT Project, has developed a lightweight GUI environment that runs on top of the CLDC that is similar to the AWT called the kAWT.

### 9.3.1 Drawing to the display with the graphics object

While there are no explicit low-level and high-level GUI APIs in KJava as there are in MIDP, the `Graphics` class can be thought of as the means to provide the low-level drawing to the screen. The `Graphics` class has a host of static methods to draw geographical shapes and bitmaps to the screen, but it also has a method to play sound if the device hosting the application is equipped with audio capability.

While the methods on the `Graphics` class are static, there is in fact, a single `Graphics` object in the system at any one time. This single object can be obtained with a `getGraphics()` method call on the `Graphics` class. Calls to display to the screen can then be made either of the instance or the class in general.

Interestingly, the `Graphics` object controls drawing not only to the screen, but can also draw to a virtual "off screen" area. This is a convenient feature for storing bitmaps temporarily, especially in graphically intensive applications such as games.

All geometric drawing methods in the `Graphics` object make use of a coordinate system. The coordinate system starts in the upper left-hand corner of the device's display as the coordinate (0, 0) with x/y values increasing from left to right and top to bottom.

The first graphical user interface operation usually performed in most applications is clearing the screen. This operation rids the display of any splash screen or leftover application image and is performed with a call to the `clearScreen()` method on the `Graphics` object.

## Drawing

Several drawing methods are provided to put geographical shapes on the display. The drawLine(int srcX, int srcY, int dstX, int dstY, int mode) and drawRectangle(int left, int top, int width, int height, int mode, int cornerDiam) methods provide the means to draw a line or rectangle based on the given coordinate starting point. In the case of drawLine(), the method is also passed the coordinate of the end point, whereas the drawRectangle() method is passed the width and height (in pixels) of the rectangle. The mode in both methods refers to one of four drawing modes provided through the Graphics class. The public static drawing mode options are PLAIN, GRAY, ERASE or INVERT. The display modes may manifest themselves slightly differently based on implementation as well as by what is being displayed. For example, the code snippet below results in the image displayed in figure 9.9. Finally, the last argument passed to drawRectangle() is the diameter. This parameter specifies the diameter, in pixels, of the imaginary circles used to form the rounded corners on each of the four corners of a rectangle. If rounded corners are not desired, simply pass zero into the method in the cornerDiam position.

```
Graphics g = Graphics.getGraphics();
g.drawString("PLAIN",75,10,Graphics.PLAIN);
g.drawRectangle(10,10,50,30,Graphics.PLAIN,0);
g.drawRectangle(0,45,160,40,Graphics.PLAIN,0);
g.drawString("ERASE",75, 50,Graphics.ERASE);
g.drawRectangle(10,50,50,30,Graphics.ERASE,0);
g.drawString("GRAY",75, 90,Graphics.GRAY);
g.drawRectangle(10,90,50,30,Graphics.GRAY,0);
g.drawString("INVERT",75, 130,Graphics.INVERT);
g.drawRectangle(10,130,50,30,Graphics.INVERT,0);
```

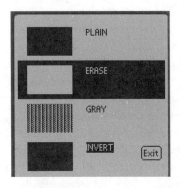

**Figure 9.9**
**This display shows the various PLAIN, ERASE, GRAY and INVERT Graphics modes for shapes and text. The top rectangle and text are done in PLAIN mode. The second rectangle and "Erase" text were drawn in ERASE mode on top of a PLAIN rectangle to provide the contrast. The final two rectangle/text combinations are drawn in GRAY and INVERT modes respectively.**

Along with methods to draw rectangles and lines, as can be seen from the code in the last example, text can also be drawn to the screen. Two drawString() methods allow for text strings to be displayed on the screen. Both require the string to be displayed along with coordinates of the top left bound of the first character in the string. The methods differ in that the drawString(java.lang.String text, int left, int top, int mode) method allows the developer to specify the mode parameter, which again refers to a choice in Graphics mode (PLAIN, GRAY, ERASE or INVERT). Both drawString() methods also return the same integer value, which is the x coordinate of the right bound of last character drawn. This can be helpful in determining where additional items can safely be placed on the screen display without appearing to be drawn over the top of the text. Two graphics helper methods are also provided to assist in displaying strings on the screen. The getHeight (java.lang.String s) and getWidth(java.lang.String s) methods can be used to determine the height and width, in pixels, for any given string displayed.

The graphic's drawBorder(int left, int top, int width, int height, int mode, int frameType) method works similar to drawRectangle(), but the developer must specify the frame type rather than the diameter for rounding the corners. The Graphics class provides two "out-of-the-box" frame types, namely SIMPLE and RAISED. However, a frame type can also be constructed with a call to the borderType() method on the Graphics object. The borderType() method builds new borders or frames given three pieces of information:

- the corner diameter (such as that specified on a rectangle)
- the width of the border shadow
- the width of the border itself.

The maximum corner diameter for a new borderType is 38, and the width of both the shadow and border can be no more than 3 pixels. Examples of borders drawn using standard and custom border types are displayed in figure 9.10, and the drawing code is shown below.

```
g.drawString("SIMPLE",75,10,Graphics.PLAIN);
g.drawBorder(10,10,50,30,Graphics.PLAIN, Graphics.SIMPLE);
g.drawString("RAISED",75, 50, Graphics.PLAIN);
g.drawBorder(10,50,50,30,Graphics.PLAIN, Graphics.RAISED);
g.drawString("Custom",75, 90,Graphics.GRAY);
g.drawBorder(10,90,50,30,Graphics.PLAIN,Graphics.borderType(2,3,3));
```

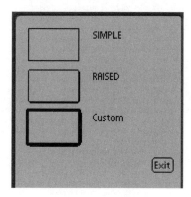

**Figure 9.10**
**Various borders can be displayed using available or newly constructed frame types. In the examples provided here, the top rectangle is drawn using drawBorder and the SIMPLE frame type, and the second rectangle is drawn with a RAISED frame type. The final border drawn is done with a custom border type using a 2-pixel diameter for the rounded corners, a 3-pixel wide border and 3 pixels for the shading on the lower and right side**

## Bitmaps

Bitmaps are drawn on the screen with the help of the drawBitmap(int left, int top, Bitmap bitmap) method sent to the Graphics object. Putting bitmaps on the display with KJava is a little trickier than displaying images or bitmaps in other Java environments. It requires a position or point on the screen to which to anchor the bitmap and it requires the bitmap itself. The first parameters to this method make up the upper left-hand coordinate or anchor point for where the bitmap is to be placed on the screen. The bitmap parameter is an instance of a wrappering class that represents the image to be displayed.

Unlike standard Java systems, the idea of a file system from which an image file can be grabbed and used by an application on a J2ME device may or may not exist. Therefore, the tricky part to using images, like bitmaps, in many of the consumer electronic and embedded devices is to first get the image into a format that can be used by the application. In KJava, bitmap data must be in the format of an array. Specifically, KJava provides a Bitmap class that is a byte array wrapper representing a bitmap in the Palm OS. Each byte of a bitmap's byte array represents 8 bits of the monochrome bitmap image (0 bit indicating that the pixel for that bit is on, 1 bit indicating the pixel is off). One provision stipulated on bitmaps is that the width (specified in bytes) of the bitmap must be even, and in the case where it is not, the bitmap is padded when displayed.

To create a Bitmap object, the width and bitmap's byte array must be passed to the constructor. The following code creates a small bitmap representing the states of California and Nevada. The image is displayed on the Palm OS screen in figure 9.11. An alternate bitmap constructor is available that allows the developer to create a Bitmap object using an array of shorts.

```
Bitmap caNV = new Bitmap((short)4, new byte[] {
    // File canv.bmp;  size: 32x32
        0,    0,    0,    0,   31,   -1,   -1,  -16,
       16,    4,    0,   16,   16,    4,    0,   16,
       16,    4,    0,   16,   16,    4,    0,   16,
       16,    4,    0,   16,   24,    4,    0,   16,
        8,    4,    0,   16,    8,    4,    0,   16,
        8,    6,    0,   16,   12,    7,    0,   16,
        6,    3, -128,   16,    3,  -64,  -64,   16,
        3, -128,   96,   16,    1, -128,   48,   16,
        1, -128,   24,   16,    0,  -64,   12,   16,
        0,  -64,    6,   48,    0,  -64,    1,  -80,
        0,   32,    1,   96,    0,   48,    0,  -32,
        0,   16,    0,   32,    0,   16,    0,   32,
        0,   30,    0,   48,    0,   15, -128,   32,
        0,    4,   96,   32,    0,    0,  -48,   96,
        0,    0, -112,   96,    0,    0,   95,  -32,
        0,    0,    0,    0,    0,    0,    0,    0
});
```

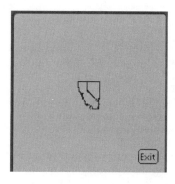

**Figure 9.11**
**In KJava, bitmaps are stored in byte arrays. This example shows the outline borders of Nevada and California depicted in a 32x32 Bitmap image converted to a byte array displayed on a Palm device.**

To draw the Bitmap object on the screen, simply call on the `drawBitmap()` method with the desired anchor coordinate position for the bitmap (the coordinate location for the upper left-hand corner of the bitmap) and the bitmap, which in this case is referenced by the `caNV` variable.

```
Graphics.drawBitmap(64,64,caNV);
```

Other than constructors, the only bitmap methods are to get a `Bitmap` object's width (in bytes) and number of rows. In the example provided previously, both the width and number of rows is 32.

### Region drawing

The `Graphics` object not only contains methods for drawing strings, shapes, bitmaps, and so forth to the screen, but it also has methods to define regions of the screen which can be copied or established as "no-draw zones" on the screen. In fact, there are actually two screens that the `Graphics` object controls. Up to this point, we have discussed methods for drawing "on screen." That is, all the display has occurred on the user-visible screen. The `Graphics` object is also in control of a virtual screen, the "off screen" area that is as big as the "on screen" area. Defined areas or regions of the "on screen" display can be copied to the "off screen" display for temporary storage. This allows image information to be quickly shuffled on and off the visible display.

A region is simply defined as a rectangular area of a screen; whether virtual—i.e. "off screen", or real—that is, "on screen." It can be used to copy a portion of the display from one area to another. In the case of the real display, it can be used to prevent drawing outside of that region. To define a region of the screen for drawing (and thus at the same time define an area prohibiting display outside of that region), use the `setDrawRegion(int left, int top, int width, int height)` method. While this method is called on the `Graphics` object, it has a global effect and prohibits other controls from displaying outside of the draw region. For example, the code section immediately following establishes a drawing region around the bitmap and exit button from the previous example. Notice how both the bitmap and exit button have been clipped in figure 9.12.

```
exitButton = new Button("Exit",135,135);
g.setDrawRegion(72, 68, 80, 80);
g.drawBitmap(64,64,caNV);
```

The draw region can be removed and the entire screen used as the drawing region by calling the resetDrawRegion() method.

Two methods are provided for copying regions of the display. The copyRegion (int left, int top, int width, int height, int dstX, int dstY, int mode) method copies one visible "on screen" region of the display to another "on screen" region of the display. The left, top, width and height parameters define the anchor coordinate, width, and height of the copied region. The dstX/dstY parameters define the destination anchor point on the screen where the copied region is to be drawn. Along with copied region and destination point of the copied region, a copy mode can be specified, which allows one to specify how the region is copied to its destination point. The copy modes are defined as static integers on the Graphics class and include OVERWRITE, AND, AND_NOT, XOR, OR, INVERT.

A region can simply overwrite whatever material was displayed previously, or logical bit operations can be used to create a display made up of bits of both the new region and existing region. Passing Graphics.AND as the mode, for example, causes the display bits from the copy-from region to be logically AND'ed with the display bits from the copy-to region. Alternately, the mode can be set to INVERT, in which case the copied region overwrites the display in the destination area, but in an inverted or reverse display fashion.

The second region copying method, copyOffScreenRegion(int left, int top, int width, int height, int dstX, int dstY, int mode, int srcWind, int dstWind), provides the capability to copy a region of the display to or from the "off screen" area. The on and off screen areas are designated through two Graphics static integers, ON_SCREEN_WINDOW and OFF_SCREEN_WINDOW. Either of these two integers can be passed as the last argument to the copyOffScreenRegion() method where they can designate either the origination and/or the destination of the region of the screen to be copied. Otherwise, the copying of regions is performed as with the copyRegion() method.

**Figure 9.12**
**Establishing a draw region can serve to clip the display. In this example, the same California/Nevada bitmap and Exit button are displayed from figure 9.11, but within a draw region. Notice that both the bitmap and button are clipped because the draw region's size is smaller than the total screen area covered by the bitmap and button items.**

## 9.3.2 Components

Unlike in many other Java user interface packages such as `javax.Swing`, `java.awt`, or even in the MIDP's `javax.microedition.lcdui`, there is no common user interface descendent from which KJava user interface widgets derive. However, many of the widgets do share similar methods. Those familiar with the standard Java user interface APIs will also find that KJava's user interface is pretty limited. However, with some work, some KJava widgets can be used in combination with each other or can be wrappered by your own code to provide more interesting and useful widgets, ultimately producing more useful interfaces.

In KJava user interface development, it is important to remember that there is no layout manager or other sophisticated display manager. Control of the location and display of widgets (or any item displayed to the screen such as a rectangle, line, or border shown throughout section 9.3.1) is at the discretion of the programmer. Therefore, if two user interface widgets are painted in too close proximity to each other, or on top of one another, the virtual machine and underlying operating system will do its best to display the items, which often times results in one widget overwriting the other.

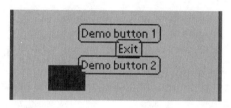

**Figure 9.13**
**Ugly overwrites of graphical elements and components can result without careful UI planning/ design as is demonstrated in this display where buttons and drawn shapes overlap.**

The following is a list of the interactive graphical elements available in the KJava user interface API:

- `Button`    a labeled button that can be used to trigger action when pressed. The label for the button can either be textual or a bitmap.

- `Caret`    the marker, designated by a blinking bar ("|") to indicate to the user the current insertion point in a text entry field. Namely, in KJava, a `Caret` object indicates the insertion point for text being entered in a `TextField`.

- `CheckBox`    a graphical component that signifies one of two states: either checked which is on/true, or unchecked which is off/false. A `CheckBox` can also be labeled.

- `RadioButton`    a two-state component such as the `CheckBox` except that a `RadioButton` object is part of a group of radio buttons, of which only one of the buttons can be in the on state at any one time. Like `CheckBoxes`, `Radio-Buttons` can be labeled.

- `RadioButtonGroup`    a collection of `RadioButtons` where exactly one `RadioButton` in the group can be in the "on" state at any given time. Pushing any `RadioButton` within the group has the effect of setting its state to "on" as well as setting the states of the other buttons to "off."

- `SelectScrollTextBox`  this extension of the `ScrollTextBox` and `TextBox` allows non-editable but selectable text to be shown on the display.

- `Slider`  a graphical user interface component that allows a user to select a value by moving a virtual lever on the component inside of a certain interval.

- `ScrollTextBox`  a means to display non-editable text on the screen. The `ScrollTextBox` is a subclass of `TextBox` and it provides for a scroll bar so that if the text to be displayed is larger than the visible text box, the user can scroll to see the remaining text displayed within the box.

- `TextBox`  a means to display non-editable text on the screen. A `TextBox` displays without a scroll bar. When too much text is displayed in a `TextBox`, the text is simply not displayed or available. In this case, it is often better to use the `ScrollTextBox`.

- `TextField`  the means for users to enter text in a single line entry field. An instance of the `Caret` class must be used in conjunction with the `TextField` in order to have an input marker provided while the user is inputting text into the `TextField`. TextFields can also be labeled.

**TEXT ENTRY ON PDAS**

Most PDA devices do not come equipped with a physical keyboard or keypad like that on cell phones. Some manufactures are starting to provide these input devices as add-on products. Without a keyboard, most PDA devices are equipped with either a virtual keyboard or a device that interprets input from a stylus moving across a sensitive surface.

A virtual keyboard is a graphical user interface display component that allows users to type out text by pushing buttons on the user interface. The component is made to look like a real keyboard so that users are comfortable with the paradigm. A virtual keyboard is displayed when a text entry field is entered. Virtual keyboards are used in Windows CE.

Palm OS devices, however, use the alternative stylus/motion detection type device. These devices have something known as Graffiti. Moving the Palm device's stylus across the pad (known as the Graffiti writing area) located on the bottom of the device's screen triggers characters or numbers to be generated and sent to the corresponding application. Graffiti is used to enter text in a text field. Certain motions of the stylus across the Graffiti area generate certain characters. If you are unfamiliar with what Graffiti is and how to use it, we would encourage you to see the Palm OS web site (www.palmos.com) for more information before developing your application targeted for these devices. (Figure 9.14)

**Figure 9.14**
The Graffiti Area is located at the bottom of the Palm OS screen. The left side of the Graffiti Area is used for entering characters. The right side is for entering numbers. In either case, one must be familiar with the Graffiti shorthand in order to enter information.

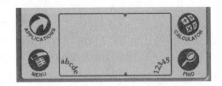

Graffiti text entry can be a little tough to use at first because one has to learn the Graffiti shorthand for characters. If you need help when entering text and you want to see the Graffiti shorthand, place the device stylus on the bottom of the screen and slide it up the entire length of the Palm device screen, keeping the stylus in contact with the screen during the motion. This will cause the Graffiti help to be displayed. When done with the help, simply press the Done button and return to your application. (figure 9.15)

**Figure 9.15**
**Graffiti help like this is displayed when the stylus is dragged from bottom to top on the device screen. The help shows how to enter the various characters and numbers by providing an indication of where the stylus must be started and how to drag it across the Graffiti Area to get the desired input.**

The typical Palm OS device also offers virtual keyboards for entering alphanumeric characters. The virtual keyboards are available by touching the small "abcde" and "12345" areas in the Graffiti area of the device. However, this feature is not yet supported in KJava.

---

• ValueSelector  unique to KJava, the ValueSelector allows users to specify an integer value with the use of increment and decrement buttons (see figure 9.16). The increment and decrement buttons are labeled with "+" and " – " labels respectively. A third button is also provided, labeled with a "?", which generates a random value between the minimum and maximum values allowed for the selector.

**Figure 9.16**
**A ValueSelector allows for integer value entry. In the figure displayed above, the Value Selector has a label of Score and a current value of 1. The "-" and "+" buttons will increment and decrement the value respectively. The "?" button, when pushed, sets the value to a randomly assigned value.**

In order to demonstrate how these components appear and behave within a device, a small Spotlet example has been provided in listing 9.1. While simple in nature, this mock employee information form demonstrates how to create and set up many of the widgets listed previously. The results of successfully compiling and linking this application are depicted in figure 9.17 on page 236.

Listing 9.1   Widgets.java

```
import com.sun.kjava.*;

public class Widgets extends Spotlet {

    Graphics g = Graphics.getGraphics();

    private Button exitButton;                              ❶
    private CheckBox employedBox;
    private boolean cbState = false;
    private RadioGroup genderGroup;
    private RadioButton mButton;
    private RadioButton fButton;
    private ScrollTextBox performanceBox;
    private TextField ageField;
    private Slider salSlider;
    private ValueSelector kidsValSelect;

    public static void main (String args[]) {
        new Widgets().drawWidgets();
    }

    private void drawWidgets() {
        register(NO_EVENT_OPTIONS);
        g.clearScreen();
        g.drawString(" Simple Widgets Example ", 5, 10, g.INVERT);
        //example check box
        employedBox = new CheckBox(10, 25, "Employed");    ❷
        employedBox.paint();
        //example radio button and radio button  group
        mButton = new RadioButton(10, 40, "Male");
        fButton = new RadioButton(50, 40, "Female");       ❸
        genderGroup = new RadioGroup(2);
      ' genderGroup.add(mButton);
        genderGroup.add(fButton);
        genderGroup.setSelected(mButton);
        mButton.paint();
        fButton.paint();
        //example scroll text box
        performanceBox = new ScrollTextBox("No record of missed work.  ❹
        Meets or exceeds on all performance reviews.", 10, 55, 140, 25);
        performanceBox.paint();
        //example text field
        ageField = new TextField("Age", 10, 85, 50, 20);   ❺
        ageField.paint();
        //example slider
        g.drawString("Salary Level: ",10,105);
        salSlider = new Slider(90, 105, 50, 1, 5, 1);       ❻
        salSlider.paint();
        //example value selector
        kidsValSelect = new ValueSelector("Kids: ", 1, 5, 1, 10, 125);  ❼
        kidsValSelect.paint();
        exitButton = new Button("Exit", 10, 140);           ❽
        exitButton.paint();
    }
}
```

```
public void penDown(int x, int y) {
    if (exitButton.pressed(x,y)) {
            System.exit(0);
    } else if (employedBox.pressed(x,y)) {
        employedBox.handlePenDown(x,y);
    } else if (mButton.pressed(x, y)) {
        genderGroup.setSelected(mButton);
    } else if (fButton.pressed(x, y)) {
        genderGroup.setSelected(fButton);
    } else if (performanceBox.contains(x,y)) {
        performanceBox.handlePenDown(x,y);
    } else if (ageField.pressed(x,y)) {
        ageField.setFocus();
    } else if (salSlider.contains(x,y)) {
        salSlider.handlePenDown(x,y);
    } else if (kidsValSelect.pressed(x,y)) {
    }
}

public void keyDown(int keyCode) {
    if (ageField.hasFocus()) {
        ageField.handleKeyDown(keyCode);
    }
}
}
```

❾

❶ Declaring the various graphical user interface elements

❷ Creating and displaying a CheckBox

❸ Creating and displaying a set of RadioButtons and RadioGroup

❹ Creating and displaying a ScrollTextBox

❺ Creating and displaying a TextField

❻ Creating and displaying a Slider

❼ Creating and displaying a ValueSelector

❽ Creating and displaying a Button

❾ Handling user interface events (covered later in this chapter)

Notice that with most graphical user interface components, the component must be created and then "painted" to the display. A common error when creating a user interface in KJava is to create a user interface object, but then forget to have it displayed with a call to the paint() method. You may also notice that KJava does not provide any type of display or layout management. This is reflected in how a pixel coordinate location must be provided to each component, usually through its constructor, before it can be displayed. Most of the components also are equipped with a setLocation(int x, int y) method for relocating the items. Again, you the

**Figure 9.17**
KJava offers a variety of user interface components/ widgets, many of which are shown in this display. More sophisticated user interface components can often be created out of combining these items into your own new component.

developer, must manage the display and make sure that widgets or other graphical drawing are not displayed on top of each other.

Most components or widgets have only a few operations. All of the components have a method for displaying themselves. Usually this is the `paint()` method. This method is important since a Spotlet does not have a means to refresh or redraw its display. Instead, the developer must explicitly call this method each time a component needs to be seen.

Besides the `paint()` method, most graphical user interface components (or controls) carry methods to get/set representative data values as well as a way to locate or move the component on the display. Finally, actions and reactions to the user interactions with various components on the display give rise to a set of event-handling methods that are covered later in this chapter.

**CARET CARE** It is worth mentioning that `Caret` objects are runnable threads. That is, the `Caret` class extends java.lang.Thread. When an instance of the `TextField` is created and given focus with a call to the `setFocus()` method, the method starts a caret thread to get the caret to blink. Subsequently, when the `TextField` loses focus, which can be done manually with a call to `loseFocus()` on the text field, the caret stops blinking. A call to `killCaret()` actually stops and kills the associated caret thread.

In most cases, the management of TextFields and their associated Caret instances do not require any extra work on the part of the developer. However, because of the threaded nature of carets, care should be taken when working with the `TextField` components, especially with regard to getting and setting focus, so as to avoid conditions where Caret instances are not properly stopped and garbage collected. Improper use of the component can lead to the slow yet steady leak of memory resulting in eventual application failure. When working with an application that is going to contain a lot of TextFields, it is a good idea to display the return value of `Runtime.getRuntime().getFreeMemory()` method calls in your application while testing to ensure caret instances are not being inadvertently held onto when they are no longer required.

## Dialogs

There is only one Spotlet with focus at any given time and this Spotlet controls the display of components and drawing to the screen. Unlike many other user interface systems with multiple windows on which to display graphical components, a Spotlet has only one window, namely the full screen. There are only two minor deviations to this display mechanism in KJava.

A `Dialog` component acts as a modal pop-up message box or window to display a string of text shown in a scrolling text box. It can be used to provide error or warning messages or to display text that may be too long to display nicely in a screen surrounded by other components. The text in the display is non-editable.

There is a single constructor, `Dialog(DialogOwner o, String t, String str, String buttonText)` for dialogs. The first and second string parameters passed to the constructor are the title of the dialog and message text to be displayed. The title string is not displayed on the screen; it is just used to label the dialog. When created, a dialog is automatically outfitted with a single dismiss button labeled via the `button-Text` string parameter used in the constructor.

A dialog box must have an owner. The owner is an object that is notified when the `Dialog` object is dismissed by pressing the dismiss button. The owning object is specified during the construction of a `Dialog` and it must implement the `DialogOwner` interface. This simple interface consists of a single `dialogDismissed(String title)` method that is the method called when the `Dialog` is dismissed. The string title parameter of the `dialogDismissed(String title)` is the title of the Dialog that was dismissed. If an object is the owner of multiple `Dialog` boxes, this parameter allows the object to discern which dialog was dismissed. The owner can then respond appropriately and possibly uniquely to each `Dialog` object dismissal. Again, remember that a Spotlet has no refresh or any similar concept, so after a dialog is dismissed, the Spotlets components will have to be redisplayed in order to show up on the screen. This often involves invoking the `paint()` method on all the contained components.

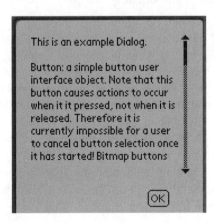

**Figure 9.18**
**A Dialog can be used to display informational text in a scrollable area. The dismissal button (the "OK" button) is automatically provided and is used to close the Dialog.**

In many cases, a Spotlet is made the owner of the dialog. Here is a small bit of code that displays and reacts to an example dialog, the result of which can be seen in figure 9.18.

```
public class DialogExample extends Spotlet implements DialogOwner {
  ...
  public void showDialog() {
   Dialog info = new Dialog(this,"Info","This is an example Dialog.\n\n" +
   "Button: a simple button user interface object. Note that this button "+
   "causes actions to occur when it is pressed, not when it is released. " +
   "Therefore it is currently impossible for a user to cancel a button " +
   "selection once it has started! Bitmap buttons do not have a border " +
   "drawn around them. If you want your bitmap button to have a border, " +
   "include the border in the bitmap.", "OK");
   info.showDialog();
  }
  public void dialogDismissed(java.lang.String title) {
    if (title.equals("Info")) {
      //...do something
    }
  }
}
```

Similar to the Dialog window, the HelpDisplay window displays text in a ScrollTextBox before an application begins. As its name implies, a HelpDisplay is intended to display application user help. A HelpDisplay object does not have an owner like the Dialog. Instead the class name of the Spotlet is passed into the constructor, so that an instance of the Spotlet can be created and run when the HelpDisplay is dismissed.

### Scrolling

KJava also provides vertical scrolling capability. Given the device's usually limiting display size, this can come in handy. The VerticalScrollBar is another component just like the components listed previously. However, a scroll bar differs in that it must have an owner. The owner of a scroll bar is another component that implements the ScrollOwner interface. The owner component is notified whenever the scroll bar is used.

The constructor provided to create a VerticalScrollBar is VerticalScroll-Bar(ScrollOwner so, int x, int y, int h, int min, int max, int initVal). Like most other GUI components, the size and coordinate location of the Vertical-ScrollBar are specified when the object is constructed. However, it is also necessary to provide the owner of the scroll bar. The min, max and initVal parameters specify the minimum, maximum, and initial values or scroll locations. A Vertical-ScrollBar has a paint() method like other components that also causes the widget to display on the screen.

The ScrollOwner interface is very simple. It has only one event-handling method, setScrollValue(int value), which must be implemented by a component serving as the owner of the scroll bar. This method is called in the event the user presses or moves the scroll bar.

### 9.3.3 Custom components

The KJava user interface does the job, but is not exactly the world's most luxurious API. If your application is left wanting for more, you can explore third party alternatives, or you can also grow your own widgets and components. This usually entails using a combination of the drawing features surrounding the Graphics class and pre-existing components. As an example, we had the need in one of our applications for a scrolling list of items that could be checked off. Using a set of CheckBoxes, VerticalScrollBar, and the Graphics object we were able to create the rather sophisticated component displayed in figure 9.19.

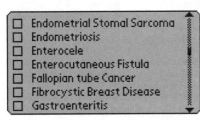

**Figure 9.19**
The richness of the user interface in a KJava application can be enhanced by creating your own custom components, either from scratch or by using a combination of existing UI components. Here, a custom KJava User Interface component was developed using the KJava's CheckBox, Vertical Scroll Bar and Graphics.

When building your own components, consider two valuable resources: memory and performance/application speed. User interfaces can take up a considerable amount of precious memory. It does not matter how pretty the GUI is if it cannot fit on the device. Furthermore, the virtual machine on many small devices may operate at one third or less of the speed of the standard Java runtime environment. Depending on the sophistication of the homegrown component, the virtual machine may be stressed when trying to display it. This can lead to some real performance issues when running your application.

In some cases, a KJava component attribute or method may be protected. "Protected," in Java, implies that the method or field is available for use by subclasses and classes within the same package. This means that there are methods or fields that your application may want or need, but to which it may not have direct access. In this case, you may want to consider developing a wrapping class that subclasses the KJava component and grants access to the desired method or field to the outside world. Care should be taken when exposing protected material. There was a reason it was deemed protected in the first place and you should learn why it was protected before allowing your application free access to it.

### 9.3.4 KJava collection classes

There are a couple of miscellaneous collection classes unique to KJava. Although not user interface components, these classes can be handy when developing Spotlet applications and we wanted to make sure to mention them. Care should be taken when using these classes with code that has a high probability of being ported to another device and Java API since they will not be available in other environments.

### IntVector

An `IntVector` is a simple expandable vector containing integers. Unlike standard Java vectors (`java.util.Vector`) in J2SE or other Java environments, these vectors contain the base type integer elements and not objects (`java.lang.Object`). Unfortunately, there are no enumerators or iterators that can be obtained directly from instances of this class, so there is no convenient means to loop through the integers contained in an `IntVector`. Adding integers to the `IntVector` is accomplished with the `append(int i)` method while getting an integer out of the vector is done by calling on the `valueAt(int index)` method. The `size()` method provides a count of the number of integers stored in the vector.

### List

The `List` class is a smaller and simplified version of the `java.util.Vector` class. Objects can be added to a `List` collection using the `append(java.lang.Object obj)` or `setElementAt(java.lang.Object o, int pos)` methods. Objects are extracted from a `List` instance using `elementAt(int index)`. Again, the `size()` method returns the number of elements in a `List` instance.

## 9.4 THE INVESTMENT QUOTE APPLICATION'S USER INTERFACE IN KJAVA

Time now to put the KJava user interface API to use. We are going to build the user interface of the investment tracking tutorial application using KJava and CLDC. When developing the user interface for MIDP devices, as was seen in chapter 5, the screen was so small that several screens had to be implemented in order to interact with the customer and display the investment quote prices. The screen size of a Palm OS device is huge in comparison to the 96×54 pixel limit on MIDP devices. Therefore, we can actually have the entire user interface displayed on a single screen, as opposed to several screens with MIDP.

As with our MIDP implementation, we will have two separate applications. One application, the ObtainQuoteSpotlet, will obtain an investment symbol from a customer and wirelessly seek the price of the investment represented by the symbol entered by the customer. This price will then be stored to a database and displayed to the customer. A second application, RetrieveQuoteSpotlet, will retrieve historical prices for a given investment symbol from the database and graphically display the historical prices for the investment to the customer.

### 9.4.1 Creating and displaying components

The first step in building our UI in KJava will be to import the required classes. All of the KJava user interface components are located in the `com.sun.kjava` package. In fact, all of the classes of KJava are located in this single package. Therefore, at the top of the ObtainQuoteSpotlet.java file, we have the required import statement

```
import com.sun.kjava.*;
```

Having already created the ObtainQuoteSpotlet application in section 9.3, we begin building the user interface by first declaring the reference variables required to hold all the necessary GUI components.

```
private TextField symbolField = null;
private RadioButton stockButton = null;
private RadioButton fundButton = null;
private RadioGroup investmentChoice = null;
private ScrollTextBox resultsBox = null;
private Button exitButton = null;
private Button getButton = null;
```

These components will serve in a fashion similar to the high-level user interface components in the MIDP tutorial. The TextField will allow the customer to enter an investment symbol. The stockButton and fundButton radio buttons allows the customer to signify whether the investment of concern is a stock or mutual fund. These radio buttons will be made part of the investmentChoice radio button group, thereby allowing only one option to be selected at any given time. After obtaining the quote for the investment symbol entered by the customer, the price (or other information if an error occurred) can be displayed in the ScrollTextBox called resultsBox. Finally, two buttons are provided on the Spotlet screen to allow the customer to signal when it is time for the application to go "get" the price or when to leave the application.

**PALM OS APPLICATIONS**   An exit button on a Palm OS application is not entirely necessary. The paradigm of Palm OS applications is to simply move to another application or the application selection screens rather than actually requesting to leave an application. Pressing the Applications soft key is an indication in the Palm OS that it is time to leave the current app.

Inside the ObtainQuoteSpotlet constructor, the components described above are created and initialized. Notice the use of the Graphics object to get the width of strings to be displayed. Remember, as a J2ME developer, you are the layout manager, so this method can come in handy when attempting to space things on the screen appropriately. Also notice how instances of RadioButton are created and then added to an instance of a RadioGroup.

```
public ObtainQuoteSpotlet() {
    String tfLabel = "Symbol";
    symbolField = new TextField(tfLabel,5,25,Graphics.getWidth(tfLabel) + 40,
        Graphics.getHeight(tfLabel));                              ❶
    stockButton = new RadioButton(50,45,"Stock");                  ❷
    fundButton = new RadioButton(100,45,"Fund");
    investmentChoice = new RadioGroup(2);
    investmentChoice.add(stockButton);                             ❸
    investmentChoice.add(fundButton);
    investmentChoice.setSelected(stockButton);
    resultsBox = new ScrollTextBox("",8,65,137,45);               ❹
    exitButton = new Button("Exit",5,140);
    getButton = new Button("Get Quote", 105,140);                  ❺
}
```

**①** Using the Graphics object to determine width of the field

**②** Creating the radio buttons

**③** Associating radio buttons to a group

**④** Creating the scrolling text box

**⑤** Creating the exit and get quote buttons

To kick off an instance of the `ObtainQuoteSpotlet` and create all of these marvelous components, we need a main method. Unlike MIDP application control, the Spotlet's `main` method is what gets called and started from the virtual machine. Our example `main` method, provided earlier in this chapter, creates a new instance of `ObtainQuoteSpotlet`. However, if we were to use the `main` method as it stands, none of our new components would be displayed. Why? We need to invoke the paint method on the components in order for them to display. Therefore, improving on the main method for `ObtainQuoteSpotlet`, we simply create an instance of `ObtainQuoteSpotlet` and then call on a new private method, `displayForm()` that will display the components.

```
public static void main (String args[]) {
    ObtainQuoteSpotlet quoteSpotlet = new ObtainQuoteSpotlet();
    quoteSpotlet.displayForm();
}
```

While displaying the components would provide the user interface with the means to get a symbol from the customer and display price information, a screen without some supplementary text and shapes would probably just confuse the customer. Therefore, in the `displayForm()` method, appropriate text and other geographical shapes will be displayed to make the application more user-friendly. We use the `Graphics` object to conduct this work.

```
private void displayForm() {
  Graphics.clearScreen();
  Graphics.drawString("Obtain Investment Quote",5,10,Graphics.INVERT);
  Graphics.drawString("Type:",5,45, Graphics.PLAIN);        Display the appli-  ①
  symbolField.paint();                                        cation title and
  stockButton.paint();      ② Paint the components          radio button label
  fundButton.paint();          to the screen
  resultsBox.paint();
  exitButton.paint();                              Display a border around  ③
  getButton.paint();                               the results ScrollTextBox
  Graphics.drawBorder(5,60, 150, 55, Graphics.PLAIN, Graphics.SIMPLE);
}
```

Why put all of the paint and drawing methods in a separate method like `display-Form()`? As we shall see, the `displayForm()` method contains all the calls to display and redisplay the screen. Again, remember that Spotlets and KJava have no refresh mechanism. Therefore, as the developer, you must provoke refreshes of the screen at appropriate times. Thus, we need methods such as displayForm() that exist outside of the Spotlet instance creation so that appropriate screen refreshes can occur without creating a whole new instance of the application.

That is about all there is to do at this time, save a little work in preparation for future activity with regard to our Spotlet. You may recall in the development of the MIDlets, the application checked to insure a symbol name ended in "X" if the customer selected the investment type of "fund." Mutual fund symbols are up to five letters in length, and a mutual fund symbol ends in the letter 'X'. In MIDP, we produced an Alert if the customer inappropriately provided a symbol without an 'X' at the end of the name but also pushed the Fund radio button. In KJava, an instance of Dialog will do the work of the Alert in the MIDP version of the application.

To use Dialog boxes you need an owner. The Spotlets are going to serve as the owner for all Dialogs in the tutorial application. Therefore the ObtainQuoteSpotlet and RetrieveQuoteSpotlet must implement the DialogOwner interface. The new class declaration for ObtainQuoteSpotlet resembles the line below.

```
public class ObtainQuoteSpotlet extends Spotlet implements DialogOwner {
```

The Spotlet must also implement the DialogOwner's one method, dialog-Dismissed(). In every instance, since the Dialog is serving to describe an error or other warning to the customer, the only thing that the Spotlet need do when a Dialog is dismissed is repaint the screen. Ah hah! The need for our displayForm() method becomes a little clearer.

```
public void dialogDismissed(java.lang.String title) {
    this.displayForm();
}
```

To check the customer-entered investment symbol against the customer-selected investment type, a simple test method is provided to examine the data obtained from the components. In the checkSymbol() method, notice how the text value and radio button value are obtained directly from the corresponding components. A Dialog instance is created and shown if the mutual fund name error condition exists.

```
private boolean checkSymbol() {
    if ((investmentChoice.getSelected().equals(fundButton)) &&
        !(symbolField.getText().toUpperCase().endsWith("X"))){
        Graphics.playSound(Graphics.SOUND_ERROR);
        Dialog symbolAlert = new Dialog(this,"Alert",
          "Check Symbol\n\nMutual Funds end in 'X'","OK");
        symbolAlert.showDialog();
        return false;
    }
    return true;
}
```

This code, and the dialogDismissed() method code, is not used yet, but it will be used once user interactions with the various GUI components are handled.

To see ObtainQuoteSpotlet's user interface, we use Jbed to build our application. First make sure the ObtainQuote project is in use. Go to the Projects menu bar option and make sure the ObtainQuote project is checked. Next, open the ObtainQuote-Spotlet.java file by selecting the File menu bar option and selecting the Open... menu item. After finding and selecting the ObtainQuoteSpotlet.java in the Open dialog box, add the code discussed above to the Java program in the text editor. To compile the application, select Java from the menu bar and select the Compile item. Finally, to link the application, select Jbed from the menu bar and select the Link item. This will result in the creation of an ObtainQuoteSpotlet.prc that is about 95K in size.

Test out your application by loading the newly-linked PRC file into the emulator. Success in these steps should result in an application that looks similar to the image in figure 9.20.

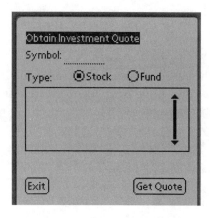

**Figure 9.20**
**The user interface of the ObtainQuote Spotlet is shown. Unlike in MIDP, the user interface of the ObtainQuote Spotlet can all be displayed on one screen. A request is made to get an investment quote and the results get displayed in the ScrollTextBox located in the middle of the display.**

You may try to operate the application and find that none of the buttons or text fields work. Do not panic. We address handling events at the end of this chapter. Proper event handling will bring the application to life. For now, to exit the application, simply tap on the Applications soft key button on the emulator (to the left of the Graffiti area).

## 9.4.2 Drawing with graphics

Much of the Spotlet used to retrieve already-obtained quotes and to display historical quotes in a graph for the customer is similar to the ObtainQuoteSpotlet. The customer is required to provide the investment quote symbol and investment type. The only difference in this application is that the price for the investment will be retrieved from a database rather than from a service over the wire. Since the information required to retrieve a quote from the database is the same, we can copy and use much of the same code developed for ObtainQuoteSpotlet. A code listing for the new RetrieveQuoteSpotlet is provided in listing 9.2.

Listing 9.2     RetrieveQuoteSpotlet.java

```
import com.sun.kjava.*;

public class RetrieveQuoteSpotlet extends Spotlet implements DialogOwner{
    private TextField symbolField = null;
    private RadioButton stockButton = null;
    private RadioButton fundButton = null;
    private RadioGroup investmentChoice = null;
    private Button exitButton = null;
    private Button getButton = null;

    public RetrieveQuoteSpotlet() {
        String tfLabel = "Symbol";
        symbolField = new TextField(tfLabel,5,25,Graphics.getWidth(tfLabel)
          + 40, Graphics.getHeight(tfLabel));
        stockButton = new RadioButton(50,45,"Stock");
        fundButton = new RadioButton(100,45,"Fund");
        investmentChoice = new RadioGroup(2);
        investmentChoice.add(stockButton);
        investmentChoice.add(fundButton);
        investmentChoice.setSelected(stockButton);
        exitButton = new Button("Exit",5,140);
        getButton = new Button("Get Quote", 105,140);
    }

    public static void main (String args[]) {
        RetrieveQuoteSpotlet quoteSpotlet = new RetrieveQuoteSpotlet();
        quoteSpotlet.displayForm();
    }

    private void displayForm() {
        register(NO_EVENT_OPTIONS);
        Graphics.clearScreen();
        Graphics.drawString("Retrieve Investment Quote",5,10,
          Graphics.INVERT);
        Graphics.drawString("Type:",5,45, Graphics.PLAIN);
        symbolField.paint();
        stockButton.paint();
        fundButton.paint();
        exitButton.paint();
        getButton.paint();
    }

    private boolean checkSymbol() {
        if ((investmentChoice.getSelected().equals(fundButton)) &&
            !(symbolField.getText().toUpperCase().endsWith("X"))){
            Graphics.playSound(Graphics.SOUND_ERROR);
            Dialog symbolAlert = new Dialog(this,"Alert",
              "Check Symbol\n\ nMutual Funds end in 'X'","OK");
            symbolAlert.showDialog();
            return false;
        }
        return true;
    }

    public void dialogDismissed(java.lang.String title) {
        this.displayForm();
    }
}
```

Because we are not going to display a single price, but rather a graph of the prices for the investment, the only change in the code in listing 9.2 is the removal of the Text-Box called resultsBox. In place of this component on the screen, we want to graphically display the prices of the current and historical quote. In the MIDP tutorial application, we made use of the low-level user interface API to draw to the screen. Although KJava does not have an explicit and distinguishable low-level user interface API, we will make use of some of the code developed for MIDP application.

In order to draw the bar charts for the retrieved quotes, the application will need some information about where to position the chart. This information is defined in some static integer variables at the top of the application.

```
static final int MAX_BAR_SIZE = 150;
static final int START_X_POSITION = 5;
static final int START_Y_CURRENT = 97;
static final int START_Y_HISTORIC = 122;
static final int BAR_HEIGHT = 5;
```

The prices will be displayed as horizontal bars drawn starting from the left of the display to a position on the right that is dependent on the price of the investment. The START_X_POSITION is the unchanging x pixel position coordinate for each rectangle. Correspondingly, the START_Y_CURRENT and START_Y_HISTORIC values provide the static starting y pixel locations for our two rectangles depicting the current and historical prices. The BAR_WIDTH variable provides the static height of all bars.

In order to actually draw the price bars on the display, we borrow two methods from the MIDP tutorial application implementation. The first, paintChart(), is a modified version of the Canvas paint() method in the MIDP application. This method is supplied with the investment symbol and price data. With this data, it utilizes the Graphics object to draw strings, rectangles and lines to display the price graph. (listing 9.3)

---

**Listing 9.3   The paintChart method in RetrieveQuoteSpotlet**

```
public void paintChart(String sym, int currentPrice, int historicPrice) {
  Graphics.drawRectangle(5,60,155,70,Graphics.ERASE,0);                    ❶
  Graphics.drawString(sym + " Performance",5,60,Graphics.PLAIN);
  Graphics.drawString("current vs. historic",5,73,Graphics.PLAIN);        ❷
  Graphics.drawString("$" + currentPrice, 5, 85, Graphics.PLAIN);
  Graphics.drawString("$" + historicPrice, 5, 110, Graphics.PLAIN);
  int[] prices = {currentPrice, historicPrice};
  int[] lengths = determineLengths(prices);
  Graphics.drawRectangle (START_X_POSITION, START_Y_CURRENT,
    lengths[0],BAR_HEIGHT, Graphics.PLAIN, 0);                            ❸
  Graphics.drawRectangle (START_X_POSITION, START_Y_HISTORIC,
    lengths[1],BAR_HEIGHT, Graphics.PLAIN, 0);

  for (int i = 30; i < MAX_BAR_SIZE; i = i + 30) {
    Graphics.drawLine (i, START_Y_CURRENT - 2, i,                        ❹
      START_Y_HISTORIC + BAR_HEIGHT + 2, Graphics.PLAIN);
  }
}
```

① Clearing the region of the screen

② Drawing text to display the current and historical prices

③ Drawing the bars representing each price

④ Adding "tick" marks to graph

The paintChart() method reuses the determinesLengths() method, without change, developed in chapter 5 to help determine the pixel length of each bar in the graph. A copy of this code is provided in listing 9.4.

**Listing 9.4   The determineLengths method in RetrieveQuoteSpotlet**

```
private int[] determineLengths (int[] prices) {

    int ratio, higherPrice, lowerPrice;
    boolean currentHigher;

    if (prices[0] < prices[1]) {
        higherPrice = prices[1];
        lowerPrice = prices[0];
        currentHigher=false;
    } else {
        higherPrice = prices[0];
        lowerPrice = prices[1];
        currentHigher=true;
    }

    ratio = higherPrice/MAX_BAR_SIZE + 1;
    while (ratio > 1) {
        higherPrice = higherPrice/ratio;
        lowerPrice = lowerPrice/ratio;
        ratio = higherPrice/MAX_BAR_SIZE + 1;
    }

    if (currentHigher) {
        int[] ends = {higherPrice, lowerPrice};
        return ends;
    } else {
        int [] ends = {lowerPrice, higherPrice};
        return ends;
    }
}
```

At this time, the components and drawing methods are not hooked up to customer actions. We will look at how to do this in KJava in the next section of this chapter. However, to see the bar graph drawing methods do their work, simply add a call to the paintChart() method, such as the one immediately following, to the bottom of the displayForm() method:

```
paintChart("MMM",75,110);
```

With this code entered into the RetrieveQuoteSpotlet.java file, use Jbed to compile and link the application just as you did with the ObtainQuoteSpotlet. If you have been following the directions throughout this chapter, do not forget that the RetrieveQuoteSpotlet is a separate project; namely the RetrieveQuote project. Successfully compiling, linking and deploying the application to an emulator should result in a display that looks similar to that in figure 9.21.

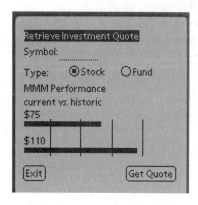

**Figure 9.21**
**The RetrieveQuote Spotlet user interface depicts the current and historical prices in a bar graph. Based on screen size, the MIDlet RetrieveQuote application required several displays to handle the same needs.**

Again, the application will not react to any attempted interaction. We look at KJava event handling next.

## 9.5 HANDLING USER INTERACTIONS IN KJAVA

Handling events in KJava is a very simple affair. All event handling is done through the Spotlet. As we mentioned in the beginning of this chapter, while an application can be made up of more than one Spotlet (which is often the case), one and only one Spotlet can have "focus" at any given time. All events are sent to the Spotlet with focus (called the current Spotlet) via a set of methods. These event-handling methods are similar to the type of event-handling methods provided in the original Java AWT.

In KJava, there are no listener or command objects such as in MIDP. Instead, the Spotlet is registered for events. Each Spotlet subclass must also override the event-handling methods that process the events in which it has interest.

### 9.5.1 Spotlet event-processing methods

A Spotlet becomes the Spotlet with focus and is registered for events with a call to the `register()` method. Once registered, the Spotlet then handles and reacts to an event by implementing one or more of the following methods:

- `keyDown(int keyCode)` Called to handle and process a user pressing any of the hard or soft keys or entering a character in the Graffiti editor. When using the emulator, this method is also triggered with standard keyboard input. The keyCode is the ASCII value of the character entered or button pressed.

- `penDown(int x, int y)` Invoked whenever the user places the pen on the display screen. The x and y parameters specify where the user touched the screen.
- `penMove(int, int)` Invoked whenever the user moves the pen across the display screen. In this case, the x and y coordinates indicate the final or destination point in the movement.
- `penUp(int x, int y)` Called when the user has removed the pen from the display. The x and y coordinates specify the last position held as the pen was removed.
- `unknownEvent(int event, java.io.DataInput in)` The catchall processing method for unknown events.

You may have noticed that no events are ever triggered directly on user interface components. Components, such as the `TextField` and `RadioButton` do have event-handling or processing methods; they simply have to be forwarded news of the event by the Spotlet. Therefore, the Spotlet serves as the central processing facility for events, and forwards or triggers reaction to events onto other components by calling on their event-handling methods.

Not all components are interested in or react to all the events. For example, a `CheckBox` component has no interest in whether the pen moved on it, in it or near it. Spotlets must be programmed to trigger or call on the appropriate event-handling method of each type component. This is made somewhat easier in that the component event-handling methods have the same name as the Spotlet event processing method except they are preceded by the word "handle." Below is a list of the various user interface components and their available event-handling methods.

**Table 9.1 User interface component event-handling methods.**

| KJava User Interface Component | Available Event-Handling Methods |
| --- | --- |
| Button | None |
| CheckBox | handlePenDown |
| RadioButton | handlePenDown |
| ScrollTextBox | handlePenDown<br>handlePenMove<br>handleKeyDown |
| SelectScrollTextBox | same as ScrollTextBox through inheritance |
| Slider | handlePenDown<br>handlePenMove |
| TextBox | None |
| TextField | handleKeyDown |
| ValueSelector | None |
| VerticalScrollBar | handleKeyDown<br>handlePenDown<br>handlePenMove |

Since there are no listeners, how does the Spotlet know which components to forward an event call to? Widgets with concern for actions have methods that help the Spotlet determine whether an action, such as a penDown action, occurred over a particular component's part of the display. For example, the RadioButton component has a pressed(int x, int y) method that the Spotlet can use to determine if the user in fact pressed inside of the RadioButton instance spot on the screen. If so, the Spotlet can trigger the RadioButton's handlePenDown(int x, int y) method.

**Table 9.2   User interface component event-handling helper methods.**

| KJava User Interface Component | Event Helper methods |
| --- | --- |
| Button | pressed(x,y) |
| CheckBox | pressed(x,y) |
| RadioButton | pressed(x,y) |
| ScrollTextBox | contains(x,y) |
| SelectScrollTextBox | contains(x,y) |
| Slider | contains(x,y) |
| TextBox | None |
| TextField | pressed(x,y)<br>hasFocus() |
| ValueSelector | pressed(x,y) |
| VerticalScrollBar | contains(x,y) |

### 9.5.2    Handling beaming events

Most Palm OS devices are equipped with infrared ports. A special processing method on the Spotlet class is provided to allow Spotlets to receive data via this port. The beamReceive(byte[] data) method is called on the Spotlet whenever the Spotlet has focus and the device is receiving beamed data. Spotlets can also beam data to another device using the infrared port by calling on the beamSend(byte[] data) method.

## 9.6    HANDLING THE EVENTS OF THE INVESTMENT QUOTE APPLICATION IN KJAVA

In the first part of this chapter, we were able to display some very nice user interfaces using the KJava user interface API. However, the displays did not allow for any user interaction. We could not even enter text in the TextField. In this portion of the tutorial, we add methods to override the event-handling methods in the Obtain-QuoteSpotlet and RetrieveQuoteSpotlet classes, which allow for customer interaction with the application.

### 9.6.1    Handling key entry events

In both the ObtainQuoteSpotlet and RetrieveQuoteSpotlet we have a text field for accepting the user's desired investment symbol. As a first step toward full interaction, we will implement the necessary `keyDown()` overriding method implementations in our Spotlets to handle Graffiti input or button presses on the device.

From table 9.1, we see that there are two components in ObtainQuoteSpotlet that we are using that might be interested in keyDown activity, namely the text field and scroll text box components. In the RetrieveQuoteSpotlet, only the text field is concerned with keyDown. In the case of the text fields, it is obvious that we want to capture the keyCode, or in other words, character being entered, and pass that to the component for display. Why would the text box be concerned with the activities handled in the keyDown event-handling method? When developing your application, don't forget about the buttons, both soft and hard, on the device. In the case of the scroll text box, we will want to move the text displayed in the box if the customer presses the directional keys at the bottom of the device.

**Scroll up**

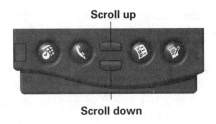

**Scroll down**

**Figure 9.22**
**Buttons at the bottom of the device allow for easier navigation through elements in a scrollable component. However, in order to use these buttons in combination with a Spotlet application, the Spotlet must be programmed to handle the keyDown event generated by these buttons.**

Pushing the top key is an indication from the user that the display should be scrolled up. Pushing the bottom key is an indication from the user that the display should be scrolled down. We use conditionals inside of the `keyDown()` method to check which area of the display and/or which key has been pressed in order to respond appropriately.

```
public void keyDown (int keyCode) {
    if ((keyCode == 11) || (keyCode == 12)){
        resultsBox.handleKeyDown(keyCode);
    } else if (symbolField.hasFocus()) {
        symbolField.handleKeyDown(keyCode);
    }
}
```

In the case when the scroll-up (key code equals 11) or scroll-down (key code equals 12) key is pushed, we forward the event onto the `resultsBox`'s `handleKeyDown()` method. Otherwise, when the `symbolField TextField` has focus, we want the key input to be sent to the `symbolField`'s `handleKeyDown()` method. In this application, we are not concerned with other hard or soft key presses, but your application might be. Put conditions and handling in the `keyDown` event-handling method if your application wants or needs to react to the Applications, Menu, Calculator, or Find soft keys or to the Calendar, Address Book, To Do List and Memo hard keys.

The keyDown() method in the RetrieveQuoteSpotlet is even easier since there is no scrolling text box. Instead, we just need to handle key entry for input of the investment symbol.

```
public void keyDown (int keyCode) {
    if (symbolField.hasFocus()) {
        symbolField.handleKeyDown(keyCode);
    }
}
```

### 9.6.2    Handling pen taps

Our application is looking better. Now, at least, the customer can enter the investment symbol into the text field. With PDA devices, however, most interactions with the device do not occur with the Graffiti editor or by pushing the devices buttons. Most interactions occur with PDA devices by using the stylus or pen instrument in contact with the display screen. This is often referred to as "tapping" on the screen and it is usually the preferred interaction with the device because it is quick and easy. Handling interactions via the pen is the job of the Spotlet's penDown(), penMove() and penUp() methods. An example of the penDown method is provided in listing 9.5.

In our application, we have all sorts of reactions to pen actions and motion, depending on which component is being interacted with. Two important interactions are when the user taps or presses one of the two buttons (Exit, Get Quote) on the display. We can tell if a tap has fallen on one of these buttons by checking to see if the x, y coordinate passed into the penDown() method is inside the button space. If a button is tapped, the component does not have any handling methods. We, as the developers, must determine what action is going to occur any time a Button is pressed. In this case, if the exitButton is pressed, we simply exit the application. If the "Get Quote" button is pressed, then things get a little more interesting.

#### Listing 9.5    The penDown method in ObtainQuoteSpotlet

```
public void penDown(int x, int y) {
    if (exitButton.pressed(x,y)){
        Graphics.playSound(Graphics.SOUND_CONFIRMATION);    ❷  ❶
        System.exit(0);
    } else if (getButton.pressed(x,y)) {                         ❸
        symbolField.loseFocus();
        if ((symbolField.getText().length() > 0) && (checkSymbol())) {
            Graphics.playSound(Graphics.SOUND_STARTUP);
            String sym = symbolField.getText().toUpperCase();    ❷
            //later on, get the price from a quote service here
            int[] price = {75, 55};
            //later on, store the price in the database here
            resultsBox.setText("The price of " + sym + " is $"
            + price[0] + "." + price[1]);
            resultsBox.paint();
        }
    } else if (symbolField.pressed(x,y)) {
```

```
        symbolField.setFocus();
    } else if (stockButton.pressed(x,y)) {
        symbolField.loseFocus();
        stockButton.handlePenDown(x,y);
    } else if (fundButton.pressed(x,y)) {
        symbolField.loseFocus();
        fundButton.handlePenDown(x,y);
    } else if (resultsBox.contains(x,y)) {
        resultsBox.handlePenDown(x,y);
    }
}
```

**4**

**5**

**6**

❶ Check if a button has been pressed

❷ Sound to indicate action confirmation

❸ Handling a Get Quote command request

❹ When the TextField is pressed, give it focus

❺ Handling radio button presses

❻ If the scroll bar is tapped, scroll the text box

When getButton has been pressed, we first check to see that the customer has provided a symbol and that the symbol is valid (checking that a symbol ending in 'X' is for a mutual fund). If the symbol were valid, we would ordinarily get the price from our quote service. Since this part of our application is not yet available, we mock up getting the price by assigning a price ($75.55) to our investment and passing this on to the resultsBox to be displayed. We would also store the price in a database. The topic, obtaining a price and storing it in a database, will be discussed in chapter 10. Notice that whenever a button is pressed we have the device provide an audible signal. The Graphics object performs this task.

The penDown() method on RetrieveQuoteSpotlet is similar. On the user's press of the Get Quote button in this Spotlet, however, a little more work needs to occur. When Get Quote is pressed, the application must attempt to retrieve the existing quote. If a historical quote exists, then the application will display the bar graph depicting the historical and current quote. If a historical quote does not exist, then the application simply prints the current price. Finally, the customer may have asked for a quote for which the system does not yet have any quote. In this case, an appropriate error message must be displayed to the screen. All of this activity is handled by the displayChart() method (shown in listing 9.6) if the user pushes the Get Quote button and the symbol is valid.

Listing 9.6   The displayChart method in RetrieveQuoteSpotlet

```
private void displayChart(String currentSymbol) {
    //later on, get prices from a database here
    int[] prices = {75,55,110,45};      ❶
    if (prices != null) {
        if (prices.length > 2) {
            paintChart(currentSymbol,prices[0],prices[2]);      ❷
        } else {
            Graphics.drawRectangle(5,60,155,70,Graphics.ERASE,0);
            Graphics.drawString("Recorded price for " + currentSymbol + "
                is: $" + prices[0] + "." + prices[1], 5, 65, Graphics.PLAIN);
            Graphics.drawString("No historical data exists.", 5, 80,
                Graphics.INVERT);      ❸
        }
    }

    else {
        Graphics.playSound(Graphics.SOUND_ERROR);      ❹
        Dialog noDataAlert = new Dialog(this,"Alert",
          "No price exists for " + currentSymbol,"OK");
        noDataAlert.showDialog();
    }
}
```

❶ The same fake prices for all investments for now

❷ With both a historical and current price, display the bar graph

❸ With only a single current price, display the price and a message

❹ With no prices, tell the customer that no prices exist

Again, because the application is not yet hooked up to a database or quote service, we provide a set of phony current and historical prices for every symbol of $75.55 and $110.45. This will be changed later so as to get the prices from a database on the device.

With the displayChart() method handling most of the details surrounding what and how to display price quotes, the Spotlet's penDown() method must orchestrate calls to the appropriate handling mechanisms as shown in listing 9.7.

Listing 9.7   The penDown method in RetrieveQuoteSpotlet

```
public void penDown(int x, int y) {
    if (exitButton.pressed(x,y)){
        Graphics.playSound(Graphics.SOUND_CONFIRMATION);
        System.exit(0);
    } else if (getButton.pressed(x,y)) {
        symbolField.loseFocus();
        if ((symbolField.getText().length() > 0) && (checkSymbol())) {
            Graphics.playSound(Graphics.SOUND_STARTUP);
            String sym = symbolField.getText().toUpperCase();
            displayChart(sym);
        }
```

```
    } else if (symbolField.pressed(x,y)) {
        symbolField.setFocus();
    } else if (stockButton.pressed(x,y)) {
        symbolField.loseFocus();
        stockButton.handlePenDown(x,y);
    } else if (fundButton.pressed(x,y)) {
        symbolField.loseFocus();
        fundButton.handlePenDown(x,y);
    }
}
```

In the case of our two applications, we are not concerned with the penUp events. However, if we were, we would simply override the penUp(int x, int y) method and react to the events as necessary.

### 9.6.3 Handling pen movement

We need to handle one final event that our ObtainQuoteSpotlet may see. We have handled the customer's desire to scroll the price quote results scroll text box by either pushing the scroll-up or scroll-down buttons at the bottom of the device through the keyDown() implementation. We have also handled the customer's desire to scroll the same scroll text box by tapping the scroll bar on the component. But what if the user attempts to drag the position indicator of the scroll bar up or down? In order to handle this last event, we must implement the penMove() method. Since a scroll text box already knows how to handle this event, we need to check that any movement with the pen occurs within the instance of the ScrollTextBox and if it does, forward the event on to the component's handling method.

```
public void penMove (int x, int y) {
    if (resultsBox.contains(x,y)) {
        resultsBox.handlePenMove(x,y);
    }
}
```

This method is absent from the RetrieveQuoteSpotlet since the Spotlet has no scroll text box and therefore no need to react to pen movement.

Our applications' user interfaces have been completed. The full code for our two Spotlets is displayed in listings 9.8 and 9.9 as follows.

> **Listing 9.8   The complete ObtainQuoteSpotlet.java**

```
import com.sun.kjava.*;

public class ObtainQuoteSpotlet extends Spotlet implements DialogOwner {

    private TextField symbolField = null;
    private RadioButton stockButton = null;
    private RadioButton fundButton = null;
    private RadioGroup investmentChoice = null;
    private ScrollTextBox resultsBox = null;
```

```
    private Button exitButton = null;
    private Button getButton = null;

    public ObtainQuoteSpotlet() {
        String tfLabel = "Symbol";
        symbolField = new TextField(tfLabel,5,25,Graphics.getWidth(tfLabel)
            + 40, Graphics.getHeight(tfLabel));
        stockButton = new RadioButton(50,45,"Stock");
        fundButton = new RadioButton(100,45,"Fund");
        investmentChoice = new RadioGroup(2);
        investmentChoice.add(stockButton);
        investmentChoice.add(fundButton);
        investmentChoice.setSelected(stockButton);
        resultsBox = new ScrollTextBox("",8,65,137,45);
        exitButton = new Button("Exit",5,140);
        getButton = new Button("Get Quote", 105,140);
    }

    public static void main (String args[]) {
        ObtainQuoteSpotlet quoteSpotlet = new ObtainQuoteSpotlet();
        quoteSpotlet.displayForm();
    }

    private void displayForm() {
        register(NO_EVENT_OPTIONS);
        Graphics.clearScreen();
        Graphics.drawString("Obtain Investment Quote",5,10,Graphics.INVERT);
        Graphics.drawString("Type:",5,45, Graphics.PLAIN);
        symbolField.paint();
        stockButton.paint();
        fundButton.paint();
        resultsBox.paint();
        Graphics.drawBorder(5,60, 150, 55, Graphics.PLAIN, Graphics.SIMPLE);
        exitButton.paint();
        getButton.paint();
    }

    private boolean checkSymbol() {
        if ((investmentChoice.getSelected().equals(fundButton)) &&
            !(symbolField.getText().toUpperCase().endsWith("X"))){
            Graphics.playSound(Graphics.SOUND_ERROR);
            Dialog symbolAlert = new Dialog(this,"Alert",
                "Check Symbol\n\nMutual Funds end in 'X'","OK");
            symbolAlert.showDialog();
            return false;
        }
        return true;
    }

    public void penDown(int x, int y) {
        if (exitButton.pressed(x,y)){
            Graphics.playSound(Graphics.SOUND_CONFIRMATION);
            System.exit(0);
        } else if (getButton.pressed(x,y)) {
            symbolField.loseFocus();
            if ((symbolField.getText().length() > 0) && (checkSymbol())) {
```

```
                    Graphics.playSound(Graphics.SOUND_STARTUP);
                    String sym = symbolField.getText().toUpperCase();
                    //later on, get the price from a quote service here
                    int[] price = {75, 55};
                    //later on, store the price in the database here
                    resultsBox.setText("The price of " + sym + " is $" +
                        price[0] + "." + price[1]);
                    resultsBox.paint();
                }
            } else if (symbolField.pressed(x,y)) {
                symbolField.setFocus();
            } else if (stockButton.pressed(x,y)) {
                symbolField.loseFocus();
                stockButton.handlePenDown(x,y);
            } else if (fundButton.pressed(x,y)) {
                symbolField.loseFocus();
                fundButton.handlePenDown(x,y);
            } else if (resultsBox.contains(x,y)) {
                resultsBox.handlePenDown(x,y);
            }
        }

    public void keyDown (int keyCode) {
        if ((keyCode == 11) || (keyCode == 12)){
            resultsBox.handleKeyDown(keyCode);
        } else if (symbolField.hasFocus()) {
            symbolField.handleKeyDown(keyCode);
        }
    }

    public void penMove (int x, int y) {
        if (resultsBox.contains(x,y)) {
            resultsBox.handlePenMove(x,y);
        }
    }

    public void dialogDismissed(java.lang.String title) {
        this.displayForm();
    }
}
```

Listing 9.9   The complete RetrieveQuoteSpotlet.java

```
import com.sun.kjava.*;

public class RetrieveQuoteSpotlet extends Spotlet implements DialogOwner{

    static final int MAX_BAR_SIZE = 150;
    static final int START_X_POSITION = 5;
    static final int START_Y_CURRENT = 97;
    static final int START_Y_HISTORIC = 122;
    static final int BAR_HEIGHT = 5;

    private TextField symbolField = null;
```

```java
private RadioButton stockButton = null;
private RadioButton fundButton = null;
private RadioGroup investmentChoice = null;
private Button exitButton = null;
private Button getButton = null;

public RetrieveQuoteSpotlet() {
    String tfLabel = "Symbol";
    symbolField = new TextField(tfLabel,5,25,Graphics.getWidth(tfLabel)
        + 40, Graphics.getHeight(tfLabel));
    stockButton = new RadioButton(50,45,"Stock");
    fundButton = new RadioButton(100,45,"Fund");
    investmentChoice = new RadioGroup(2);
    investmentChoice.add(stockButton);
    investmentChoice.add(fundButton);
    investmentChoice.setSelected(stockButton);
    exitButton = new Button("Exit",5,140);
    getButton = new Button("Get Quote", 105,140);
}

public static void main (String args[]) {
    RetrieveQuoteSpotlet quoteSpotlet = new RetrieveQuoteSpotlet();
    quoteSpotlet.displayForm();
}

private void displayForm() {
    register(NO_EVENT_OPTIONS);
    Graphics.clearScreen();
    Graphics.drawString("Retrieve Investment Quote",5,10,
        Graphics.INVERT);
    Graphics.drawString("Type:",5,45, Graphics.PLAIN);
    symbolField.paint();
    stockButton.paint();
    fundButton.paint();
    exitButton.paint();
    getButton.paint();
}

private boolean checkSymbol() {
    if ((investmentChoice.getSelected().equals(fundButton)) &&
        !(symbolField.getText().toUpperCase().endsWith("X"))){
        Graphics.playSound(Graphics.SOUND_ERROR);
        Dialog symbolAlert = new Dialog(this,"Alert",
            "Check Symbol\n\nMutual Funds end in 'X'","OK");
        symbolAlert.showDialog();
        return false;
    }
    return true;
}

private void displayChart(String currentSymbol) {
    //later on, get prices from a database here
    int[] prices = {75,55,110,45};
    if (prices != null) {
```

```java
            if (prices.length > 2) {
                paintChart(currentSymbol,prices[0],prices[2]);
            } else {
                Graphics.drawRectangle(5,60,155,70,Graphics.ERASE,0);
                Graphics.drawString("Recorded price for
                    " + currentSymbol + " is:  $" + prices[0] + "."
                      + prices[1], 5, 65, Graphics.PLAIN);
                Graphics.drawString("No historical data exists.", 5, 80,
                    Graphics.INVERT);
            }
        }
        else {
            Graphics.playSound(Graphics.SOUND_ERROR);
            Dialog noDataAlert = new Dialog(this,"Alert",
              "No price exists for " + currentSymbol,"OK");
            noDataAlert.showDialog();
        }
    }


    public void paintChart(String sym, int currentPrice, int historicPrice)
    {
        Graphics.drawRectangle(5,60,155,70,Graphics.ERASE,0);
        Graphics.drawString(sym + " Performance",5,60,Graphics.PLAIN);
        Graphics.drawString("current vs. historic",5,73,Graphics.PLAIN);
        Graphics.drawString("$" + currentPrice, 5, 85, Graphics.PLAIN);
        Graphics.drawString("$" + historicPrice, 5, 110, Graphics.PLAIN);

        int[] prices = {currentPrice, historicPrice};
        int[] lengths = determineLengths(prices);
        Graphics.drawRectangle (START_X_POSITION, START_Y_CURRENT,
          lengths[0], BAR_HEIGHT, Graphics.PLAIN, 0);
        Graphics.drawRectangle (START_X_POSITION, START_Y_HISTORIC,
          lengths[1], BAR_HEIGHT, Graphics.PLAIN, 0);

        for (int i = 30; i < MAX_BAR_SIZE; i = i + 30) {
            Graphics.drawLine (i, START_Y_CURRENT - 2, i, START_Y_HISTORIC +
                BAR_HEIGHT + 2, Graphics.PLAIN);
        }
    }

    private int[] determineLengths (int[] prices) {

        int ratio, higherPrice, lowerPrice;
        boolean currentHigher;

        if (prices[0] < prices[1]) {
            higherPrice = prices[1];
            lowerPrice = prices[0];
            currentHigher=false;
        } else {
            higherPrice = prices[0];
            lowerPrice = prices[1];
            currentHigher=true;
        }

        ratio = higherPrice/MAX_BAR_SIZE + 1;
```

```
        while (ratio > 1) {
            higherPrice = higherPrice/ratio;
            lowerPrice = lowerPrice/ratio;
            ratio = higherPrice/MAX_BAR_SIZE + 1;
        }

        if (currentHigher) {
            int[] ends = {higherPrice, lowerPrice};
            return ends;
        } else {
            int [] ends = {lowerPrice, higherPrice};
            return ends;
        }
    }

    public void penDown(int x, int y) {
        if (exitButton.pressed(x,y)){
            Graphics.playSound(Graphics.SOUND_CONFIRMATION);
            System.exit(0);
        } else if (getButton.pressed(x,y)) {
            symbolField.loseFocus();
            if ((symbolField.getText().length() > 0) && (checkSymbol())) {
                Graphics.playSound(Graphics.SOUND_STARTUP);
                String sym = symbolField.getText().toUpperCase();
                displayChart(sym);
            }
        } else if (symbolField.pressed(x,y)) {
            symbolField.setFocus();
        } else if (stockButton.pressed(x,y)) {
            symbolField.loseFocus();
            stockButton.handlePenDown(x,y);
        } else if (fundButton.pressed(x,y)) {
            symbolField.loseFocus();
            fundButton.handlePenDown(x,y);
        }
    }

    public void keyDown (int keyCode) {
        if (symbolField.hasFocus()) {
            symbolField.handleKeyDown(keyCode);
        }
    }

    public void dialogDismissed(java.lang.String title) {
        this.displayForm();
    }
}
```

As was done earlier in this chapter, use Jbed to compile and link the applications producing two PRC files. These PRC files can then be deployed to the emulator and finally to the actual devices. However, our application is not yet complete. We still need to hook up our applications to a persistent storage mechanism on the PDA device for storing and retrieving the investment quote information. Furthermore, we will utilize the QuoteService developed in the MIDP section to obtain live investment quotes wirelessly.

## 9.7   SUMMARY

In this chapter, we examined the KJava's graphical user interface and event handling mechanisms. Unlike the MIDP APIs, the KJava API has no high-level or low-level user interface or event handling mechanisms and is often considered a fairly simplistic API. Again, remember that KJava was designed and developed to be a demonstration API. Therefore, its sophistication and capabilities must be viewed in that light when comparing  it to a full J2ME profile. This chapter also provided us an opportunity to see and use an IDE, Jbed by esmertec, for developing our applications. IDEs can simplify a number of the tedious tasks associated with creating the application. They can also offer assistance in debugging and sometimes offer deployment options.

# CHAPTER 10

# KJava data storage

PDA devices are getting bigger and stronger. Many of the leading database vendors have started to recognize this fact and are now shipping mini-versions of their relational databases for these devices. More information on these databases is provided in chapter 15.

Today, however, many PDA manufacturers also have their own proprietary databases on the device. Palm OS devices utilize Palm database files (PDB files) for several applications that run on the device, including the Address Book, Calendar and To Do List applications.

In the future, access to more standard relational databases on these devices will come via JDBC access. Access to the proprietary databases requires the development of a new standard such as the MIDP RMS or a special Java API that serves as a wrapper around the device's databases.

In chapter 6, we examined the MIDP Record Management System. The RMS established a contract for persistent data storage on small devices, in this case typically cell phones and pagers. Under this contract the platform vendor can implement storage of data on a device they deemed fit so long as the J2ME application could access data via the RMS API. KJava, on the other hand, was developed as a demonstration/testing capability for Palm OS devices. Given this beginning, it should come as no surprise that the KJava persistent storage mechanism is aimed at one specific implementation of a database, specifically Palm OS databases. The KJava `Database` class is a wrapper class for Palm OS databases. In this chapter, we look at how to create and utilize Palm OS databases through the KJava API and in particular, we examine:

- some background on the Palm database.
- the API for accessing and storing data through KJava's `Database` class

Lastly, as we have done in all of the API chapters, we will add what we have learned in this chapter to the tutorial application. In this case, we will add KJava Database access to the tutorial application. In this particular example, we will add a Palm OS database to our KJava applications from chapter 9 for the purposes of storing and retrieving investment price data. Finally, we will also reuse our QuoteService built in the MIDP implementation. As we will see, the Generic Connection Framework is available across the various APIs in J2ME.

## 10.1 PALM OS DATABASES

A Palm OS database is actually a very rudimentary data storage mechanism. On the device, a Palm OS database is a set of possibly non-contiguous memory chunks managed as a single unit by a Data Manager. These chunks, or records as they are called by Palm, are finite in size. This allows the operating system's Data Manager to access and update information in place on the disk as opposed to reading data from the file into a memory buffer. Given the RAM resource constraints of the Palm OS device, attempting to transfer large amounts of data in and out of dynamic memory would create many difficulties and would not be optimal. Managing the databases then becomes an exercise in allocating, deleting, and resizing the various records on the part of the Data Managers.

### 10.1.1 Different types of Palm OS databases

In fact, there are two types of databases in the Palm OS device. Record databases often contain user data and are managed by the Data Manager. Address book, calendar, memo data, and the like are all stored in record databases. Records inside of a record database are ordered, with the index of records in a record database starting at 0. Resource databases, on the other hand, are used by applications to store user interface elements such as images, fonts, user interface layouts, and so forth. The memory chunks in a resource database are called resources and are managed by the Resource Manager. There is no order assigned to resources in a resource database. The KJava database API does not properly allow for access of resource databases. Therefore, the rest of this chapter will concern itself with Palm OS record databases.

### 10.1.2 Palm OS record database

The Palm OS API for accessing and handling record databases and records is extensive. The KJava API does not expose much of this API to Java developers. However, it is helpful to understand a little bit about how Palm OS databases are structured.

## Header

Each Palm OS database has a header. The header contains some basic information about the database and a list of all the records belonging to it. The record list is a list of local IDs that can be converted to a memory handle by the Data Manager when the record is requested. Other information in the header includes, but is not limited to, the information in table 10.1.

**Table 10.1   The header in a Palm OS database contains information about its type, name and capacity among other properties.**

| Header Information | Restrictions/Structure |
| --- | --- |
| The name of the database | Limited to less than 32 characters (31 bytes plus a null terminator) and it must be unique to all other databases |
| The modification number | This is incremented every time a record in the database is deleted, added or modified |
| Version number of the database | System determined version number of the database |
| The database type | A four character (4 byte) field identifying the purpose of the database. At least one of the four characters must be uppercase. |
| The database creator | A four character (4 byte) field identifying the creator of the database |
| Number of records in the database | Count of the records in the database |

Type and creator require a little explanation. As an example, the type of the address book database associated with the Address Book application that comes standard with all Palm OS systems is "DATA" and its database creator or Creator ID is "addr".

## Creator ID

Every application, database, library, or other resource file on a Palm OS device should have a four character Creator ID identifying its author. Palm maintains a Creator ID database and allows Palm OS developers to register their desired ID over the Internet. The Creator ID Database search and online registration form are available at http://dev.palmos.com/creatorid. If you are going to be developing KJava or other Palm OS applications, it is a good idea to go to this site and register your intended Creator ID. If you and the other Palm OS developers do this, it will prevent your application or database from conflicting with applications and databases already on these devices.

It takes about two minutes to check and register your Creator ID. Palm, Inc. reserves Creator IDs consisting of lowercase letters for their use. Thus a Creator ID of "addr" immediately identifies the database as a creation of Palm. Catapult Technologies has a registered Creator ID of "CATT". Therefore all of the examples in this book will carry this Creator ID.

## Records

Again, a record is simply a block of data on the device that is referenced by a database. This block cannot exceed 64K and all records for a single database must reside on the same memory card. Today, this last rule is easily enforced since current products have only one card (called card 0). However, in the future, more than one memory card may exist in each device. Along with the header, a database contains a series of record references. Each record reference, or record entry as it is also referred to, has three fields stored in 8 bytes.

**Table 10.2  Each Record in a Palm OS database has an eight-byte Record Reference. The Record Reference contains the IDs of the record as well as attribute information such as whether the record is dirty.**

| Record Field | Size |
| --- | --- |
| The local ID of the record | 4 bytes |
| The record attributes | 1 byte |
| The unique ID for the record | 3 bytes |

The local ID is used by the Data Manager to determine the location or handle to the record from this ID. The unique ID, on the other hand, is the ID of the record with regard to other records in the database. It must be unique to all records within a database and it never changes for the life of the record, regardless of any modifications to the record. Finally, the record attribute stores information about the condition of each record. Bits inside of the record attribute indicate whether the record is dirty (being updated), busy (an application currently has the record locked), secret (the record should not be displayed before a user has provided a password), or deleted (the record has been deleted but not yet cleared from the database).

Details about the Palm OS record databases, database header, and records are not terribly significant to developing applications in KJava since the API does not provide direct access to many of these details. However, understanding the database and its elements helps to explain a number of methods, parameters, and features associated with the KJava `Database` wrapper class.

## 10.2   *KJAVA DATABASE API*

The KJava persistent storage API consists of one class. Specifically, the `Database` class is a wrapper class to the Palm OS Data Manager, and it provides minimal support for accessing Palm OS databases.

### 10.2.1   Opening and creating databases

The single constructor, `Database(int typeID, int creatorID, int mode)`, opens a Palm OS database represented by an instance of `Database`. The `creatorID` is your registered Palm Creator ID represented in two-digit hexadecimal form. Thus, "CATT" becomes 0x43415454.

**Table 10.3   Creator ID CATT converted to hex.**

|  | C | A | T | T |
| --- | --- | --- | --- | --- |
| Hex | 0x43 | 0x41 | 0x54 | 0x54 |

In the same way, the typeID, which represents the type or purpose of the database, must be converted to hex. In our tutorial application, the type ID is "INVS" for "investments." When converted to hex value the "INVS" string becomes 0x494E5653. The mode passed in as the last constructor parameter refers to the access granted to the database user. There are three mode options, each defined by a Database static int: READONLY, READWRITE, WRITEONLY.

If the database specified in the constructor does not exist, however, no exception is thrown. Instead, a Database instance is still returned, but no Palm OS database is opened. To check if the Database object returned from the constructor is truly open, call the isOpen() method on the returned instance. This method returns a boolean, with a true value indicating the database does exist and was successfully opened.

If the database does not exist, it is necessary in many circumstances to create it. To create a new Palm OS database through the Database class, use the static create (int cardNo, java.lang.String name, int creatorID, int typeID, boolean resDB). The first parameter in this method is the memory card location for the database. As indicated earlier, at this time there is only one memory card for Palm OS devices and it is labeled card 0. Therefore, until this situation changes, the cardNo is always 0. The second parameter is the database name. The name must be unique with regard to all databases on the Palm OS device, and is limited to 31 characters. The creatorID and typeID, as per the constructor method, specify the registered Palm Creator ID and type ID represented in two-digit hexadecimal form. The final parameter supplied to the create() method is a boolean indicating whether to create a resource database. Again, the KJava database API does not provide a means to address resource databases. Therefore, this value should always be set to false signifying the creation of a record database.

In many cases, the Database constructor (which opens but does not create a database), the isOpen() method and the create() method are used together to ensure that a database is opened or created before continuing the application. Consider the common database initialization code as follows.

```
String dbName = "SomeDatabase";
int dbType = 0x494E5653;     //'INVS'
int dbCreator = 0x43415454;  //'CATT'
com.sun.kjava.Database quoteDB = new Database (dbType, dbCreator,
  Database.READWRITE);     ❶
if (!quoteDB.isOpen()) {                                        ❷
  Database.create(0, dbName, dbCreator, dbType, false);
  quoteDB = new Database (dbType, dbCreator, Database.READWRITE);
}
```

❶ Attempt to open the investment database

❷ If opened, use the database, otherwise create it

Notice how the constructor is used first to attempt to open the database, and then, if the attempt is unsuccessful, the constructor is used again to open the newly created database. It may look strange to see the new keyword being used when attempting to open an existing database, but remember, the Database class is simply a wrapper to the actual Palm OS database. Therefore, the call to the constructor, in either case, is not creating a database. It is merely attempting to open the existing or just-created database when it was found not to exist. The create() method returns a boolean. You may want to check this return value after sending the create() message to ensure that the database really did get created.

To close a database after you have finished using it, use the close() method on the database object.

> **WARNING** The close() method on the database object will close the actual Palm OS database; however, the isOpen() method will still return true on the Database object reference.

## 10.2.2 Accessing the database

There are several methods to access a Palm OS database through the wrapper objects. Most importantly are the methods to CRUD (create, read, update and delete) records. Through the eyes of a Database object, a Palm OS record is simply a byte array. Thus, a byte array (byte[]) is what is used to add, update or delete the database and a byte array is returned when requesting records from the database. Given the fact that the Palm OS database is really just a collection of memory chunks, it should come as little surprise that KJava treats records as simple bytes of data.

All of the database-modifying record operations (add, update, delete) will return a boolean indicating whether the particular database operation was successful. To add a new record to the database use the addRecord(byte[] data) method. For example, the following code stores the string "HelloDatabase" into the quoteDB database opened earlier in this chapter.

```
byte[] someData = "HelloDatabase".getBytes();
quoteDB.addRecord(someData);
```

In a similar fashion, to remove a record from the same database, call on the delete-Record(int recordNumber) method. The index refers to the ordered sequence or index of the record in the database. The record index numbers start at 0. Updating a record in the database requires the use of setRecord(int recordNumber, byte[] data).

Finally, to just read a record from the database, call the getRecord(int recordNumber) method. Unlike the other access methods, this method returns the byte array that is the data in the specified record in the database at the index location specified through the method parameter. Use caution when referring to any record in the database via its index. Notice that the methods to access the database do not throw exceptions. In fact, if an attempt is made to access a record at an index that does not exist, the Palm OS Data Manager crashes. The error in figure 10.1 is the result of attempting access to a record at an index that does not exist on the emulator. The error on a real device will require a soft reset of the device.

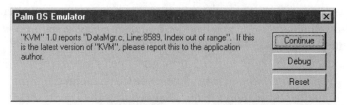

Figure 10.1   Attempting to access non-existent records in a Palm OS database can create real problems. Attempting to access a record in the database at an unused index location results in this error message. On a real device, the problem is even worse and requires a soft reset of the device.

To get the actual number of records in a database, and thus know the upper bound on the record indexes, call the `getNumberOfRecords()` method. It is a good idea to use this method to check an index before attempting to access a record with an index.

## 10.3   *IMPLEMENTING THE INVESTMENT QUOTE PERSISTENT STORAGE IN KJAVA*

The `Database` class is our means to store and retrieve data in Palm OS databases. With this wrapper class, let's update the tutorial application developed in chapter 9 to store and retrieve investment price quotes.

In the RetrieveQuoteSpotlet, you may remember that we stubbed out calls to retrieve data by simply returning the same current and historical prices all the time. Now we can fix this and really store data when obtained through the ObtainQuoteSpotlet and retrieve data when requested in the RetrieveQuoteSpotlet.

In the design of the application, recall that the ObtainQuote and RetrieveQuote use cases made use of two other use cases, namely SavePrice and RetrievePrice. These use cases stored and fetched investment price information in and out of the persistent mechanism. As we did in the MIDP application, we will create the code that implements these use cases using KJava's `Database` class in this chapter.

### 10.3.1   The stock/mutual fund record

As was learned in this chapter, a record is nothing more than a byte array. Throughout the tutorial, an investment record consists of the stock or mutual fund symbol along with the current and historical price, usually contained within a delimited string.

As mentioned previously, the CLDC, on which KJava relies, does not support floating point numbers. Therefore the use of Java's double or float base types cannot be used to represent dollar/cent prices of most stock and mutual fund quotes. Instead, we use two integers to represent one price. For example, if the stock price were $120.55, then the price must be stored as two integers, 120 and 55. One integer represents the dollars associated with the price while the second represents the cents of the price. Remember that the application must be able to store a current and a historical price for each stock or mutual fund. Therefore, along with a symbol to identify the stock or mutual fund, two sets of dollar and cent integer values must be stored. In order to store all this data in a single string, a marker or delimiter is needed to indicate where one value stops and the next data value begins. For this tutorial, we choose the semi-colon as a data delimiter. So, the string representing a current price of $120.55 and a historical price of $113.45 for 3M would look like the following:

MMM;120;55;113;45

In the case where only one price has been obtained for the stock or mutual fund, the last two trailing integers are left off. So, using our previous example, when the first price of $113.45 was obtained for 3M, the original record string would have been represented as:

MMM;113;45

The string record that contains the stock or mutual fund price quotes and investment symbol needs to be converted to a byte array before being stored as a record in the record store. This can easily be accomplished using the method getBytes() on any String object.

## 10.3.2 Storing investment quotes

The ObtainQuoteSpotlet controls all aspects of getting and storing stock or mutual fund quotes. In the user interface chapter, where the quote service and database were not available, we simply used arbitrary numbers to simulate the getting of prices. From inside the penDown() method of ObtainQuoteSpotlet, in reaction to a Get Quote button press, the following code was run:

```
if ((symbolField.getText().length() > 0) && (checkSymbol())) {
  Graphics.playSound(Graphics.SOUND_STARTUP);
  String sym = symbolField.getText().toUpperCase();
  //later on, get the price from a quote service here
  int[] price = {75, 55};
  //later on, store the price in the database here
  resultsBox.setText("The price of " + sym + " is $" + price[0] + "." +
   price[1]);
  resultsBox.paint();
}
```

**Trigger the saving of the price data here** ❶

Our goal now is to implement the storage of the price data for use by the RetrieveQuoteSpotlet later on.

To begin, we need an open Palm OS database. We saw earlier in this chapter how to open, and create if necessary, a database. We start a new method called storePrice(String symbol, int[] price). This method will fulfill the SavePrice use case described in our tutorial application design. It is passed the investment symbol and price of the quote for the investment of concern. From inside this method we open the database:

```
String dbName = "QuoteData";
int dbType = 0x494E5653;    //'INVS'    ❶
int dbCreator = 0x43415454; //'CATT'    ❷

com.sun.kjava.Database quoteDB = new Database (dbType, dbCreator,
 Database.READWRITE);                                              ❸
if (!quoteDB.isOpen()) {
  Database.create(0, dbName, dbCreator, dbType, false);
  quoteDB = new Database (dbType, dbCreator, Database.READWRITE);
}
```

❶ The database typeID

❷ The database creatorID

❸ Open or create the investment database

With the open database, we first determine if there is an existing record for the given symbol. Unlike in the MIDP RMS, there are no convenience objects for filtering the database or enumerating through records. In KJava, enumerating through the database must be done using a loop, reading, and checking each record in the database. Inside of a for loop that starts at 0 and potentially goes to the full number of records in the database, we must read each record with a call to getRecord(int recordNumber) and determine if the record contains the symbol provided by the customer.

```
boolean found = false;
int n = quoteDB.getNumberOfRecords();
for (int i = 0; i<n; i++) {
  byte[] raw = quoteDB.getRecord(i);
  if ((new String(raw)).startsWith(symbol + ';')) {
    found = true;
    newRecord += ';' + getLastPrice(raw);
    byteRec = newRecord.getBytes();
    quoteDB.setRecord(i, byteRec);
    break;
  }
}
```

The data stored in a Palm OS database comes out as a byte array. Because the symbol of the investment is stored in the front part of the data, we can simply check to see if the data, converted to a string, begins with the investment symbol. If so, we have a matching database record, indicating that a previous quote is stored in the database.

When updating an existing record, the last current price becomes the new historical price. (Figure 10.2)

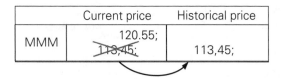

**Figure 10.2**
**When the application retrieves a new investment price for which an existing price already exists in the database, then the old price is made the historical price and the new price is made the current price.**

To assist in getting this data from the existing byte array record, another method is used to convert the byte array back to a string and to extract the last price from the string.

```
private String getLastPrice(byte[] rec) {
  String recString = new String(rec);

  int dollarPos = recString.indexOf(';');
  int centPos = recString.indexOf(';',dollarPos+1);
  int centEnd = recString.indexOf(';',centPos + 1);

  if (centEnd > 0) //had a historical price
    return recString.substring(dollarPos+1,centEnd);
  else    //no previous historical price
    return recString.substring(dollarPos+1);
}
```

**①** Get the position of the last price within the string

**②** Return the current price string, regardless of a historical price

The getLastPrice() method, developed in the MIDP tutorial application implementation, is a byte array-to-string converter with some string manipulation to find the appropriate dollar and cent values stored in between the appropriate ';' character delimiters.

In the case where no investment record is found for an investment symbol provided, a new record must be added to the database. This is accomplished using the addRecord() method. The argument passed to the addRecord() method is the new record data converted into a byte array.

```
if (!found) {
  byteRec = newRecord.getBytes();
  quoteDB.addRecord(byteRec);
}
```

Finally, don't forget to close the database with a call to the close() method after storing or updating the investment quote. All together, the new two methods added to the ObtainQuoteSpotlet look like the code in listing 10.1.

**Listing 10.1   The getLastPrice and storePrice methods in ObtainQuoteSpotlet**

```
private String getLastPrice(byte[] rec) {
  String recString = new String(rec);

  int dollarPos = recString.indexOf(';');
  int centPos = recString.indexOf(';',dollarPos+1);
  int centEnd = recString.indexOf(';',centPos + 1);

  if (centEnd > 0) //had a historical price
    return recString.substring(dollarPos+1,centEnd);
  else    //no previous historical price
    return recString.substring(dollarPos+1);
}

private void storePrice(String symbol, int[] price) {
  String newRecord = symbol + ";" + price[0] + ";" + price[1];
  byte[] byteRec;
  String dbName = "QuoteData";
  int dbType = 0x494E5653;    //'INVS'
```

```
    int dbCreator = 0x43415454;   //'CATT'

    com.sun.kjava.Database quoteDB = new Database (dbType, dbCreator,
      Database.READWRITE);
    if (!quoteDB.isOpen()) {
      Database.create(0, dbName, dbCreator, dbType, false);
      quoteDB = new Database (dbType, dbCreator, Database.READWRITE);
    }

    boolean found = false;

    int n = quoteDB.getNumberOfRecords();
    for (int i = 0; i<n; i++) {
      byte[] raw = quoteDB.getRecord(i);
      if ((new String(raw)).startsWith(symbol + ';')) {
        found = true;
        newRecord += ';' + getLastPrice(raw);
        byteRec = newRecord.getBytes();
        quoteDB.setRecord(i, byteRec);
        break;
      }
    }
    if (!found) {
      byteRec = newRecord.getBytes();
      quoteDB.addRecord(byteRec);
    }
    quoteDB.close();
}
```

The only other change required to have the ObtainQuoteSpotlet now work with the
Palm OS database is to have the penDown method call the storePrice() method
after the price, or in this case, the phony price, has been obtained.

```
if ((symbolField.getText().length() > 0) && (checkSymbol())) {
  Graphics.playSound(Graphics.SOUND_STARTUP);
  String sym = symbolField.getText().toUpperCase();
  //later on, get the price from a quote service here
  int[] price = {75, 55};
  storePrice(sym, price);       ❶ Call to store the price quote when obtained
  resultsBox.setText("The price of " + sym + " is $" + price[0] + "." +
    price[1]);
  resultsBox.paint();
}
```

To see the KJava database wrapper in action, we go back to Jbed to rebuild our appli-
cation. First make sure the ObtainQuote project is in use. Go to the Projects menu bar
option and make sure the ObtainQuote project is checked. Next, open the Obtain-
QuoteSpotlet.java file by selecting the File menu bar option and selecting the
Open... menu item. After finding and selecting the ObtainQuoteSpotlet.java in the
Open dialog box, add the code discussed previously to the Java program in the text editor.
In particular, add the two new methods, storePrice() and getLastPrice(),

as well as the changes to the penDown() method. Then, to compile the application, select Java from the menu bar and select the Compile item. Finally, to link the application, select Jbed from the menu bar and select the Link item. This will result in the creation of an ObtainQuoteSpotlet.prc that, with these additions, is up to about 118 KB in size.

### 10.3.3 Retrieving records

Having the data stored in a database does no good unless it is saved for later retrieval. In this part of the tutorial, the stock and mutual funds can be retrieved to display the current and historical prices of a given investment. Recall that in the exploration of the KJava user interface, we even developed a means to graphically depict the current and historical prices in a comparison bar chart using KJava's Graphics object.

As with the ObtainQuoteSpotlet, the RetrieveQuoteSpotlet was written to demonstrate the user interface capabilities and so the actual investment symbol and quote were simply passed as fake parameters to the display methods. From earlier in our tutorial, the penDown() event handling method called on the displayChart() when the "Get Quote" button was pushed to display the quote chart. In order to test the display, fake current and historical prices ($75 and $110) were put in an integer array as if they were pulled from a database from inside of the displayChart() method.

```
//later on, get prices from a database here
int[] prices = {75,55,110,45};
```

It is now time to retrofit the RetrieveQuoteSpotlet to open the quote database and retrieve stored quotes placed in the database by the ObtainQuoteSpotlet. We start by developing a method called retrievePrices(String symbol) to get quotes from the database based on a symbol supplied by the caller. This method, as shown in listing 10.2, will satisfy the RetrievePrice use case specified in the tutorial application design.

**Listing 10.2   The retrievePrices method in RetrieveQuoteSpotlet**

```
private int[] retrievePrices(String symbol) {

  int[] dollars = null;

  String dbName = "QuoteData";
  int dbType = 0x494E5653;    //'INVS'
  int dbCreator = 0x43415454; //'CATT'
  com.sun.kjava.Database quoteDB = new Database (dbType, dbCreator,
    Database.READWRITE);
  if (!quoteDB.isOpen()) {
    Database.create(0, dbName, dbCreator, dbType, false);
    quoteDB = new Database (dbType, dbCreator, Database.READWRITE);
  }

  boolean found = false;
```

**Open the ❶
Palm OS database
(creating it if it
does not exist)**

```
int n = quoteDB.getNumberOfRecords();
for (int i = 0; i<n; i++) {
  String raw = new String(quoteDB.getRecord(i));
  if (raw.startsWith(symbol + ';')) {
    found = true;
    byte[] rec = quoteDB.getRecord(i);
    dollars = parsePrices(rec);
    break;
  }
}
if (!found) {
  dollars = null;
}
quoteDB.close();
return dollars;
}
```

**2** If a record for the investment is found, return the current and historical prices

**3** If a record for the investment is not found, return null signifying no prices and no record

At first glance, the retrievePrices() method looks a lot like the storePrice() method from the ObtainQuoteSpotlet. In fact, they both use a loop to locate a record. However this time, instead of updating or adding the record, the retrievePrices() method simply extracts the current and historical dollar prices from any matching record found.

Extracting the dollar prices from a record is again a matter of string manipulation and character matching. It is handled by the parsePrices(byte[] quoteRec) method, which was also developed and used in the MIDP tutorial application. Each record contains the symbol for the investment and up to two sets of integers for the dollars and cents of each price quote (current and possibly historical price). The current and historical prices are extracted from the record and returned in an integer array. If the investment has only one price stored for it, then the array returned contains two integers: the dollar and cents of the currently known price for the investment. If a historical price is also known for the investment, the integer array will have four numbers representing the current dollars and cents price as well as the historical dollars and cents price respectively. (Listing 10.3)

**Listing 10.3   The parsePrices method reused in the RetrieveQuoteSpotlet**

```
private int[] parsePrices(byte[] quoteRec) {
  String rec = new String(quoteRec);
  int dollar1Pos = rec.indexOf(';');
  int cent1Pos = rec.indexOf(';',dollar1Pos+1);
  int dollar2Pos = rec.indexOf(';',cent1Pos + 1);

  if (dollar2Pos > 0) { //had a historical price
    int cent2Pos = rec.indexOf(';',dollar2Pos + 1);
    int currentDollars = Integer.parseInt(rec.substring(dollar1Pos + 1,
      cent1Pos));
    int currentCents = Integer.parseInt(rec.substring(cent1Pos + 1,
      dollar2Pos));
```

```
    int historicalDollars = Integer.parseInt(rec.substring(dollar2Pos + 1,
      cent2Pos));
    int historicalCents = Integer.parseInt(rec.substring(cent2Pos + 1));
    int[] returnPrices = {currentDollars, currentCents, historicalDollars,
      historicalCents};
    return returnPrices;
  } else {    //no previous historical price
    int currentDollars = Integer.parseInt(rec.substring(dollar1Pos + 1,
      cent1Pos));
    int currentCents = Integer.parseInt(rec.substring(cent1Pos + 1));
    int[] returnPrices = {currentDollars, currentCents};
    return returnPrices;
  }
}
```

With these two methods added to the RetrieveQuoteSpotlet, the only remaining task is to have the `retrievePrices()` method called when the Get Quote button is pushed. This is accomplished inside of the Spotlet's `displayChart()` method. Now, instead of generating an `int` array containing phony prices, the `display-Chart()` method just calls the `retrievePrices()` method with the symbol supplied by the customer.

```
int[] prices = retrievePrices(currentSymbol);
```

With this code entered into the RetrieveQuoteSpotlet.java file, use Jbed to compile and link the application just as you did with the ObtainQuoteSpotlet. Do not forget that the RetrieveQuoteSpotlet is a separate Jbed project, namely the RetrieveQuote project.

## 10.4  REVISITING THE CONNECTION TO THE INTERNET

Our Spotlet version of the tutorial application is nearly complete. We have a user interface and data being stored to Palm OS databases. What's left to implement? In the MIDP version of the tutorial application, we implemented a means, the Quote-Service, to connect to the Internet and pull down investment prices.

Because KJava runs on top of the CLDC, and because we implemented the Quote Service as generically as possible, we can reuse this service without modification. The foundation of the Quote Service lies in the Generic Connection Framework and the `java.io` package. While the MIDP offers some enhancements to the GCF, we choose not to use them in order to keep the implementation of the Quote Service as portable as possible.

Therefore, in order to get the ObtainQuoteSpotlet connected to the World Wide Web for investment price information, we simply have to have the Spotlet call on the already developed QuoteService. This entails replacing the following line in the `penDown()` method

```
//later on, get the price from a quote service here
int[] price = {75, 55};
```

with a call to the service. Because we are no longer using the phony price array that always returns the same results, some routine condition handling is now in order. The QuoteService may not return a price. This is the case if the service is not available (maybe the quote Web site is down), or if the customer has provided an incorrect symbol. Therefore, add a conditional check that the price array return is not null. If the price is null, an appropriate message is displayed to the customer in the form of a dialog.

```
String sym = symbolField.getText().toUpperCase();
int type;

if (investmentChoice.getSelected().equals(fundButton))
  type = 1;
else
  type = 0;
int[] price = QuoteService.getPrice(sym,type);
if (price != null) {
  storePrice(sym, price);
  resultsBox.setText("The price of " + sym + " is $"
  + price[0] + "." + price[1]);
  resultsBox.paint();
} else {
  Graphics.playSound(Graphics.SOUND_ERROR);
  Dialog symbolAlert = new Dialog(this,"Alert",
    "Check Symbol and Type.\n\nNo quote found.","OK");
  symbolAlert.showDialog();
}
```

**❶** Get which investment type of radio button is selected

**❷** Get the price from the QuoteService, passing the symbol and type

**❸** If a price is found, store the price and display the price to the customer

**❹** If no price is found, display an indication that the price is not found.

In order to use the QuoteService in the tutorial application, we must add the `Quote-Service` class and a few other Jbed GCF implementation items to our application. To do this, we need to return to the ObtainQuote project in Jbed.

Start the Jbed IDE, select Projects from the Jbed menu bar and select ObtainQuote in order to set the current project to the ObtainQuote project. Edit the project properties file by selecting the Edit Project menu option from the same Projects menu after the project has been set. In the LINKER section of the properties displayed, add the following classes just before the ObtainQuoteSpotlet:

```
com.jbed.microedition.protocol.SocketFactory
com.jbed.microedition.protocol.HttpFactory
com.jbed.net.DnsImpl
QuoteService
```

The QuoteService class is the service and this class file must be located in the same place as the ObtainQuoteSpotlet. We will compile this file in a moment. The other class files are Jbed-provided classes for implementing the GCF. (GCF was introduced in chapter 7 and will be discussed in more detail in chapter13). The `SocketFactory` and `HttpFactory` classes provide a factory service built by esmertec for implementing HTTP connectivity through the GCF `Connector`. `DnsImpl` allows the framework to use domain name services (DNS) as an option in the connections. With DNS, the program can reference domains by name, whereas without this class, the application would only be able to use IP numbers, such as 204.221.213.98, when connecting.

After adding the previous entries, the LINKER section of the project should look like that displayed in figure 10.3.

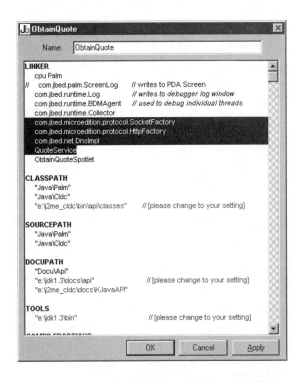

**Figure 10.3**
**Additions, highlighted here in black, must be made to the Jbed project properties in order to connect ObtainQuote to the Internet. These additions provide the necessary classes for our ObtainQuoteSpotlet to connect to the Internet via the HTTP protocol.**

Before linking the application into a PRC file, the `QuoteService` class must be compiled. If you already entered the QuoteService.java code during the MIDP implementation, simply copy the file (the QuoteService.java file) to the \Jbed\Java\Palm directory and open the file in the Jbed IDE. If this file has not been entered, open a new file from within Jbed and enter the QuoteService.java code as it was provided in chapter 7. To compile the Quote Service, with the .java file open and selected in the IDE, select the Java menu bar option and select Compile (or press Ctrl+L).

Make certain the ObtainQuoteSpotlet.java file is also compiled and then link the entire application by selecting Jbed and then Link (or press Ctrl+Q). The KJava implementation of the tutorial application, complete with access to the same external quote service, is now available for testing on the POSE and eventual deployment to a Palm OS device.

The complete ObtainQuoteSpotlet.java and RetrieveQuoteSpotlet.java are provided below to bring all the material in this chapter together. As mentioned before, the QuoteService did not change and therefore the complete QuoteService.java file from chapter 7 can be reused.

```
import com.sun.kjava.*;

public final class ObtainQuoteSpotlet extends Spotlet implements DialogOwner {

    private TextField symbolField = null;
    private RadioButton stockButton = null;
    private RadioButton fundButton = null;
    private RadioGroup investmentChoice = null;
    private ScrollTextBox resultsBox = null;
    private Button exitButton = null;
    private Button getButton = null;

    public ObtainQuoteSpotlet() {
        String tfLabel = "Symbol";
        symbolField = new TextField(tfLabel,5,25,Graphics.getWidth(tfLabel) +
            40, Graphics.getHeight(tfLabel));
        stockButton = new RadioButton(50,45,"Stock");
        fundButton = new RadioButton(100,45,"Fund");
        investmentChoice = new RadioGroup(2);
        investmentChoice.add(stockButton);
        investmentChoice.add(fundButton);
        investmentChoice.setSelected(stockButton);
        resultsBox = new ScrollTextBox("",8,65,137,45);
        exitButton = new Button("Exit",5,140);
        getButton = new Button("Get Quote", 105,140);
    }

    public static void main (String args[]) {
        ObtainQuoteSpotlet quoteSpotlet = new ObtainQuoteSpotlet();
        quoteSpotlet.displayForm();
    }

    private void displayForm() {
        register(NO_EVENT_OPTIONS);
        Graphics.clearScreen();
        Graphics.drawString("Obtain Investment Quote",5,10,Graphics.INVERT);
        Graphics.drawString("Type:",5,45, Graphics.PLAIN);
        symbolField.paint();
        stockButton.paint();
        fundButton.paint();
        resultsBox.paint();
        Graphics.drawBorder(5,60, 150, 55, Graphics.PLAIN, Graphics.SIMPLE);
        exitButton.paint();
        getButton.paint();
    }
```

```
    private boolean checkSymbol() {
        if ((investmentChoice.getSelected().equals(fundButton)) &&
            !(symbolField.getText().toUpperCase().endsWith("X"))){
            Graphics.playSound(Graphics.SOUND_ERROR);
            Dialog symbolAlert = new Dialog(this,"Alert",
              "Check Symbol\n\nMutual Funds end in 'X'","OK");
            symbolAlert.showDialog();
            return false;
        }
        return true;
    }

    private String getLastPrice(byte[] rec) {
        String recString = new String(rec);

        int dollarPos = recString.indexOf(';');
        int centPos = recString.indexOf(';',dollarPos+1);
        int centEnd = recString.indexOf(';',centPos + 1);

        if (centEnd > 0) //had a historical price
            return recString.substring(dollarPos+1,centEnd);
        else     //no previous historical price
            return recString.substring(dollarPos+1);
    }


    private void storePrice(String symbol, int[] price) {
        String newRecord = symbol + ";" + price[0] + ";" + price[1];
        byte[] byteRec;

        String dbName = "QuoteData";
        int dbType = 0x494E5653;    //'INVS'
        //'CATT' Palm-registered database creator id
        //for Catapult Technologies.  Assigned hex value
        int dbCreator = 0x43415454;

        com.sun.kjava.Database quoteDB = new Database (dbType, dbCreator,
        Database.READWRITE);
        if (!quoteDB.isOpen()) {
            Database.create(0, dbName, dbCreator, dbType, false);
            quoteDB = new Database (dbType, dbCreator, Database.READWRITE);
        }

        boolean found = false;

        int n = quoteDB.getNumberOfRecords();
        for (int i = 0; i<n; i++) {
            byte[] raw = quoteDB.getRecord(i);
            if ((new String(raw)).startsWith(symbol + ';')) {
                found = true;
                newRecord += ';' + getLastPrice(raw);
                byteRec = newRecord.getBytes();
                quoteDB.setRecord(i, byteRec);
                break;
```

```
                }
            }
            if (!found) {
                byteRec = newRecord.getBytes();
                quoteDB.addRecord(byteRec);
            }
            quoteDB.close();
        }

        public void penDown(int x, int y) {
            if (exitButton.pressed(x,y)){
                Graphics.playSound(Graphics.SOUND_CONFIRMATION);
                System.exit(0);
            } else if (getButton.pressed(x,y)) {
                symbolField.loseFocus();
                if ((symbolField.getText().length() > 0) && (checkSymbol())) {
                    Graphics.playSound(Graphics.SOUND_STARTUP);
                    String sym = symbolField.getText().toUpperCase();
                    int type;
                    if (investmentChoice.getSelected().equals(fundButton))
                      type = 1;
                    else
                      type = 0;
                    //later on, get the price from a quote service here
                    int[] price = QuoteService.getPrice(sym,type);
                    if (price != null) {
                        storePrice(sym, price);
                        resultsBox.setText("The price of " + sym + " is $" +
                          price[0] + "." + price[1]);
                        resultsBox.paint();
                    } else {
                        Graphics.playSound(Graphics.SOUND_ERROR);
                        Dialog symbolAlert = new Dialog(this,"Alert",
                          "Check Symbol and Type.\n\nNo quote found.","OK");
                        symbolAlert.showDialog();
                    }
                }
            } else if (symbolField.pressed(x,y)) {
                symbolField.setFocus();
            } else if (stockButton.pressed(x,y)) {
                symbolField.loseFocus();
                stockButton.handlePenDown(x,y);
            } else if (fundButton.pressed(x,y)) {
                symbolField.loseFocus();
                fundButton.handlePenDown(x,y);
            } else if (resultsBox.contains(x,y)) {
                resultsBox.handlePenDown(x,y);
            }
        }

        public void keyDown (int keyCode) {
            if ((keyCode == 11) || (keyCode == 12)){
                resultsBox.handleKeyDown(keyCode);
            } else if (symbolField.hasFocus()) {
```

```
            symbolField.handleKeyDown(keyCode);
        }
    }

    public void penMove (int x, int y) {
        if (resultsBox.contains(x,y)) {
            resultsBox.handlePenMove(x,y);
        }
    }

    public void dialogDismissed(java.lang.String title) {
        this.displayForm();
    }
}
```

**Listing 10.5   Complete RetrieveQuoteSpotlet.java**

```
import com.sun.kjava.*;

public final class RetrieveQuoteSpotlet extends Spotlet implements DialogOwner{

    static int MAX_BAR_SIZE = 150;
    static int START_X_POSITION = 5;
    static int START_Y_CURRENT = 97;
    static int START_Y_HISTORIC = 122;
    static int BAR_HEIGHT = 5;

    private TextField symbolField = null;
    private RadioButton stockButton = null;
    private RadioButton fundButton = null;
    private RadioGroup investmentChoice = null;
    private Button exitButton = null;
    private Button getButton = null;

    public RetrieveQuoteSpotlet() {
        String tfLabel = "Symbol";
        symbolField = new TextField(tfLabel,5,25,Graphics.getWidth(tfLabel) +
                                    40, Graphics.getHeight(tfLabel));
        stockButton = new RadioButton(50,45,"Stock");
        fundButton = new RadioButton(100,45,"Fund");
        investmentChoice = new RadioGroup(2);
        investmentChoice.add(stockButton);
        investmentChoice.add(fundButton);
        investmentChoice.setSelected(stockButton);
        exitButton = new Button("Exit",5,140);
        getButton = new Button("Get Quote", 105,140);
    }

    public static void main (String args[]) {
        RetrieveQuoteSpotlet quoteSpotlet = new RetrieveQuoteSpotlet();
        quoteSpotlet.displayForm();
    }
```

```
private void displayForm() {
    register(NO_EVENT_OPTIONS);
    Graphics.clearScreen();
    Graphics.drawString("Retrieve Investment Quote",5,10,Graphics.INVERT);
    Graphics.drawString("Type:",5,45, Graphics.PLAIN);
    symbolField.paint();
    stockButton.paint();
    fundButton.paint();
    exitButton.paint();
    getButton.paint();
}

private boolean checkSymbol() {
    if ((investmentChoice.getSelected().equals(fundButton)) &&
        !(symbolField.getText().toUpperCase().endsWith("X"))){
        Graphics.playSound(Graphics.SOUND_ERROR);
        Dialog symbolAlert = new Dialog(this,"Alert",
            "Check Symbol\n\nMutual Funds end in 'X'","OK");
        symbolAlert.showDialog();
        return false;
    }
    return true;
}

private int[] parsePrices(byte[] quoteRec) {
    String rec = new String(quoteRec);
    int dollar1Pos = rec.indexOf(';');
    int cent1Pos = rec.indexOf(';',dollar1Pos+1);
    int dollar2Pos = rec.indexOf(';',cent1Pos + 1);

    System.out.println("=====> " + rec);

    if (dollar2Pos > 0) { //had a historical price
        int cent2Pos = rec.indexOf(';',dollar2Pos + 1);
        int currentDollars = Integer.parseInt(rec.substring(dollar1Pos +
            1, cent1Pos));
        int currentCents = Integer.parseInt(rec.substring(cent1Pos + 1,
            dollar2Pos));
        int historicalDollars = Integer.parseInt(rec.substring(dollar2Pos
            + 1, cent2Pos));
        int historicalCents = Integer.parseInt(rec.substring(cent2Pos
            + 1));
        int[] returnPrices = {currentDollars, currentCents,
            historicalDollars, historicalCents};
        return returnPrices;
    }
    else {   //no previous historical price
        int currentDollars = Integer.parseInt(rec.substring(dollar1Pos
            + 1, cent1Pos));
        int currentCents = Integer.parseInt(rec.substring(cent1Pos + 1));
        int[] returnPrices = {currentDollars, currentCents};
        return returnPrices;
    }
}

private int[] retrievePrices(String symbol) {
```

```
        int[] dollars = null;

        String dbName = "QuoteData";
        int dbType = 0x494E5653;    //'INVS'
        //'CATT' Palm-registered database creator id
        //for Catapult Technologies.  Assigned hex value
        int dbCreator = 0x43415454;

        com.sun.kjava.Database quoteDB = new Database (dbType, dbCreator,
          Database.READWRITE);
        if (!quoteDB.isOpen()) {
            Database.create(0, dbName, dbCreator, dbType, false);
            quoteDB = new Database (dbType, dbCreator, Database.READWRITE);
        }

        boolean found = false;

        for (int i = 0; i<quoteDB.getNumberOfRecords(); i++) {
            String raw = new String(quoteDB.getRecord(i));
            if (raw.startsWith(symbol + ';')) {
                found = true;
                byte[] rec = quoteDB.getRecord(i);
                dollars = parsePrices(rec);
                break;
            }
        }
        if (!found) {
            dollars = null;
        }
        quoteDB.close();
        return dollars;
    }

private void displayChart(String currentSymbol) {
    int[] prices = retrievePrices(currentSymbol);
    if (prices != null) {
        if (prices.length > 2) {
            paintChart(currentSymbol,prices[0],prices[2]);
        } else {
            Graphics.drawRectangle(5,60,155,70,Graphics.ERASE,0);
            Graphics.drawString("Recorded price for " + currentSymbol +
                " is:  $" + prices[0] + "." + prices[1],
                5, 65, Graphics.PLAIN);
            Graphics.drawString("No historical data exists.", 5, 80,
                Graphics.INVERT);
        }
    }
    else {
        Graphics.playSound(Graphics.SOUND_ERROR);
        Dialog noDataAlert = new Dialog(this,"Alert",
          "No price exists for " + currentSymbol,"OK");
        noDataAlert.showDialog();
    }
}
```

```java
public void paintChart(String sym, int currentPrice, int historicPrice) {
    Graphics.drawRectangle(5,60,155,70,Graphics.ERASE,0);
    Graphics.drawString(sym + " Performance",5,60,Graphics.PLAIN);
    Graphics.drawString("current vs. historic",5,73,Graphics.PLAIN);
    Graphics.drawString("$" + currentPrice, 5, 85, Graphics.PLAIN);
    Graphics.drawString("$" + historicPrice, 5, 110, Graphics.PLAIN);

    int[] prices = {currentPrice, historicPrice};
    int[] lengths = determineLengths(prices);
    Graphics.drawRectangle (START_X_POSITION, START_Y_CURRENT, lengths[0],
       BAR_HEIGHT, Graphics.PLAIN, 0);
    Graphics.drawRectangle (START_X_POSITION, START_Y_HISTORIC,
       lengths[1], BAR_HEIGHT, Graphics.PLAIN, 0);

    for (int i = 30; i < MAX_BAR_SIZE; i = i + 30) {
       Graphics.drawLine (i, START_Y_CURRENT - 2, i, START_Y_HISTORIC +
          BAR_HEIGHT + 2, Graphics.PLAIN);
    }
}

private int[] determineLengths (int[] prices) {

    int ratio, higherPrice, lowerPrice;
    boolean currentHigher;

    if (prices[0] < prices[1]) {
       higherPrice = prices[1];
       lowerPrice = prices[0];
       currentHigher=false;
    } else {
       higherPrice = prices[0];
       lowerPrice = prices[1];
       currentHigher=true;
    }

    ratio = higherPrice/MAX_BAR_SIZE + 1;
    while (ratio > 1) {
       higherPrice = higherPrice/ratio;
       lowerPrice = lowerPrice/ratio;
       ratio = higherPrice/MAX_BAR_SIZE + 1;
    }

    if (currentHigher) {
       int[] ends = {higherPrice, lowerPrice};
       return ends;
    } else {
       int [] ends = {lowerPrice, higherPrice};
       return ends;
    }
}

public void penDown(int x, int y) {
    if (exitButton.pressed(x,y)){
       Graphics.playSound(Graphics.SOUND_CONFIRMATION);
       System.exit(0);
```

```
        } else if (getButton.pressed(x,y)) {
            symbolField.loseFocus();
            if ((symbolField.getText().length() > 0) && (checkSymbol())) {
                Graphics.playSound(Graphics.SOUND_STARTUP);
                String sym = symbolField.getText().toUpperCase();
                displayChart(sym);
            }
        } else if (symbolField.pressed(x,y)) {
            symbolField.setFocus();
        } else if (stockButton.pressed(x,y)) {
            symbolField.loseFocus();
            stockButton.handlePenDown(x,y);
        } else if (fundButton.pressed(x,y)) {
            symbolField.loseFocus();
            fundButton.handlePenDown(x,y);
        }
    }

    public void keyDown (int keyCode) {
        if (symbolField.hasFocus()) {
            symbolField.handleKeyDown(keyCode);
        }
    }

    public void dialogDismissed(java.lang.String title) {
        this.displayForm();
    }
}
```

## 10.5  ACCESSING PALM OS APPLICATION DATABASES

Palm OS devices have a rich set of applications that many Palm OS device users have come to know and love. These include the Address Book, Calendar, To Do List and Memo applications. These applications, in particular, are hardwired to the hard keys at the bottom of the device.

A common question is often raised in J2ME circles as to whether a Java application, or more precisely a KJava application, can access the databases of these applications. In fact, the Database class is just a wrapper for any Palm OS database. All that is required is to have the database type and creator IDs. While it is possible to access these databases, care should be taken when doing so. As we have seen, the KJava Database wrapper is an interface to the Palm OS databases, and you can easily destroy the databases for these precious applications.

As a small example of how to access one of these databases, we open the Address Book database and count the number of records it has in listing 10.4.

To create this application, open a new Jbed project. We copied the ObtainQuote project and called our project CountAddresses. In the LINKER section of the New Project editor, replace the ObtainQuoteSpotlet class with the new CountAddress class.

Listing 10.6   Accessing the Palm Address Book

```
import com.sun.kjava.*;

public class CountAddress extends Spotlet {
  Button exitButton;
  ScrollTextBox results;
  Database addressDB;
  int dbType = 0x44415441;    //'addr'
  int dbCreator = 0x61646472; //'DATA'

  public static void main(String[] args) {
      new CountAddress().count();
  }

  public void count() {
      register(NO_EVENT_OPTIONS);
      exitButton = new Button("Exit",10,130);
      results = new ScrollTextBox("",5,10,150,100);
      Graphics.clearScreen();
      addressDB = new Database(dbType, dbCreator, Database.READWRITE);
      int numRec = addressDB.getNumberOfRecords();
      addressDB.close();
      results.setText("The # of recs in the Address
        Book Database is:  " + numRec);
      exitButton.paint();
      results.paint();
  }
  public void penDown(int x, int y){
      if (exitButton.pressed(x,y))
              System.exit(0);
  }
}
```

**1** The type and creator IDs are established by Palm

**Open the Address Book database 2**

**3** Get the number of addresses

**4** Don't forget to close the Address Book database

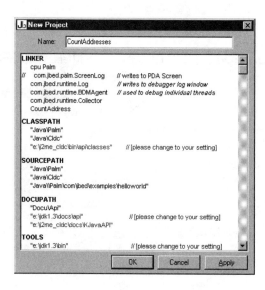

**Figure 10.4**
To create a new Jbed project for the CountAddress application, apply project properties similar to those depicted here. We copied ours from the ObtainQuote project.

*CHAPTER 10   KJAVA DATA STORAGE*

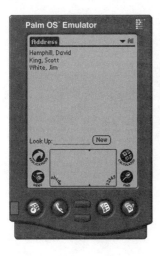

**Figure 10.5**
**If the Address Book contains three names as suggested on the left, the results of running CountAddress are shown on the right.**

Open a new file editor and enter the code from above. Save the file as CountAddress.java. Compile this file by selecting Java from the Jbed menu bar and then selecting the Compile menu item. After the application compiles successfully, link the application to produce the CompileAddresses.prc. This is done by selecting Jbed from the menu bar and Link from the dropdown menu. When the application is deployed to either an emulator or device, results similar to those depicted in figure 10.5 should appear.

## 10.6 SUMMARY

In this chapter, we explored the Palm OS database and KJava's wrapper Database class to allow KJava applications access to them. While certainly not as feature-rich as the MIDP RMS, the Database class provided the basic support necessary to store, update and retrieve information on Palm OS devices.

Without so much as a single line of code change in the QuoteService of chapter 7, we connected the KJava version of the tutorial application to an external price quote web site. This was accomplished through the use of the Generic Connection Framework. Finally, we looked at using the KJava Database wrapper class to access other Palm OS application databases.

# PART 4

# Developing for the enterprise: beyond the specifications

The next few chapters are dedicated to helping developers and architects design J2ME applications that can be used in an enterprise setting. This part of the book provides a more comprehensive examination of Java and other server-side technologies such as Servlets, Java ServerPages, XML, HTTP and small footprint relational databases. Additionally, there are two chapters that provide a more in-depth examination of J2ME networking and the J2ME runtime environment. The final chapter provides a starting point for investigating products that can assist developers in creating J2ME applications.

# Real-world design

When new technology emerges into the marketplace, a fair amount of information tends to surface about how to use the technology itself, such as how the APIs are organized, how the pieces are put together, and so forth. However, there tends to be a gap between information on how the technology works versus how to build applications with it.

The intent of this chapter is to provide guidance from an application architecture perspective. The information in this chapter is based on our real-world experience in building J2ME and Java applications for mobile devices. Although J2ME comprises more than mobile and wireless devices, such as Internet TV set-top boxes and other fixed devices, the focus here is on mobile and wireless devices. However, many of the lessons can be applied to applications that use the J2ME APIs, regardless of the actual device.

To begin, we will discuss the critical issue of dealing with stakeholders. Stakeholders are the reason for building software. Among other interested parties, they are the managers, end users, and financiers of software development. To be successful with developing mobile and wireless solutions, stakeholders must be familiar with what it means to develop for the mobile and wireless paradigm.

## 11.1 DEALING WITH STAKEHOLDERS

The concepts involved in building J2ME applications for devices that are as constrained and varied as cellular phones and set-top boxes often requires a shift in thinking for developers. For non-technical people that are sponsoring, recommending or providing the business vision for the development of such applications, the required shift in thinking may not come as naturally or as quickly as desired.

Keeping with the chapter focus on mobile and wireless devices, stakeholders must be informed and knowledgeable about the paradigm of mobile and wireless computing. Developing mobile and wireless applications requires people to think differently about how tasks are performed on computing devices. For nontechnical people who are used to desktop or even mainframe, terminal-based computers, the shift to mobile and wireless devices can be difficult. The familiar way of doing things may not make sense, be appropriate or even be possible on a mobile device. When dealing with stakeholders it is essential to understand the motivation behind creating a mobile and wireless solution.

In some cases, the initial thinking for developing mobile applications may be something along the lines of:

- providing access to the enterprise on a cellular phone or PDA
- decreasing the need for a mobile worker to be in the office
- improving communication in the field
- replacing expensive laptop computers with smaller, cheaper devices

All of these visions have merit. However, the job of an architect is to balance the needs and desires of the sponsors with what is possible and practical on the chosen devices. Many problems developing mobile and wireless devices can be avoided by educating the stakeholders and conducting some analysis of the underlying problems that are to be solved. How much functionality are stakeholders willing to forego in favor of mobility? Different devices have different limitations. But if the desired or necessary capabilities cannot be placed into some kind of J2ME device, the next step up is a laptop or PC.

### 11.1.1 Get them familiar with the devices early

During initial meetings with stakeholders it is important to level the field. Make certain each decision maker understands the nature of the device or devices that are being discussed. A good approach is to get one of these devices in the hands of stakeholders. Let them use the applications and features that come with the device. This will provide an opportunity to see if the stakeholders even like the device. They can test the data entry capabilities, such as Graffiti, virtual keyboards, alphanumeric entry on a 10-digit keypad, and so forth. If the device supports a wireless connection, how do they like reading their email on the smaller screen, creating messages and replying, and the amount of time required to download messages? By putting devices in the hands of a stakeholder they become familiar with the paradigm, which may help them to start thinking differently about these devices. It is also a good idea to put the candidate devices in the hands of the end users as well. If the end users like the device, they are positioned to get behind your project. If they hate the device, you can avoid deploying a wonderful application onto a device that the users hate, before the organization commits to buying the devices.

When stakeholders are new to the mobile and wireless paradigm it is important to point out language that is commonly taken for granted in discussing computer applications. For example, avoid terminology that may be inappropriate for the candidate devices such as "We save this data into the file…" or "From this menu…" It is quite possible that the candidate devices do not support a file system or menu system.

### 11.1.2 Set expectations

Mobile and wireless devices are slower than desktops. They probably always will be, relatively speaking. Currently, wireless access to the Internet typically ranges between a fiery 9600 bps to 19.2 kbps. Battery life of the devices is affected by the applications and batteries will need to be recharged. Many devices require charging both the modem and the device separately. If the device loses its charge completely you may lose data in permanent storage. If the device is lost, how accessible or secure is the data? Discuss issues with single-task and single-processor devices. These devices will not be able to allow users to open and switch between multiple windows or run multiple applications concurrently.

### 11.1.3 Gathering requirements

Encourage stakeholders to be open to new options and different methods of dealing with information. Also, encourage exploration into and focus on functionality that is made possible by the mobile and wireless paradigm that cannot be implemented on a fixed desktop computer.

As an architect, it is important to make certain that stakeholders have identified and are focused on solving a specific problem. The problem should be clearly stated in terms of the business, not in terms of technology. For example, allowing order entry to be performed on a cellular phone may be a good idea, but what does it mean to the business? Will the business actually benefit by putting this functionality onto a device? Will the benefit justify the expense of doing the work? Above all, you need to make sure that J2ME is not in the picture simply because it is Java, or that the organization is going mobile just to be mobile. Without an underlying business need, it becomes difficult, as an architect, to make appropriate design trade-off decisions.

### 11.1.4 State of the organization

Before embarking on a J2ME project, it is important to consider what kind of technological position an organization is in. If an organization currently does not have a commitment to Java or if this mobile and wireless solution is to be the first Java endeavor of the organization, the implications could be more than expected. J2ME is not necessarily a good place to introduce Java to a team of developers due to the variances in devices and the implementations within the J2ME architecture required to support a wide range of devices. Also, once the J2ME solution is in the field, will the organization be able to adequately support the implementation?

Another important consideration that is often overlooked is whether or not the organization is ready for a mobile and wireless solution. Are there issues with the existing infrastructure that make it difficult for the J2ME applications to access the necessary data? Does the organization want to implement a mobile and wireless solution to compensate for an existing infrastructure that is insufficient? In other words, if the infrastructure problems were fixed, would there be a need for a mobile and wireless solution?

As with any software development project, it is essential to have stakeholders involved early in the process. It is equally important that stakeholders understand how their organization and workflows will benefit or be impacted by mobile and wireless solutions. The next section illustrates the early stages of a typical development scenario.

## 11.2  A DEVELOPMENT SCENARIO

Developing wireless, mobile and Internet appliance applications differ, in some cases significantly, from more traditional desktop and enterprise application architectures. This section illustrates an early phase of a fictional project using the following scenario:

A national landscaping company by the name of The Greener Grass Corporation provides custom lawn and landscaping services to residential homes and commercial businesses. Over the last two years, the Greener Grass Corporation has invested a fair amount of time, effort and money in their Java Servlet-based inventory and order-entry system. The system is accessible over the Internet and provides customers with a catalog of their products and provides a way to order supplies. The basic architecture of this system is depicted in figure 11.1.

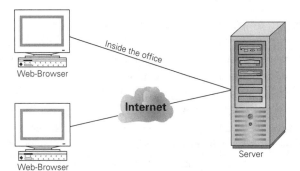

**Figure 11.1**
**The existing software configuration that allows users to access the enterprise server resources through a browser. Access to the system is available from inside the office over the local area network as well as outside the office over the Internet.**

In addition to selling landscaping supplies, the Greener Grass Corporation also sells landscaping services. The field workers they employ must come into the office routinely to drop off orders and to obtain supplies. Recently, however, since the inventory and order entry systems are online, some are opting to submit orders over the Internet from home. In order to streamline their business, the Greener Grass Corporation would like to provide this information to their field staff. Furthermore, they would like to be able to monitor status and automate their project scheduling process as much as possible.

After a series of meetings, the Greener Grass Corporation has arrived at the conclusion that what they need is to put their inventory and order entry system, along with the scheduling enhancements, onto a cell phone. They feel cell phones are a good choice since their staff already has cell phones and this would not introduce another device that they would need to carry. The proposed architecture for including wireless cell phone access to the corporate systems is shown in figure 11.2.

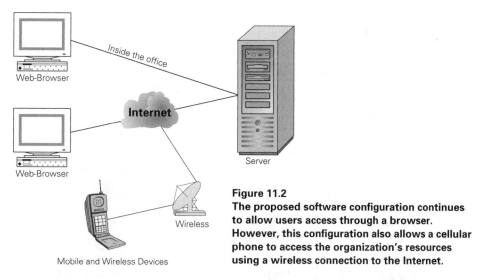

**Figure 11.2**
**The proposed software configuration continues to allow users access through a browser. However, this configuration also allows a cellular phone to access the organization's resources using a wireless connection to the Internet.**

The next step is to hire a consultant to come in and build their system. This is where we come into the picture.

First, we need to fully understand the context and history of what needs to be built. From there we can determine if J2ME is a good fit or recommend other options. From the scenario, we know that Greener Grass has an existing commitment to Java. Furthermore, a version of the order entry system already exists, which serves as a basis for our application. However, there are some interesting points to consider.

### 11.2.1 Analysis

We are led to believe that they want their entire inventory and order-entry systems on a cell phone, not to mention the scheduling enhancements. We need to investigate the feasibility of doing this. To begin, we analyze the existing system to capture some vital metrics.

### Display

For each screen, how much data does the existing system need to display? Compare this to the limits of a cellular phone's graphical capabilities. How many columns of data do most lists need to be useful? How many data entry fields need to be on a screen to fulfill something useful? Chances are, since this is an inventory system, that there is a fair amount of searching and displaying of large data lists. This may not fit onto a cell phone screen.

### Navigation

How much screen navigation is the user required to do in order to complete useful tasks on the existing system? It may be a good idea to map out the general flow of tasks the application performs to gain a conceptual picture. How would this map into a device with only a jog dial and two soft buttons?

### Data entry

How much data is required for an order to be submitted? How easily can this be to do on a device with a 10-digit keypad? Are there screens that require multiple selections from lists by holding the control-key or by extensively scrolling through the list?

## 11.2.2 Options

From the looks of our analysis thus far, there may be a gap between what the Greener Grass Corporation wants to do and what is feasible. Although there are other factors to investigate, at this point it would be best to set some expectations.

To help explain the situation, the Greener Grass Corporation is presented with a J2ME-supported cellular phone. For comparison, a PDA is also provided for their examination. This will allow the stakeholders to familiarize themselves with the devices. Additionally, providing an overview of the device's limitations from an end-user perspective is also a good idea. It may be useful for your stakeholders to know that the cell phone they are considering has no file system, that there are only 10 keys with which to enter data, and that the screen is less than one and a half square inches. Also, this would be a good time to investigate if the existing phones they intend to use support J2ME.

### Identifying a good feature set

Putting the entire enterprise application onto a cellular phone, or any J2ME device may not be practical, therefore:

- consider starting with a smaller set of functionality to pilot the devices in the field, and
- focus on the business problem to solve, rather than simply mobilizing the enterprise.
- remember that the key problems which the Greener Grass Corporation is looking to solve are:
  - allow orders to be submitted from the field
  - allow access to inventory in the field
  - provide scheduling information to field workers
  - monitor project status in the field

After some consideration, the Greener Grass Corporation identifies that their key problem is supplying about five different materials to worksites in a timely fashion. These materials range from black dirt and rock to fertilizer and lawn care products. The company is organized into teams that focus on a particular type service. Although the types of materials each team works with can vary, any one team only needs about five types of materials at any given time. Furthermore, it is discovered that most of the reason the Greener Grass Corporation would like to know the status of each project is to improve the distribution of these materials.

## Revised requirements

From this perspective, a new set of requirements is proposed in order to create an application that the company can give to their field workers as a test pilot. The new requirements are as follows:

- field workers will be able to select a type of product from a list of five to ten items.
- what products make up the list will be determined be the type of team the user works on. For example, if the field worker is on a lawn care team, they will have a different list than a landscaping team. Product lists are preconfigured through a browser using their existing system.
- after the product is selected, a quantity is entered as a number.
- multiple products can be ordered at a single time.
- a summary of the order is provided before submitting.
- a confirmation that the order was received is provided after submitting the order.
- an order status report will be implemented on the existing system to help manage the status of the field projects.

## Focusing on the problem to solve

Although this is a fictional example, it illustrates some key issues with extending the enterprise. One of the lessons we could draw from this is that extending the enterprise is not really a problem; it is more of a solution. If we had gone forward and implemented what the stakeholders were originally asking for, it may have turned out poorly. However, by flushing out a business problem that could be solved through the use of mobile and wireless devices, we were able to minimize risk and focus on improving the company's bottom line.

Remember that extending the enterprise does not necessarily mean moving the enterprise to, or rebuilding the enterprise on, a mobile device. Although technology is advancing rapidly, the underlying problems and purposes for technology tend to remain relatively constant. In general, most companies are looking to improve their business practices in ways that lead to better accountability and more efficient and functional workflows.

At this point, we leave the Greener Grass Corporation scenario behind and discuss general characteristics that an architect needs to address when designing and building mobile applications.

## 11.3 GUIDELINES FOR BUILDING J2ME APPLICATIONS

Throughout this book we have discussed the issues facing the J2ME technology space. However, in prior chapters these issues were discussed in the context of the technology or the devices. In this chapter we revisit these issues from an architectural point of view, as well as introduce a few issues that come into the picture once our perspective is expanded beyond the scope of the device itself. The following sections discuss the architectural characteristics and constraints of building J2ME applications. Available options and consequences are also discussed as appropriate.

### 11.3.1 The user interface

One of the first, and obvious, constraints in the J2ME space is the user interface. Some of these issues surfaced in the Greener Grass Corporation scenario. A general guideline when designing user interfaces for the J2ME device space is to measure the "pokeability" factor. Pokeability refers to the ability for a user to tap or select information as a means of working with the application. The goal is to provide pokeability for 80% of the application functionality, forcing the user to another means of input, such as keyboard or keypad text entry, in rare or optional cases. Pokeability is important in the mobile space since most devices do not support a full alphanumeric keyboard or the means to easily enter a large amount of alphanumeric data.

#### User interface—display

Display sizes and screen resolutions vary. Some devices support rich color schemes; others have grayscale support while still others have black and white or monochrome screens. This is known as screen depth. A screen depth of 1 is usually a black and white display. Also, if the device is used outdoors, the flat panel display may suffer from glare and washout in full sunlight. In many cases, different devices are more suited to particular widget sets than others.

Due to these variations, portability can be an issue. Moving a MIDP application between a cell phone and a pager, for example, may cause undesirable effects simply due to the screen becoming shorter and wider. Soft buttons may get mapped differently.

Adjusting for the environment, as in the case of a MIDP application, is largely handled by the high-level user interface profile implementation and the virtual machine. For example, in a MIDP application, the developer does not have to specify the location of a text entry widget on the screen. The location is determined by the profile implementation and virtual machine. Therefore, when an application containing a text entry field is ported to another device, in theory no developer work is needed to adjust for a possibly different screen size. However, if you include low-level user interface features, such as drawing lines on a canvas, adjustments may be needed when the application shows up on another MIDP device. For this reason it is a good idea to stay within the bounds of the high-level user interface widgets as much as possible.

## User interface—navigation

Navigation techniques vary between devices. Cell phones and pagers have buttons; PDAs have touch screens. Since display size is an issue on smaller devices, there is a high probability for an application to require several screens to accomplish what another device could do in a single screen. If navigation becomes too complex, users can become lost in the application, or forget where certain options are located. A feature-rich application is not very useful if the features cannot be found. Obviously, the goal is to keep things simple. Subsets of functionality that are device-appropriate may be helpful in paring down the navigation tree.

## Exploring navigation designs

As a design guideline, it is often useful to map out the navigation for an application. You can do this by drawing a tree structure that represents how users navigate to all the features on the device. Once the navigation tree is mapped, run through usage scenarios and record the number of screens users will be required to navigate in order to accomplish a task. This is an important metric to understand before developing a J2ME application that may help you avoid a lot of rework later down the line. The following examples show an initial navigation tree for a MIDP application and the subsequent redesign after running a few scenarios. The navigation tree models the Greener Grass application.

Figure 11.3 shows the initial screen design with arrows indicating the navigation paths. The shallowness of the tree allows all the application options to be displayed on the main menu. Upon first glance this seems to be a decent design. The user is always within one to two screens from any information or functionality required. However, when we begin to run through scenarios to test the design, some problems arise.

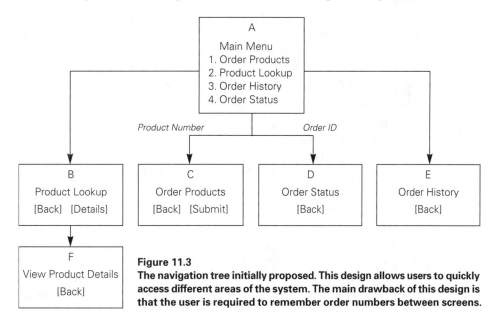

**Figure 11.3**
**The navigation tree initially proposed. This design allows users to quickly access different areas of the system. The main drawback of this design is that the user is required to remember order numbers between screens.**

### Test the design

To test the design, trace the navigation paths for ordering products and checking on an order status. Notice that each screen has been assigned a letter. These letters are used to document the path as we trace through the scenario.

Using the design in figure 11.3 to order a product, the user must do one of two things. He must either have the product number memorized and enter it in the Order Products screen, or he must traverse the screen sequence to find the product ID, memorize the product number, navigate back to the main menu, and then go to the Order Products screen and enter the product number. If the user knows the product number, the navigation is trivial: A, C. If the product number must be looked up the navigation gets more complicated: A, B, F, B, A, C. In this scenario it is assumed that the Product Lookup screen just displays the product description as there is probably not enough room to display both the product number and a description.

### Understand the users

If the users are likely to have the product numbers memorized, this may not be a bad design at all. In fact, if the product numbers are numeric rather than alphanumeric this may be ideal. However, if the product numbers must be looked up a majority of the time, the user is forced into doing two rather annoying tasks. First, he is required to remember the product number after looking it up. Second, he must manually enter the product number on the order screen. If there are multiple products to be ordered, this sequence of tasks becomes rather cumbersome.

Tracing the navigation for checking the status of an order has similar problems. The user must first look up the order ID using the Order History screen, remember the order ID, navigate to the Order Status screen and manually key in the order ID. In the case of Order Status, even expert users would not have the order number memorized in most cases since these are dynamically assigned.

### Exploring alternatives

Using what we have learned, the design is reworked into what is displayed in figure 11.4. This design has eliminated the need, as well as the ability, for a user to directly type a product number into the Order Products screen. This change has also increased the depth of the hierarchy. The user is required to traverse the same number of screens regardless if he is an expert user (a user that would have the product numbers memorized) and a casual user (a user that would need to look up the product number). However, in the case where the product number must be looked up before ordering, the navigation path has become simpler: A, B, C, D. There are now four screens to navigate instead of six, plus the fact that the user does not need to key in the product number also saves keystrokes.

Checking an order status has undergone similar changes. The user now navigates to the Order History screen, chooses and orders and then views the Order Status details.

If the majority of users fall into the casual or novice category, then we could consider this design to be an improvement. If the majority of users are experts, then this design probably has made things worse since the product number can no longer be directly entered. Additionally, all the application options are no longer displayed on the main menu. A user must discover or know where the Order Products screen is, given the choices Product Lookup and Order History.

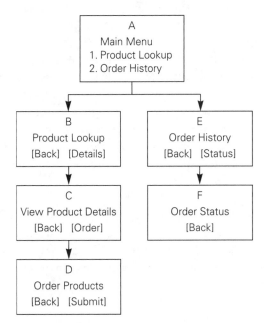

**Figure 11.4**
**This is a refined design of the navigation tree. This design organizes the system features in a much deeper tree structure. The advantage for the user is that information does not need to be remembered between screens. The drawback is that the user must traverse a number of screens to get the information needed.**

Upon further investigation, reworking the screens creates another design. This new design is shown in figure 11.5. In this design, the Product Lookup screen has replaced the main menu. A soft button now navigates to the Order History screen while the product selection navigates to the View Product Details screen. This has eliminated a step in navigating to the Order Products screen, making the path traversal only three steps: A, C, D. The rationale for eliminating the main menu is that with only two options, a menu was not required. The Product Lookup screen was chosen based on the assumption that this screen would be more frequently used than the Order History screen.

The Order History scenario remains unchanged except that the initial navigation is now from a soft button rather than a menu.

### Examining the options

By taking a few moments to flush out the navigation of the user interface we have potentially saved ourselves some coding rework. Which design is appropriate, however, depends on the users and uses of the system. As previously mentioned, if the users are likely to become experts with the system, keying in a numeric product ID could be the ideal design. If the users are not likely to become experts with the system, the design shown in figure 11.3 is likely to be a better choice. Also, there are a number of design variations that have not been considered that may work even better.

When designing user interfaces it is also a good idea to test the design on some of the eventual users of the system. This can be done by mocking up screens on paper and presenting them to the users, asking them to move through a particular scenario. As each screen is presented, the user describes what they would do (press a button, enter data, etc.). Upon making a choice, you present them with the next screen or mimic the system behavior by describing what certain options do.

If the users are able to navigate to the correct locations easily, the design probably holds. If they end up hunting around a fair amount, ask them questions to understand their thinking such as, "What are you expecting to see when you press button 'X'?"

One important lesson to remember is that users can be unpredictable. It is not unusual to discover that a seemingly good user interface design does not suit the needs of the end users. Paper prototyping helps to resolve these issues in a much more cost-effective manner than when actually implemented. A few moments taken to validate the user interface helps reduce risk down the line during product acceptance testing.

### User interface—user input

The ability to input data on most J2ME devices is significantly constrained from the desktop environment where a keyboard and mouse are available. In the case of cell phones, entering a four-character stock ID can push the limits of what the user is willing to do, considering that to enter a letter "L," for example, involves cycling the "5" button three times.

### Use of lists

List selection is a good idea as data can be easily entered with a few key presses. However, if the user is forced to move through large scroll lists this may become tedious. In some cases, more than one column of data needs to be displayed in order to allow the user to correctly choose an option. Since J2ME displays can be limited this could incur horizontal scrolling. Horizontal scrolling is something to avoid whenever possible.

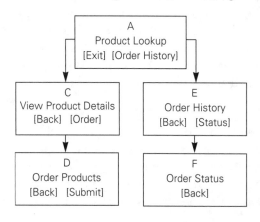

**Figure 11.5**
**Another design that further refines the navigation tree. In this design the main menu is replaced by the Product Lookup screen, allowing the navigation tree to be condensed. This design assumes that most tasks begin by looking up a product or going to the Order History screen.**

### Multiselecting

Multiselection from lists can be accomplished using check boxes. Keep in mind that many devices are designed to be used "one-handed." A cell phone, for example, is not designed to use control keys to alter the keyboard state in order to perform tasks such as multi-selection. Furthermore, even if this were an acceptable approach for your application, you may find that such devices do not support the ability to detect control key states, or have control keys.

### Entering text

If the device you are considering supports Graffiti, make certain that this is an acceptable method of input for your use. Graffiti, if supported, should not be the only means for entering data.

When text data is required on a touch screen device, such as a PDA, a "virtual keyboard" can be provided. In some case, as with Windows CE, a virtual keyboard is provided by the underlying operating system. In other cases, such as Palm OS, a virtual keyboard must be implemented by the application. Virtual keyboards provide one of the best ways to enter text data on a touch screen device. However, you may be forced to give up nearly half your display in order to get the entire (US-English) alphabet displayed. A method for showing and hiding the virtual keyboard is a good idea, allowing the user control when the keyboard is available. In this scenario you want to be sure that the text entry field is also visible when the virtual keyboard is visible.

### Be creative

Other types of data entry problems can be solved using a different approach from what is typically found in desktop and enterprise software environments. Password-protecting the application is such an example. Rather than forcing the user to enter a

**Figure 11.6**
**The combination lock example on Palm OS. This design allows a user to tap a sequence of buttons (1-8) to gain access to an application. This metaphor allows an application to be password-protected without burdening the user with character-based passwords. This design takes advantage of the pen-based user interface.**

password using alphanumeric characters, consider a "combination lock" metaphor where the user must tap a sequence of buttons to gain access to the application. An example of this approach is shown in figure 11.6. Each user has a different combination that is entered to gain access to the application.

### 11.3.2 The network

From a wireless architecture perspective, proving the network infrastructure is a crucial step in building wireless applications of any sort. There are many variables that must be in line.

The profiles you intend to use must support the protocols you need or wish to use. Additionally, the devices must support the profiles and protocols you wish to use. In some cases, such as MIDP 1.0, support of sockets and datagrams is optional. Only HTTP is required in MIDP 1.0. The device must support some type of wireless connectivity over a protocol such as CDPD or CDMA in the United States.

The next thing to check is the service provider options. In some cases there may only be a single provider for a particular device. Is service coverage provided in the areas in which the applications will be used? The wireless service must provide a network connection to the network you will need to access, such as the Internet. Make sure that the service provider's infrastructure allows you to effect the necessary connections and is not limited to the service provider's proprietary services.

If there are multiple devices in the picture you must make certain the same service provider can support all devices, or find a combination of service providers that fulfills

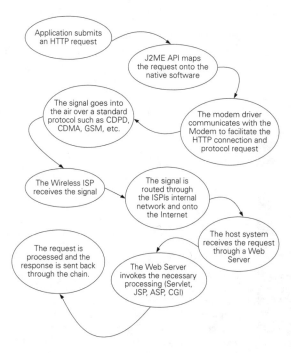

**Figure 11.7**
**The chain of responsibility in a wireless architecture. There are a number of pieces that all must come together in order for a signal to be processed through a wireless device and onto a wireless network, namely, the J2ME implementation must interact with the native operating system and the modem software to establish the wireless link.**

your needs. If supporting multiple devices means implementing to multiple J2ME profiles, all of these variables listed in the previous paragraphs should be verified for each profile.

Flushing out these details before designing your application minimizes risk. You do not want to go to the trouble of developing for a particular device or set of devices only to discover that the networking is insufficient for your needs on some of your target devices. Figure 11.7 illustrates the path a network connection must travel. At each transition point, between devices, service providers and network interfaces, there is a potential breaking point for the architecture. Be sure to trace through the architecture in order to verify that the proposed solution is possible. Figure 11.8 illustrates the components of a wireless architecture when connecting to the Internet.

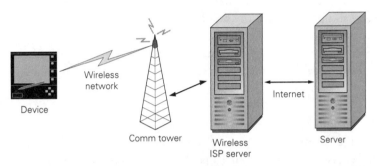

**Figure 11.8   The pieces of a wireless architecture. A device communicates over a wireless network operated by a Wireless Internet Service Provider. The WISP moves the wireless signals onto the public Internet so it can interact with the desired server.**

It is important to understand the subtle distinction between network coverage and network availability. Coverage is what the service provider indicates as areas of service on a map. Availability has more to do with the quality of service in a particular area. For example, two different cities may fall into the coverage map of a wireless service provider but one city may have intermittent connectivity and more unavailable service time than the other city.

Before getting too far into design, it is important to understand the bandwidth metrics of the architecture. It is worthwhile running some tests to understand how much data you can move across your connection and at what speed. Knowing this up front may affect your design when it comes time to flush out the data communication and synchronization pieces. Many PDAs support a 19.2 kbps connection. However, you should not expect that rate all the time. In some cases, J2ME devices may connect at as low a rate as 9600 bps. In these circumstances you may opt to spend some effort on minimizing network access and dependency. In some cases, differences in connection speeds may impact your choice in using XML vs. a comma-delimited format for transmitting data, as XML can become rather bloated in comparison.

### 11.3.3　Data exchange formats

Once you have a means for obtaining a network connection, you need to plan how the connection will be used. Typically there are two things that move over the network between a J2ME client and a server: data and commands. In most cases, each transmission involves both, as the receiving system must be given some instruction as to the action the sender is requesting. For example, sending a new order for supplies will invoke different functionality than sending a request to check order status. The distinction is made here in order to consider different design scenarios. In some cases, the transmission will consist of mostly data, while in other cases the only data passed may be the parameters of the command.

Whether you plan to use sockets, datagrams or HTTP, you need to devise a format in which to send data across the network. The format of the data is something that must be agreed upon by both the sending and receiving system in order to interpret the data correctly and consistently.

There are many approaches to formatting data for network transmission. The four approaches addressed here are XML, delimited, fixed position and name-value.

#### XML

Extensible Markup Language (XML) is a tool for creating data structures that can be stored in a file or transmitted over a network connection using a common syntax. The actual data structure of a particular XML document or transmission format is not specified by the XML specification but rather is user-defined based on what the implementation requires.

XML consists of tags, similar to HTML, that are enclosed by brackets ("<" and ">"). Each tag may contain attributes in the form of name=value pairs in order to provide information about a tag. The fundamental difference between XML and HTML is that HTML defines the syntax and the meaning for each tag. The intent of an HTML tag is to be interpreted and rendered consistently between browsers. XML simply defines the syntax and rules of the language itself but leaves the meaning and interpretation of the format up to the implementer. In other words, the interpretation and rendering of an XML document or transmission format is the responsibility of the XML reader or writer. XML uses tags to delimit data but imposes no meaning to the data. The meaning and interpretation of XML is determined by the applications using the XML format.

Since the interpretation of a specific XML format must be determined and understood by the creators and users of the XML format, this format must have a definition. This is referred to as the schema. An XML schema is a specific format that defines some type of content. An XML schema is what allows an instance of an XML document or transmission to be created and interpreted between systems. The schema is the contract agreed upon by the creating and interpreting systems.

The XML syntax itself is derived from Standard Generalized Markup Language (SGML). SGML was adopted as an ISO standard in 1986. XML is a subset of SGML that is intended to be as powerful as SGML but easier to use.

XML has gained a lot of popularity as well as hype in the last few years. There are good reasons for this, since some of the work of formatting and syntax can be provided to a system in a standardized way that allows the system to parse out the information in which it is interested. From an industry hype perspective, creating a mobile architecture that uses XML is quite attractive. However, there are some issues to consider. First of all, XML by itself simply allows a way for structuring data. How systems interpret and manipulate the content of an XML structure depends on the underlying system.

In order to share information between systems both the producer and consumer of the XML content must agree on a common schema. This schema can be validated using a Document Type Definition (DTD) describing the items that make up a valid document for your particular case. Although some standard XML schemas for various industries are emerging it is unlikely, at this point, that simply choosing XML for data transport is the total solution. At a minimum, you need to build or buy a component capable of formatting data into your XML format and extracting or parsing the data out of the documents. More than likely, you will need to devise your own schema.

If you are in a position where you need to define your own schema it may be a good idea to reexamine why you are using XML. After all, if you are defining the schema, the format of your XML will be proprietary. Make certain you understand what XML is buying you.

### Caveats and tradeoffs of XML

There are a number of considerations that need investigating before choosing XML as the solution. In some cases, XML is appropriate, but not always.

If you are targeting CLDC-class devices, XML may be difficult to support. Many of the parsers require as much as 45 kilobytes of binary code space on the device. Due to restrictions of the device, a CLDC application may not have the luxury of binary code space or processing power to support an XML parser, not to mention the memory required to perform parsing.

Most lightweight XML parsers support the Simple API for XML (SAX) approach for parsing documents as opposed to the Document Object Model (DOM) approach. In many cases, this is the only parsing approach available due to the memory advantages of SAX. The main difference is that with DOM, the entire XML tree is constructed in memory where a SAX parser throws events to an application as the data is parsed, allowing the application to deal with the data immediately. By delegating the data handling immediately, a SAX parser does not need to hold onto the data being parsed. A SAX parser simply provides a means for inspecting and dealing with the data contained in the XML document. What happens to the data is entirely the responsibility of the application or component using the SAX parser.

If you are targeting CDC devices, deploying an XML parser with your application may not increase the application footprint beyond the limits of the device as CDC devices tend to have, on average, at least 2 MB of space available. These devices tend to have more processing power as well, which is important for running XML parses since, in J2ME terms, parsing can become resource-intensive.

## XML over networks

Regardless of whether CDC or CLDC devices are being used, the network connection rate must be considered as well. XML requires quite a bit of information beyond the data itself, such as the tags, header information, and so forth. While this information may be useful in some applications, it can be considered bloated when compared to a comma-delimited format. This may impact transmission time if the formatting is complex.

## XML and existing systems

There are a number of reasons for choosing XML as a data transport format. For example, if there is an existing system that the device must communicate with that requires an XML interface you may have little choice. Also, there are advantages to reusing the existing XML portal. The architectural tradeoff is between reusing the server interface vs. slimming down the transport format and requiring an XML parser on the device.

## Home-grown parsing

One thing to point out, as another option, is that using XML as a data transportation format does not necessarily require an XML parser to construct and parse XML streams. You may be able to get away with parsing the XML yourself, using the `String` function `indexOf()` and grabbing what you are interested in.

## Data complexity

XML also becomes attractive when complex data formats are involved, such as a format with lots of nested data. An example of this might be a customer record that contains a list of orders. An undetermined number of orders will be enclosed within the customer record. Furthermore, each order may contain nested information such as a list of addresses, some of which are optional such as billing address, shipping address, home office address, and so forth.

If you do not require a complex format, or a complex format can be divided into smaller, less complex formats, you may want to reconsider the use of XML as a data transport format. However, if validating the data format is critical to the application, XML may be a good choice since XML can validate an XML document against a DTD.

Table 11.1 lists a few of the XML parsers available for J2ME devices. More information on these APIs can be found in chapter 15.

**Table 11.1    Small footprint XML parsers**

| XML Parser | Description |
|---|---|
| NanoXML | Non-validating parser written in Java with a minimum footprint of 6 kilobytes. NanoXML is available at nanoxml.sourceforge.net. |
| TinyXML | Non-validating parser written in Java with a minimum footprint of 16 kilobytes. TinyXML is available at www.gibaradunn.srac.org/tiny/index.shtml. |
| Aelfred | DTD-aware parser supporting event-based parsing. Aelfred is available at www.opentext.com/microstar. |
| kXML | Parser with optional WAP Binary encoded XML parsing capabilities (WBXML). Binary encoding allows the XML stream to be made smaller to improve network efficiency over sending the XML as ASCII text. kXML is available at www.kxml.org. |

## Example of an XML format

The following example shows the use of XML for submitting a product order. Since most lightweight parsers are non-validating, the example is provided without a DTD. Furthermore, for efficiency, the format uses attributes rather than elements to contain the data. Parsers can deal with attributes more efficiently. The drawback of not using elements is that the document cannot be validated against a DTD. Even if the J2ME client does not validate records, there may be reasons you want to perform this step on the server.

```
<OrderRecord>
  <Order id=4444>
    <Product id=1001 />
    <Quantity value=4 />
  </Order>
  <Order id=4445>
    <Product id=3003 />
    <Quantity value=2 />
  </Order>
  <Order id=4446>
    <Product id=4004 />
    <Quantity value=8 />
  </Order>
</OrderRecord>
```

## Delimited formats

If XML is not a viable solution due to the API footprint, network bandwidth or processing power issues, a delimited stream format may be an option. A simple delimited markup can be devised using one or two well-chosen delimiters. By well-chosen, we mean that you must be careful to pick a delimiter that will not interfere with the protocol over which the data is being sent. Additionally, the delimiter must be uniquely distinguishable within the data stream. Using a comma or semi-colon as a delimiter may not work if these characters appear in the data itself as punctuation marks.

Using delimiters allows the data format to be rather compact, since the length of the data elements does not need to be defined in order to create or parse the streams.

The downside to using a delimited format is that the sender and receiving systems must both understand what data is in what positions, or a header must be sent to provide this information. If you are in control of both sender and receiver, it may be possible to reuse the code that packages the data and unpackages the data for transmission on both the client and the server.

Without enclosing the format in the header, the format must be hard-coded into the classes themselves. If header data is included as part of the format, you may want to revisit using XML since this is what XML excels at providing. However, even with a header involved, this format can still be slimmer than XML-formatted data. The following is an example of delimited syntax. This particular format uses semi-colons as the primary delimiter and commas as a nested delimiter.

*Header:*

```
OrderNumber, ProductNumber, Quantity
```

*Data Example:*

```
4444,1001,4;4445,3003,2;4446,4004,8
```

In the preceding example each record contains three data elements. A semi-colon separates each record.

### Name-value formats

A common method for sending data over the Internet is the use of name=value pairs. Most browsers and web applications utilize this format. The benefit is that the format is rather agile and can be used to send arbitrary sets of data. For example, if a data element is empty or does not apply in some cases, it can be omitted from the stream. In comparison, null values in delimited or XML formatted data must be represented by a null marker or an empty value.

This is one of the simplest solutions and may not require a lot of thought. However, there are some implications if the data sets are large or the data format is complex.

If the data sets are large, the field information (the name) must be repeated for each record. In the delimited scenario, the field information can be specified once, in the header or in the software itself. If the transmission is sending multiple records in a name=value format there may be quite a bit of redundant data being sent over the connection unnecessarily. The following examples show data formats for name=value pair streams. In this case, in order to identify data elements as a record, the order of elements is meaningful or the OrderNumber must be included as part of the name. In the first example, the parser assumes that all data following an OrderNumber belongs to that order.

```
OrderNumber=4444
ProductNumber=1001
Quantity=4
OrderNumber=4445
```

```
ProductNumber=3003
Quantity=2
OrderNumber=4446
ProductNumber=4004
Quantity=8
```

In this next example, the order number is omitted as an entry and is combined with the name portion of the syntax. This relieves the order dependency but introduces an assumption that the OrderNumber is part of, and repeated for, each element name.

```
ProductNumber.4444=1001
Quantity.4444=4
ProductNumber.4445=3003
Quantity.4445=2
ProductNumber.4446=4004
Quantity.4446=8
```

### Fixed-position formats

Fixed-position formats are common in many legacy mainframe computing environments. In many cases, these formats were chosen for the same reasons you may opt to use them in a J2ME application: namely for reducing data size. Like J2ME applications, mainframe software developed years ago needed to pay much more attention to data size characteristics for storage and resource reasons. Fixed-position formats provide a predefined amount of space for each field in the format. The parser recognizes a subset of the data to represent an individual record or field. The benefit to using a fixed-position format is that there are no delimiters to worry about. All that is sent is the data, along with perhaps some header information depending on the design. The drawbacks tend to be in the rigidity of the format. If the data stream is off by as little as one character the entire stream can be corrupted. Furthermore, altering the data format to include a new field can be tedious since programming changes to the parsing code itself may be necessary.

Fixed-position formats rely heavily on position and the order of data elements. An order number is expected at certain offsets. Data contained within those offsets are assumed to belong to the preceding order number.

The size of the formatted data itself can be rather compact. However, empty and null values must be specified in order to preserve the position of the fields. Furthermore, there will be wasted space within fields since the field positions must specify the maximum field length. So, if you need to send a lot of memo type text, with fields that can handle lots of characters, you may incur a fair amount of overhead. For comparison, a memo field that allows up to 500 characters to be entered requires 500 character positions in the fixed format, where in the other formats the space required is the length of the memo text itself. The following example illustrates the order submission data using a fixed-position format. The header could be included as part of the format or coded into the software.

*Header:*

```
OrderNumber[4],ProductNumber[4],Quantity[3]
```

*Data Example:*

```
444410010044445300300244464004008
```

From this example we can see that one last drawback to using fixed-position formats is readability. During development and to correct defects in the application, programmers are likely to be investigating problems using the formatted data. This format is the most difficult to work with from a developer perspective unless the code that handles these formats can be automated or generated in some fashion.

### 11.3.4 Data synchronization

Data synchronization is often referred to as the Achilles' heel of mobile computing. This is due to the fact that if a mobile device is to operate in a state that is disconnected from the network, the device is likely to need a local copy of data in which to work. The key problem that arises in this situation has to do with the word "copy." Once you have a copy of data within the architecture, you have data synchronization issues to deal with. Most of the stickiest data synchronization issues tend to involve situations where data is updated on both the device as well as the server. However, read-only data can have synchronization issues as well. How "fresh" does the data need to be, for example? In situations where the system must rely on the user to trigger the data synchronization, problems can become amplified since the amount of data to synchronize can become rather large if the user does not perform synchronizations frequently.

There are a number of factors that an architect should weigh when considering data synchronization issues.

First of all, is synchronization required? If a copy of data is not stored or buffered on the device, data synchronization should not be an issue. Systems in this situation make use of a persistent connection to the server, always dealing with the server data directly rather than getting a copy for their own use. This situation, however, depends upon a reliable network connection.

Second, if there are data synchronization requirements, to what extent does the architecture need to deal with them? For example, what is the likelihood of a dirty write occurring? A "dirty write," in a mobile context, is when the copy of data on the device and the copy of data on the server have both been independently modified. When the device attempts to update the server with its data there are two sets of changes that are in competition: the modifications made to the device data and the modifications made on the server data. To resolve these issues, the architecture should enforce some type of policy. This policy could be as simple as "last one wins." In other words the last write to the database becomes the current version of the data, even if previous changes are overwritten causing them to be lost. This is by far the most simple, as well as the most optimistic method of dealing with these types of synchronization issues.

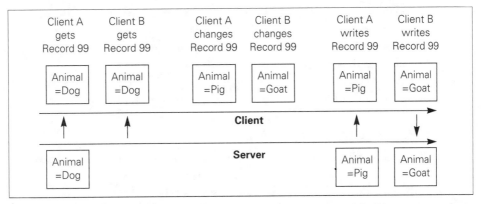

**Figure 11.9**  This figure illustrates a scenario where no locking is used. In this case, access to any record is always granted. Conflicts between clients are not resolved and thus the last client to modify the record determines the state of the record. This is also known as "last one wins."

However, depending on the nature of the data and the updates that are occurring, this approach may be unacceptable to the users or the business. Figure 11.9 illustrates a scenario that uses a non-locking scheme.

Another way of dealing with the "dirty write" issue is to implement a locking policy. There are many variations for locking data and only a few of the most common are discussed here.

### Optimistic locking policies

Using an optimistic locking model, a timestamp could be employed to note the last time the data on the server was updated. When the data is copied out to the device, this timestamp would be copied as well. When the device sends modifications back to the server, the device and server timestamps are compared. If they are equal, the

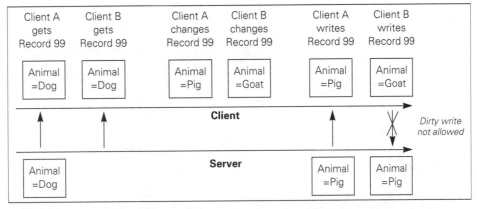

**Figure 11.10**  This figure illustrates an optimistic locking model. In this model read access to any record is always granted. However, when an update is to take place, the record must be unmodified for write access to be granted. If the record has been modified since the client read the record, the update is not allowed.

update is allowed to occur. If the server timestamp is later than the device timestamp, the server data has been modified by another source and the updates from the device are rejected. Usually, this results in sending a reply to the device indicating that the update cannot occur. The responsibility is now thrust upon the users to resolve the issues for themselves, often through much confusion, frustration and loss of data. An example of this locking model is shown in figure 11.10.

### Pessimistic locking policies

This situation can be avoided using a pessimistic locking model. In this model, when the data is copied to the device, the server version is marked with a flag indicating that the device "has" the data. The only updates that can occur at this point must come from the device. Although this eliminates the possibility of dirty writes, it also ties up the data for an unspecified amount of time. What makes a pessimistic locking model unattractive in a mobile environment is that there is no guarantee that the device will ever release the lock condition on the server. What if the device is lost? Or the user simply neglects or forgets to perform synchronization?

### Lease-locking policies

Recently, the concept of a lease has entered the field of data synchronization technology. A lease is a contract between two elements in a computing environment. These can be physical machines, components, software, or any combination of these things. What is interesting about a lease is that there is a time period associated with this agreement. The contract remains in effect between the two computing elements until the lease expires or is renewed. The concept of a lease can be used to deal with data synchronization in a mobile environment as well. Consider the pessimistic locking

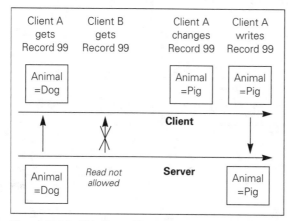

**Figure 11.11** This figure illustrates a pessimistic locking model. This is the most restrictive locking model available and only allows one user to access a record at a time. If one client reads a record, a lock is set so that no other clients can access the record until the lock is released. This lock is incurred regardless of whether or not an update takes place.

model just discussed. If a lease were introduced as part of the locking policy, the device could lock the data on the server for a specified time period. During this period of time, no reads or updates from other sources than the device holding the lease would be allowed to occur. However, if the device does not synchronize its copy of the data with the server during the leased time period, and the device does not renew the lease, the lease expires. Once the lease expires the lock is released on the server copy of the data, making it available to others. An example of a lease-locking policy is shown in figure 11.12.

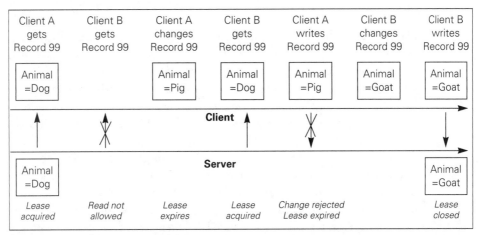

**Figure 11.12** **This figure shows an example of a lease-locking model. This model is similar to a pessimistic model in that when a client acquires a lease, and reads a data record, no other clients can obtain a lease or gain access to the data until the lease expires or is cancelled by the client. The main advantage of a leasing model is that a lease can expire, thus freeing up the data after a specific period of time.**

There are many variations that can be imposed on the samples provided here. For example, a leasing model could allow read access much like an optimistic model, but a client must obtain a lease in order to have write privileges.

Depending on how fine-grained the control is over the data, there may be other options for synchronization. If data can be synchronized on a field-by-field basis, as opposed to a record basis, the chance of a dirty write is reduced. This would allow a record to be updated by multiple users as long as the same fields were not modified. However, regardless of how fine-grained the control over data synchronization is, there still needs to be a policy in place for reconciling dirty write situations.

### Factors influencing data synchronization

Who is in control of synchronization: the software or the user? In other words, is synchronization triggered by an action taken by the user (that is, a user pressing a button or taking some action) or does the software perform synchronization automatically in a manner unknown to the user? If the software is in control when synchronization takes

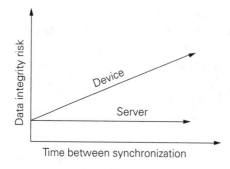

**Figure 11.13**
As the time between synchronizations increases the synchronicity gap of data on the device and on the server increases. When synchronization occurs, more effort is required, along with larger transactions and longer connection times, in order to bring the two environments back into synchronicity. In some cases, this can impact the business process as well as the data integrity.

place, data synchronization can occur in a well-defined manner. If triggering the synchronization process is the responsibility of the user, the timeliness of synchronization as well as the amount of data to be synchronized becomes an unknown. In either circumstance, synchronization is dependent on the ability to establish a network connection.

What about adding and deleting data? So far, we have discussed updates to existing data. However, there are often more than data changes to consider. When adds and deletes come into the picture there are other scenarios to consider. For example, what happens when a new record is added and then deleted on the device before synchronization occurs? First of all, if our synchronization architecture is sophisticated enough it can determine that nothing needs to occur for that record on the server. If the architecture cannot detect this situation, the application must be capable of preserving the order of the operations. If the record was added and then deleted, we do not want the application to perform the delete first (which does nothing on the server, since the record does not exist), and then perform the add, which would create a duplicate record. The other problem that comes into the picture is that a true delete on the device means that we physically remove the data from the device. In this situation, how do we tell the server what to delete if the record is completely missing from the device? The best solution is not to delete anything on the device. Instead, mark the item for deletion. When synchronization occurs, the system will be able to resolve the delete between both the client and the server.

How often can you synchronize? Ideally, synchronization takes place frequently. By synchronizing frequently, smaller chunks of data can be synchronized, possibly working behind the scenes and not even attracting or requiring the user's attention. The more time between synchronizations the more risk to data integrity. As the number of data changes grow, the gap between the server data and the device data widens. To synchronize data between the systems after a long period of time takes more work and processing. Figure 11.13 illustrates this principle.

### Synchronization tools

There are several things that can help to deal with data synchronization issues between a J2ME device and the server. Many third party, small-footprint databases have synchronization either built into their products or have add-on products that aid synchronization. Two of these database products are Pointbase and Cloudscape. These products are discussed in more detail in Chapter 15.

Possibly more interesting is the emerging synchronization protocol SyncML. SyncML is an open synchronization specification that is being developed by industry leaders such as IBM, Lotus, Motorola, Ericsson, Palm, Nokia, Panasonic, Psion, and Starfish. SyncML is an XML-based markup language that describes synchronization tasks between mobile devices and their data sources. The specification will allow third-party software vendors to create synchronization software to an open standard.

## 11.3.5   Data storage

Data storage between profiles and devices can vary widely. In some cases, such as MIDP, a byte array may be all that is available. In the CDC environment, it is quite likely that a relational database management system (RDBMS) or an object database (ODBMS) can be installed.

### *Byte arrays*

Byte array data storage provides fine-grained control over data storage because the developer must write the storage operations. There are some third-party APIs available that provide some convenient and more productive interfaces for dealing with byte array storage. However, when you are dealing with byte arrays you are most likely dealing with a limited device in the CLDC space. Building or using an API to deal with byte array formats may require more overhead than you can allow.

Byte arrays provide a simple means of storing data. There is no inherent format or structure to the data storage other than that a byte array is accessed by a key, usually an `int` or a `String`. A single byte array could be used to store a large quantity of data, or the byte arrays can be partitioned into a finer structure where each field or element is contained within its own array. Usually, the best option for data storage lies somewhere in between these two options.

To determine a good record size it is worth looking at not only the type and quantity of data the application stores but also how the data needs to be accessed. Consider the following scenarios.

If data is stored on the device only for the purposes of eventually submitting it to a server application, and the only data access required is to store the data and retrieve it during transmission, then the record size does not benefit by being broken into smaller chunks. In fact, it would be best, perhaps, to store the data in the format in which it is transmitted.

When an application requires the data store to be queried, the record size becomes more important. Unlike with a relational database, in order to query a byte array the array must be read into memory and compared to the search criteria. Depending on how this is handled, significant resources may be required to perform the necessary operations, such as heap memory and CPU processor cycles. Furthermore, if the data needs to be sorted, this is something the application will need to do as well.

### Data storage and performance

One of the most expensive operations in computing environments tends to be accessing the storage system. In order to limit going to the database you may choose to cache data records in memory. In doing so, you gain faster access to the data. The drawbacks are that it takes precious memory resources and if the application terminates unexpectedly or the device is reset, the cached data can be lost. In some cases a balance needs to be found between performance and resource utilization. On a limited device, these decisions are best made on a case-by-case basis. However, as a general rule, static data, such as the content for dropdown lists (codes and descriptions) can be cached without worry since the data is never updated on the device. By caching this type data, the data access can be performed once and the information can be stored in a pre-sorted manner.

### Format of the stored data

The format of the data itself is another consideration. If the data can be stored in the format that is used to send and receive the data between the J2ME device and external systems, some efficiencies are gained. First of all, processor time can be minimized when transmitting data over the network since reformatting is not necessary. Likewise, when the device receives data it can be placed into storage immediately without modification. This can be a tremendous advantage if your application is tight on heap memory since each record could be read from storage and placed directly onto the network output stream and vice versa. This minimizes the amount of data that needs to reside in memory at any given time during the transmission.

### Flat files

Some J2ME environments will provide support for accessing a file system on a device instead of simple byte arrays. On such systems, the standard java.io classes are used to access file data. This means that you can take advantage of storage techniques that may be more familiar to you. However, this may mean you will need to implement the concept of a record and provide the means to create, read, update and delete these records.

### Small footprint databases

There are several databases surfacing on the market that provide relational database support on J2ME devices. Many of these products support a full set or subset of SQL syntax to access the data. Table 11.2 lists a few of the available products.

If your application needs to store a lot of information on the device and the application needs to create, update, delete as well as run queries across the data, a relational database may be worth its weight many times over, even if the application is left a little strained for resources.

However, if you do not need to perform much data access or do not need to store much data, a relational database may be overkill.

**Table 11.2    Small footprint databases**

| Database | Description |
| --- | --- |
| Pointbase | An all-Java database with a footprint of 45 kilobytes that is designed to fit into CLDC and CDC devices, as well as run in the J2SE environment. Pointbase is available from Pointbase, Inc. More information can be found at their website, www.pointbase.com. |
| Cloudscape | An all-Java database that works as both a relational database and an object database. Although this database ships with the J2EE it can be used within a more constrained environment such as J2ME. Cloudscape is owned by IBM. More information can be found at their website, www.cloudscape.com. |
| SQL Anywhere | A small footprint database provided by Sybase. More information can be found at their website,  www.sybase.com/products/mobilewireless/anywhere. |
| Oracle Lite | A small footprint version of Oracle. More information can be found at their website, www.oracle.com/ip/deploy/database/8i/8ilite. |

Regardless of how data is stored on the device there will be a data mapping issue that needs to be dealt with for moving data over a network connection. Unless there is a JDBC driver that can run over your network connection, the data from the external system needs to be mapped into the network transmission format and then mapped from that format into the device's internal storage format. Simply running an RDBMS on both the J2ME client and the server (or other system) may not relieve you of this mapping task since the network format sits in between the two databases.

Another item to consider is that some database products, such as Cloudscape and Pointbase, offer data synchronization features and complementary products to help keep the device data and the server data synchronized. This solves the network data format issues automatically.

### 11.3.6    Memory

How memory is allocated and utilized varies between devices. In the J2ME device space, the familiar notion of runtime memory (RAM) and disk capacity as it is understood on desktop and laptop systems usually does not hold for the simple reason that many J2ME devices do not have a hard disk. In fact, many do not support a file system. In many cases, the runtime memory and the storage memory are simply partitions of the same memory resource, such as Flash Memory. Devices running Palm OS, for example, partition memory into two heaps, the dynamic heap, and the storage heap. The dynamic heap is used for application runtime. The contents of this memory partition do not survive a device reset. The storage heap is used for persistent data storage. The contents of this memory partition will survive a device reset (excluding a hard reset which will revert the device to its original manufacturer settings).

Understanding how memory is utilized on your target devices becomes important since your application must fit into the memory constraints of each device as well as stay within the storage limitations of the devices. For example, if your target devices support 8 MB of memory you cannot assume that all the memory is available to your application. You are sharing it with other applications stored on the device as well as the data of other applications. In many cases, the amount of runtime memory is significantly less than the total memory. On a PalmVx, which has 8 MB of memory, the runtime heap is allocated 256 KB. If networking is enabled, this consumes an additional 32 KB of this space. The KVM requires as much as 80 KB of runtime memory. This leaves less than 144 KB of runtime memory available for your application.

Since the memory limitations are likely to vary across a set of target devices, you are forced to develop your application to the lowest common denominator or alter functionality based on memory constraints.

In many cases, memory issues can be managed within an application using programming techniques. For example, when uploading data to the device, rather than holding the data in memory until the transmission is complete, the data could be immediately written to memory. In general, this is a good programming practice to follow. Another important issue to consider with J2ME applications is to create as little garbage for the garbage collector as possible. There are two reasons for this. First of all, creating a lot of garbage incurs a lot of work for the garbage collector. The garbage collector steals processing power from the application in order to run. Second of all, J2ME garbage collectors vary in their implementation and some are better than others. If the garbage collector cannot effectively clean up memory you will have memory leaks robbing you of precious runtime memory. Therefore, it is important to pay attention to how you use memory in operations and what is happening behind the scenes in the virtual machine. For example, if you need to dynamically build a `String`, you are better off assembling the `String` using `StringBuffer.append()` than concatenating `String` objects using += (e.g, s += "append to end"). This is because `String` is immutable and each concatenation actually creates a new `String` object that combines the two concatenated `String` objects. `StringBuffer`, on the other hand, allows its contents to be changed, thus fewer objects are created in the string assembly process.

### 11.3.7  Portability between profiles

In general, there are three main areas of functionality that networked device applications need to consider: user interface, data storage, and network connectivity. Since network connectivity is supported at the configuration layer by the generic connection framework, network connectivity is likely to be the most portable of the three. Data storage can vary since some devices only support byte arrays while others have file systems or can run a relational database. The user interface is quite vulnerable; however, the architecture of J2ME is set up to reduce inconsistencies between user interface APIs. The key issues with user interface portability have to do with managing a consistent set of GUI widgets, a consistent method of laying out components, and a common event model. While the types of GUI widgets may vary between J2ME profiles, it is likely that J2ME will maintain consistency in widgets between profiles. For example, if two profiles support a TextField component, the method signatures and behavior of the component can be similar, even if the implementation on the profile needs to change. This reduces a significant amount of rewriting between profiles.

Furthermore, because J2ME profiles participate in an overarching J2ME architecture, the methods of GUI component layout and event handling can be implemented in a common way. However, the actual implementation of J2ME user interfaces between profiles, and how portable applications are between profiles, is something yet to be discovered as J2ME profiles emerge.

From a practical point of view, however, it is worth discussing some non-J2ME APIs and the real-world porting issues we have encountered to date. This discussion is valuable on two levels. First of all, you may need to write an application for a device that does not yet have J2ME support, such as a PDA. Second of all, in the future you may want to move your application into the J2ME architecture or port it to another device. The following information may be valuable in designing the application today and understanding portability issues in this space.

### Portability between other Java environments

Outside of J2ME, the user interface is generally the most vulnerable part of a J2ME application with regard to portability. This is mainly due to the differences in user interface widgets that are supported or appropriate for particular devices. Currently, PDA applications for Windows CE devices can be developed using PersonalJava, the KJava API can be used to develop applications for Palm OS devices and MIDP can be used to develop applications for cellular phones, pagers, and Palm OS PDAs.

From our experience, moving a KJava application to the PersonalJava platform, the user interface portion of the application generally requires a fair amount of rewriting, but the remainder of the application code can remain intact. In fact, if your application does a good job of separating business and application logic from user interface logic, most of the business and application logic can be ported without modification.

Between the KJava and PersonalJava APIs the event model changes as well. PersonalJava uses a publish-subscribe approach to event handling that allows listeners to register with objects to receive notification when something happens. As we saw in chapter 9, the KJava API requires that specific methods, such as penDown() and penMove() be overridden by a Spotlet descendent class in order to respond to events.

Finally, the last major difference in the two APIs is how components are laid out. The PersonalJava API provides Layout Managers to handle this task. The KJava API requires components to be painted at x, y coordinates on the screen.

Because of the differences in how the user interface APIs are put together in KJava and PersonalJava, there will be little user interface code that can survive the port. However, we also have found that rebuilding a KJava user interface in PersonalJava can go rather quickly. Once the user interface and events are in place, the rest of the application can usually be hooked up easily.

Moving a KJava or PersonalJava application to MIDP incurs similar work. You need to consider the event models as well as the layout managing techniques. In MIDP, the concept of a layout manager is built directly into the components and is rather limited, as the devices themselves are rather constrained. The available GUI widgets vary along with their behavior between these environments. When moving from a PDA environment to MIDP it is worth doing some prototyping to make sure that the MIDP application will satisfy your requirements. MIDP is designed mainly with cellular phones and pagers in mind. MIDP for Palm OS is simply another device implementation for MIDP, but may prove to be too limited for your needs in a PDA environment.

### Data storage portability

Data storage is another area where portability issues may arise. For example, a Windows CE device supports a file system and there is no support provided for byte array storage. Why would you need a byte array if you have a file system? As a result, moving an application from an environment that only has a byte array storage facility to one that has a file system, and no byte array storage API requires this inconsistency to be addressed. The solution we have used successfully, to make porting go more quickly, is to implement the byte array storage API using the file system. If you are moving from a byte array storage system to a file system, this works well. However, this may not be the ideal way to store data on the device that supports a file system. What is appropriate and how much work you want to incur during the port needs to be decided on a case-by-case basis.

Several of the third-party database products mentioned in chapter 15 are available on many of the popular devices. For the price of the product, these products can be used to eliminate data storage portability issues among various platforms.

### 11.3.8   Security

J2ME provides basic security on the device through the virtual machine. In CLDC, preverification provides a minimal level of security to help ensure the safety of the device and that an application that is being loaded has not been tapered with. However, the responsibility of securing the device itself has been left to the manufacturer. Likewise, securing the application and data is left to the developer.

J2ME currently does not support a network security mechanism such as SSL (Socket Security Layer). In the CLDC, security is handled primarily by omitting unsafe classes that could potentially expose security risks in the absence of a full security model. In CDC, the Java security model is present and verification is handled in a similar manner to how class verification is handled in the J2SE environment.

As a J2ME software developer, there are several areas of security to address. The first is transporting data over the network. Since SSL is not readily available through the J2ME specifications at this time, you need to do one of three things: do nothing, encrypt the data yourself, or employ a third-party solution. One third-party solution that has recently become popular is Bouncy Castle, an open source cryptography package available at www.bouncycastle.org. Keep in mind that encryption can reduce the efficiency of an application. You may want to identify key pieces of information that need to be encrypted rather than blindly encrypting all of your data. For example, how meaningful is a patient's medical record if there is nothing to connect a patient to some test results, and so forth. The point here is that encrypting the patient's ID, name, etc. may be sufficient under some circumstances.

Once you have achieved a satisfactory level of security over the network, you should consider how safe the data is on the device. One consideration for protecting data on the device is to password-protect your application. Should the device become lost or stolen a person would need to gain access to the password in order to use the application. If the data stored on the device is particularly sensitive, you may opt to store the data in an encrypted format, making it difficult for someone to access the data in a meaningful way. On some devices, where data is stored in a file system for example, you application may not be the only means of accessing the data. On a Windows CE device, data files can be accessed with a text editor on the device. Furthermore, data files can be pulled off of mobile devices onto desktop computers that have more powerful options for viewing data and files.

If password-protecting your application sounds like something you need, you will want to investigate ways for making password entry as painless as possible for your users. One thing to remember is that entering alphanumeric data on a cellular phone or PDA can be rather tedious. In the case of a PDA you may want to investigate other ways to capture a password, such as the combination lock metaphor shown in figure 11.4.

### 11.3.9    Internationalization

J2ME provides basic support for some internationalization capabilities. Basic internationalization support is comprised of character encoding as well as the ability to localize the application to a specific language, country and time zone.

#### *Character encoding and localization*

Character encoding is the process of converting character data to a series of bytes and back again. This mechanism is used by java.io.Reader and java.io.Writer classes to read and write character-based data to and from the underlying byte stream. Character encoding provides the ability for an application to display characters specific to a particular language or subset of standard character sets. Localization deals with formatting currency, dates, times, and time zone issues.

The support for internationalization differs between the CLDC and CDC environments. The CDC provides character encoding as well as locale support where the CLDC environment does not support the concept of a locale. Implementations of both the CDC and CLDC must support "Latin 1" (ISO8859_1) character encoding. However, this is the only encoding type that is required. Depending on the manufacturer and their market, additional encoding types may be provided. Utilizing different types of encoding may cause your application to fail between different J2ME implementations. If a converter for the specified encoding cannot be found, an UnsupportedEncodingException is thrown.

The following can be used to determine the current character encoding at runtime:

```
String characterEncoding = System.getProperty("microedition.encoding");
```

## Time zones

When dealing with mobile applications, time zones can become an issue since the application may be used across multiple time zones as the user wanders from time zone to time zone. This is especially problematic when times and dates are part of the data communicated between devices and servers. For example, what happens when the mobile device user views time-sensitive information that a server application stored within a different time zone? Will the proper adjustments be handled? For example, if an appointment is scheduled for 10:00 AM CST and transmitted to a device in PST, will the appointment show up as 8:00 AM as it should?

Within both the CDC and CLDC environments, the following line of code can be used to determine the current time zone for the system. Note, however, that how time zone information is obtained can vary per implementation. On cellular phones, for example, the current time zone may be updated automatically while a PDA may only recognize the time zone specified by the user when the device is configured.

```
TimeZone tz = TimeZone.getDefault();
```

Furthermore, devices vary in which time zones are supported. To obtain a list of supported time zones use the following code:

```
String[] s = TimeZone.getAvailableIDs();
```

## Calculating between time zones

The `java.util.Date` object from the J2SE environment automatically adjusts the date according to the default time zone associated with the current environment. The `Date.getTime()` method returns a `long` representation of the date. This `long` is an offset, in milliseconds, from the date January 1, 1970, 00:00:00 GMT.

Dates in J2ME operate in the same manner. However, it is important to note that some time zones may not be supported on a particular device. In some cases only Greenwich Mean Time (GMT) and Coordinated Universal Time (UTC) are supported. Under this circumstance, converting between GMT and local time must be performed manually by adding or subtracting an offset, in milliseconds.

**ABOUT TIME**   GMT and UTC are similar in that they both represent a common time in which to base offset local time zones. GMT and UTC are different in that UTC is based on the atomic clock where GMT is based on astronomical observations.

If the time zones you require are supported on the devices you are deploying to, the calculations between time zones will be handled automatically as long as dates are passed as representations of the java.util.Date class or the `long` representation provided by the `Date.getTime()` method.

**NOTE**   Not all devices and J2ME implementations support the same set of time zones. Make sure that your target devices support GMT or UTC and the necessary local time zones. Otherwise you may need to perform time zone calculations on your own.

*CHAPTER 11   REAL-WORLD DESIGN*

### Locale

Since the CDC environment supports the concept of locale, adjustments in formatting can be dealt with obtaining format-related classes using the locale parameter. For example, obtaining a locale-specific Calendar instance would look something like the following, where "EN" represents the language "English" and "us" represents the country:

```
Calendar c = Calendar.getInstance(new Locale("EN", "us"));
```

Ironically, even though CDC supports locale, the only required locale is us-EN. This means that different manufacturers can support different sets of locales. Your applications will need to deal with the situation where an expected locale is not supported by a particular J2ME implementation.

When using the CLDC environment, the same formatting classes are available, but you will need to make the necessary adjustments for localization yourself.

## 11.4 ARCHITECTURAL TOOLS AND TECHNIQUES

To develop mobile and wireless applications successfully and consistently, there are a number of tools that can be employed to facilitate the process early on in the project lifecycle. This section discusses a few of these tools and techniques. The first of these techniques is a questionnaire designed to understand if a mobile and wireless solution is a good fit for an organization.

### 11.4.1  Questionnaire: assessing if mobile and wireless is a good fit

This short quiz contains questions indicating symptoms that a mobile and wireless solution may be a good fit for a particular situation. The set of questions is intended to quickly gather information about an organization's business process to discover where mobile and wireless solutions may be of help. Keep in mind, however, the factors indicated by this quiz do not immediately validate or invalidate the need for a mobile and wireless solution. The quiz is not intended to be scored or provide empirical data; it is simply a quick gauge that can be used to promote discussion.

- Do workers deal with a lot of forms in their workflows and business processes?
- Is there a lot of faxing of data between members of the organization or different locations?
- Are workers that collaborate or interact distributed across different locations?
- Is there a time lag between data coming from the field into a central office?
- Is there a time lag distributing current information or data from a central office into the field?
- Are there often inconsistencies or inaccuracies with data gathered in the field?
- Would members of your workforce benefit by having a device at the point of service?
- Is there a lot of re-entering of data in workflows and business processes?

### 11.4.2 Mobile application models

Different types of applications have inherently different types of characteristics. It is often helpful to categorize these characteristics in terms of a model or pattern. The following models provide a high-level categorization for applications that can be helpful for communicating during design and development.

One helpful tool in architecting applications for mobile and wireless devices is to understand the model that your application falls into. This text identifies four general models. Understanding the application model will help to determine the importance of J2ME features such as data storage, network connectivity, and so forth.

#### Standalone

This model describes applications that are downloaded from a network connection or installed via other means, such as a cradle, and do not require further communication with other systems or network resources to operate. Many games fall into this category. Figure 11.14 illustrates this application model.

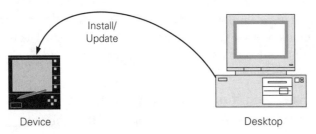

**Figure 11.14   A Standalone application model only connects to another computing environment in order to obtain applications or data. This is a one-way transaction. Under the standalone model, information is never transmitted to another computing environment.**

#### Cradle-Synchronized

This model describes applications that rely on a non-network type of interaction with other systems for installing the application and exchanging data. Data synchronization and exchange is often performed between the device and another system while the device is in a cradle, connected by a physical wire or communicating over an Ir port. Figure 11.15 illustrates this application model.

#### Persistent Network-Aware

This model describes applications that depend on a network connection to operate. If a network connection is unavailable the application cannot function. A microbrowser is an example of such an application in that the application renders data provided by the server and submits information captured by the browser to the server. Applications of this nature can either be downloaded each time the application is requested by the user or permanently installed. Downloading the application each

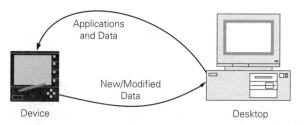

**Figure 11.15** A Cradle-Synchronized application obtains applications and data from another computing environment and sends back any data modified on the device. Under this model, new data elements may originate from either environment (in this example, the desktop or the device). New data elements are added to the originating environment upon synchronization. There is no wireless exchange of applications or data under this model. The device is mobile, but is synchronized through a cradle or a wire connection to another environment.

time reduces the client-server compatibility issues that arise with a persistently installed application, but does incur the overhead of obtaining the application each time. Without a persistent network connection being available this application cannot be used.

The primary advantage of this model is that very little information would need to be stored on the device, if any at all. Since network connectivity is persistent, applications under this model would favor reading data directly from the server and updating the server with any changes made on the device immediately. This model provides for more real-time interaction between the client and server environments as changes can be immediately represented on the server and data is always up to date since data is read directly from the server rather than local storage on the device. This model applies to any type of wireless network connection, which includes local area networks (such as an 802.11b wireless LAN) as well as a wireless connection to the public Internet. Figure 11.16 illustrates this application model.

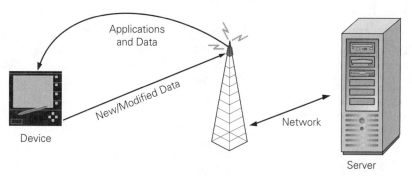

**Figure 11.16** A Persistent, Network-Aware application model depends on a constant wireless connection between the device and the network. This model relies on a wireless network connection for delivering applications and data to the device. Under this model, data is less likely to be stored on the device, in favor of interacting directly with the server environment. It is expected that changes made to the data on the device would be immediately reflected on the server. If this connection is unavailable the application cannot function.

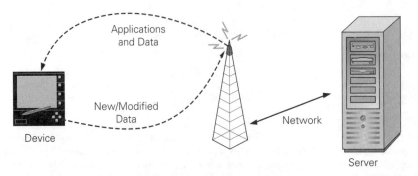

**Figure 11.17** Using an Intermittent, Network-Aware application model relieves the dependency of requiring a constant connection to the network while keeping the advantages of using a wireless network for data exchange between the device and server as well as application delivery. Since network connections are allowed to be intermittent or unreliable under this model, enough data must be stored locally on the device for the application to be used when there is no network connection available. When a connection is available, the network can be utilized to synchronize data between the device and server or to update applications.

## Intermittent Network-Aware

This model describes applications that require network communication for exchanging data and interacting with network services. However, this application has the ability to either fully or partially operate in the absence of a network connection. As with Persistent Network-Aware applications, Intermittent Network Aware applications can either be downloaded each time the application is requested by the user or permanently installed. If the application must be downloaded upon startup each time, the network connection must be available for this portion of the runtime. If the application is permanently installed, no network connection is required to perform most tasks, or the network-dependent tasks can be deferred until a connection is available.

Identifying an application model will also help communicate design strategies to stakeholders during the early phases of the project. Defining a high-level application model assists everyone in understanding the important characteristics of the application and how applications and data will be loaded and synchronized. This model applies to any type of wireless network connection, which includes local area networks (such as an 802.11 wireless LAN) as well as a wireless connection to the public Internet. Figure 11.17 illustrates this application model.

### 11.4.3   Architect's checklist

The following is an architect's checklist that can be used as a quick reference to make sure important issues that characterize a mobile and wireless application have been considered. Each of the following should be considered with respect to each candidate device.

Memory

- ❏ total memory for each device
- ❏ memory models for each device (runtime vs. storage allocation)
- ❏ upper limited footprint for application (compiled, installed code)
- ❏ estimated runtime memory requirements

Data Storage

- ❏ types of storage (byte array, file system, RDBMS)
- ❏ upper limit for data storage on each device
- ❏ anticipated amount of data on the device

Data Synchronization

- ❏ potential for dirty writes
- ❏ locking mechanisms (optimistic, pessimistic, none?)
- ❏ conflict resolution (what happens when you have a dirty write situation?)

Network

- ❏ coverage (from where will users need to connect?)
- ❏ availability (how good or reliable is the service?)
- ❏ data transmission (how much, how often?)
- ❏ speeds of connection
- ❏ data transmission format (XML, delimited, name=value, fixed position, etc.)
- ❏ who controls data transmission (user, device or both?)
- ❏ intermittent or persistent connection required?

Portability

- ❏ how much is required?
- ❏ estimated effort to support desired platforms?
- ❏ is J2ME available?

User Interface

- ❑ screen display area of devices
- ❑ data entry mechanisms of devices
- ❑ navigation mechanisms
- ❑ rank of the general navigational complexity of the application (low, medium, high)
- ❑ display areas that may get covered (e.g., virtual keyboard or Graffiti)

Computational Power

- ❑ calculations
- ❑ data manipulation
- ❑ encryption

Power Supply

- ❑ battery or plugged in
- ❑ how long does the application need to function between charges?

Security

- ❑ encryption (data transmitted over the network)
- ❑ encryption (data on device)
- ❑ password protection

Internationalization

- ❑ locales
- ❑ encoding
- ❑ time zones

Application Model

- ❑ Stand-Alone
- ❑ Non-Network Synchronized
- ❑ Persistent Network-Aware
- ❑ Intermittent Network-Aware

Checklists are helpful at all phases of a project to reduce risk by ensuring critical aspects of a project have been considered. Not every item in the checklist provided will pertain to every project. It is the team's responsibility to assess the applicability of each item and the degree to which it needs to be considered. The checklist should be expanded and modified on each project, as the team learns more about what needs to be considered on each project. This allows the organization one method for improving how software is developed and to learn from past mistakes.

## 11.5  SUMMARY

Developing for the mobile and wireless paradigm requires a shift in thinking from more traditional client-server computing environments. It is important that both application developers as well as stakeholders understand the differences of this paradigm. The areas of user interface, data storage, and networking tend to be where the issues of developing mobile and wireless systems are most apparent. However, there are many things to consider nested within these areas such as data synchronization, security, portability, processing power and memory utilization. In this chapter we have focused on some of these issues so they can be considered early in a project lifecycle. Where appropriate, guidelines have been provided for handling various situations.

In many cases, solving problems in the mobile and wireless environment involves different approaches both from a technical point of view as well as a business point of view. Identifying the critical business tasks and workflows that apply to a mobile and wireless solution tends to be an important aspect of a successful application. Furthermore, it is important to understand that the set of device-appropriate features is likely to vary between devices. The most essential features must be joined with the most appropriate and practical devices. When developing J2ME applications the stage is typically set by defining a feature set, choosing devices, and picking one or more profiles.

# Integrating the server

Moving the enterprise into the mobile space is an attractive venture for many organizations. Providing the ability to access organizational resources on a cell phone, pager, or PDA, for example, could enhance communication and productivity significantly. In doing so, however, consideration of the paradigm needs to be taken into account. For example, how much of the enterprise can practically be put on a cell phone or other small device? What device is the best fit? Will multiple devices and device types need to be supported? In other words, will there be cell phones from multiple manufacturers or a mix of devices such as cell phones and PDAs? Also, once you have a set of devices, how will you connect and interact with the enterprise systems?

Developing J2ME applications that connect to network and enterprise resources is the subject of this chapter. We will discuss issues with extending the enterprise into the mobile space and provide two examples. The first example is a MIDlet that interacts with a Java Servlet. The second example is a MIDlet that accesses an XML data source implemented using a JavaServer Page.

## 12.1 EXAMINING SERVER INTEGRATION

The key to successfully extending the enterprise into the mobile space is to identify and focus on the problem that a mobile solution solves. A statement such as, "Extending the enterprise into the mobile space," in and of itself, is not a goal that describes something beneficial to the business.

By focusing on specific business objectives, rather than technology solutions, an organization can begin to flush out the beneficial pieces that need to be included in a mobile architecture. In many cases, the mobile portion of the architecture turns out to be many "portlets" rather than one big mobile portal. It may be better to have several smaller applications that have a specific focus rather than one large mobile enterprise application.

### 12.1.1 Avoid monolithic applications

From an architecture and project perspective, one of the most important decisions is determining how the applications will be put together. For example, do you plan to develop a single application that is capable of performing multiple tasks or would it be better to develop a single application for each task? These are the two ends of the spectrum. The eventual solutions probably lie somewhere between these two extremes. However there are advantages to making each application as granular as possible and developing a suite of applications rather than one single application.

From a usage perspective, a more focused application does not require the complex navigation that a larger, multi-purpose application must have in order to navigate to the starting point of a task or operation. For example, an application menu bar that exists in many of today's large desktop applications is not possible or very inconvenient on many small devices. Furthermore, the smaller applications approach allows users to install only the applications that are necessary for them to perform their work.

From a systems perspective, given that mobile devices often have limitations on memory, processing power, storage and so forth, developing a suite of applications allows developers to avoid these limitations more effectively. For example, if the target device only has 150 KB of runtime memory available for your application, a single application must fit entirely within this 150 KB restriction. However, breaking the application into multiple applications will allow each application, running separately, 150 KB of runtime (heap) memory. Because applications on these small devices may be upgraded via wireless connections, smaller applications can also be more easily replaced.

From a project perspective, partitioning the functionality into multiple applications allows for smaller release cycles. Developing five smaller applications instead of one large one allows each application to be released as it becomes available, rather than waiting for all the functionality to become available in the larger application. Having a new product available every three months is usually more attractive to stakeholders than having a single, monolithic product available within 15 months. Iteratively releasing product functionality throughout the life of the project can reduce risk since smaller units of functionality are being released. The problems that are encountered can be resolved in a smaller context and avoided on subsequent releases of the other applications. Furthermore, getting functionality in the hands of users elevates the visibility of the project earlier allowing the organization to rally behind the project.

## 12.2  WHAT TECHNOLOGY TO CONNECT TO?

Embarking on a J2ME project to extend the enterprise involves establishing an architecture or protocol to connect the enterprise with the J2ME space. It is important to understand that building a J2ME mobile solution does not require the enterprise to be running Java. For example, if the enterprise communicates with a web browser using HTTP, then whether the enterprise application is using Java Servlets, JavaServer Pages (JSP), Active Server Pages (ASP), Common Gateway Interface (CGI) scripts or some other means of HTTP support does not matter. This is because HTTP is application-independent. The only thing that the client and server need to understand is the format of the data being exchanged. They do not require any knowledge of how each is implemented. For this reason, HTTP is an attractive communication protocol since it abstracts the client and the server rather nicely.

HTTP is not the only protocol available in the J2ME environment; there is also support for connectively using sockets and datagrams. Regardless of the communication mechanism used, you should verify that connection protocols are supported by the J2ME profiles to which you are developing. In some case, certain protocols are optional. For example MIDP 1.0 requires only HTTP, leaving sockets and datagrams as an optional feature for profile implementers. Although many vendors support all three protocols, you are not always guaranteed that sockets and datagrams are available on all MIDP 1.0 compliant devices.

> **WARNING**  Connection protocols may be optional under certain profiles. Be sure to verify whether or not the protocols you need are required or optional. For example, MIDP 1.0 supports sockets, datagrams, and HTTP connection protocols but only requires an implementation to support HTTP.

## 12.3  SERVLET EXAMPLE

HTTP is a popular protocol and common to many enterprise architectures using Java servlets. Servlets act as a controller between the client and backend components. In this example, we demonstrate how this middleware can be used to interface J2ME clients to backend systems.

This example uses a client MIDP application called `EnterpriseClient` to contact a Servlet called `EnterpriseServletExample`. The client provides a menu option for sending a message over HTTP using either a `GET` or a `POST` method. The message must be formatted differently depending on the HTTP method being used. This is necessary to allow the servlet engine to process the request properly. In the case where the message is sent using a `GET` method, the message is passed on the parameter string. For the POST method, the message is passed as part of the HTTP stream itself. As a general rule, when data, other than parameters, are passed from a client to a server, a POST method is the proper HTTP method to use.

**WARNING** The J2ME implementation of the HttpConnection protocol supports HTTP version 1.1. If the server software does not provide full HTTP 1.1 support you may experience flaky and inconsistent behavior.

In the example, the EnterpriseClient allows a text message to be entered. The servlet processes the request by incrementing a counter, which is tracked using a cookie, and echoes the submitted text back to the client.

In order to run this example you will need a servlet engine of some sort that provides full support of the HTTP 1.1 protocol. This example uses WebLogic 6.1.

**WARNING** Tomcat version 3.x, a widely used open source application server, does not provide full support for HTTP 1.1. As a result, the first time the client contacts the server the request usually succeeds but subsequent attempts to contact the server tend to fail. Upgrading to Tomcat 4.0, or using another HTTP 1.1 compliant Servlet engine will solve this problem.

The setup and configuration of Servlet engines is beyond the scope of this text. For more information regarding Servlets in general please refer to *Java Servlets by Example*, by Alan R. Williamson (Manning Publications).

## Creating the servlet

The servlet we create to handle the GET and POST requests sent by the EnterpriseClient is rather straightforward. All we need to do is accept the data, increment a counter, and return a response. However, to fully understand everything that is going on, our servlet prints a fair amount of information to the console regarding each request. Specifically, the information in which we are interested is the list of parameters sent by the client, HTTP header information and any cookie data. Also, in order to know if our session tracking is working properly, we will keep a counter of how many times the servlet is accessed and print this to the console as well.

The first step in creating a servlet is to declare the class by extending the HttpServlet class that resides in the javax.Servlet.http package. The name of our Servlet is EnterpriseServletExample.

```
public class EnterpriseServletExample extends HttpServlet {
}
```

There are several methods available for dealing with connections to the Servlet, namely doGet(), doPost() and service(). The service() method is the most generic and is always called for any HTTP request. In the case of doGet(), this method is called to handle an HTTP GET request. Likewise a doPost() is called in response to an HTTP POST request. For our purposes the service() method will be used.

The following is a list of tasks performed by the servlet. As mentioned, most of the tasks listed simply print out information in which we are interested as the Servlet processes the request.

- prints initial information, such as request type, etc.
- prints parameter information
- prints HTTP header information
- prints cookie information
- processes the session counter
- processes data input
- initializes the data to be sent
- processes the response

The primary function of our servlet is to capture the data sent from the client and return a response. The data can be obtained from the HTTP stream in the same manner regardless of the method type. The following code illustrates how to do this:

```
private String processDataInput(HttpServletRequest request)
    throws IOException {
  int len = request.getContentLength()+2;                    ❶ Adjust length, MIDP
  String s = "";                                                reference imple-
  System.out.println("Request Content Length = "+len);          mentation only
  if (len > 0) {
    System.out.println("Reading data from request:");
    BufferedReader reader = request.getReader();
    char[] buffer = new char[len];
    int i  = reader.read(buffer, 0, buffer.length);
    s = new String(buffer);
    System.out.print("  Data.............:");
    System.out.println(s);
    System.out.println("  Data Length .....:"+i);
  }
  return s;
}
```

**NOTE**   Due to a bug in the reference implementation HttpConnection of MIDP 1.0, the request length of an HTTP call must be increased by 2 before reading the stream. However, this will not be necessary on other implementations.

The following code writes the response data onto the Servlet response stream:

```
private void processResponse(HttpServletResponse response, String data)
    throws IOException {
  System.out.println("Responding...");
  response.setContentType("text/plain");
  response.setContentLength(data.length()+2);
  PrintWriter writer = response.getWriter();
  writer.println(data);
  System.out.println("Response Sent");
}
```

Beyond these two code examples, the rest of the Servlet just prints information about the request to the console so we can understand what is happening. A full code listing of the servlet follows in listing 12.1:

**Listing 12.1 EnterpriseServletExample.java**

```java
package com.ctimn;

import java.io.*;
import java.util.*;
import javax.servlet.*;
import javax.servlet.http.*;

public class EnterpriseServletExample extends HttpServlet {

  public void service (HttpServletRequest request,
                       HttpServletResponse response)
                       throws ServletException, IOException {
    System.out.println(
      "Accepting data from a J2ME client. IP="+request.getRemoteAddr());
    System.out.println("Request Method...:"+request.getMethod());
    printParameterInfo(request);
    printHeaderInfo(request);
    printCookieInfo(request);
    processCounter(request);
    String data = processDataInput(request);
    String responseString =
      "Echo \"" + data + "\" sent via " + request.getMethod();
    processResponse(response, responseString);
  }

  private void printParameterInfo(HttpServletRequest request){
    System.out.println("Parameter Info:");
    Enumeration e = request.getParameterNames();
    while (e.hasMoreElements()){
      String name = (String)e.nextElement();
      System.out.println("
        Parameter........:"+name+"="+request.getParameter(name));
    }
  }
```
**Print HTTP parameters** ❶

```java
  private void printHeaderInfo(HttpServletRequest request){
    System.out.println("Header Info:");
    Enumeration e = request.getHeaderNames();
    while (e.hasMoreElements()){
      String name = (String)e.nextElement();
      System.out.println("
        Header...........:"+name+"="+request.getHeader(name));
    }
  }
```
**Print HTTP header** ❷

```java
  private void printCookieInfo(HttpServletRequest request){
    System.out.println("Cookies:");
    Cookie[] cookies = request.getCookies();
    for (int ccnt=0; ccnt < cookies.length; ccnt++){
      System.out.println(
        "  cookie...........:"+cookies[ccnt]);
```
**Print cookie information** ❸

```java
      System.out.println(
        "   cookie name......:"+cookies[ccnt].getName());
      System.out.println(
        "   cookie value.....:"+cookies[ccnt].getValue());
      System.out.println(
        "   cookie max age...:"+cookies[ccnt].getMaxAge());
    }
  }
```

**Print cookie information** ❸

```java
  private void processCounter(HttpServletRequest request){
    HttpSession session = request.getSession(true);
    Integer sessionCounter = null;
    int tempCounter = 0;
    Object obj = session.getAttribute("hit_counter");
    if (obj == null){
      sessionCounter = new Integer(1);
    } else{
      sessionCounter = (Integer)obj;
    }
    tempCounter = sessionCounter.intValue();
    System.out.println("Hit Counter........:"+tempCounter);
    tempCounter++;
    sessionCounter = new Integer(tempCounter);
    session.setAttribute("hit_counter", sessionCounter);
  }
```

**Increment the counter** ❹

```java
  private String processDataInput(HttpServletRequest request)
      throws IOException {
    int len = request.getContentLength()+2;
    String s = "";
    System.out.println("Request Content Length = "+len);
    if (len > 2) {
      System.out.println("Reading data from request:");
      BufferedReader reader = request.getReader();
      char[] buffer = new char[len];
      int i  = reader.read(buffer, 0, buffer.length);
      s = new String(buffer);
      s = s.substring(0, s.length()-2);
      System.out.print("   Data.............:");
      System.out.println(s);
      System.out.println("   Data Length .....:"+i);
    }
    return s;
  }
```

**Read the input stream** ❺

```java
  private void processResponse(HttpServletResponse response,
      String data)
      throws IOException {
    System.out.println("Responding...");
    response.setContentType("text/plain");
    response.setContentLength(data.length()+2);
    PrintWriter writer = response.getWriter();
    writer.println(data);
    System.out.println("Response Sent");
  }
}
```

**Write the response** ❻

The parameters for compiling Servlets can vary between Servlet engines depending on what libraries are required and where the class files need to be compiled. The following example is provided to get you started. However, you may need to modify it for your particular Servlet engine. The %target% parameter is an environment variable pointing to the location where the Servlet class needs to be compiled for the Servlet engine to find it.

```
javac -classpath e:\j2sdkee1.2.1\lib\j2ee.jar;
  -d %target% EnterpriseServletExample.java
```

Once you have the Servlet compiled we are ready to test it. We can do this by calling the Servlet from a browser. The first step is to get the Servlet engine up and running. Once the Servlet engine is running, invoke the Servlet using the localhost or IP address 127.0.0.1 and appending the msg parameter. When invoking the Servlet in this way from the browser, the browser invokes a GET request by default. The following is an example of the URL that can be used to test the GET functionality of our Servlet.

```
http://localhost:7001/EnterpriseServletExample?msg=Testing
```

Running the Servlet from a browser first allows the Servlet to be tested independent of the J2ME client we will be creating in order to make certain it is working properly. This way, if there are problems running the EnterpriseClient, odds are that it is the client that is causing the problems rather than the Servlet. Note, however, that the POST functionality is not tested at this point.

### Creating the client

The MIDP client application that we create will access our EnterpriseServlet-Example using an HTTP connection. How the connection is obtained differs depending on whether we are doing a GET or a POST. If the request is to be of the method type GET, parameters are included as part of the connection URL provided to the Connection.open() method. HTTP GET parameters are specified by placing a "?" on the end of the URL string. Multiple parameters are separated using the ampersand "&" character. Each parameter must also be supplied with a parameter value using the "=" sign. The following example illustrates creating a connection with two parameters: Msg1 and Msg2. Each parameter has a value associated with it. In this case the values are Test1 and Test2 respectively.

**NOTE**    HTTP parameters cannot contain spaces. Spaces in a URL denote the end of the string. It is a good idea to encode URLs to mask spaces before sending a URL.

```
String url =
  "http://localhost:7001/EnterpriseServletExample?Msg1=Test1&Msg2=Test2";
HttpConnection connection =
  (HttpConnection)Connector.open(url, Connector.READ_WRITE);
```

Once a connection has been obtained, the request method must be set. This is accomplished by calling the setRequestMethod() method on the HttpConnection instance. By default, method type is GET.

```
connection.setRequestMethod(HttpConnection.POST);
```

Since this example requires the Servlet to count how many times a specific client has accessed it, the client needs a way to identify itself to the Servlet. HTTP is a connection-less protocol, which means that each request that is sent from a client to a server occurs on a separate connection. The connection between the client and server does not remain open between HTTP calls. In order to maintain the concept of a connection across multiple HTTP calls, the concept of a session is employed. A session is a way to maintain the state of client-server interactions between HTTP calls. A session is maintained by the server and has a unique ID. Each time the client sends a request, this session ID is passed as a parameter. The session ID is used as a means for the client to identify itself, as well as what session the server should use in conjunction with the request.

Servlets typically pass a session ID using one of two methods: cookies or URL rewriting. The main difference is that cookies are maintained as part of the HTTP header information. URL rewriting embeds information into the HTML content itself in a way that the client can extract and resend the information. The use of cookies tends to perform much better and is a much cleaner way of maintaining the session ID between the client and server. URL rewriting is used in situations where cookies are not supported or cookie functionality has been turned off.

In this example, the session ID is maintained between the MIDlet and the Servlet engine using cookies. J2ME provides no inherent way to manage cookies, other than allowing access to the HTTP header information, so the session ID must be managed by the MIDlet. This session ID needs to be passed between the client and server for each HTTP request in order to maintain the logical link between the client and server. The `HttpConnection` method `getHeaderField()` is used to retrieve the session ID.

```
if (sessionId == null){
    sessionId = connection.getHeaderField("set-cookie");
}
```

**NOTE** The parameter name and value formats for cookies and session Ids will vary across application servers. This example illustrates the conventions for the BEA WebLogic servlet engine.

When submitting data to the server, the session ID needs to be set on the HTTP request we are making. The following code illustrates how this is done:

```
connection.setRequestProperty("Cookie", sessionId);
```

The `sessionId` is the string captured from the first HTTP response we received from the Servlet. The connection is the current `HttpConnection` instance.

Data is sent to the Servlet differently depending on whether we are doing a GET or a POST. As previously discussed, if the request method is GET, the data can be passed on the URL as a parameter or on the data stream. For POST requests data is passed on the data stream. The following illustrates how to send data to the servlet:

```
byte[] dataOut = data.getBytes();
DataOutputStream os = connection.openDataOutputStream();
try {
  os.write(dataOut);
  os.flush();
} finally {
  os.close();
}
```

**WARNING**  The use of the flush() method will occasionally cause problems in HTTP 1.1. In some cases, calling flush() causes the HTTP implementation to send data in chunks rather than all at once. Removing the call to flush() can remedy this problem, since closing the data stream will flush the buffer as well.

Once data is written to the HttpConnection, an InputStream is opened to wait for the response as follows:

```
StringBuffer sb = new StringBuffer();
DataInputStream is = connection.openDataInputStream();
try {
  long len = connection.getLength();
  int c = 0;
  for (int ccnt=0; ccnt < len; ccnt++){
    c = is.read();
    sb.append((char)c);
  }
  String dataIn = sb.toString();
} finally {
  is.close();
}
```

The full EnterpriseClient code listing follows in listing 12.2:

---
**Listing 12.2   EnterpriseClient.java**
---

```
package com.ctimn;

import java.io.*;
import javax.microedition.io.*;
import javax.microedition.midlet.*;
import javax.microedition.lcdui.*;

public class EnterpriseClient extends MIDlet implements CommandListener {
  private Form outputForm = new Form("Server Messages");
  private Form inputForm = new Form("Input Message");
  private TextField msgFld =
    new TextField("Msg", "Test", 15, TextField.ANY);
  private Command okCmd = new Command("OK", Command.OK, 1);
  private Command exitCmd = new Command("Exit", Command.EXIT, 1);
  private Command sendCmd = new Command("Send", Command.SCREEN, 1);
  private Display display;
  private String sessionId;
```

**Set up the**  ❶
**application**

```java
private boolean initialized = false;
private int methodType = 0;
private static final int GET = 0;
private String url = "http://localhost:7001/EnterpriseServletExample";

private static final String[] choices = {
  "1 GET Message",
  "2 POST Message"
};

private List menu = new List("Select:", List.IMPLICIT, choices, null);

protected void startApp() throws MIDletStateChangeException {
  init();
  display = Display.getDisplay(this);
  display.setCurrent(menu);
}

private void init(){
  if (!initialized){
    inputForm.append(msgFld);
    menu.addCommand(okCmd);
    menu.addCommand(exitCmd);
    outputForm.addCommand(okCmd);
    outputForm.addCommand(exitCmd);
    inputForm.addCommand(sendCmd);
    menu.setCommandListener(this);
    outputForm.setCommandListener(this);
    inputForm.setCommandListener(this);
    initialized = true;
  }
}

protected void pauseApp() {
}

protected void destroyApp(boolean unconditional)
  throws MIDletStateChangeException {
}

public void commandAction(Command cmd, Displayable displayable) {
  if (cmd == exitCmd){
      handleExit();
  } else if ((displayable == menu) && (cmd == okCmd)) {
      handleOK(((List)displayable).getSelectedIndex());
  } else if ((displayable == inputForm) && (cmd == sendCmd)) {
      sendMsg();
  } else {
      display.setCurrent(menu);
  }
}
```

**Set up the application** ❶

```
private void handleExit(){              ❷ Handle the
  try {                                    button events
    notifyDestroyed();
    destroyApp(true);
  } catch (MIDletStateChangeException x) {
    x.printStackTrace();
  }
}

private void handleOK(int idx){          ❷
  display.setCurrent(inputForm);
  methodType = idx;
}

private void sendMsg(){                   ❷
  display.setCurrent(outputForm);
  processInit();
  if (methodType == GET){
    doGet();
  } else {
    doPost();
  }
}

private void doGet(){
  String data = msgFld.getString();
  try {
    String paramString = "?msg="+msgFld.getString();
    HttpConnection connection = getConnection(paramString);
    connection.setRequestMethod(HttpConnection.GET);
    connection.setRequestProperty("Content-Length",
          String.valueOf(data.length()));
    setCookie(connection);
    sendData(connection, data);
    receiveData(connection);
    processHeaderInfo(connection);
    System.out.println("Done.");
  } catch (IOException x) {
    System.out.println("Problems sending or receiving data.");
    x.printStackTrace();
  }                                 Send HTTP GET ❸
}                                   request to server

private void doPost(){
  String data = msgFld.getString();
  try {
    HttpConnection connection = getConnection(null);
    connection.setRequestMethod(HttpConnection.POST);
    connection.setRequestProperty("Content-Length",
      String.valueOf(data.length()));
    setCookie(connection);
    sendData(connection, data);            Send HTTP POST ❹
    receiveData(connection);               request to server
    processHeaderInfo(connection);
```

```
      System.out.println("Done.");
    } catch (IOException x) {
      System.out.println("Problems sending or receiving data.");
      x.printStackTrace();
    }
  }
```

**Send HTTP POST** ④
**request to server**

```
  private void processInit(){
    System.out.println("\n");
    System.out.println("Initiating Write-Read with Servlet.");
    StringItem item = new StringItem("Contacting Servlet", "");
    outputForm.append(item);
  }
```

**Initialize message** ⑤

```
  private HttpConnection getConnection(String paramString)
      throws IOException {
    if (paramString != null)
      url += paramString;
    HttpConnection connection =
        (HttpConnection)Connector.open(url, Connector.READ_WRITE);
    return connection;
  }
```

**Obtain an HttpConnection** ⑥

```
  private void setCookie(HttpConnection connection) throws IOException {
    if (sessionId != null){
      connection.setRequestProperty("Cookie", sessionId);
      System.out.println("Cookie Set...................:"+sessionId);
    }
  }
```

**Put the session ID** ⑦
**onto the request**

```
  private void sendData(HttpConnection connection, String data)
      throws IOException {
    byte[] dataOut = data.getBytes();
    System.out.println("Data To Send.................:"+data);
    System.out.println("Length of Data To Send.......:"+dataOut.length);
    DataOutputStream os = connection.openDataOutputStream();
    try {
      os.write(dataOut);
      os.flush();
      System.out.println("Output Stream Flushed.");
    } finally {
      os.close();
    }
  }
```

**Send data to** ⑧
**the server**

```
  private void receiveData(HttpConnection connection)
      throws IOException {
    StringBuffer sb = new StringBuffer("");
    DataInputStream is = connection.openDataInputStream();
    try {
      System.out.println("Input Stream Opened.");
      System.out.println(
        "Data Length to Receive.......:"+connection.getLength());
      long len = connection.getLength();
```

**Receive the** ⑨
**response**

*CHAPTER 12  INTEGRATING THE SERVER*

```
    int c = 0;
    for (int ccnt=0; ccnt < len; ccnt++){
      c = is.read();
      sb.append((char)c);
    }
    String dataIn = sb.toString();
    StringItem item = new StringItem("Msg: ", dataIn);
    outputForm.append(item);
    System.out.println("Data Received................:"+dataIn);
  } finally {
    is.close();
  }
}


private void processHeaderInfo(HttpConnection connection)
    throws IOException {
  if (sessionId == null){
    sessionId = connection.getHeaderField("set-cookie");
  }
  System.out.println("Get Header Info:");
  for (int ccnt=0; ; ccnt++){
    String name = connection.getHeaderFieldKey(ccnt);
    if (name == null){
      break;
    }
    System.out.println("  Key=Value..................:"+name+"="+
      connection.getHeaderField(ccnt));
  }
}
}
```

**Receive the** ⑨
**response**

**Capture the** ⑩
**session ID**

The following commands can be used to compile, preverify, and JAR the application:

```
\jdk1.3\bin\javac -g:none
  -bootclasspath \midp-fcs\classes
  -d .\build EnterpriseClient.java

\midp-fcs\bin\preverify.exe
  -classpath \midp-fcs\classes;.\build -d .\verified  .\build

jar cvf io.jar -C verified .
```

To run the application, make sure the web application server is started and the Servlet has been properly deployed. Since the above commands JAR the application into a file called io.jar, this file needs to be on classpath. Figures 12.1 and 12.2 depict the EnterpriseClient submitting both a GET and a POST request.

```
e:\midp-fcs\bin\midp.exe -classpath io.jar com.ctimn.EnterpriseClient
```

**NOTE**    If the EnterpriseClient application is run multiple times without quitting, subsequent messages are appended to the screen. This requires scrolling down through the server Messages screen to see subsequent message responses.

**Figure 12.1   Running the EnterpriseClient application to perform a GET request. First the user selects "GET Message" from the main menu. Then the user enters a message to send and invokes the Send operation. The message is sent using an HTTP GET method and the response from the server is displayed.**

**Figure 12.2   Running the EnterpriseClient application to perform a POST request. First the user selects "POST Message" from the main menu. Then the user enters a message to send and invokes the Send operation. The message is sent using an HTTP POST method and the response from the server is displayed.**

The text printed to the console while running the EnterpriseClient application while doing a POST request should look something like the following:

```
Initiating Write-Read with Servlet.
Data To Send.................:POST Test
Length of Data To Send.......:9
Output Stream Flushed.
Input Stream Opened.
Data Length to Receive.......:32
Data Received................:Echo "POST Test" sent via POST
Get Header Info:
  Key=Value..................:content-type=text/html
  Key=Value..................:connection=Close
  Key=Value..................:set-cookie=JSESSIONID=
    O4K4wJSSFq2g722mh562pl91qL6XMhud82Sq1KwAAdII3Xbs
    fbuQ!4962291947788757973!168430088!7001!7002; path=/
  Key=Value..................:date=Tue, 21 Aug 2001 19:38:40 GMT
  Key=Value..................:content-length=32
  Key=Value..................:server=WebLogic WebLogic Server 6.1
    07/23/2001 22:31:20 #129251
Done.
```

The text that prints to the server console while the `EnterpriseExampleServlet` is responding to the HTTP request should look something like the following code example. Note that the first time the client submits a request there will not be a session ID. This is created during the first request. All subsequent requests will contain the session ID. The example below includes the session ID since it was captured from the second HTTP request that was submitted from the same J2ME client:

```
Accepting data from a J2ME client. IP=127.0.0.1
Request Method...:POST
Parameter Info:
Header Info:
Header..........:Cookie=JSESSIONID=O4K4wJSSFq2g722mh562pl91
  qL6XMhud82Sq1KwAAdII3XbsfbuQ!4962291947788757973
  !168430088!7001!7002; path=/
  Header..........:Host=localhost:7001
  Header..........:Content-Length=9
Cookies:
  cookie..........:javax.Servlet.http.Cookie@52e9a8
  cookie name......:JSESSIONID
  cookie value.....:O4K4wJSSFq2g722mh562pl91qL
    6XMhud82Sq1KwAAdII3XbsfbuQ!4962291947788757973!168430088!7001!7002
  cookie max age...:-1
Hit Counter........:2
Request Content Length = 11
Reading data from request:
  Data.............:POST Test
  Data Length .....:9
Responding...
Response Sent
```

## 12.4  XML

Extensible Markup Language (XML) has become rather popular in the last several years. The appeal of XML is in its ability to standardize the way that data can be represented. This is an especially powerful concept when two or more disparate systems need to share data.

An XML document is a self-describing data structure that adheres to the basic rules and syntax of the XML specification defined by the W3C. For more information on XML and related technology refer to the W3C website at www.w3c.org.

The three main parts of XML are a Schema, a Document Type Definition (DTD), and the XML document itself. The schema describes the structure of an XML document. This structure, and more importantly, the rules supporting the structure, can then be defined in a DTD. The XML document itself could be considered an instance of the schema or DTD such that the document adheres to all of the DTD rules.

A DTD is an optional component of an XML solution. However, when a DTD is available, an XML document can automatically be validated against these rules defined in the DTD. Since the rules are defined in the DTD, a standard set of APIs can be, and have been, created to deal with different XML documents and DTDs without requiring modification. Within industries where schemas and DTDs become standardized, the ability to move data between disparate systems can become a commodity.

An application deals with XML data by processing the data using an XML parser. An XML parser extracts and disassembles the content of the XML document. However, to do something meaningful with the data supplied by the parser the application will need to take action on the parsed XML in some manner. In other words, when receiving XML content, the application is the interface responsible for mapping the parsed XML content into the application environment. Conversely, when sending XML content, the application extracts the necessary data from the environment (using SQL, flatfiles, etc.) and creates an XML document or stream. The XML APIs can perform a great deal of work, but mapping the data into something meaningful to your application often requires some effort.

The two main tasks for incorporating XML into an architecture is to identify or create an XML schema (and associated DTD if one is to be used) and writing the software to generate and interpret the XML content.

### 12.4.1 Using XML

There are two primary models that are used to handle XML data. These models are commonly referred to as tree-based and event-based. Each model has its own set of strengths and weaknesses. Which model is right for an application depends on the nature of the application and the tradeoffs that best fit the situation.

At the heart of XML is a parser. An XML parser is capable of moving through XML content and presenting the data and meta-information to an application. Each XML model adopts a variation on how parsing takes place. A tree-based XML parser constructs the entire contents of an XML document or stream in memory. XML, by nature, is hierarchical, allowing the data to be represented easily in a tree structure. Consider the following example:

```
<customer id="1">
  <demograpics>
    <firstname>David</firstname>
    <lastname>Hemphill</lastname>
    <phone>555-555-5555</phone>
  </demograpics>
  <order id="6633">Grass Seed</order>
  <order id="248">Sunflower Seeds</order>
</customer>
```

Using the syntax of XML tags, the data contained in the above example can be easily represented as a collection of Java objects that are linked in a tree structure. An example of this tree structure is shown in figure 12.3.

An event-based XML parser takes a different approach. Rather than constructing a tree in memory to represent the XML data, an event-based parser moves through the XML data and triggers events as different XML tags and meta-information are

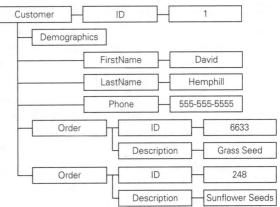

**Figure 12.3**
Tree representation of parsed XML.
A Customer contains Demographics,
and zero or more orders. A customer
also has a unique ID. Demographics
consist of a first name, last name, and
phone number. Each order consists of
an ID and a description.

encountered. When an event is triggered, the appropriate contents are passed through a programming API into an XML handler. The XML handler is part of the application that is utilizing the XML data. It is the XML handler that interprets how the XML data is used in relation to the application. A visual representation of event-based parsing is shown in figure 12.4.

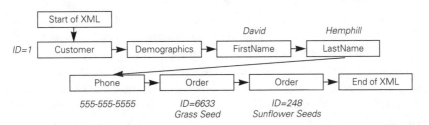

**Figure 12.4   Event-based parsing of XML data. As each XML tag is encountered, an event is triggered to allow the application to handle the data. The application can only "see" the XML data in the context of each individual event.**

The benefit of a tree-based parser is that the application has access to all of the data at the same time. The drawback is that tree-based parsers can become memory intensive since the entire XML contents must reside in memory. If your application needs to deal with large amounts of data on a small device a tree-based solution may be unfeasible. An event-based parser gets around this memory problem by allowing the XML data to be parsed without needing to hold onto the data in memory. When an event is triggered, the necessary contents are passed to the handler. The handler then takes appropriate action with the information passed through the API. This allows memory utilization to remain relatively constant regardless of how much XML data is being interpreted. The drawback of event-based parsing is that the handler only has serial access to the XML data. If an application needs to manipulate the XML data or its structure, a tree-based model may be more suitable.

## 12.4.2  Open standards of XML

The fact that XML is based on open standards is one of the most compelling arguments for using XML. The Document Object Model (DOM) is the open standard tree-based model and the Simple API for XML (SAX) is the standard for the event-based model. Both of these specifications subscribe to the XML specification defined by the W3C. Information on XML itself can be found at www.w3.org/XML. Information about SAX and the Java APIs can be found at sax.sourceforge.net.

The major components of an XML document are elements, attributes, entities and a Document Type Definition or DTD. These components are concrete in that they are part of the syntax or physical entities that can be manipulated by an XML parser or application. One important part of any XML solution is the XML schema. The schema is the format that valid XML content must adhere to. The Schema is a conceptual entity that defines the contract allowing instances of XML to be created and interpreted consistently by different systems. A DTD is a way to represent an XML schema in a way that allows an XML parser to validate XML content.

A DTD describes the structure of a well-formed XML document. This is the metadata that represents the schema for a particular document. To be a valid XML document, the contents of the document must adhere to the constraints of the DTD. Most parsers provide the ability to validate an XML document against its DTD. It is important to note, however, that a DTD is an optional part of an XML solution. If a DTD does not exist, the systems using the XML solution must adhere to the schema definition in order to process the XML content correctly.

An Element describes data within an XML document or stream. Each element can contain one or more attributes. The following are examples of elements with and without attributes. The first example is a simple element with begin and end tags that contain data in the middle.

```
<FirstName>David</FirstName>
```

The next example shows an element with three attributes. The element in this case is self-contained in that the element tag describes both the beginning and ending tag. The beginning is indicated by `<Customer` and the end of the tag is denoted by the `/>`. Attributes are specified as name=value pairs. Attribute values must be enclosed in quotes.

```
<Customer id="999" firstname="David" lastname="Hemphill" />
```

Entities in an XML document are used to describe references to other data either internal or external to the XML document. References to an image or another XML document are examples of how an external entity tag could be used. External entities are necessary since graphical data, for example, cannot be embedded into an XML document. Therefore, the document must refer to the resource. An entity also provides the means to describe what the entity is, such as a JPEG, PNG, GIF, etc. so it can be properly interpreted.

The following example uses an internal entity tag to define a character entity. This character entity can then be used through the document in element tags.

```
<!ENTITY ast "***">
```

Using &ast is then identical to using "***" within the XML document. For example, the following two lines are identical with the entity defined.

```
<separator>&ast Section 2 &ast </separator>

<separator>*** Section 2 *** </separator>
```

### 12.4.3    Consequences of XML in J2ME

There are three main issues to consider before adopting XML into your application. The first issue is the parser footprint. There are many small-footprint parsers available but each of these will consume between 9 and 40 KB of your binary code space. In some cases, this overhead may cause the application to exceed the available space on the device or impose limitations on your application.

The second issue has to do with transmitting data over a network connection. If the connection is wireless and there are a lot of data that need to move over the connection, the verbose nature of XML may impact the data transmission performance.

The third issue to consider regarding XML is whether to use a tree-based parser or an event-based parser. Due to the memory constraints of J2ME devices, the event-based parser seems like an appropriate choice; however, this is not always the case and this decision must be weighed in terms of the application requirements.

Finally, another important consideration when looking at XML for the J2ME environment has to do with DTDs. In general, small-footprint parsers ignore DTD since supporting DTDs would increase the size of the API; thus, they do not provide the ability to validate a document and enforce the rules of the DTD. Furthermore, many small-footprint XML APIs support a subset of features you would normally expect in a larger environment, such as CDATA tags (XML markup that needs to be stored as data) and external entities. If these features are important to your application make certain you choose an XML API that supports your needs.

### 12.4.4    Small-footprint parsers

There are several small-footprint parsers available. Each has different characteristics and variations on how or if the open specifications are supported. More information about small-footprint parsers is available in Chapter 15.

#### *NanoXML*

NanoXML supports both a tree-based parser interface and a SAX 1.0, event-based parser interface. The tree-based interface is proprietary. NanoXML can be found at the website nanoxml.sourceforge.net. However, this version is not J2ME compliant. There are dependencies on J2SE classes and packages, such as `java.io.File` and `java.util.Locale` among others. Eric Giguere has provided a source code version of the NanoXML 1.6.4 tree-based interface that is compatible with the CLDC. These source files have been renamed to have a lower case "k" in front of each modified class. In order to use NanoXML on the J2ME platform the NanoXML source files must be replaced with the ported source files and recompiled. If you wish to use

NanoXML's SAX interface you will need to port this yourself. The dependencies are relatively minimal.

To port NanoXML you will need the following source code elements:

- the gzipped tar file containing the source code for NanoXML 1.6.4 available at nanoxml.sourceforge.net (version 1.6.8 works as well)
- kNanoXML source files available from www.ericgiguere.com/nanoxml
- the SAX 1.0 libraries available at sax.sourceforge.net

The required changes are as follows:

- remove the J2SE dependencies on the `java.io` package (e.g., `FileInput-Stream` and `FileNotFoundException`)
- remove the dependencies on the java.net package (e.g., `URL` and `Malformed-URLException`)
- remove the J2SE dependencies on `Locale` in both the SAX 1.0 interfaces as well as `SAXParser.java`
- replace the appropriate NanoXML classes with the ported kNanoXML classes, and modify references from other source files to the "k" versions of the classes
- remove demo classes (any class containing the word "Demo") from the SAX 1.0 library

All necessary source changes can be made by commenting out code in `SAXParser.java` and `org.xml.sax.Parser`, unless you plan or need to use the `parse(String systemId)` method of the parser.

> **WARNING**  You may be tempted to create an empty class `java.util.Locale` to deal with the absence of `Locale` in `CLDC`. Although this works in the emulated environment, where the `bootclasspath` parameter can be set to include this empty class, it cannot be made to work on the actual device. Altering the core Java classes is a violation that is detected by the virtual machine since you are attempting to modify the contents `java.util` package.

By the time NanoXML is ported to J2ME, both tree-based and SAX interfaces, the footprint is around 16 KB compressed (32 KB uncompressed). This includes the SAX 1.0 APIs as well as the NanoXML classes in preverified form.

## TinyXML

TinyXML supports both a tree-based parser interface and an event-based parser interface, both of which are proprietary. Christian Sauer has provided a J2ME ported version of TinyXML that can be found at www.microjava.com/_downloads/tinyXML.zip. The main TinyXML web address is www.gibaradunn.srac.org/tiny/index.shtml. The J2ME ported version of TinyXML has a footprint after preverification of about 8 KB compressed with test classes removed (13 KB uncompressed).

**kXML**

kXML is an XML API that was built with J2ME in mind from the beginning. This is the most feature-rich of the parsers discussed here. kXML supports a version of DOM, called kDOM. There is also optional support for WAP Binary XML (WBXML) that encodes XML is binary form to reduce the size of the XML content, which is especially important when transmitting XML content over a slow network connection.

kXML supports what the authors call a "Pull Parser" rather than a SAX parser. This concept allows an application to ask for a specific XML event in the order needed, rather than having the order imposed by the document and the parser, where the event is passed to a handler.

kXML is available from www.kxml.org and has a footprint of 33 KB compressed (58 KB uncompressed).

**NOTE**     The next version of MIDP, named MIDP NG for Next Generation, is slated to contain a lightweight XML parser.

## 12.5   *XML USING JSPS EXAMPLE*

One of the useful scenarios for utilizing XML is to provide an XML-based Internet portal for mobile and wireless clients. To demonstrate this, the following example uses NanoXML's SAX API to connect to a JavaServer Page (JSP). The JSP returns an XML data stream that is parsed by the J2ME client application. NanoXML is used in this example since it supports the open-standard SAX interface, allowing other SAX-compliant parsers to be used instead of NanoXML if desired.

The context for this example uses the Greener Grass Companies business domain from Chapter 10. The application allows a customer ID to be entered. This customer ID is sent to the server. The JSP captures the customer ID and retrieves the appropriate information about what the customer has ordered (or what field workers have ordered on behalf of the customer).

To fully understand this example it is important to know something about JavaServer Pages. A JSP allows for combining Java code with ASCII content. Many implementations currently use JSPs to generate HTML content dynamically. However, JSPs are not restricted to HTML. As we will demonstrate, it is just as easy to use JSPs to produce XML content.

JSPs reside on the server and require a JSP-compliant application server, such as Tomcat or WebLogic, to run a JSP.

### 12.5.1   How JavaServer Pages work

At runtime, when the application server receives an HTTP request, if the file suffix is "jsp", the request is interpreted as a JavaServer Page request. If this is the first time the JSP is called, the JSP must be compiled (unless the JSP was precompiled when it was deployed). When a JSP is compiled, what occurs is that the application server translates the JSP into a Java Servlet. Once the Servlet is created, it is compiled, loaded into the Java Virtual Machine and called to handle the request. As a result, the first request that invokes a JSP can take longer than subsequent calls, since the JSP must be compiled. Subsequent calls simply access the Servlet that was previously generated.

In order to combine Java code with the ASCII text of the JSP, JavaServer Pages use a special set of tags for processing the JSP correctly. A quick reference regarding the syntax of these tags along with other JSP material can be found at java.sun.com/products/jsp/technical.html.

There are two tags used to denote Java code. One is called a scriptlet tag and has the following syntax:

```
<% code fragment %>
```

The other tag is called an expression and has the following syntax:

```
<%= expression %>
```

A code fragment is used to perform processing tasks within the JSP. An expression is used to replace the tag with contents returned by the expression. Examples of both tags are used in the example application.

Two other tags that will be needed by the example application are the `<jsp:use-Bean>` and `<jsp:setProperty>` tags. The `useBean` tag allows a JavaBean to be named within the JSP to help facilitate processing the page. This class that is named in the `useBean` tag must conform to the JavaBean requirements; specifically it must have a no-args constructor and must contain getter/setter methods to get and set attribute values.

The `setProperty` tag can be used to extract parameters from the HTTP request and automatically call the appropriate set methods on the JavaBean specified. Consider the following example.

```
<jsp:useBean id="helper" scope="page" class="com.ctimn.JSPHelper" />

<jsp:setProperty name="helper" property="customerId" />
```

The `useBean` tag identifies a class using the fully qualified class name. In this case we are naming the class `com.ctimn.JSPHelper`. This class must be on the application server's `classpath` so it can be found by the JSP at runtime. This class is instantiated and associated with the name `helper`. At this point, we can refer to this class instance using the name `helper` anywhere in the JSP.

The `setProperty` tag extracts the property "customerId" from the HTTP request parameters and calls the method `setCustomerId(String value)` on the class `com.ctimn.JSPHelper`, passing the value extracted from the HTTP request as a parameter. Of course this means that the `JSPHelper` class must define this method. Parameters in the HTTP request that cannot be mapped using this naming convention are ignored.

**NOTE** While it is not necessary to use JavaBeans in JSPs, it is an especially powerful feature since much of the Java code can be hidden from the JSP. As your JSP grows in complexity, mixing all of the Java code required by the JSP with the other ASCII markup (HTML or XML) can quickly become unmanageable. Also, if there are different groups of developers working on a project, one focused on HTML or XML and one focused on the Java code, the separation can work to the advantage of the team in terms of workflow and availability of source code.

To get started with this example, you will need to have a JSP-capable application server. This particular example uses WebLogic 6.1. For more information on Java-Server Pages please refer to *JavaServer Pages* by Duane K. Fields and Mark A. Kolb (Manning Publications).

### 12.5.2 Creating the JSPHelper

This example uses a JavaBean called JSPHelper to facilitate most of the dynamic, Java-based processing. This allows us to remove most of the Java code from our JSP and maintain a cleaner separation of presentation and business logic.

We will create the JSPHelper class first since it is referenced by the JSP. Within this class you would normally perform the database access and other tasks. For simplicity, this class loads some test data based on the value of the customer ID passed to the setCustomerId() method. The code for the JSPHelper is shown in listing 12.3.

**Listing 12.3  JSPHelper.java**

```java
package com.ctimn;
import java.util.*;

public class JSPHelper {

  private int customerId;

  private String firstName;
  private String lastName;
  private String phone;
  private ArrayList items = new ArrayList();

  public void setCustomerId(String id){
    customerId = Integer.parseInt(id);
    loadCustomer();
  }

  public String getCustomerId(){
    return Integer.toString(customerId);
  }

  public String getFirstName(){
    return firstName;
  }

  public String getLastName(){
    return lastName;
  }
```

**1** Get/Set data

```java
public String getPhone(){
  return phone;
}

public Iterator getItemsOrdered(){
  return items.iterator();
}

private void loadCustomer(){

  switch (customerId){
    case 1:
      firstName = "David";
      lastName = "Hemphill";
      phone = "555-555-5555";
      items.add("Grass Seed #6633");
      break;
    case 2:
      firstName = "James";
      lastName = "White";
      phone = "555-555-5555";
      items.add("Fertilizer #3345");
      items.add("Fertilizer #9976");
      items.add("Plant Food #9906");
      break;
    case 3:
      firstName = "Scott";
      lastName = "King";
      phone = "555-555-5555";
      items.add("Weed Killer #3345");
      items.add("Grass-B-Gone #998");
      break;
    case 4:
      firstName = "Amy";
      lastName = "Votava";
      items.add("Orchid Food #112");
      items.add("Grow Light #KJ44");
      phone = "555-555-5555";
      break;
    case 5:
      firstName = "Olivia";
      lastName = "Hemphill";
      phone = "555-555-5555";
      items.add("Sunflower Seeds #248");
      break;
    default:
      firstName = "Undefined";
      lastName = "Undefined";
      phone = "Undefined";
  }
 }
}
```

**❶ Get/Set data**

**❷ Obtain test data**

Make certain to compile this class to a location where the application server can find it at runtime.

### 12.5.3 Creating the JSP

The next step is to create a JSP that uses the JSPHelper to return customer order information in an XML format. The schema of the XML provides a customer first name, last name, and phone number as demographics and 0 to n orders. The structure is as follows.

```
<?xml version="1.0"?>
<customer>
  <demograpics>
    <firstname></firstname>
    <lastname></lastname>
    <phone></phone>
  </demograpics>
  <order>order 1</order>
  <order>order 2</order>
     *
     *
     *
  <order>order n</order>
</customer>
```

The JSP code required to produce the XML for a specific customer is shown in listing 12.4:

#### Listing 12.4   XMLExample.jsp

```
<jsp:useBean id="helper" scope="page" class="com.ctimn.JSPHelper" />
```
❶ **Create JSPHelper**

```
<jsp:setProperty name="helper" property="customerId" />
```
❷ **Set the customer ID from the request**

```
<%@page import="java.util.*"%>
<?xml version="1.0"?>
<customer id="<%= helper.getCustomerId() %>">
  <demograpics>
  <firstname><%= helper.getFirstName() %></firstname>
  <lastname><%= helper.getLastName() %></lastname>
  <phone><%= helper.getPhone() %></phone>
</demograpics>
```
❸ **Get customer data**

```
<%
  Iterator it = helper.getItemsOrdered();
  while (it.hasNext()) {
%>
    <order><%=it.next()%></order>
<%
  }
%>
```
❹ **Get order information**

```
</customer>
```

To test the JSP, you can invoke it from a browser. Note, however, that the URL will differ depending on the application server you are using.

Using something like the URL http://127.0.0.1:7001/XMLExample.jsp?customerId=1 returns the following output to the browser. This example uses Internet Explorer accessing the localhost IP address of 127.0.0.1.

```
<?xml version="1.0" ?>
-<customer id="1">
  -<demograpics>
    <firstname>David</firstname>
    <lastname>Hemphill</lastname>
    <phone>555-555-5555</phone>
  </demograpics>
  <order>Grass Seed #6633</order>
</customer>
```

**NOTE**  In order for the `setProperty` tag to work properly, parameter names must follow the syntax where the first letter of the parameter name begins with a lower case letter.

## 12.5.4  Creating the J2ME Client

For this example, the NanoXML API illustrates the use of a SAX-based parser to retrieve information from a J2EE, XML-based data source. NanoXML was chosen because it conforms to the SAX 1.0 standards and allows the `InputStream` to be parsed while data is coming into the device, thus using less memory. TinyXML does not lend itself to this important characteristic. Due to the nature of the API, TinyXML requires that the XML data be provided in the form of a String to the `XMLInputStream`. This means that the entire XML content must be read into memory, compromising the key benefit of an event-based parser that we are interested in: low memory utilization.

There are two classes that need to be written to get our XML client working. First, we need a MIDP application. The application allows a user to enter a customer ID using the keypad. Once the ID has been entered, another button is pressed to fetch the data from the enterprise server over the network connection. Most of the code in the MIDP client application involves the user interface, which has been covered in chapter 5 of this book. The one key aspect of the client is how the XML parser comes into play. NanoXML utilizes the SAX 1.0 factory class `ParserFactory` to construct the parser. Using this mechanism allows any SAX-compliant parser to be constructed. The parameter passed to this factory method is the fully qualified class name of the NanoXML SAX parser.

```
Parser parser = ParserFactory.makeParser("nanoxml.sax.SAXParser");
```

Once a parser is constructed, a handler needs to be created to handle the events that the parser throws. A handler using the SAX 1.0 API must either implement the `DocumentHandler` interface or extend the `HandlerBase` class. The handler we create is called `XMLHandler`. The handler must be registered with the parser before parsing can begin. This is done using the `setDocumentHandler()` method.

```
XMLHandler handler = new XMLHandler(this);
parser.setDocumentHandler(handler);
```

The next step is to obtain the XML InputStream from where the XML data is to be parsed. The SAX 1.0 API requires this source to be represented using the Input-Source class. An InputSource class is constructed by passing a java.io.Input-Stream to the constructor. This means that we have to obtain the network connection to our XML data source before we can construct the InputSource. This is done using the Generic Connection Framework.

Although the application accesses the JavaServer Page using HTTP, it is not necessary to create an HttpConnection class when all we need is the underlying InputStream associated with the connection. Since this is the case, we use the Connector's openDataInputStream() convenience method. Since we need to pass the customer ID as a parameter to the JSP, we still need to follow the syntax for submitting a parameter using an HTTP GET method, which is to append a "?" followed by the parameter name=value pair. The following example assumes that "id" is a non-null string containing the customer id.

```
String url = "http://localhost:7001/XMLExample.jsp?customerId="+id;
DataInputStream is = Connector.openDataInputStream(url);
InputSource source = new InputSource(is);
```

The InputSource object is now ready to begin reading data. Invoking the parse() method of the parser and passing the InputSource as a parameter starts this process. The following example accepts the InputSource object named source as a parameter. This invokes the JSP. The parser then begins reading the Input-Stream returned by the JSP, which in turn triggers events that are handled by the XMLHandler instance.

```
parser.parse(source);
```

The full source listing of the XMLClient application is shown in listing 12.5:

**Listing 12.5   XMLClient.java**

```
package com.ctimn;

import java.io.*;
import javax.microedition.io.*;
import javax.microedition.midlet.*;
import javax.microedition.lcdui.*;
import nanoxml.*;
import nanoxml.sax.*;
import org.xml.sax.*;
import org.xml.sax.helpers.*;

public class XMLClient extends MIDlet implements CommandListener {

  private Form outputForm = new Form("Order Information");
  private Form inputForm = new Form("Enter Customer");          Set up the  ❶
  private TextField customerFld =                                application
    new TextField("ID", "1", 15, TextField.NUMERIC);
  private Command okCmd = new Command("OK", Command.OK, 1);
```

```
private Command exitCmd = new Command("Exit", Command.EXIT, 1);
private Command getCmd = new Command("Get", Command.OK, 1);
private Display display;
private boolean initialized = false;
private static final String CONNECTION_URL =
  "http://localhost:7001/XMLExample.jsp";

protected void startApp() throws MIDletStateChangeException {
  init();
  display = Display.getDisplay(this);
  display.setCurrent(inputForm);
}

private void init(){
  if (!initialized){
    inputForm.append(customerFld);
    inputForm.addCommand(getCmd);
    inputForm.addCommand(exitCmd);
    outputForm.addCommand(okCmd);
    outputForm.addCommand(exitCmd);
    inputForm.setCommandListener(this);
    outputForm.setCommandListener(this);
    initialized = true;
  }
}

protected void pauseApp() {
}

protected void destroyApp(boolean unconditional)
  throws MIDletStateChangeException {
}

public void commandAction(Command cmd, Displayable displayable) {
  if (cmd == exitCmd){
    handleExit();
  } else if ((displayable == outputForm) && (cmd == okCmd)) {
    display.setCurrent(inputForm);
  } else if ((displayable == inputForm) && (cmd == getCmd)) {
    getCustomer();
  } else {
    display.setCurrent(inputForm);
  }
}

private void handleExit(){
  try {
    notifyDestroyed();
    destroyApp(true);
  } catch (MIDletStateChangeException x) {
    x.printStackTrace();
  }
}
```

**Set up the** ❶
**application**

**Handle** ❷
**button**
**events**

```
private void getCustomer(){
  removeStringItems();
  String id = customerFld.getString();
  display.setCurrent(outputForm);
  try {
    XMLHandler handler = new XMLHandler(this);
    Parser parser = ParserFactory.makeParser("nanoxml.sax.SAXParser");
    parser.setDocumentHandler(handler);
    InputSource source = getXml(id);
    parser.parse(source);                                    Initialize XML ❸
  } catch (Exception x){                                        handler and
    x.printStackTrace();                                         parse data
  }
}

private InputSource getXml(String id){
  InputSource source = null;
  String url = CONNECTION_URL + "?customerId="+id;
  try {
    DataInputStream is = Connector.openDataInputStream(url);
    source = new InputSource(is);
  } catch (IOException x){
    x.printStackTrace();                          Obtain the XML data ❹
  }
  return source;
}

private void removeStringItems(){
  int count = outputForm.size();
  for(int i=count-1; i >= 0; i--){
    if (outputForm.get(i) instanceof StringItem){
      outputForm.delete(i);
    }
  }
}                                               Clear output form ❺

public void append(String s){      ❻ Append output
  outputForm.append(s + "\n");
}
}
```

Before we can compile the XMLClient, we need to implement a class to handle the
events the parser triggers. A SAX 1.0 handler implements the DocumentHandler
interface. However, since many handlers do not require all the methods the DocumentHandler interface prescribes, you can opt to extend the HandlerBase class
instead. Thus, the empty methods only need to be overridden when specific functionality is required by the application. This example implements the Document-
Handler interface directly to show the full interface even though only a few methods are actually needed.

For our example, we create a document handler by passing the XMLClient instance as a parameter. We do this so that the handler can call the append() method of the XMLClient application as data is parsed. The append() method displays the data to the user. The key methods needed in order to parse the XML are as follows:

- startElement(), which is called when a beginning tag is encountered such as <Customer> or <FirstName>.

- characters(), which is called to pass the contents located between element tags.

When startElement() is called, the customer ID is captured and appended to the outputForm on the XMLClient. When characters() is called, we simply append the data passed as a parameter to the outputForm.

Listing 12.6 shows the full source listing for XMLHandler:

**Listing 12.6  XMLHandler.java**

```java
package com.ctimn;

import java.util.*;
import org.xml.sax.*;

public class XMLHandler implements DocumentHandler {

  private XMLClient app;
  private String customerId;

  public XMLHandler(XMLClient client){        ❶ Reference the
    app = client;                                application
  }

  public void characters(char[] ch, int start, int length) {
    String data = new String(ch);              ❷ Process
    System.out.println("characters: "+new String(ch));   XML
    app.append(data);                             content
  }

  public void endDocument() {
    System.out.println("Finished parsing document.");
  }
                                               Note XML ❸
                                                 events
  public void endElement(java.lang.String name) {
    System.out.println("endElement: "+name);
  }

  public void ignorableWhitespace(char[] ch, int start, int length) {
    System.out.println("ignorableWhitespace: "+new String(ch));
  }

  public void processingInstruction
      (java.lang.String target, java.lang.String data) {
    System.out.println("processingInstruction target="+target+
      " data="+data);
  }
```

*CHAPTER 12   INTEGRATING THE SERVER*

```
public void setDocumentLocator(Locator locator) {
  System.out.println("setDocumentLocator: "+locator);
}

public void startDocument() {
  System.out.println("Starting to parse document.");
}

public void startElement(java.lang.String name, AttributeList atts) {
  System.out.println("startElement: "+name);
  for (int i = 0; i < atts.getLength(); i++) {
    if (atts.getName(i).toLowerCase().equals("id")){
      customerId = atts.getValue(i);
    }
    System.out.println("  Attribute Name = "+atts.getName(i));
    System.out.println("  Attribute Type = "+atts.getType(i));
    System.out.println("  Attribute Value = "+atts.getValue(i));
  }
  if (name.toLowerCase().equals("customer")){
    app.append("Customer "+customerId);
  }
}
}
```

**❸ Note XML events**

**Handle XML start tag event ❹**

To the XMLClient application you must first make sure the JSP is deployed and the application server is running. The output from the XMLClient application is depicted in figure 12.5.

**Figure 12.5**
**XMLClient accessing XMLExample.jsp. On the first screen the user enters the Customer ID and presses the Get button. The application makes an HTTP request to the JSP to return information pertaining to Customer ID 1. The data returned is displayed.**

The output to the console from XMLClient looks like the following:

```
setDocumentLocator: nanoxml.sax.SAXLocator@fd5e38
Starting to parse document.
startElement: customer
  Attribute Name = ID
  Attribute Type = CDATA
  Attribute Value = 1
startElement: demograpics
startElement: firstname
characters: David
```

```
endElement: firstname
startElement: lastname
characters: Hemphill
endElement: lastname
startElement: phone
characters: 555-555-5555
endElement: phone
endElement: demograpics
startElement: order
characters: Grass Seed #6633
endElement: order
endElement: customer
Finished parsing document.
```

## 12.6  SUMMARY

When two or more systems use a standard protocol, such as HTTP, to communicate, the two systems do not need to be written in a common language or need to understand the intricate details of how each works. This is a major benefit and one of the core purposes behind using open standards. A J2ME client could access an Active Server Page (ASP) just as easily as it could access a JSP to interact with the enterprise environment. Incorporating XML has the potential for bringing standardization to the data itself as opposed to the communication protocol only. Simple Object Access Protocol (SOAP) and SyncML are two examples of open, XML-based protocols of which a J2ME application could take advantage.

In this chapter the concepts of using Java Servlets and JavaServer Pages were demonstrated along with the ability to transfer information in an XML format. These tools address important aspects of extending an enterprise environment using J2ME over a network, namely the connection protocol and the data format. However, it is important to remember that there are many methods for connecting two systems across a network and the best solution is likely to vary for each implementation.

# CHAPTER 13

# *The network connection*

One of the most critical aspects of J2ME is network connectivity. Although J2ME devices can be useful when they are not connected to a network, the ability to make a network connection provides a means to tap into the powerful resources available on a network. Even more significant are the emerging capabilities to establish a wireless network connection. Many J2ME devices support this capability, which opens the door to providing features on devices that go beyond sending and receiving email, such as extending the enterprise into the mobile space. J2ME applications, in this regard, become more than simple communication devices. They become another client capable of interfacing with the enterprise systems, databases, corporate intranets and the Internet. An insurance agent could file and adjust claims interactively while talking to customers. Medical staff could interact with the hospital and clinical systems at the point of care. Inspectors could file reports on site. Salespeople could submit orders, check inventory, and calculate deals in the field. Schedules could be dynamically updated and adjusted for mobile workers.

**Table 13.1  GCF interfaces**

| GCF Interface | Purpose |
| --- | --- |
| Connection | The most basic type of connection in the GCF. All other connection types extend Connection. |
| ContentConnection | Manages a connection, such as HTTP, for passing content, such as HTML or XML. Provides basic methods for inspecting the content length, encoding and type of content. |
| Datagram | Acts as a container for the data passed on a Datagram Connection. |
| DatagramConnection | Manages a datagram connection. |
| InputConnection | Manages an input stream-based connection. |
| OutputConnection | Manages an output stream-based connection. |
| StreamConnection | Manages the capabilities of a stream. Combines the methods of both InputConnection and OutputConnection. |
| StreamConnectionNotifier | Listens to a specific port and creates a StreamConnection as soon as activity on the port is detected. |

While mobile applications are nothing new to the technology market, J2ME provides the ability for organizations with a commitment to Java to easily move into the mobile space. J2ME also makes it possible to run the same application on multiple devices, providing flexibility among vendors. In cases where applications are publicly released, the number of devices on which the application can run becomes an important selling point.

The network capabilities of J2ME complements other emerging technologies such as Bluetooth, which provides wireless local area network capabilities through radio frequency communication, and Jini, which provides spontaneous networking capabilities. Using Jini and Bluetooth, a J2ME device could automatically register itself on a wireless local area network as the user enters a room and unregister the user when he leaves the room. While connected to the wireless network, the user would have access to a number of network services such as printers, fax machines, email, network file systems, databases, enterprise systems, and other devices currently registered with the network. Which services a user has available depends on who the user is, of course, and how the user or device is presented to the network.

Since network connectivity is so vital to J2ME it is important that the architecture be extendible to many different protocols while allowing applications to be portable across many devices. The piece of software within the J2ME architecture that addresses network connectivity is called the Generic Connection Framework (GCF).

## 13.1  ABOUT THE GENERIC CONNECTION FRAMEWORK

The Generic Connection Framework provides the foundation for all network communications within the J2ME architecture. Within the configuration layer the Generic Connection Framework interface is defined along with a number of basic interfaces. The Generic Connection Framework provides no protocol implementations.

The vendors supplying the profile must implement the necessary Generic Connection Framework interfaces.

The Generic Connection Framework resides in the `javax.microedition.io` package and consists of:

- one class (`Connector`)
- one exception (`ConnectionNotFoundException`)
- eight interfaces (table 13.1)

The relationships of these interfaces are depicted in figure 13.1.

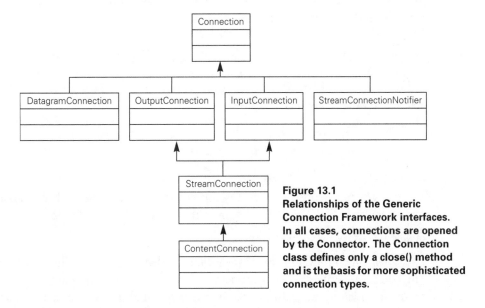

**Figure 13.1**
**Relationships of the Generic Connection Framework interfaces. In all cases, connections are opened by the Connector. The Connection class defines only a close() method and is the basis for more sophisticated connection types.**

### 13.1.1 Where the Generic Connection Framework lives

The Generic Connection Framework is defined at the configuration layer of the J2ME architecture. By implementing the framework at this level, the same `Connector` and interfaces are available across all the profiles.

Both the CDC and the CLDC support the Generic Connection Framework. Due to the nested arrangement of configurations, the connection interfaces are provided throughout the J2ME architecture. This increases the compatibility across configurations.

**NOTE** By definition, all J2ME configurations must adhere to a nested relationship. In other words, the CLDC fits completely inside the CDC. There are no classes, methods or other functionality in the CLDC that are not also in the CDC.

### 13.1.2    Working with the Connector class

The `Connector` class is used to create instances of a connection protocol using one of `Connector`'s static methods. The instance returned is an implementation supporting the `Connection` interface or one of its descendents.

The `Connector` class is not designed to be instantiated. It is simply used to create instances of a connection protocol. All of the methods `Connector` defines are static and serve this purpose.

The `Connector` defines three variations of an `open()` that return a `Connection` instance. The `Connector` also defines methods that return input and output streams. These methods will be discussed later in this chapter. For now, we will concentrate on the `open()` method.

The `open()` method returns an instance of type of `Connection`. However, the instance returned is most likely to be a subclass of `Connection` that is more sophisticated. It is the responsibility of the calling application to know what class to expect and to coerce the returned instance to the correct object type as necessary. The open method has the following signatures:

- `open(String name)`
- `open(String name, int mode)`
- `open(String name, int mode, boolean timeouts)`

The name is essentially a URI and is composed of three parts: a scheme, an address, and a parameter list. The general form of the name parameter is as follows:

`<scheme>:<address>;<parameters>`

The scheme identifies how the connection is made (socket, http, file, datagram, etc.). The address identifies what to connect to (www.ctimn.com, myfile.txt, etc.) and the parameters identify other information that is required by the protocol to establish a connection such as a connection speed. The parameters, when needed, are specified as name=value pairs. Some examples of the name URI are shown in the following list. Note that in some cases the parameter is not necessary and thus the ";" is not always present:

- http://www.ctimn.com:8080
- socket://localhost:8080
- file:c:/myfile.txt (Windows only)
- file:/myfile.txt (Unix)
- datagram://127.0.0.1:8099
- comm:0;baudrate=9600

The mode parameter allows the connection to be established in various access modes, such as read-only, read-write and write-only. These modes are defined by the `Connector` constants `READ`, `READ_WRITE`, and `WRITE`.

The `timeouts` parameter is a flag indicating whether or not the connection should throw an `InterruptedIOException` if a timeout occurs. The application is then responsible for handling this exception gracefully.

The `Connector` class is the only mechanism for creating the various types of connections using the Generic Connection Framework. Specific protocol implementations are designed to be created directly.

The other methods defined by the `Connector` interface are:

- `openInputStream()`
- `openOutputStream()`
- `openDataInputStream()`
- `openDataOutputStream()`

These are convenient methods for creating different types of input and output streams at the same time the `Connection` is created. In most cases, applications are not concerned with the `Connection` instance itself, but rather the stream that can be read from or written to. By using one of these four methods, the application can obtain the stream directly, without needing to be concerned about the connection instance. The following example illustrates the difference between the two ways of obtaining streams:

```
try {
  OutputConnection connection =
      (OutputConnection)Connector.open("socket://127.0.0.1:8888");
  OutputStream os = connection.openOutputStream();
  os.close();
  connection.close();
} catch (IOException x) {
    //Handle the exception
}
```

This first way to obtain an `OutputStream` is rather verbose and requires us to deal with the `Connection` simply for the purpose of calling the `openOutput-Stream()` method. We are also forced to cast the return type to `OutputConnection`. If you do not need to interact with the `Connection` instance itself, you can abbreviate how a stream is obtained.

```
try {
  OutputStream os =
    Connector.openOutputStream("socket://127.0.0.1:8888");
  os.close();
} catch (IOException x) {
    //Handle Exception
}
```

This second way of obtaining the `OutputStream` connection is much more concise and eliminates lines of code that deal directly with the `Connection` instance. Furthermore, there is no coercing of the return type on our part. However, there is one troubling aspect that comes into the picture when using `openOutputStream()`: Who closes the connection? In this case, the connection has already been closed by the `openOutputStream()` method when the stream is returned. A connection is established just long enough to obtain an output stream. Once the stream has been obtained, the connection can be closed. It is important to understand that this works for stream-based connections only. The connection must remain open for some connection types, such as Datagrams, that rely more heavily on the underlying connection.

> **NOTE** In the case where a stream is obtained directly, using `openInput-Stream()` or `openOutputStream()`, the connection `close()` is called immediately after the stream is obtained. However, the actual connection remains open until all the streams are closed as well. This is handled internally by the `Connection`, using a counter to track the number of opens and closes performed. When `open()` is called, the counter is incremented. When `close()` is called the counter is decremented. When the number of closes returns to zero, the connection is actually closed. This is why invoking `close()` on the `Connection` can take place without affecting the streams and still allow the connection resources to be cleaned up properly.

### 13.1.3 The Connector is a factory

The concept employed by `Connector` for creating connection protocol instances is often referred to as a factory. A factory is a class that has the sole purpose of creating and possibly configuring a set of classes supporting a common interface. Factories provide the ability to return different implementations of an interface while hiding these details from the application code. The actual implementation returned depends on what parameters are passed into the static method (an open method in this case) and possibly the state of the system. The factory then deciphers the parameters and system state and determines which class to create. The object created must implement the interface specified by the static method's return type (`Connection`, in this case). However, the interface does not need to be directly supported. For example `DatagramConnection` subclasses `Connection` and is therefore a `Connection` as well.

Factories provide a level of indirection or decoupling that allows the implementation of the interface to vary somewhat independently of the class using the interface. Put more simply, the class using `Connector` does not need to know about the actual (concrete) class that is created. This example of loose coupling is an extremely important aspect of the Generic Connection Framework because it provides flexibility and extendibility.

### 13.1.4 How the Connector finds the correct class

When the URI (name) is passed to the `Connector.open()` method, the `Connector` parses the URI into its various parts `<scheme>:<address>;<parameters>`. The key piece of information that the `Connector` is looking for at this point is the scheme. It is the scheme, in combination with other information such as the root package name and a platform identifier that allows the `Connector` to determine the appropriate `Connection` implementation to create. Once this information is determined, a fully qualified class name is concatenated.

The root package and platform information are system properties identified by `microedition.protocolpath` and `microedition.platform`, respectively. The values of these properties are obtained using the `System` class.

```
String rootPackage = System.getProperty("microedition.protocolpath");
String platform = System.getProperty("microedition.platform");
```

By design, the Generic Connection Framework distinguishes different protocol implementations by package name rather than class name. This is necessary since every protocol implementation is written in a class named `Protocol.java`. Keeping the class name the same relieves the `Connector` class from having to know the names of each implemented class. The classes are differentiated by the location in which they reside. For example, a socket protocol could be defined by the class `com.sun.cldc.io.j2me.`**`socket`**`.Protocol.class` and an http protocol could be defined by the class `com.sun.cldc.io.j2me.`**`http`**`.Protocol.class`. Even though the names of the classes are identical, the full qualification (package name and class name) of the class allows the two implementations to be distinguished from one another. In this example, the root package is `com.sun.cldc.io` and the platform is "j2me".

In the case of the CLDC reference implementation, the fully qualified class name for a protocol is constructed as follows using the root package name + platform + protocol name + `Protocol`, or more specifically `com.sun.cldc.io.[j2se, j2me, palm].[socket, datagram, http].Protocol`. The following example illustrates the process for creating a datagram protocol instance:

```
DatagramConnection connection =
        (DatagramConnection)Connector.open("datagram://127.0.0.1:9090");
```

The `Connector` extracts the scheme "datagram" and obtains the platform from the `System` properties. In this case, we will assume the platform is j2me. The fully-qualified class name is `com.sun.cldc.io.j2me.datagram.Protocol`. The `Connector` then loads this class into the virtual machine and creates an instance using statements similar to the following.

```
Class c = Class.forName("com.sun.cldc.io.j2me.datagram.Protocol");
Connection connection = (Connection)c.newInstance();
```

Once the `Protocol` instance is created the open method of the actual `Protocol` class is called to configure the instance. The Protocol's open method returns the configured instance to the caller. The caller then coerces the instance to the expected connection type, which is `DatagramConnection` in this case.

It is important to note that the protocol implementations do not reside in the `java.*` or `javax.*` package. This is due to the fact that protocol implementations, such as HTTP, are the responsibility of the profile implementer, not the creators of J2ME. Furthermore, protocols must be implemented differently for specific platforms, such as Palm OS or a Motorola phone. In many cases native calls into the underlying device APIs are required. Because of this device dependency of protocol implementations, the Generic Connection Framework does not provide any specific protocol implementations.

The primary goal of the Generic Connection Framework is to generalize how connectivity is handled so that it is extensible and coherent.

## 13.2  USING THE GENERIC CONNECTION FRAMEWORK

In the sections that follow, various protocols supported by the Generic Connection Framework are examined using examples for each protocol. The example will demonstrate the ability to send and receive messages over a network connection. For simplicity, and ease of learning, the same implementation will be provided for HTTP, socket and datagram connections.

The Generic Connection Framework is available in both the CDC and the CLDC configurations. For these examples, the MIDP will be used, which uses the CLDC at the configuration. Since the CLDC is completely nested inside the CDC, the GCF functionality in these examples will work for both configurations.

We begin by examining HTTP. This example application will be expanded to illustrate sockets and datagrams later on in the chapter.

## 13.3  HTTP-BASED CONNECTIONS

To establish HTTP GET connections, when you are not interested in HTTP-specific information, such HTTP header information, the GCF ContentConnection interface can be used. This example shows how a MIDlet can be used to read a page of HTML from a website and display the title of the document in a Form.

### 13.3.1  Establishing a connection

The ContentConnection interface enables connections to deal with rich data exchanges, such as HTTP. This type of connection extends the StreamConnection interface and defines methods that allow an application to determine the type of connection, the length of content and the encoding used through the following methods:

- String getEncoding()
- long getLength()
- String getType()

In most cases, ContentConnection is not used directly but serves as a base interface for a protocol-specific connection types, such as an HttpConnection interface.

The following example shows how to use ContentConnection with HTTP as the underlying protocol:

```
ContentConnection connection = (ContentConnection) Connector.open(
    "http://www.catapult-technologies.com/ctimain.htm", Connector.READ);
```

In this example we want to read a page of HTML at a specified URL (www.catapult-technologies.com). The connection takes place over the default HTTP port, port 80. Since this is the default port it does not need to be specified. Since this example only reads the page, the connection is opened in read-only mode.

Once the connection is established, we obtain the input stream:

```
DataInputStream is = connection.openDataInputStream();
```

In this particular example we could have simply obtained an input stream without creating the connection directly, using the `openDataInputStream()` method of the `Connector`. However, the methods stated earlier that provide content length, content type and the encoding reside on the `ContentConnection` instance. Therefore it is necessary to hang onto the connection instance beyond the creation of the input stream.

The `ContentConnection` methods can be used as follows to obtain information about the connection:

```
System.out.println("encoding: "+ connection.getEncoding());

System.out.println("length: "+ connection.getLength());

System.out.println("type: "+ connection.getType());
```

### 13.3.2   Using the connection

Once a connection is established it can be used to retrieve data. The following example illustrates how to use the content connection to read a page of HTML from a network connection. Since the amount of data retrieved is substantial in this case, our application will parse out only a meaningful portion of the data returned to display on the cell phone emulator. The entire contents of the read, however, will be displayed to the console so the progress can be monitored. The class we will create is named `MsgClient` and will be used throughout this chapter as a basis for demonstrating different types of connections. The full source listing for the MsgClient is shown in listing 13.1.

**Listing 13.1   MsgClient.java**

```
package com.ctimn;

import java.io.*;
import javax.microedition.io.*;
import javax.microedition.midlet.*;
import javax.microedition.lcdui.*;

public class MsgClient extends MIDlet implements CommandListener {

    private Form outputForm;
    private Display display;
    private List menu;
    private Command okCmd = new Command("OK", Command.OK, 1);
    private Command exitCmd = new Command("Exit", Command.EXIT, 1);
```

```java
 private static final String[] choices = {
   "1 HTTP Example"
 };

protected void startApp() throws MIDletStateChangeException {
   display = Display.getDisplay(this);
   outputForm = new Form("Server Messages");
   menu = new List("Select:", List.IMPLICIT, choices, null);
   menu.addCommand(okCmd);
   outputForm.addCommand(okCmd);
   outputForm.addCommand(exitCmd);
   menu.addCommand(exitCmd);
   outputForm.setCommandListener(this);
   menu.setCommandListener(this);
       display.setCurrent(menu);
   }

   protected void pauseApp() {
   }

   protected void destroyApp(boolean unconditional)
           throws MIDletStateChangeException {
   }

   public void commandAction(Command cmd, Displayable displayable) {
       if (cmd == exitCmd){
     handleExit();
   } else if ((displayable == menu) && (cmd == okCmd)) {
     handleOK(((List)displayable).getSelectedIndex());
   } else {
       display.setCurrent(menu);
       }
    }

private void handleExit(){
   try {
     notifyDestroyed();
     destroyApp(true);
   } catch (MIDletStateChangeException x) {
     x.printStackTrace();
   }
}

private void handleOK(int idx){
   display.setCurrent(outputForm);
   getHttpMessage();
}


private void getHttpMessage(){
   int c = 0;
   String dataIn = null;
   StringItem item = new StringItem("Reading from URL", "");
   outputForm.append(item);
```

```
    try {
      ContentConnection connection = (ContentConnection)                ➋
        Connector.open(
        "http://www.catapult-technologies.com/ctimain.htm",
        Connector.READ);
      DataInputStream is = connection.openDataInputStream();           ➌
      try {
        System.out.println("encoding: "+ connection.getEncoding());    ➍
        System.out.println("length: "+ connection.getLength());
        System.out.println("type: "+ connection.getType());
        StringBuffer sb = new StringBuffer("");
        for (int ccnt=0; ccnt < connection.getLength(); ccnt++){       ➎
          c = is.read();
          sb.append((char)c);              ➏

        }
        dataIn = sb.toString();
        item = new StringItem("Title: ", getTitle(dataIn));
        outputForm.append(item);
      } finally {
        is.close();
      }

    } catch (IOException x) {
      System.out.println("Problems sending or receiving data.");
      x.printStackTrace();
    }
  }

  private String getTitle(String data){
    String titleTag = "<TITLE>";                                       ➐
    int idx1 = data.indexOf(titleTag);
    int idx2 = data.indexOf("</TITLE>");
    return data.substring(idx1 + titleTag.length(), idx2);
  }
}
```

➊ Set up the user interface

➋ Open a connection

➌ Open an input stream

➍ Display connection information

➎ Read the input

➏ Convert bytes to characters

➐ Extract the title

**BEST PRACTICE** Note the use of the try..finally construct in the example. As a general practice, it is a good idea to use a try..finally construct to handle the closing of resources. This ensures that the close() operation always takes place, whether an exception is thrown or not.

The try should be placed immediately after the resource has been opened. Placing the open statement within the try..finally block is likely to cause problems if the open process throws an exception. This is because the flow of control would be routed through the close() statement while the connection is in an unstable state, and was probably never opened.

The steps to compile and run this example follow. Since we are only dealing with a single class, the MsgClient, there is no need to JAR this application in order to run it.

### 13.3.3 Compiling and running the application

Use the following command line to compile the application:

```
>e:\jdk1.3\bin\javac -g:none -bootclasspath e:\midp-fcs\classes -classpath
  .\build -d .\build MsgClient.java
```

Use the following command to preverify the application:

```
>e:\midp-fcs\bin\preverify.exe
  -classpath e:\midp-fcs\classes;.;.\build  .\build
```

Use the following command to run the application:

```
>e:\midp-fcs\bin\midp.exe -classpath e:\midp-fcs\classes;
  .com.ctimn.MsgClient
```

The first screen to appear when running the application is the menu options of the MsgClient application. This is shown in figure 13.2.

**Figure 13.2**
**MsgClient main menu**

Pressing the OK button reads the information from the URL provided. The encoding, content length, and content type are displayed to the console so that we can inspect the values. The "Title" of the HTML page is then parsed and displayed to the screen. The MIDlet output is depicted in figure 13.3.

The output to the console is as follows:

```
encoding: null
length: 176
type: text/html
```

In this case, the encoding is not known, the length, in bytes, is 176 and the content type is HTML.

## 13.4   SOCKET-BASED CONNECTIONS

Sockets can be used to implement communication between two systems and allow the network connection to be treated as a stream. Once a socket is established the stream can be read from, using an `InputStream`, or written to, using an `OutputStream`.

The Generic Connection Framework provides two interfaces for working with streams, `StreamConnectionNotifier` and `StreamConnection`. `StreamConnectionNotifier` is used by a server to monitor a port for clients wanting to establish a connection. `StreamConnection` is used to establish a socket connection.

The `StreamConnection` interface extends both `InputConnection` and `OutputConnection`, allowing both read and write capability on a single connection. In general, the interfaces `InputConnection`, `DataInputConnection`, `OutputConnection`, and `DataOutputConnection` are used in combination throughout the Generic Connection Framework to build more sophisticated connection types. Individually, they are not terribly useful since most connection protocols support both read and write capabilities.

Before a client can request a socket connection to a listener, the listener must be listening to a designated port. To bind a socket listener application to a port using `StreamConnectionNotifier` the following syntax for the open command is used:

```
StreamConnectionNotifier connection = (StreamConnectionNotifier)
    Connector.open("serversocket://:4444", Connector.READ_WRITE);
```

The `Connector` knows to open a `StreamConnectionNotifier` by looking for the "serversocket" scheme. The port number is specified after the ":" in the address portion of the name. The port chosen is arbitrary so long as both the client and the socket listener use the same port number. Also, if the specified port number is unavailable, or another service is already bound to the port, the connection will be refused.

Once a `StreamConnectionNotifier` is established, the socket listener waits for a client to attempt a connection using the `acceptAndOpen()` method.

```
StreamConnection sc = connection.acceptAndOpen();
```

When a client attempts to connect to the socket listener, the `acceptAndOpen()` method verifies that the connection can be established and opens a `StreamCon-`

**Figure 13.3**
**Reading the HTML page**
**with a ContentConnection.**

nection socket. Once a `StreamConnection` is established, the socket listener is ready to read and write data from and to the stream. In order for the connection to be accepted by the listener, the client attempting the connection must be attempting to establish a socket connection. Other types of connections that the listener cannot handle or does not understand are refused.

Clients connect to socket listeners by directly opening a `StreamConnection`.

```
StreamConnection connection = (StreamConnection)
    Connector.open("socket://127.0.0.1:4444", Connector.READ_WRITE);
```

To open a socket from the client side, the "`socket`" scheme is used and both the host and port number must be specified in the address portion of the name. Note that the port numbers must be exactly the same when the connection is opened for both the client and the socket listener. If they are different you will not be able to establish a connection. Furthermore, if the socket listener at the host address is not listening to this port, or another type of service that cannot handle sockets is bound to this port, the connection will be refused with an exception stating that the connection was refused. If the connection is successful, the socket is ready to write and read data to and from the socket's input and output streams.

Generally, the client is the first to write data to the stream, even if only to issue a command to the listener; however, this is not a requirement of sockets. Once a connection is successful, either side may initiate the conversion.

Sockets provide a very useful means of communicating between systems; however, sockets only define the connection and the low-level data transport mechanisms, such as TCP/IP. How the client and socket listener deal with each other must be defined by the client and listener applications.

### 13.4.1 Writing to sockets

Once we have a successful connection, an output stream may be obtained from the `StreamConnection` using the `openOutputStream()` or `openDataOutput-Stream()` methods.

```
OutputStream os = connection.openOutputStream();
DataOutputStream os = connection.openDataOutputStream();
```

Once an output stream is obtained, the application can begin writing data using one of the various methods of the `OutputStream`. To make life easier, an `Output-Stream` can be wrapped inside of other stream classes that provide richer data support when writing to the stream. For example, an `OutputStream` could be passed to a `OutputStreamWriter` to provide the means for dealing with character-based stream content rather than byte-based content. The `OutputStreamWriter` acts as a filter, converting the characters passed to the `OutputStreamWriter` methods into a byte representation of the data and passing this on to the appropriate `Output-Stream` method.

### OutputStream

`OutputStream` provides the basic methods necessary for writing byte data onto a stream, flushing the stream and closing the stream. All other output stream classes either extend or wrapper instances of `OutputStream`.

### DataOutput

`DataOutput` is an interface that defines the methods for converting data from primitive types, such as `int`, `long`, `boolean`, etc. to an array of bytes that can be written to an output stream. This interface also provides the ability to convert Java `Strings` to UTF-8 format that in turn is written as a byte array to an output stream.

### DataOutputStream

`DataOutputStream` extends `OutputStream` and implements the `DataOutput` interface to provide the ability to deal with byte, character and UTF encoded data in a machine-independent manner.

### ByteArrayOutputStream

A `ByteArrayOutputStream` extends `OutputStream` and provides dynamic buffering capabilities for writing to byte streams. As data is written to the `ByteArrayOutputStream`, the buffer grows automatically. This class supplies two useful methods for retrieving the data as a byte array, using `toByteArray()`, or as a `String`, using the `toString()` method.

### Writer

`Writer` is an abstract class that provides support for writing to character streams as opposed to bytes. Java uses a naming convention of "Writer" in the `java.io` package to denote classes that act as a bridge between byte streams and character-based streams. The fundamental benefit of using a `Writer` (or its counterpart, a `Reader`) is that character encoding is automatically translated between the byte representation of the data and the character representation of the data. All other writer classes extend `Writer`. Since this class is abstract it cannot be used directly by applications. Applications requiring `Writer` capabilities should use `OutputStreamWriter`.

### OutputStreamWriter

`OutputStreamWriter` extends `Writer` and provides the necessary implementation for applications to write characters to an output stream. With the exception of the `write()` methods, all characters written to the stream through this class are buffered, requiring a call `flush()` in order to actually place the data on the stream.

### PrintStream

PrintStream is a convenience class that extends OutputStream and provides means for easily printing stream data. Most notably, PrintStream introduces a println() with various signatures for printing different data types. The println() methods automatically append a '\n' (new line) character to the data printed. Furthermore, PrintStream does not throw IOExceptions but rather sets an internal flag if errors occur. The error state is checked by a call to the checkError() method.

## 13.4.2 Reading from sockets

The API for reading from a socket is similar to the output APIs but performs reads instead. Once an input stream is obtained, there are a number of classes that help facilitate retrieving data from a stream.

### InputStream

InputStream provides the basic methods necessary for reading byte data from a stream and closing the stream. All other input stream classes either extend or wrapper instances of InputStream.

### DataInput

DataInput is an interface that defines methods for reading a stream of bytes and converting this series of bytes to Java primitive types such as int, long, short, char, boolean, etc. This interface also defines the ability for creating a Java String from a UTF-8 format.

### DataInputStream

DataInputStream extends InputStream and implements the DataInput interface, providing an implementation for reading and converting java primitives from a series of bytes on an input stream. This class also provides the ability to deal with UTF encoded data in a machine independent manner.

### ByteArrayInputStream

ByteArrayInputStream extends InputStream and provides buffering capabilities while reading from a byte input stream. The number of bytes read by this class is determined by the buffer size provided to the constructor.

### Reader

Reader is an abstract base class for other readers in the API. Java uses a naming convention of "Reader" in the java.io package to denote classes that act as a bridge between byte streams and character-based streams. The fundamental benefit of using a Reader is that character encoding is automatically translated from the byte representation of the data to the character representation of the data during the read operations. All other reader classes extend Reader. Since this class is abstract it cannot be used directly by applications. Applications requiring `Reader` capabilities should use `InputStreamReader`.

### InputStreamReader

`InputStreamReader` extends `Reader` and provides an implementation for reading character data from a byte stream, thus providing a layer of translation between byte and character data. This class also provides capabilities for returning UTF-encoded data. `InputStreamReader` automatically supports buffering. Each read operation will cause one or more bytes to actually be read from the stream, regardless of the data to be returned by the method.

### 13.4.3    When to use sockets

Sockets are a primitive but lightweight method of connecting two systems and exchanging data. Due to the low overhead of sockets, this can be one of the fastest methods of exchanging data and issuing commands between two systems. However, the lightweight nature of sockets comes at the price of needing to define a protocol of how the two systems communicate. In other words, sockets provide the connection, but the format of the information exchanged is something left to the implementer. As a result, there are few restrictions on what you can do with sockets; however, everything you do will need to be determined and built.

Sockets are useful in cases where speed is more important than adhering to open protocol standards. In other words, using sockets probably means you will be implementing a proprietary data transport mechanism. (Note, however, that the protocol HTTP can be, and often is, implemented using sockets.) If your system needs to subscribe to open communications standards or you are not in control of both the client and the server, sockets may not be a good way to implement communication capabilities in your application. In these cases, something like HTTP may be more appropriate. There are exceptions to this case, however. Since sockets purely provide the transportation mechanism, another data format or protocol could be used in conjunction with sockets. For example, sockets could be used in combination with XML. This would allow an application to take advantage of sockets while using a nonproprietary or publicly defined XML schema. You should be aware, however, that this still requires coordination between client and server applications since they both need to support the same connection types. If the systems implementing a standardized XML data exchange expect an HTTP connection, implementing a socket solution would not be acceptable.

### 13.4.4    Client-server socket example

The following example enhances the `MsgClient` application used earlier to include socket communication capabilities. This example illustrates how to establish a connection between a client and a socket listener (server) and send data between the two systems. Figures 13.4 and 13.5 illustrate communication links between two systems.

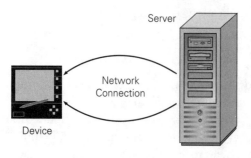

**Figure 13.4**
**A client-server relationship that allows data to be exchanged between the two systems. Generally, the client (in this example, the device) participates by triggering the communication events and asking the server for information. The server simply listens for incoming messages and responds appropriately.**

Since we are dealing with J2ME, the two systems in this case are cellular phones that send messages to each other. However, it is definitely possible to use sockets to connect to a J2SE or J2EE server application.

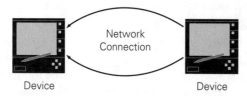

**Figure 13.5   A client-server relationship where both systems are mobile devices. This is the scenario used for the socket and datagram examples so that both sending and receiving data in a J2ME environment can be demonstrated. In this situation, one of the devices would be designated the client and the other the server. The device acting as the server will listen for incoming messages and respond appropriately. For example, two devices could communicate with each other using an infrared link between the two devices.**

### Modifying the client

The first step in incorporating socket capabilities in the MsgClient application is to modify the user interface so that the socket behavior that we will be writing can be invoked. This requires two changes. First, we add a menu item to our list of menu choices called "Socket Message". This becomes the second option in the list.

```
private static final String[] choices = {
  "1 HTTP Example",
  "2 Socket Message"
};
```

Next we enhance the handleOK() method to be able to respond appropriately when the "Socket Message" menu option is chosen.

```
private void handleOK(int idx){
  display.setCurrent(outputForm);

  switch (idx) {
    case 0:
      getHttpMessage();
      break;
```

```
    case 1:
      socketMessage();
      break;
  }
}
```

The only thing left on the client side is to implement the `socketMessage()` method to send and receive data. To open a socket connection, the following scheme is used.

```
StreamConnection connection = (StreamConnection)
  Connector.open("socket://localhost:4444", Connector.READ_WRITE);
```

The input and output streams are obtained immediately, since both will be required. Once this is done, the connection's `close()` method can be called.

```
DataOutputStream os = connection.openDataOutputStream();
DataInputStream is = connection.openDataInputStream();
connection.close();
```

The complete `socketMessage()` method of implementation is shown in listing 13.2:

**Listing 13.2  socketMessage() method**

```
private void socketMessage(){
  StringBuffer sb = new StringBuffer("");
  String dataIn = null;
  String dataOut = null;
  int c = 0;
  try {
    StreamConnection connection = (StreamConnection)
      Connector.open("socket://localhost:4444", Connector.READ_WRITE);
    DataOutputStream os = connection.openDataOutputStream();
    DataInputStream is = connection.openDataInputStream();
    connection.close();  -                          ❶ Open a socket
    try {                                              connection
      dataOut = "Message from the client.";
      os.writeUTF(dataOut);                 ❷ Write
      os.flush();                             data
      dataIn = is.readUTF();                           ❸ Read
      System.out.println(dataIn);                        data
      StringItem si = new StringItem("Msg: ", "'"+dataIn+"'");
        outputForm.append(si);
    } finally {
      is.close();       ❹ Close the
      os.close();          socket
    }
  } catch (IOException x) {
    System.out.println("Problems sending or receiving data.");
    x.printStackTrace();
  }
}
```

## Creating the socket listener

Now that we have a client that can connect to a service that is listening to a particular port, we need to create that service. To do so, we will implement another MIDlet that will listen to a designated port. When a client sends a message, the message is displayed by the MIDlet and a response is returned.

The listener MIDlet will be used in this example as well as the datagram example, so we will create the user interface with the ability to handle both cases. To modularize the design, the protocol-specific behavior will be encapsulated in separate classes. This allows the listener application to easily employ many different services without becoming monolithic. The listener application has the responsibilities of providing the means to start a particular service, socket listener, or datagram listener, and displaying the messages as they are handled by the service. The full source listing for the listener application is provided in listing 13.3.

### Listing 13.3 MsgListener.java

```java
package com.ctimn;

import java.io.*;
import javax.microedition.io.*;
import javax.microedition.midlet.*;
import javax.microedition.lcdui.*;

public class MsgListener extends MIDlet implements CommandListener {

    private Form outputForm;
    private Display display;
    private List menu;
    private Command okCmd = new Command("OK", Command.OK, 1);
    private Command exitCmd = new Command("Exit", Command.EXIT, 1);
    private SocketListener socketListener;

    private static final String[] choices = {
        "1 Socket Listener",
        "2 Datagram Listener"          ❶ Provide menu options
    };
    protected void startApp() throws MIDletStateChangeException {
        display = Display.getDisplay(this);
        outputForm = new Form("Messages");
        menu = new List("Select:", List.IMPLICIT, choices, null);
        outputForm.addCommand(okCmd);
        menu.addCommand(okCmd);
        outputForm.addCommand(exitCmd);
        menu.addCommand(exitCmd);
        outputForm.setCommandListener(this);
        menu.setCommandListener(this);
        display.setCurrent(menu);
    }

    protected void pauseApp() {
    }
```

*CHAPTER 13   THE NETWORK CONNECTION*

```
protected void destroyApp(boolean unconditional)
    throws MIDletStateChangeException {
  System.out.println("Destroy App.");
  if (socketListener != null){
    socketListener.shutdown();
  }
}

public void commandAction(Command cmd, Displayable activeDisplay) {
  if (cmd == exitCmd) {
    handleExit();
  } else if ((activeDisplay == menu) && (cmd == okCmd)) {
    handleOK(((List)activeDisplay).getSelectedIndex());
    return;
  }
  display.setCurrent(menu);
}

private void handleExit(){
  try {
  System.out.println("exit.");
    destroyApp(true);
    notifyDestroyed();
  } catch (MIDletStateChangeException x){
    x.printStackTrace();
  }
}

private void handleOK(int idx){
  display.setCurrent(outputForm);
  switch (idx) {
    case 0:
      socketListener();
      break;
    case 1:
      datagramListener();
      break;
  }
}
```

❷ **Handle the menu event**

```
private void socketListener(){
  if (socketListener == null){
    socketListener = new SocketListener(outputForm);
    socketListener.start();
  }
}
```

❸ **Start the socket listener service**

```
private void datagramListener(){
}
```

❹ **Create a placeholder for the datagram example**

## Creating the service class

The next step is to implement the `SocketListener` service class. This is where all the socket listener behavior will be encapsulated. Listening for messages is slightly different than sending messages because the listener can never be sure of when or if the client will attempt to connect. As a result, if we simply listened for the connection and the data to be sent on the same thread that the application is running on, our application would appear to hang until the connection was terminated. For this reason, it is best to implement the connection listening part of the application on a separate thread. This allows the application to continue functioning while waiting and receiving messages. By handling messages on a separate thread, the data received by the message handler can be displayed immediately as well, rather than having to wait until the connection finished transmitting data. This is especially important if two devices require that the users provide input during the data exchange. If a separate thread is not used, a connection would need to be established each time the user entered a piece of data, since the connection and the data entry must share the same thread.

The `SocketListener` class extends `Thread` to provide the ability to create and run the listener on its own thread.

```
public class SocketListener extends Thread
```

The `Thread` class requires that the main thread loop be implemented in a method named `run()`. For our purposes, this is where the connection will be established and the listener loop will be implemented.

To start a thread in Java using the `Thread` class, the `start()` method is called. In our case, the `SocketListener` thread is started by the `MsgListener` application. This is already in place as we can see by revisiting the code listing for `MsgListener.java`.

Since the `SocketListener` will be running on its own thread, we need a way to shut down the thread when we are finished. A public `shutdown()` method is provided to perform this step from the `MsgListener` application. However, the best we will be able to do at this point is set a `boolean` flag indicating that the `SocketListener` should shut itself down at the earliest point possible. This is because the `SocketListener` class will be occupied by its task of listening for incoming messages. The best opportunity for checking the shutdown state is when the listener times out. We then have the opportunity to check the shutdown state and either exit the thread or restart the listener connection.

In some implementations of the J2ME virtual machines, there is only one underlying native thread that is actually being used on the device. This is the thread the virtual machine is running on. In these situations multithreading behavior is handled internally by the virtual machine using what are called green threads. Green threads are explained in more detail in chapter 14. In these situations all threads will be terminated automatically when the application exits without the need for invoking any thread shutdown operations. However, it is always a good idea to have thread shutdown functionality in place, since each J2ME virtual machine has different characteristics and may implement threading differently. Failing to properly terminate threads could result in memory leaks or worse. In our example, failing to shut down a listener would lock the port that the listener is bound to, requiring the device to be restarted in order to release the port resource.

**NOTE** The KVM provided with the MIDP reference implementation implements multithreading entirely within the virtual machine (green threads). As a result, all listener threads are terminated when the application exits. Therefore, there is no way to actually illustrate the threads terminating on their own since they are shut down automatically.

Unlike a socket client, the socket listener must listen to a designated port for any clients wishing to establish communications. This is implemented using a `Stream-ConnectionNotifier`.

```
StreamConnectionNotifier connection = (StreamConnectionNotifier)
    Connector.open("serversocket://:4444", Connector.READ_WRITE);

StreamConnection socketConnection = connection.acceptAndOpen();
```

**WARNING** Sockets can be created on any port supported by the platform. However, it is important to note that on Unix you must be signed in as the root user to create a port below 1024. This means that your application would be required to run as root to create a `StreamConnection` or `StreamConnectionNotifier` using port 999 on Unix. Furthermore, you will be deploying applications into network environments where other services are also using ports. If you attempt to establish a connection to a port that is already in use an exception will be thrown and your application will be unable to bind to the port. Although changing a port may be an easy modification to your code, it is nice to find problems like this before your application ships. Therefore it is advisable to do a bit of research on the platforms and environments that an application is targeting before choosing the port number.

The `StreamConnectionNotifier` is first created using the `serversocket` scheme and designating a port. The mode in which to open socket connections is also specified. Once we have a `StreamConnectionNotifier`, the `acceptAndOpen()` method is called. The `acceptAndOpen()` method causes the server to sit idle until a client attempts to connect to the server. There is no socket connection at this point.

When a client contacts the server, the server determines if a socket connection can be established. This takes place within the `acceptAndOpen()` method. If a socket connection can be established, `acceptAndOpen()` returns a `SocketConnection`. Since we specified that `READ_WRITE` sockets should be created when we created the `StreamConnectionNotifier`, the `SocketConnection` returned can be used for both receiving and sending data to the client.

If the client connection cannot be established, the connection is refused. An exception is thrown on the client side. The server, however, continues listening for other clients.

With a client-server socket connection established, the server is reading to receive and send data. To do this, an `InputStream` and an `OutputStream` are obtained.

```
InputStream is = socketConnection.openInputStream();

OutputStream os = socketConnection.openOutputStream();
```

### Reading from a stream

Data can be read from a `DataInputStream` as a UTF-8 encoded `String` using the method `readUTF()`. The data read using the method, however, must be sent using UTF-8 encoding in order to read the data successfully. This requires the client and server to coordinate on how the data is sent. Alternately, the data can be read as an array of bytes. Examples of both techniques are provided below. This first example reads UTF-encoded data:

```
String dataIn = is.readUTF();
```

The following example demonstrates reading bytes from the stream. This example assumes that the data is character data in byte form and coerces the data before appending it to a `StringBuffer`:

```
int ch = 0;
StringBuffer sb = new StringBuffer();
while (ch != -1) {
  ch = is.read();
  if (ch == -1){
    break;
  }
  sb.append((char)ch);
}
String dataIn = sb.toString();
```

### Writing to a stream

To write data to the output stream we will use the `writeUTF()` method along with a `DataOutputStream`. This method encodes the data as UTF-8 before sending it to the destination. Since the listener is expecting a UTF-8 encoded String it is necessary that the client provide the data in this format. If the application on the other end is not expecting UTF-8 encoded data, it may not be able to handle the data properly. In this case, unexpected behavior in the stream interactions can result. If the client cannot handle UTF-encoded data, the data can be sent as a byte array.

The following code demonstrates how to write to the `DataOutputStream`. When you are finished, the output stream must be flushed. This forces bytes within the buffer to be written to the stream, if the stream supports buffering. How data is buffered in an output stream differs between different types of streams. In some cases, no buffering may be applied at all. However, it is always a good practice to call `flush()` when you have finished writing to a stream.

```
String data = "Test Message";
os.writeUTF(data);
os.flush();
```

The next example demonstrates writing a byte array to the stream. This is useful when sending raw bytes to another system.

```
String data = "Test Message";
byte[] b = data.getBytes();
os.write(b, 0, b.length);
os.flush();
```

### Opening a client connection

Once an application is listening to a port, a client can attempt to open a connection to the listening application using the following syntax:

```
StreamConnection connection = (StreamConnection)
    Connector.open("socket://127.0.0.1:4444", Connector.READ_WRITE);
```

Unlike the socket listener example, the client must specify a host address as well as a port. If the open() is successful, a StreamConnection is returned. If the socket connection cannot be established, a ConnectException is thrown indicating that the connection was refused. A connection can be refused for a number of reasons. Typically, this occurs when there is no application listening to the port or another type service that does not or cannot deal with sockets is listening to the port and refuses the connection.

With a StreamConnection open, the client is ready to send and receive data. At this point, the code is the same as the server examples provided earlier.

### Shutting down the listener thread

Since the SocketListener is implemented on its own thread, it supports the ability for an external object to shut it down. In our example, MsgListener makes the call to shutdown() when the application exits. Since the shutdown() method is invoked by a thread different from the one that our socket listening code is running, all we can really do is set a flag so that the thread within the listen-respond loop can check the status of this flag periodically during execution and take appropriate action.

There is a problem with this, however. Most likely, when shutdown() is called, the thread that we need to shut down is busy listening for connections within the acceptAndOpen() method. The thread will remain at this spot in the code until one of two things happens: a socket connection is accepted or a timeout occurs. Since these are the only two cases where the listening thread will have the opportunity to check the status of the shutdown flag, we use these situations to our advantage. The easiest way to trigger the shutdown process is for the listener to respond to timeout conditions. This is done by specifying the appropriate value in the Connector's open() method.

```
StreamConnectionNotifier notifier = (StreamConnectionNotifier)
    Connector.open("serversocket://:4444", Connector.READ_WRITE, true);
```

This signature of the open method allows for setting a `boolean` indicating we want to be notified when a timeout occurs. The timeout can then be detected by catching an `InterruptedIOException`. When this exception occurs, after the timeout expires the `StreamConnectionNotifier` connection, the `SocketListener` can take appropriate action based on the value of the shutdown flag. If the flag is true, indicating we should shut down, the method exits (using a return statement). If the value is false, the `SocketListener` continues listening for connections. If the `Socket-Listener` is to continue listening, however, the `StreamConnectionNotifier` must be reestablished. The code to perform shutdown flag monitoring is as follows:

```
try {
  StreamConnection connection = notifier.acceptAndOpen();
} catch (InterruptedIOException x){
  if (shutdownFlag){
    return;
  } else {
    notifier = createNotifier();
  }
}
```

In this example the `createNotifier()` method returns an instance of `Stream-ConnectionNotifier`.

```
private StreamConnectionNotifier createNotifier()throws IOException {

  return (StreamConnectionNotifier)
      Connector.open("serversocket://:4444", Connector.READ_WRITE, true);
}
```

The full-source listing of `SocketListener` is shown in listing 13.4. To simulate connecting over a network connection, the localhost address will be used, 127.0.0.1.

**WARNING** In some implementations of the Generic Connection Framework it is necessary to specify the IP address rather than the domain name.

---

**Listing 13.4  SocketListener.java**

```
package com.ctimn;

import java.io.*;                                    ❶ Reference to
import javax.microedition.io.*;                         the MsgListener
import javax.microedition.midlet.*;                     output form
import javax.microedition.lcdui.*;

public class SocketListener extends Thread{          ❷ Flag indicating if
  private Form outputForm;                              the service has
  private boolean shutdownFlag = false;                been shut down
  private StreamConnectionNotifier notifier;

                                                     ❸ Socket
  public SocketListener(Form outputForm){              connection
    this.outputForm = outputForm;
  }
```

```
private StreamConnectionNotifier createNotifier() throws IOException  {
  return (StreamConnectionNotifier)
    Connector.open("serversocket://:4444",                  Create the socket ❹
    Connector.READ_WRITE, true);                              connection
}

public void run(){
  String dataIn = null;
  String dataOut = null;
  int counter = 1;
  StringItem item = new StringItem("Listening to Socket", "");
  outputForm.append(item);
  StreamConnection connection = null;             ❺ Establish the listener
  try {                                              connection with
    notifier = createNotifier();                     timeout exceptions
    while (true) {          ❻ Do these steps "forever"
      try {
        connection = notifier.acceptAndOpen();   ❼ Wait for a client message
      } catch (InterruptedIOException x){
        if (shutdownFlag){
          return;                          ❽ Check shutdown status on timeout.
        } else {                              Return if shutdown=true
          notifier = createNotifier();   ❾ Return if shutdown=false,
        }                                   restart the listener connection
      }
      DataInputStream is = connection.openDataInputStream();
      DataOutputStream os = connection.openDataOutputStream();  ❿ Get the I/O
      connection.close();    ⓫ Call close on the connection       streams
      try {                     obtained by acceptAndOpen()
        dataIn = is.readUTF();
        System.out.println(dataIn);
        item = new StringItem("Msg: ", "'"+dataIn+"'");
        outputForm.append(item);
        dataOut = "Message " + counter + " from the server.";
        counter++;
        os.writeUTF(dataOut);
        os.flush();                             Form and write a ⓭
      } finally {        ⓮ Flush the output     response message
        os.close();         stream buffer
        is.close();                              Read and display ⓬
      }          ⓯ Close the I/O streams          the message
    }                                             from the client
  } catch (IOException x) {
    System.out.println("Problems sending or receiving data.");
    x.printStackTrace();
  }
}

public void shutdown(){      ⓰ Set the shut-
  shutdownFlag = true;          down flag
}
}
```

### Compiling and preverifying and running

The entire example, including the classes `MsgClient`, `MsgListener`, and `Socket-Listener` is now ready to be compiled and preverified. In order to run the application, since there is more than a single class involved, all the classes will need to be packaged into a JAR file. The following batch file shown in listing 13.5 can be used to build the application and bundle it as a single JAR file.

---
**Listing 13.5   Build.bat**

```
e:\jdk1.3\bin\javac -g:none
  -bootclasspath e:\midp-fcs\classes
  -classpath .\build
  -d .\build *.java

e:\midp-fcs\bin\preverify.exe
  -classpath e:\midp-fcs\classes;.;.\build  .\build

jar cvf io.jar -C output .
```
---

The `MsgClient` and `MsgListener` applications must be run from separate command windows. The following commands are necessary for starting the `MsgListener`. The first command allows all protocols to be made available to our MIDlet. Without this flag set to true, only the HTTP connections are available since this is the only connection type that must be supported by MIDP.

```
>set ENABLE_CLDC_PROTOCOLS=true

>e:\midp-fcs\bin\midp -classpath e:\midp-fcs\classes;.\io.jar
com.ctimn.MsgListener
```

The `MsgListener` presents a menu listing the available options. Choosing the "Socket Listener" option invokes the `SocketListener` and binds the listener to port 4444. Figure 13.6 shows the running `MsgListener` application.

Use the following command to run the `MsgClient`:

```
>set ENABLE_CLDC_PROTOCOLS=true

>e:\midp-fcs\bin\midp -classpath e:\midp-fcs\classes;.\io.jar
com.ctimn.MsgClient
```

**Figure 13.6**
**Running MsgListener for the first time. The MsgListener creates a StreamConnectionNotifier and waits for activity on the specified port.**

**Figure 13.7**
**MsgClient sending and receiving messages using sockets. The MsgClient initiates communication by opening a socket connection. The receiving system acknowledges the connection, allowing the MsgClient to pass data onto the stream represented by the connection.**

Choosing the second option sends a message from the MsgClient to the MsgListener. The MsgListener then returns a response to the MsgClient-. This is shown in figure 13.7.

The client initially displays a menu as well, which is shown in figure 13.7. Selecting the second option "Socket Message" triggers the client code to send a message to the server. The server responds with a message. The messages are displayed in the output forms of each emulator. The output from the MsgListener is shown in figure 13.8.

**Figure 13.8**
**MsgListener receiving a message over a socket connection. The MsgListener monitors a specified port for socket activity. When the MsgClient initiates a connection, the MsgListener establishes the other half of the connection and gets ready to receive data. When the MsgClient transmits data, the MsgListener responds appropriately.**

Additionally, we placed some System.out.println() statements into our code to monitor progress from the command line. These results are shown in figure 13.9.

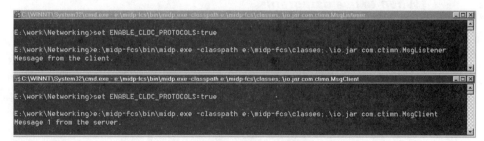

Figure 13.9   Command line results from running MsgClient and MsgListener.

## 13.5  DATAGRAM-BASED CONNECTIONS

Datagrams are designed for sending packets of data over a network. Datagrams work much differently than sockets in that a hard connection is not established between the two systems. In the case of sockets, if a client tries to connect to a system that does not support sockets or is not listening for socket connections, an exception is thrown. Datagrams, on the other hand, allow data to be sent over a connection regardless of whether the listener on the other end is capable of handling datagrams or even exists. In all cases, when sending data using Datagrams, the transmission is assumed to be successful. Furthermore, unlike sockets, the data sent using Datagrams is considered to be unreliable in that if a packet is lost it is not resent automatically by the protocol implementation, and when multiple packets are sent there is no guarantee that the packets will arrive in the same order they were sent. Datagrams do not provide support for reassembling data packets into the order in which they were sent. For these reasons, Datagrams are termed to be an unreliable data transport mechanism. The term unreliable in this case is not necessarily a negative term. It simply means that the protocol does not inherently support mechanisms to guarantee that data arrives in the order it was sent or that the data arrives at all. There is nothing stopping an application from implementing these features itself, however.

So why use Datagrams? Speed is one primary reason. Datagrams do not incur the overhead of ensuring that packets arrive in the correct order or that they arrive at all. In some applications, such as audio streaming, a missing data packet may appear as static. Raw speed is more important in this case than data integrity.

There are several datagram protocols available. The most common is User Datagram Protocol (UDP). This is the protocol implementation provided by the reference implementation of the Generic Connection Framework. However, the `Datagram` and `DatagramConnection` interfaces of the Generic Connection Framework are designed to allow implementations of different types of datagram protocols. Other such protocols include IP and WDP along with proprietary beaming protocols that take advantage of the packet nature of datagrams for transmitting data.

### When to use datagrams

At first glance, datagrams seem to have a lot of marks against their use, especially since there is no reliability of data delivery, flow-control and error handling. However, the raw speed benefits of datagrams may outweigh the data integrity issues for some applications. Applications that stream real-time audio or video may be more concerned with speed than getting every byte of data transported and in a certain order. If data is missing there may be some static over the speaker or on the screen momentarily. Although static is not a desirable feature in such applications, the alternative would require the application to wait for all the data to arrive and to place it into the correct receiving order based on how the packets were sent before the data could be officially received. This speed degradation is likely to be unacceptable in applications that are streaming audio or video content.

Since UDP does not provide guarantees of packet delivery or packet receiving order, the headers and metadata required are simpler than a reliable protocol such as TCP. Therefore, datagrams are most useful when speed of delivery is crucial. In the J2ME environment, datagrams can be useful due to their simplicity as a lighter weight data transport alternative to TCP. For example, datagrams might be useful when beaming data over an Ir port between two devices.

Another feature of datagrams is that the programmer controls the packet size of the transmission. If you want to send a large amount of data in a single packet, you can (up to 64kB). If you want to send a single byte in a packet, you can.

### Handling datagram unreliability

Although UDP datagrams do not inherently provide guaranteed delivery and packet reordering, you can implement this at the application level. For example, a client that sends a datagram and does not receive a response for a specified period of time could assume the packet was not received and try to resend the information or indicate an error. Furthermore, the data encapsulated by the datagram could include tags indicating how to reassemble the data on the receiving side. For example, if the first packet received contains the information "packet 4 of 7" the receiver would understand it needs 7 packets in all before attempting to order the data. If less than 7 packets are received and a certain amount of time passed without receiving another packet, the receiver could ask the sender to resend the missing packets.

Alternatively, a client could send packets one at a time and wait for the receiver to respond with a success code indicating that the packet was correctly received before sending the next packet.

Of course in doing this the sender and receiver need to understand how to communicate. In other words, you need to define your own protocol. This does not mean, however, that you are duplicating the functionality of TCP and eliminating the benefits of datagrams. Obviously, there will be some additional overhead in providing flow-control and data delivery error handling in datagrams. However, a custom protocol has the advantage of accommodating a specific case, rather than the more generalized case that TCP is required to address, and this specificity can improve efficiency. If you are working in a closed system, where you have control of both the sender and the receiver, you also have the ability to define how the sender and receiver communicate.

### How datagrams work in J2ME

Datagrams have been generalized in the Generic Connection Framework so that different types of datagram connections can be used. As a result, the datagram API is much different in J2ME than in J2SE.

The two classes involved with datagrams in the Generic Connection Framework are `DatagramConnection` and `Datagram`. The `DatagramConnection` class is used to bind the application to a port and the `Datagram` class is used to transport data over this port connection. It is important to understand that datagrams do not behave like streams. Although the datagram is ultimately sent across the network connection in some fashion, datagrams themselves are packets of data placed onto the protocol as a whole. The difference is that with a stream, each byte written to a stream immediately becomes part of the stream and is sent to whatever the stream is hooked up to, assuming there is no buffering taking place. With datagrams, all of the data resides in the datagram buffer until the datagram is placed on the `DatagramConnection`. Once the datagram is placed on the connection, the connection transmits the data to the specified target.

**NOTE** The J2SE `DatagramSocket` class is analogous to the J2ME `DatagramConnection` class and the J2SE `DatagramPacket` class is analogous to the J2ME `Datagram` class. In J2SE, you bind the application to a socket using the `DatagramSocket` class and transport data over this connection using a `DatagramPacket` class.

To send a datagram using the J2ME API, your application needs to supply three things: the address to send the datagram, the port on which the receiving system is listening, and the data. The port used by the application sending data (the client) is always dynamically allocated.

The `DatagramConnection` instance is created using a slightly different name parameter depending on whether you are a datagram client or server. To open a connection as the client the target host must be specified. The following example opens a `DatagramConnection` in "client mode."

```
datagram://127.0.0.1:5555
```

To open the connection on the receiving side, only the port is specified.

```
datagram://:5555.
```

When establishing a client connection, the application is specifying the host as well as the port on which the host is expected to be listening. The port that the client is using on the system is hidden from the developer and is dynamically assigned.

When opening the connection on the receiving side, the receiving application binds itself to a port. If these ports are not identical, data sent from the client will be lost since it will not be transmitting to a port on which the service is listening. Since datagrams do not guarantee packet delivery, the client sends the data once and is never informed that anything is wrong.

Once a `DatagramConnection` is established, multiple `Datagrams` can be sent over this single connection. However, a single datagram is good for one read and one write, allowing an application to receive a message and send a response. A datagram response is sent using the same `Datagram` instance used to receive data. This instance contains the necessary host and port information required to send the response message.

In this scenario, a new datagram is created for each incoming message. There is no attempt to prevent a single Datagram instance from incorrectly being used multiple times; however, unexpected results can occur since the buffer is not designed for reuse beyond the receive-response sequence. Therefore, it is the responsibility of the application to manage when a Datagram needs to be created and when a datagram can be reused.

In order for a receiving application to respond to a datagram, the same datagram instance must be used for the outgoing message. Although, in theory, it would be possible to construct a new Datagram for the send operation, the Generic Connection Framework Datagram interface does not support the ability to obtain the sender's port number. The port number for a DatagramConnection opened in client mode is dynamically assigned. Thus, there is no way to properly construct a new Datagram to reply to a client application even if we wanted to.

## 13.5.1 Datagram example

The following example is a simple application that uses datagrams as the means of transmitting data between two systems.

In this example we will create the client (the datagram sender) first. To begin, a DatagramConnection between the client to the listener must be established. This is done using the Connector.open() method and the datagram scheme.

```
DatagramConnection connection = (DatagramConnection)
  Connector.open("datagram://127.0.0.1:5555", Connector.READ_WRITE);
```

A client connection must specify both the host address as well as the port. The connection is opened in read-write mode, allowing the client and server to pass data back and forth.

The client, in this example, is the first to send a message. To send a message over a DatagramConnection, a datagram object is needed. Datagrams are created using the DatagramConnection method newDatagram(). There are several signatures of newDatagram() available. These are provided for convenience. At a minimum, newDatagram() requires a buffer size to be specified. We will create a Datagram with a buffer size of 100 bytes.

```
Datagram datagram = connection.newDatagram(100);
```

Once the datagram is created, the buffer must be populated with data. Datagrams only deal with data in a byte form. Below we create a String and convert it to a byte array. Once we have a byte array of data, this data can be placed into the datagram using the setData() method.

```
byte[] data = "Message 1 from the Client".getBytes();
datagram.setData(data, 0, data.length);
```

In the setData(String) method, the first parameter is the byte array of data, the second parameter is an offset, indicating where to begin sending data from when the datagram is actually sent. The third parameter is the actual length of the data.

With a `DatagramConnection` and a `Datagram` containing our data, the only thing left to do is send the data. The `DatagramConnection` class provides a `send(Datagram)` method to trigger the data transmission. This method is called by passing our Datagram instance as a parameter.

```
connection.send(datagram);
```

The `DatagramConnection` `send(Datagram)` method automatically flushes the buffer and transmits the data. There are no additional steps we need to take. As long as no exceptions were thrown, the data has been transmitted through the network. What we cannot assume, however, is that the message was actually received. As mentioned, datagrams do not guarantee data transmissions. If there is no system listening on the designated port or the system is unable to handle datagrams, the data is sent into empty space and our client receives no indication of this situation.

However, there are ways to detect if a message was actually received. To do this, our client must be capable of receiving a response from the system to which the message is sent. To set up the client to receive a message, the `DatagramConnection` method `receive(Datagram)` is used. We will also need a new `Datagram` instance to hold the incoming data.

Create a new `Datagram` using the `newDatagram()` method.

```
Datagram datagram = connection.newDatagram(100);
```

Then pass this new datagram to the receive method. The receive method waits idly for data to be sent.

```
connection.receive(datagram);
```

If there is no system listening on the host port, as currently is the case with our example, the client will appear to hang as it waits for the response. To handle this situation you could create the connection and specify that you wish to be notified if there is a timeout on the connection.

```
DatagramConnection connection = (DatagramConnection)
  Connector.open("datagram://127.0.0.1:5555", Connector.READ_WRITE, true);
```

By opening the connection with the ability to be notified of timeouts, the client will not wait indefinitely for the listener's response. However, our application must be ready to deal with the timeout situation as well by handling the exception thrown when the connection times out.

Once the datagram is received, the data can be extracted from the `Datagram` instance, which is accessed using the `Datagram` method `getData()` which returns the data as a byte array. This byte array can then be converted to an appropriate data type. The data type involved depends on what kind of data the transmitting system actually sent. In this example, the data is assumed to be a `String`.

```
String data = new String(datagram.getData());
```

## Enhancing the MsgClient

To incorporate the ability to send and receive datagrams from our MsgClient, the following changes will be needed, starting with the user interface, then adding the datagram option to the menu as the third option:

```
private static final String[] choices = {
  "1 HTTP Example",
  "2 Socket Message",
  "3 Datagram Message"
};
```

Next, we add the necessary lines of code to the handleOK method to trigger a datagram message to be sent.

```
private void handleOK(int idx){
  display.setCurrent(outputForm);
  switch (idx) {
    case 0:
      getHttpMessage();
      break;
    case 1:
      socketMessage();
      break;
    case 2:
      datagramMessage();
      break;
  }
}
```

To handle the functionality of sending and receiving datagrams, three more methods are introduced to the MsgClient: datagramMessage(), receiveDatagram() and sendDatagram(). The datagramMessage() method is called to handle requests from the menu to send and receive a message. The latter two methods handle the receiving and sending of specific functionality. The code for sending and receiving datagrams is shown in listing 13.6.

### Listing 13.6   Sending and receiving datagrams from the MsgClient

```
private void datagramMessage() {
  String msg = null;
  try {
    DatagramConnection connection =                              ❶
      (DatagramConnection)Connector.open(
        "datagram://localhost:5555", Connector.READ_WRITE);
    Datagram datagram = null;
    try {
      datagram = connection.newDatagram(100);
      sendDatagram(connection, datagram, "Message from the Client");   ❷
      datagram = connection.newDatagram(100);
      msg = receiveDatagram(connection, datagram);      ❸
    } finally {
      connection.close();      ❹
    }
```

```
    } catch (IOException x) {
      x.printStackTrace();
    }
    StringItem item = new StringItem("Msg: ", msg);        ❺
    outputForm.append(item);
}

private void sendDatagram(DatagramConnection connection,
      Datagram datagram, String msg) throws IOException{   ❻
    byte[] data = msg.getBytes();          ❼
    datagram.setData(data, 0, data.length);        ❽
    connection.send(datagram);         ❾
}

private String receiveDatagram(DatagramConnection connection,   ❿
      Datagram datagram) throws IOException{
    connection.receive(datagram);          ⓫
    System.out.println("Address="+datagram.getAddress());
    System.out.println("Length="+datagram.getLength());
    System.out.println("Offset="+datagram.getOffset());
    byte[] byteData = datagram.getData();
    byte b = 0;
    StringBuffer sb = new StringBuffer();
    for (int ccnt=0; ccnt < byteData.length; ccnt++){
      if (byteData[ccnt] > 0){                                  ⓬
        sb.append((char)byteData[ccnt]);
      } else {
        break;
      }
    }
    String data = sb.toString();
    System.out.println("Data="+data);
    return data;
}
```

❶ Create the Datagram connection

❷ Create a new datagram and send a message

❸ Create a new datagram and receive a message

❹ Close the connection

❺ Display the message received

❻ Prepare a datagram and send a message

❼ Get the message in a byte format

❽ Load the message into the datagram

❾ Send the datagram

❿ Receive and display a datagram message

⓫ Receive the incoming datagram

⓬ Retrieve the contents of the datagram

## Datagram listener

Now that we have a client application sending datagrams to another system, we now need to implement a `DatagramListener` class that can handle the message and return a response from the `MsgListener` application we wrote earlier. This listener behaves a lot like the socket listener from the previous example only it handles datagrams and uses a different port. Listening for socket messages and datagram messages on different ports allows the listener application to monitor for both socket and datagram client connections simultaneously.

The only difference between a datagram client and a datagram receiver (server) in J2ME is how the connection is established. In the client example, we needed to specify both the host address as well as the host port. When establishing a listening connection, only the port needs to be specified.

```
DatagramConnection connection = (DatagramConnection)
  Connector.open("datagram://:5555", Connector.READ_WRITE, true);
```

Once the connection is established, the server is ready to read information sent from the client. Reading and writing data to a `DatagramConnection` on the server is exactly the same as using datagrams on the client. First a datagram is created in which to place the data, then the datagram's `receive()` method is invoked.

```
Datagram datagram = connection.newDatagram(100);

connection.receive(datagram);
```

To send data back to the client a `Datagram` is created, populated with the data and placed onto the connection using the `send(Datagram)` method.

```
Datagram datagram = connection.newDatagram(100);
byte[] data = "Message 1 from the Server".getBytes();
datagram.setData(data, 0, data.length);
connection.send(datagram);
```

Listing 13.7 shows the implementation of the `DatagramListener` class that handles receiving and responding to datagram messages on behalf of the `MsgListener` class we created earlier.

### Listing 13.7   DatagramListener.java

```
package com.ctimn;

import java.io.*;
import javax.microedition.io.*;
import javax.microedition.midlet.*;
import javax.microedition.lcdui.*;

public class DatagramListener extends Thread {

  private Form outputForm;
  private boolean shutdownFlag = false;
```

```
public DatagramListener(Form outputForm){
  this.outputForm = outputForm;
}

public void run(){
  Datagram datagram = null;
  String msg = null;
  StringItem item = new StringItem("Listening for Datagrams", "");
  outputForm.append(item);
  try {
    DatagramConnection connection =  (DatagramConnection)      ❶ Create a
      Connector.open("datagram://:5555", Connector.READ_WRITE);    Datagram
    try {                                                          connection
      while (true) {        ❷ Run "forever"
        datagram = connection.newDatagram(100);
        try {
          msg = receiveDatagram(connection, datagram);
        } catch (InterruptedIOException x){
          if (shutdownFlag){
            return;                             Wait for a  ❸
          }                                     datagram
        }
        item = new StringItem("Msg: ", msg);
        outputForm.append(item);
        sendDatagram(connection, datagram, "Message from the server");
      }
    } finally {
      connection.close();
    }
  } catch (IOException x) {
    System.out.println("Problems sending or receiving data.");
    x.printStackTrace();
  }
}

private String receiveDatagram(DatagramConnection connection,
    Datagram datagram) throws IOException{
  connection.receive(datagram);
  System.out.println("Address="+datagram.getAddress());
  System.out.println("Length="+datagram.getLength());
  System.out.println("Offset="+datagram.getOffset());
  byte[] byteData = datagram.getData();
  byte b = 0;
  StringBuffer sb = new StringBuffer();
  for (int ccnt=0; ccnt < byteData.length; ccnt++){
    if (byteData[ccnt] > 0){
      sb.append((char)byteData[ccnt]);     ❹ Receive a
    } else {                                  datagram
      break;
    }
  }
  String data = sb.toString();
  System.out.println("Data="+data);
  return data;
}
```

```
    private void sendDatagram(DatagramConnection connection,
        Datagram datagram, String msg)   throws IOException{
      byte[] data = msg.getBytes();                          ❺ Send a
      datagram.setData(data, 0, data.length);                  response
      connection.send(datagram);
    }

    public void shutdown(){        ❻ Set the
      shutdownFlag = true;             shutdown
    }                                  condition
}
```

In this example, the client sends a message to the DatagramListener and the
DatagramListener responds with a message of its own. When the client finishes
running, it closes the connections and the application exits. The DatagramListener, however, continues running and waits for another message.

### Shutting down the listener thread

As with the SocketListener, DatagramListener is implemented on its own
thread and therefore must support the ability for an external object to shut it down.
In our example, MsgListener makes the call to shutdown() when the MsgListener application exits. Since the shutdown() method is invoked by a thread different from the one that our socket listening code is running, all we can really do is
set a flag so that the thread within the listen-respond loop can check the status of this
flag periodically during execution and take appropriate action.

The same problem that existed with SocketListener applies to the DatagramListener. At the point shutdown() is called the DatagramListener is
most likely to be waiting for an incoming message. As a result, the listening thread is
unavailable to check the status of the shutdown flag. The only events that allow the
listener to stop listening for incoming messages and inspect the shutdown status are
if a datagram connection is made or a timeout occurs. To take advantage of this situation, the listener requests to be notified of timeouts when the Datagram connection is opened. If a timeout occurs, an InterruptedIOException exception is
thrown. By catching this exception and checking the status of the shutdown flag the
DatagramListener can respond appropriately.

### Enhancing the MessageListener

The next step is to enhance the MessageListener created during the socket example to be able to listen for datagrams as well. The following lines of code are required
to create a DatagramListener instance when the datagram option is selected from
the menu. The following method was intentionally left blank on the previous exercise. Now that we have a DatagramListener, we can fill in the details.

```
private datagramListener() {
  if (datagramListener == null) {
    datagramListener = new DatagramListener(outputForm);
    datagramListener.start();
  }
}
```

We will also need to add a member variable to hold onto the DatagramListener reference. The following line of code needs to be added to the top of the Message-Listener class.

```
private DatagramListener datagramListener;
```

## Building the applications

At this point we can compile, preverify, and run both the MsgClient and MsgListener (which invokes DatagramListener) and send messages between the two applications. The commands for building the examples are essentially the same as for building the MsgClient.

Compile the DatagramListener and MsgListener classes.

```
>e:\jdk1.3\bin\javac -g:none -bootclasspath e:\midp-fcs\classes
  -classpath .\build -d .\build DatagramListener.java MsgListener.java
```

If the classes compiled successfully, preverify them using the following command. This command preverifies all classes in the .\build directory (the directory where we just compiled the code) and places the preverified version of the classes into an \output directory off of the current directory.

```
>e:\midp-fcs\bin\preverify.exe -classpath
  e:\midp-fcs\classes;.;.\build  .\build
```

Use the following to JAR the application into a file named io.jar.

```
jar cvf io.jar -C output .
```

Now we are ready to run both the client and the listener applications and send datagrams back and forth. Remember to set the ENABLE_CLDC_PROTOCOLS environment variable before running the applications. Without this variable set, the emulator will report that the datagram protocol is unavailable.

Since we are running two applications that need to communicate with each other, you will need to run each application from a separate command window. Use the following commands to run the applications. The example to run the listener is shown first.

```
>set ENABLE_CLDC_PROTOCOLS=true
```

```
>e:\midp-fcs\bin\midp.exe -classpath e:\midp-fcs\classes;.\io.jar
  com.ctimn.MsgListener
```

**Figure 13.10**
**MsgListener menu.**

**Figure 13.11**
**Listening for**
**a Datagram.**

The menu displays the options for listening. Choosing the second option, "Datagram Listener" invokes our code that binds to port 5555 and listens for an incoming datagram. Examples of running the datagram listening service from `MsgListener` are shown in figures 13.10 and 13.11.

With the `DatagramListener` running from within the `MsgListener` application we are ready to run the `MsgClient` application and send a datagram message. Run the `MsgClient` from the other window using the following commands. When the main menu appears, choose the second option, "Datagram Message".

```
>set ENABLE_CLDC_PROTOCOLS=true

>e:\midp-fcs\bin\midp.exe -classpath e:\midp-fcs\classes;.\io.jar
   com.ctimn.MsgClient
```

Selecting the "Datagram Message" option sends a message to the listener. The listener then displays the message and responds with a message for the client. The results of sending and receiving messages using the `MsgClient` and `MsgListener` are shown in figure 13.12.

Additional information is shown on the command line as messages are sent back and forth. The output from the command windows is shown in figure 13.13.

**Figure 13.12   Running the MsgClient and MsgListener passing datagrams.**
The MsgListener waits for activity on a specified port. When a datagram is sent from the MsgClient, the MsgListener receives the datagram and responds appropriately.

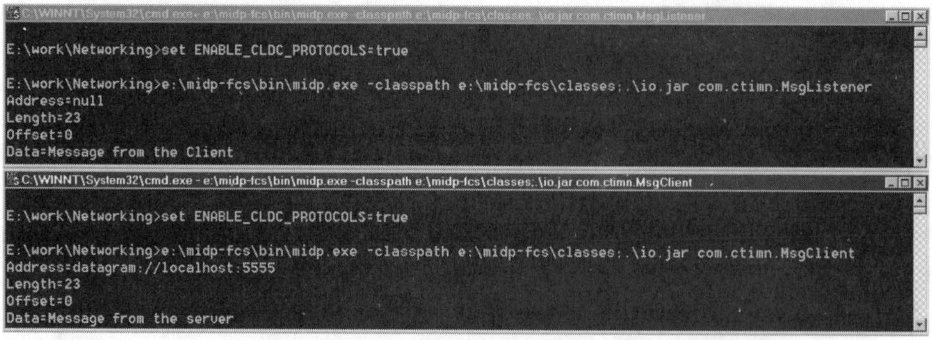

**Figure 13.13   Command line results from running the MsgListener and MsgClient.**

## 13.6   SUMMARY

This chapter explored the Generic Connection Framework in detail. The Connector class is the factory that allows vendor-specific implementations of each GCF connection to be instantiated at runtime. By using a factory to instantiate the actual classes, the GCF can effectively abstract the device-dependent aspects of establishing network connections. This architecture greatly enhances portability across applications that make use of the network since the connection implementations are allowed to vary but the interface remains consistent.

Examples were provided using common network connections such as HTTP, sockets and datagrams. In the case of sockets and datagrams, multiple threads were used to monitor a port for incoming messages in the background so that the use of the device would not be affected.

Since J2ME provides support for HTTP connections, J2ME clients can connect to any server environment that understands HTTP and is not restricted to interacting with Java services. As a result, a J2ME client can be used with non-Java technologies such as ASP and CGI.

**C H A P T E R   1 4**

# J2ME runtime environment

If you have worked with Java for any amount of time you are probably familiar with the Java Virtual Machine (JVM) and understand its responsibilities. However, if you are new to Java, the concept of a virtual machine may also be new. A virtual machine is essentially a computer implemented in software. The Java Virtual Machine sits within a layer between the host operating system and the application. In Java, the primary runtime component is the Java Virtual Machine.

The JVM is the key to Java's portability across environments since the JVM can be ported to a number of different operating systems. The virtual machine handles the operating-system-specific dependencies and differences rather than the application. As a result, Java applications can be easily ported to any environment supporting a Java Virtual Machine by simply copying the compiled application to the appropriate location.

## 14.1 THE JAVA RUNTIME ENVIRONMENT

In principle, the Java Virtual Machine knows little to nothing about Java the programming language. What the JVM understands is something called Java byte codes. Java byte codes are sets of instructions generated by the Java compiler (javac). Java byte codes are generally stored in a file with the ".class" extension and are interpreted at runtime by the virtual machine. The virtual machine then uses these instructions to interact with the operating system to produce the desired effect for the application. Figure 14.1 illustrates the basic steps involved in creating an application that the JVM can interpret.

The Java Virtual Machine Specification defines the characteristics and responsibilities to which a JVM implementation must adhere. In the case of J2ME, however, some exceptions to the JVM Specification have been made in order to create a JVM suitable for smaller devices, such as those supported by the CLDC. However, before we get into the J2ME-specific runtime environments we first discuss the responsibilities of a JVM and then show how these principles are applied within the J2ME environment.

**Figure 14.1**
**Process of creating a Java application for use by a virtual machine. First the source code is created and placed in a file with a .java extension. Next the java compiler is used to transform the Java syntax into the executable byte codes used by the virtual machine at runtime. Byte codes are stored in a file with a .class extension. At runtime, the virtual machine reads the contents of the class file and translates the byte code instructions appropriately for the current platform.**

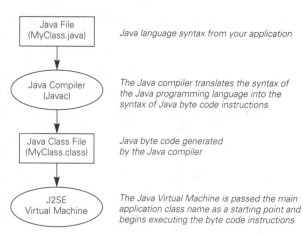

Java language syntax from your application

The Java compiler translates the syntax of the Java programming language into the syntax of Java byte code instructions

Java byte code generated by the Java compiler

The Java Virtual Machine is passed the main application class name as a starting point and begins executing the byte code instructions

### 14.1.1 Lifecycle of the Java Virtual Machine

The Java Virtual Machine runs as an application on top of the host operating system. In this section we discuss the basic lifecycle of a JVM and the tasks it performs. The basic activities during the lifecycle of the virtual machine are starting up, loading classes, linking, creating new objects and shutting down.

#### Starting up

The JVM begins execution by loading a designated application class. This class must define a `public static void main(String[] args)` method. Once the virtual machine is running and this first class is loaded, the main method is invoked.

Not all Java applications are started using a `main` method. In some cases, such as with MIDlets and Applets, the application level class is instantiated by the system through other means and an instance method is called, such as `startApp()` or `start()` respectively. For the purposes of this chapter, however, application startup will be discussed using the static `main` method.

## Loading classes

Class loading is the process of finding the byte code form of a class or interface and loading it into memory as a Java binary construct. Once a class or interface is discovered, the virtual machine loads the class by performing the linking and initialization processes. Figure 14.2 depicts the class loading process.

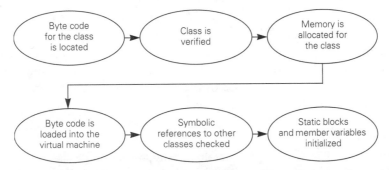

**Figure 14.2    Class loading process used by the virtual machine at runtime. The first step is to locate the byte code, which is typically in a .class file. The next step is to verify that the byte code is safe to be loaded and executed from within the virtual machine. If the class is determined to be safe, memory is allocated for the class and the byte code is loaded into the virtual machine. Finally, additional initialization is performed before making the class accessible within the virtual machine, such as checking symbolic references with other classes used by the class to be loaded and initializing static blocks and variables.**

## Linking

Linking consists of three activities known as verification, preparation and resolution. Verification is the process of ensuring that each class or interface loaded by the virtual machine is a valid Java class or interface and that it will not harm the machine. The steps taken by the verification process are to ensure that each byte code instruction has a valid operation code, that each branch instruction branches to the start of another instruction (as opposed to the middle of an instruction), that every method signature is valid, and that every instruction adheres to the Java type definitions. If the verifier detects anything invalid about the class or interface, the loading process is aborted and an exception is thrown. In some cases classes are preloaded or cached. In this scenario it is the responsibility of the virtual machine to throw such an exception at a point appropriate for the executing application to handle the exception.

Preparation is the process of allocating the proper amount of memory for static storage and data structures used internally by the JVM. It is at this point that static variables are initialized to their standard default values. For example, an int is set to 0 and a boolean is set to false.

Resolution is the process of checking symbolic references to other classes and interfaces to ensure these references are correct. Depending on the VM implementation, this may require the referenced classes and interfaces to be loaded as well. How and when resolution occurs is entirely up to the implementer of the virtual machine. Alternatively, the virtual machine may choose to load these related classes only when needed. Often during resolution the symbolic reference to a related class or interface is replaced with a direct reference. This allows the referenced class to be processed by the virtual machine more efficiently, especially when the reference is used repeatedly.

## Initialization

Initialization is when the virtual machine initializes static blocks and member variables. The variables are initialized in the order they appear and before any constructor or static method can be invoked. If a new instance of the class is being created the class constructor is invoked. If the class being initialized is the main application class (i.e., the first application class loaded by the runtime environment), the JVM invokes the static main(String[] args) method.

## Reloading classes

By default, most Java virtual machines do not support reloading classes, a process also known as dynamic class loading. Virtual machines that support dynamic class loading can reload classes without restarting the virtual machine. Without dynamic class loading, a class is loaded once during the lifecycle of the virtual machine. If you compile and deploy a new class, overwriting the old class, these changes are not reflected until the JVM is restarted. If the JVM supports dynamic class loading, a class may be reloaded into the JVM many times during the lifecycle of the virtual machine.

By implementing a custom class loader, the default class loading behavior can be changed. For example, you may want to allow modifications to be deployed to a machine without having to restart it. To make the virtual machine aware of the newly deployed class files, these class files must be reloaded into the virtual machine.

By default, the primary class loader of a virtual machine does not reload classes. However, some third-party vendors have implemented virtual machines that support class reloading. Often this is called dynamic class loading. It is also possible to implement a custom class loader that provides this capability.

The core Java classes, java.* and javax.* packages, are always loaded by the primary class loader. Furthermore, per the JVM specification, these core classes cannot be reloaded during the lifecycle of a Java Virtual Machine. Altering or replacing the core Java classes is viewed a security risk. Substituting any of the core Java classes could compromise the security model, particularly since much of Java's security is implemented within these classes. For this reason, custom class loaders are restricted to classes outside the java.* and javax.* packages.

### Shutdown

The virtual machine exits when one of the two criteria is met:

- All non-daemon threads terminate
- One of the executing threads invokes the exit() method of the Runtime or System classes. In this case, the security manager must grant exit privileges.

As part of the virtual machine shutdown process, finalization may be run on any objects that have not already run their finalizers. Finalization is the process that allows objects to clean up any resources they may be using just prior to being garbage collected. By default, finalization does not run when the JVM is terminating; however, this can be changed by the executing application by invoking the System.runFinalizers-OnExit(boolean) method and passing the value true. The ability for an application to use this method depends on the permissions granted by the security manager.

**WARNING**  Finalization is unreliable in that it is tied to the garbage collection process. There are no guarantees as to when the garbage collector will run or if a particular object will be collected. Even when garbage collection is explicitly requested using System.gc(), the garbage collector does not run immediately. The call to System.gc() simply requests garbage collection as soon as possible. This may never occur if other threads take priority. As a result, a resource such as a database connection or an I/O stream, will be tied up as the object that used the resource awaits finalization.

## 14.1.2   Java Virtual Machine responsibilities

In addition to managing classes and other lifecycle-related tasks, the JVM performs activities such as creating objects, garbage collection, security management and multithreading.

### Creating objects

Objects are instances of a class that exist only at runtime. Classes are sometimes referred to as a template for creating objects. This processes is illustrated by figure 14.3.

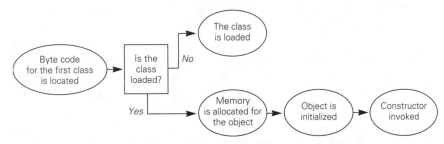

**Figure 14.3   The process used by the virtual machine to create objects at runtime. For each object, the class must first be loaded into the virtual machine and memory for the instance must be allocated. Once memory is allocated the object is initialized and the constructor is invoked.**

Objects are typically created using the new keyword or the static newInstance() method on the Class class. When an object is created, the JVM allocates enough memory for all the instance variables as well as all of the instance variables in all of the superclasses from which the object inherits. Once memory is allocated, the instance variables are initialized to their default values. If there is not enough memory available the object creation process aborts with an OutOfMemoryError.

The next step that the JVM performs on a newly created object is to run the constructor specified by the creation statement. Regardless of the constructor that is invoked, a constructor for each superclass in the hierarchy must run. This can happen explicitly by referencing another constructor from within a constructor using the keywords this or super. However, if this or super is not specified, the default constructor is invoked implicitly by the JVM, thus guaranteeing that at least one constructor will execute within each superclass.

Methods can be invoked during object initialization, both during the initialization of instance variables themselves and during the constructor execution. The JVM specifies no rules or limitations as to when a method can be invoked.

## Garbage collection and memory management

One of the key features of the Java programming language is that the runtime environment manages memory allocation and deallocation automatically. This greatly eases the burden on developers from having to account for and track memory allocations in order to free memory once an object is no longer needed by the application.

In some languages, such as C, programmers are required to allocate the proper amount of memory for an object and keep track of where this memory is so the memory block can be deallocated when the object is no longer needed. Failure to clean up unused memory results in what are known as memory leaks. If an application has a number of memory leaks, the application will slowly use up memory in the system. In cases where an application runs for long periods of time, and memory leaks are present, the system could begin to experience out-of-memory errors since there is no way to reclaim this memory. The only way to correct this problem is to terminate the application or, in some cases, reboot the system.

In Java, the JVM performs the memory accounting activities in a manner that is invisible to developers. When an application requests that a Java object be created (e.g., new MyObject()), the virtual machine allocates the proper amount of memory required for the object as part of the construction process. Once the object is no longer used by the application it becomes eligible for garbage collection. The JVM detects classes that are no longer in use by periodically scanning object references in the heap. A Java object becomes eligible for garbage collection when all other objects in the system no longer hold a reference to it.

The garbage collector itself runs on a low priority background thread and becomes active periodically throughout the lifecycle of the virtual machine. Garbage collection can be explicitly requested by an application with a call to Runtime.gc() or System.gc().

However, it is important to understand that making one of these calls does not immediately start garbage collection. Instead, these calls request that garbage collection be scheduled as soon as possible. When garbage collection actually runs is up to the virtual machine. Thus, the time span between the request for garbage collection and when the garbage collector actually runs can vary greatly depending on what the system is doing.

The Java Virtual Machine Specification does not define the algorithm for garbage collection or specify any criteria as to how garbage collection is accomplished. How garbage collection is implemented is up to the developer implementing the JVM. In some cases, the virtual machine does not implement garbage collection at all but rather defines an interface to plug in a garbage collector. Different JVMs employ different garbage collecting techniques depending on their needs. These techniques vary significantly from vendor to vendor. As a result, the precision of garbage collection varies, as do other factors, such as the periods between garbage collection cycles and the duration of each garbage collection cycle.

### Multithreading and synchronization

A key feature of the Java language is that multithreading is built into the language itself making threads easier to deal with. Depending on the implementation of a particular JVM, and the operating system it runs on, threads are implemented in different ways. In some cases, threading may be implemented entirely within the JVM itself. These are referred to as "green" threads. In other cases, the virtual machine may map threading capabilities to the underlying operating system to take advantage of the native multithreading capabilities. By default, the standard virtual machine uses green threads. However, native threading can be employed on specific operating systems, such as Solaris, by installing a native threads service pack.

**WARNING**    Multithreading is one of the areas most vulnerable to application portability. This is often due to the JVM making use of native threads on different operating systems. This is especially true in the case of thread scheduling and prioritization. For example, the Windows operating systems define seven thread priorities, Solaris defines $2^{32}$ and the JVM specifies nine. This requires two of Java's nine priorities to be mapped to the same value on Windows while on Solaris each of Java's nine priorities is unique. As a result, the multithreading behavior of an application is subject to change if thread scheduling is employed.

In the case where green threads are used it is important to understand that all multithreading capabilities are implemented within the virtual machine. This means that even though your application is multithreaded, ultimately, the entire application is running on a single native thread, which is the thread acquired by the JVM at startup. Whether or not green threads are used is a virtual machine implementation decision. The decision to use green threads may allow the virtual machine implementation to be more portable, since green threads eliminate the need to map native thread support to each operating system. Also, green threads may be employed in cases where multithreading is not supported by the native operating system.

In the cases where native threads can be used, a multiprocessing environment such as Solaris could schedule threads across parallel processors for increased efficiency.

> **NOTE** In general, it is considered good practice to make any class you develop thread-safe. A well-designed object has the potential to be reused in situations not originally anticipated. Some of these situations may involve multithreading and if the object is not thread-safe it may not behave well in a multithreaded situation.

When an application employs threading, your application needs to ensure that its classes are thread-safe. This is done using the keyword `synchronized`. Synchronization can be used at the method level or on a section of code within a method. Generally, synchronization is employed to guarantee that only one thread at a time can access and modify variables within a specific block of code. Use of the `synchronized` keyword should be done judiciously. Each time a section of code is placed within a synchronized block, only one thread at a time is allowed to enter this section of code. All other threads are blocked until the synchronized code is released. Carelessly synchronizing your code can have a significant impact on the running application. It may even negate the benefit of a multithreading environment or cause the system to deadlock. As a rule of thumb, you should always know why you are specifying a synchronized block of code and this block should be kept as small as possible.

> **NOTE** If `synchronized` is used on a static method, the entire class is synchronized, preventing its use by other threads during this timeframe. When instance methods are synchronized, it is the object that blocks other threads and the class is still accessible.

### Finalization

Finalization allows objects the opportunity to release resources before being destroyed. Resources such as device contexts, network connections and database connections are examples of resources that often need to be relinquished explicitly by Java objects since these resources are not automatically reclaimed as a result of the object being removed from memory.

Finalization is invoked by the virtual machine on an object through a call to the object's `finalize()` method. This is known as automatic finalization to differentiate explicit calls to the `finalize()` method made by the application. During automatic finalization no assumptions can be made as to when this method will be invoked, in what order, or by what thread. The virtual machine is only required to execute finalization prior to reusing the memory area allocated to the object.

When implementing a `finalize()` method, it is considered good practice to always invoke finalization on the superclass with a call to `super.finalize()`. Unlike with constructors, the finalization on superclasses is not automatically performed.

### Security

Networks, and more specifically the Internet, tend to be prime delivery mechanisms for Java applications. When applications are used and delivered in a shared, network environment, security becomes a concern.

Much of the Java runtime security model is implemented in class libraries that run inside the JVM rather than in the JVM itself. However, the security model must be initialized, or bootstrapped, by the JVM. This initialization prevents the `java` and `javax` packages from being replaced at runtime or allowing the security model to be altered by unauthorized means. As discussed previously, the JVM is responsible for ensuring only valid class files are loaded into memory.

## 14.2  THE J2ME RUNTIME ENVIRONMENT

The J2ME runtime environments are specified by the J2ME configurations. Each configuration determines the characteristics that a virtual machine must adhere to. The specification allows, and encourages, third parties to develop JVMs that adhere to the same characteristics but run on other platforms or provide an improved JVM for an existing platform.

Sun provides virtual machine reference implementations for the existing configurations. The CLDC reference implementation virtual machine is named the Kilobyte Virtual Machine (KVM) and the CDC reference implementation virtual machine is named the C-Virtual Machine or CVM.

> **NOTE**  For simplicity, the terms CLDC-Compliant Virtual Machine and KVM are used interchangeably unless noted. Likewise, we do the same for the terms CDC-Compliant Virtual Machine and CVM. It should be noted, however, that the KVM and the CVM are not *the* virtual machines for the J2ME but are simply reference implementations. While device manufacturers have the option to port these reference implementations to their devices in order to support J2ME, they also have the option to create their own virtual machines that adhere to the Java Virtual Machine Specification and the configuration specifications.

## 14.3  CLDC-COMPLIANT VIRTUAL MACHINES (THE KVM)

The KVM is designed with smaller, more constrained devices in mind. The key design features for the KVM implementation are as follows:

- small footprint. The core of the virtual machine requires between 40 kilobytes and 80 kilobytes depending on compilation options and the target platform.
- capable of running applications in as little as 128 kilobytes of memory.
- capable of running on both 16 and 32-bit RISC/CISC processors.
- clean, well-commented source base that is highly portable.
- modular and customizable architecture.
- as complete and as fast as possible without compromising other design goals.

### 14.3.1    KVM lifecycle

The lifecycle of the KVM is similar to the standard virtual machines with a few exceptions. The class file verification process is the most noticeable difference. We discuss this in a moment. Also, in some cases like with MIDP, an application is not started by calling a static `main(String[] args)` method, but rather the instance method `startApp()`. Under this model of application management, the device is responsible for starting the virtual machine and then calling the application's instance method.

### Class loading

The default class loader performs all class loading in the CLDC environment. This is the class loader provided by the virtual machine implementer. The default class loader cannot be substituted or manipulated in any way in the CLDC environment. All class loading takes place internally to the virtual machine and custom class loaders are not permitted in the CLDC for security reasons. The CLDC lacks a full Java security model as the classes `java.security.*` are not part of the CLDC libraries. Allowing custom class loaders would pose a security risk to the CLDC environment.

Likewise, the class lookup order and classpath is internal to the virtual machine. This means classpath cannot be defined or altered by developers in the CLDC environment. This is done for two reasons: first of all, many devices in the CLDC space do not have a file system that allows classpath to be meaningful. Second, allowing developers to manipulate classpath in any way posses a security risk in that the core `java.*` and `javax.*` classes could be substituted by altering the class lookup order.

As with the J2SE virtual machine, classes are typically loaded using the `new` keyword or the `newInstance()` method on the `Class` class.

### Class file verification

In some cases, CLDC virtual machines implement class file verification much differently than standard virtual machines. J2SE virtual machines require an excessive amount of resources, in CLDC terms, in order to verify classes before they are loaded. Specifically, the J2SE verifier has a minimum footprint of 50 KB and requires at least 30 to 100 KB of RAM at runtime. This feature alone could consume a majority of the available resources on smaller devices. Therefore, an alternative method for performing class file verification is provided for the CLDC environment. This alternative method breaks class file verification into two steps: preverification and in-device verification. The virtual machine is responsible for performing in-device verification that will be discussed in a moment.

### 14.3.2    Preverification

Preverification is typically performed off of the device, either on a developer's workstation, staging area, or the server used to deploy the applications. Preverification is accomplished by running a preverify utility. This step handles most of the "heavy lifting," thus easing the burden of verification performed on the device at runtime.

The preverify utility that ships with the CLDC reference implementation is a modified version of the J2SE class file verifier. The preverify utility modifies class files generated by the Java compiler and produces new class files.

Although the class file is modified, the modified classes are still compatible with the J2SE virtual machines. The modifications are extensions of the standard class file format defined by the Java Virtual Machine Specification. These modifications increase the size of class files by about five percent.

During preverification, subroutines are inlined, which is the process of eliminating subroutine calls by systematically embedding the code from one call into the other. Inlining subroutines reorganizes the code to be more efficient and reduces the number of subroutine calls or branches that need to take place at runtime. Attributes, called "stackmaps," are added to the class file during the preverification step. Stackmaps are specific to the CLDC and serve as a way to catalog sets of instructions within the byte code. Each entry in the stackmap table catalogs variables and operations that reside on the interpreter's stack at runtime, hence the name "stackmap." During the creation of stackmap data, the class's sequence of instructions is inspected, making sure that each branching instruction (if-then-else, switch, method call, etc.) jumps to the start of another instruction (as opposed to the middle of an instruction) and that the class does not attempt to access resources outside the virtual machine heap space.

The stackmaps are stored in the class file and are used during the in-device verification step.

## 14.3.3 In-device verification

Due to the fact that class files arrive on the device in preverified form, the in-device verification process is simpler than the J2SE verification process. In-device verification needs only to perform a single-pass scan of the class, where the J2SE verifier must iteratively scan class files to complete a full verification. This simplification allows the verification process to use fewer resources and perform better.

During in-device verification, byte codes are scanned to make sure each instruction is valid and has a stackmap entry. If any instruction does not have a stackmap entry, the class is rejected and the verifier reports an error. Furthermore, each method must end with a return instruction (unconditional jump) to ensure control does not fall through any methods.

In addition to verifying the class byte codes, the in-device verifier must distinguish between newly created objects and existing objects that have already had their constructors invoked. It becomes the verifier's responsibility to ensure an object's constructor is invoked only once.

The process for creating CLDC-based applications is shown in figure 14.4.

## 14.3.4 Security

In the interest of reducing the footprint of the CLDC, much of the standard security model has been excluded from the CLDC. In fact, the CLDC contains no java.security.* packages. The security APIs distributed with the J2SE provide

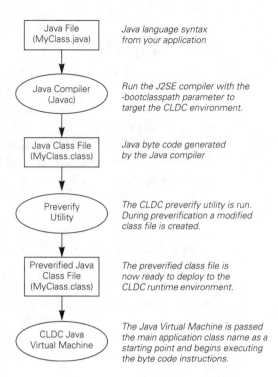

**Figure 14.4**
**The process for creating a CLDC application is similar to creating applications for the J2SE environment with the additional task of preverifying the class. In the CLDC environment, class file verification takes place in two steps, preverification and in-device verification. Preverification is performed on a developer's workstation or a server used to distribute CLDC applications. The result is a partially verified class file. Once the class is installed onto the device, additional class verification is required as the class is loaded into the CLDC-compliant virtual machine, but the verification process is significantly reduced increasing the efficiency in which classes can be loaded while running on the devices.**

the ability to safely move beyond the sandbox security model. Due to the diminished J2SE security features, the CLDC supports a sandbox security model. The sandbox security model tends to be as restrictive as it is simplistic. In many cases, the security features provided by the sandbox model come at the expense of reducing programming features and options by either removing or restricting the use of certain features. Characteristics of the sandbox security model under the CLDC are described as follows:

- All classes must be properly verified as valid Java classes before being loaded into the virtual machine. Classes that do not satisfy the criteria of class file verification must be rejected by the virtual machine.

- Any classes that depend on the security APIs or any other missing security features are not included in the CLDC.

- Downloading, installing and managing of class libraries are handled by the device natively. These processes, such as class loading, are not visible or modifiable by the Java developer.

- The set of native functions provided by the CLDC is closed. Developers can only use APIs defined by the CLDC and the supported profiles. Native functionality cannot be added or replaced beyond what the CLDC and profiles provide. More simply, the java.* and javax.* packages cannot be replaced or modified in any way. Furthermore, the class lookup order is hidden from the application and cannot be modified.

The CLDC identifies two main categories of security, low-level device security and application security.

Low-level device security is provided by class file verification. The class file verifier is responsible for ensuring only valid classes are loaded and these classes do not attempt to access memory outside of the Java heap space.

Application-level security is concerned with how applications are allowed to access device services such as data storage, file systems, infrared ports, networks and peripherals. This level of security is necessary to ensure the safety of the device while the application is running. The J2SE security model employs a security manager to monitor access to these services. However, in the CLDC environment, the security model is much diminished. The CLDC does not support the concept of a security manager. As a result, the sandbox security model defines application-level security.

### 14.3.5    Unsupported Java features

Since the CLDC purposefully omits functionality commonly found in the standard Java environments, all CLDC-compliant virtual machines must adhere to these restrictions as well. As a result, a number of features are not supported by the CLDC runtime environment. Here are the features of the CLDC that pertain to the virtual machine:

#### Floating-point data types

Floating-point data types are not supported since many of the devices in the CLDC space do not support this capability. Furthermore, the designers of the CLDC thought floating-point support is too expensive in terms of memory and binary code space to support this capability.

#### Finalization

Objects used within CLDC applications do not have the `Object.finalize()` method available. The rules of finalization make garbage collection more complicated since each object can be finalized exactly once, which requires some accounting on the part of the garbage collector. Furthermore, in some circles of the Java community, finalization has become something to avoid for several reasons. Finalization is not guaranteed. You do not know when it will run, if it will run or in what order objects will be finalized. Furthermore, by default the JVM does not run finalization during the JVM shutdown process. This means that if your application is exiting, and causes the JVM to exit as well, finalization is still not guaranteed to run.

#### Error handling reduced

The CLDC-compliant virtual machines generally support exception handling; however, the number of errors recognized by the CLDC virtual machines is limited. Java defines an `Error` as a type of exception in which the system is not expected to recover. How individual devices deal with these types of errors is highly device-specific.

In some cases, a device may attempt to recover from an error while another device automatically performs a soft-reset. Furthermore, error handing, as defined by the Java Virtual Machine Specification, is expensive to implement and support. For these reasons only a small number of errors are recognized by CLDC virtual machines.

### Java Native Interface (JNI)

Java Native Interface (JNI) is not supported in the same sense as the standard virtual machines support JNI. In the CLDC environment, only the virtual machine implements native calls. These native calls are part of the API support provided directly by the virtual machine. Custom JNI capabilities are not exposed to developers. There are a couple of reasons for not supporting JNI. First of all, in order to ensure the safety of the system, JNI relies on the Java security model. Most of the standard security model APIs are not supported by the CLDC, thus posing a security risk. Furthermore, JNI is considered to be resource-expensive.

### User-defined class loaders

In the CLDC, the virtual machine defines one class loader that cannot be replaced, overridden or reconfigured by developers. Having the class loading take place within the virtual machine, and unreachable by developers, is necessary to ensure the safety of the system in the absence of a fully Java security model. This ensures that the class loading order cannot be tampered with and that the core `java.*` and `javax.*` packages cannot be replaced at runtime.

### Reflection

Reflection allows an application to inspect classes, objects, methods, fields and other items residing in the virtual machines at runtime. Due to the absence of reflection, the CLDC runtime does not support RMI, serialization, JVM debugging interface or a JVM profiler interface.

> **NOTE**   Although reflection is not available, the ability to create classes using `Class.forName()` is supported by the CLDC environment. This provides the ability to create instances of classes that define a zero-args constructor.

### Weak references

A weak reference is the ability of an application to hold a reference to an object while still allowing the object to be a candidate for garbage collection. Weak references are often useful in caching situations and scheduling cleanup operations. Supporting weak references requires the garbage collector to be able to notify the application when a weak referenced object becomes eligible for collection. As with finalization, there is a fair amount of accounting that the virtual machine and garbage collector need to perform in order to handle weak references.

### 14.3.6 Multithreading

The KVM does not use multithreading capabilities of native environments. All threading is implemented in the virtual machine using green threads. This makes porting the KVM much easier since native threads do not need to be supported. Furthermore, many of the devices in the KVM space are not multiprocessor devices. Forcing a device to support native thread capabilities in these cases is not practical.

However, this does not mean all CLDC-compliant virtual machines use green threads. The choice of thread implementation is entirely up to the implementer of the virtual machine. As mentioned previously, multithreading can be a portability issue, causing your application to behave differently on different multithreaded platforms. This is especially true when thread scheduling is used. If your application uses multithreading you should test the robustness of the threading employed by the application on all of your target devices.

The KVM employs a deterministic method of task management in its threading implementation. Threads are switched after a certain number of byte codes are executed.

### 14.3.7 Garbage collection

As with threading, garbage collection in the KVM has been implemented entirely within the virtual machine. However, the code for the garbage collector has been carefully partitioned from the virtual machine code so that it can easily be replaced by other garbage collection techniques.

Implementing garbage collection within the virtual machine makes porting the KVM easier since there are no system dependencies to deal with. However, garbage collection algorithms and implementations are decisions made by the virtual machine implementer. Each implementation of CLDC-compliant virtual machines may choose to handle garbage collection differently.

A CLDC-compliant virtual machine, as is the case with the KVM, should be optimized for small heap sizes, usually on the order of tens of kilobytes.

As with any Java environment, the precision and efficiency of the garbage-collector will vary depending on the implementation. In the case of small devices where memory is a premium, garbage collection is rather important. Unfortunately, the effectiveness of the garbage collector cannot be guaranteed across different devices and different virtual machines implementers. Furthermore, regardless of the efficiency of the garbage collector, reclaiming memory comes with the price of consuming processing cycles. Therefore, it is important to observe good programming practice and to incur as little work as possible, or as is reasonable, for the garbage collector. Adhering to this rule will better prepare your application for dealing with particularly bad garbage collectors. Additionally, it will assist the overall efficiency of your application by not incurring large amounts of garbage to begin with. This does not mean you should avoid good programming practice in order to make your code more garbage-collector friendly; however, you should be aware of how much garbage you are incurring.

For example, String manipulation tends to incur a fair amount of garbage. In these cases, you should favor `StringBuffer` instead. Also, remember that `String s = ""` is the same as `String s = new String()`; which is different from `String s = null`, which does not create a `String` instance.

### 14.3.8 Internationalization

The CLDC provides support for Unicode characters. The `InputStreamReader` and `OutputStreamReader` classes support translating between Unicode characters and a sequence of bytes. Both classes support a constructor that allows the encoding to be specified. The default encoding is described by the system property `micro-edition.encoding`. The CLDC does not support any other internationalization features. Most notably, the CLDC does not support localization. As a result, there is no feature set that supports formatting for date, time, currency, etc. based on locale. These features are considered outside the scope of the CLDC at this time.

### 14.3.9 Application management (JAM)

The Java Application Manager (JAM) manages the lifecycle of an application on a device. The JAM is implemented natively per device, usually in C, and defines the basic interactions between the device and a J2ME application with respect to downloading, installing, launching, inspecting, updating and uninstalling applications. Since the devices within the J2ME space tend to be used for a special purpose and are not general computing devices, many of the standard utilities and services found on desktop computers, such as a file system, are not always available. The JAM provides the ability to deal with the lack of these services on the devices.

In the CLDC runtime environment the JAM is optional. Often a JAM is utilized in conjunction with some type of micro-browser on the device that allows the user to access applications that can be downloaded and installed over the network.

The JAM has two basic techniques for dealing with applications. The first technique is to download the application and install it onto the device, allowing the user to run the application many times before uninstalling it. Alternately, an application may be downloaded to the device, loaded directly into memory and thrown away once the user exits the application.

A JAM makes use of two basic components, a JAR file and a descriptor file. The JAR file consists of a manifest and the class files and resources used by the application. The descriptor file contains name=value pairs in a plain-text file. The name=value pairs in table 14.1 are required for any JAM descriptor file:

Specific profiles may introduce more or different name=value pairs depending on their needs. Additionally, developers can add additional name=value pairs to provide customized properties to the applications on the device. These properties can be accessed at runtime using `System.getProperty(String key)`.

**Table 14.1   The JAM descriptor file provided by the CLDC specification**

| | |
|---|---|
| **Application-Name** | A text description of the application. This text will be displayed on the device screen and is limited to what the device can display. |
| **Application-Version** | Specifies the version information of the application. This allows the JAM to reconcile the version currently installed and the version on the server to know if an application update is necessary. The format of this field follows a major.minor[.micro] convention (e.g., 1.2.05) where the micro portion is optional. If version information is omitted, the information is assumed to be 0. |
| **KVM-Version** | This field is used to reconcile the application compatibility with the virtual machine implementation on the device. Note that this may not be the KVM, but rather an implementation subscribing to the same specifications. This value can be a list of version strings delimited by commas. The items in this value are compared to version information retrieved by the system property `microedition.configuration`.<br>An exact match must be found between these version resource strings before the application will be allowed to run. |
| **Main-Class** | The name of the main class to run. |
| **JAR-File-Size** | The size of the JAR file specified in bytes. This field must be an integer value. |
| **JAR-File-URL** | Specifies the URL to the JAR file. This can be a URL relative to the descriptor file. |
| **Use-Once** | Indicates whether or not the application is retained after running the first time. The format for this field is `[yes|no]`. |
| **Help-Page-URL** | A location of a help page associated with the application. |

The JAM descriptor is accessed over a network connection using a MIME type. This MIME type can vary for different profile specifications. In general, a JAM MIME type is specified as `application/x-jam` where the descriptor has the extension ".jam". Note, however, that the MIDP specifies that descriptor files have the extension ".jad" and the mime type is `text/vnd.sun.j2me.app-descriptor`. The content of the descriptor also changes.

## 14.3.10   Java Code Compact (JCC)

The Java Code Compact is a utility that allows application classes to be statically linked into the virtual machine. In doing this, application startup time can be significantly reduced. The memory required by the application can also be reduced. This technique is also known as ROMizing.

This utility is run against your applications classes to create a C file. This C program file can then be compiled and linked with the virtual machine. The KVM supports this utility, which is located in the tools\jcc directory of the CLDC distribution. If you are using another virtual machine, the implementers of the CLDC-compliant virtual machine must have included support for the Java Code Compact as well.

Since the JCC generates C code, you must specify a target environment for the completed product. Currently, the KVM only supports prelinking for the Unix, Windows, and Palm OS.

### 14.3.11  Deployed classes

A CLDC-compliant virtual machine must support compressed JAR files. Since network bandwidth is an issue for CLDC devices, compressing classes into a JAR file format helps reduce the size of an application by as much as 50 percent.

The CLDC specification makes a distinction between "publicly represented" and "non-publicly represented" applications and resources. A publicly represented application is stored on a publicly accessible server that can be accessed by open standards, such as HTTP. When an application is represented publicly, it must be in the compressed JAR format. Conversely, a non-publicly accessible application, that is, an application that resides on a private network or closed system, is not required to be represented in JAR format, compressed or otherwise.

The JAR files comprising an application can also contain resources used by the application, such as graphics, icons, media files, reference data, and so forth. These resources are accessed using the method call `Class.getResourceAsStream (String name)` that returns an `InputStream`.

> **NOTE**  Java class files are designed to be independent units that contain all the necessary elements to run without making assumptions about the availability of class-specific resources. As a result, each class file contains its own symbol table as well as method, field, and exception tables and some other information. The encapsulation of these elements also makes Java class files easy to extend at runtime. However, this flexibility comes with the cost of supporting redundant information structures. If a set of class files were to be delivered as a unit unto themselves, much of these redundancies could be removed, making for a much smaller application size. This possibility is desirable in the CLDC space due to bandwidth limitations. Additionally, such a format could also allow applications to be executed "in-place" without the need for a loading process, making for a similar application runtime model that could improve performance. The creators of the CLDC recognize this opportunity and this capability may find its way into the CLDC on a future version.

### 14.3.12  Debug support

Sun Microsystems has developed a number of debugging architectures and interfaces that are compatible with Java Virtual Machines. The Java Debug Wire Protocol (JDWP) is an interface that allows any JVM to be plugged into development and debugging environments. The Java Platform Debugging Architecture (JPDA) supports the infrastructure for building JVM-compatible debugging tools. Communication between the development environment and the virtual machine using the JDWP is typically done using sockets.

Due to memory restrictions, the KVM does not fully support the Java Debug Wire Protocol. Instead, a subset of the JDWP is supported by an interface named the KVM Debug Wire Protocol (KDWP).

By supporting the KDWP, a development environment equipped with a JPDA-compliant debugger can interface to the KVM debug features through a proxy. This proxy issues debug commands to the KVM and interfaces with the KVM to retrieve debug data values. The proxy is invisible to the development environment. To the development environment, it looks like the debugger is communicating with a fully compliant implementation of the Java Debug Wire Protocol interface.

## 14.4   *CDC-COMPLIANT VIRTUAL MACHINES (THE CVM)*

The CVM is designed for devices that have more resources available and are not as constrained as CLDC devices. The CDC runtime environment is a superset of the CLDC runtime environment and provides full support for the Java Virtual Machine Specification as well as the Java Language Specification. The C-Virtual Machine (CVM) is the reference virtual machine implementation for the CDC environment. This virtual machine is based on the J2SE and PersonalJava virtual machines; however, the CVM is more modular and easier to extend than the J2SE and PersonalJava virtual machines. Since the CVM is a fully compliant virtual machine, its lifecycle is identical to the J2SE virtual machine. Unlike the CLDC virtual machines, class file verification is handled entirely on the device. As with the KVM, the CVM is a reference implementation virtual machine. Device manufacturers can choose to port the CVM or build their own virtual machine from the ground up. The key design features for the CVM are as follows:

- Designed for devices with at least 512 KB of ROM and 256 KB RAM. However, most devices in this space support at least 2 megabytes of total memory available for the CVM and the CDC libraries.

- Full-featured virtual machine that completely supports the Java Virtual Machine Specification and the Java Language Specification.

- Runs on 32-bit processors

- Supports network connectivity

- Based on the Personal Java Virtual Machine and the J2SE Virtual Machine; however, the CVM is designed to be more modular and extendible.

- Targets communicator class devices such as pocket PCs, PDAs, smart phones, small retail payment terminals and Internet appliances.

### 14.4.1 Garbage collection and the CVM

The CVM does not implement garbage collection directly but rather provides an interface so that garbage collection can be plugged into the virtual machine independently without needing to modify the virtual machine source code. The CVM is carefully designed to separate the virtual machine's operational code from the memory management code.

The default garbage collector that ships with the CVM is designed to be as precise as possible. The collector employs the concept of "exactness" in order to precisely understand all pointer information during garbage collection passes. Exactness uses fewer handles per object, allows for full compacting of the heap during each collection pass, reduces the amount of "guess work" in collecting objects and allows for more garbage collection algorithm options.

Exactness is implemented by requiring all threads to manage themselves between two states, gc-safe and gc-unsafe. By default, threads operate in the gc-unsafe state a majority of the time. While in this state, objects may operate on and within the heap and perform gc-unsafe operations. However, each thread is required to periodically place itself into a gc-safe state in order for the garbage collector to perform collection operations. When a thread becomes gc-safe, it must make all of its pointers explicitly known to the garbage collector.

The garbage collector can only execute if all threads are in a gc-safe state. This requires the CVM to bring all threads in the system to a gc-safe state before allowing the garbage collector to proceed. As each thread becomes gc-safe, the thread suspends itself and makes all of its pointers available.

The interpreter contains what are called gc-safe points in order to allow garbage collection to take place periodically. The gc-safe points are implemented periodically within the interpreter instruction set. Specifically, the interpreter implements gc-safe points when methods are invoked, on returns from method calls, memory allocation points and class loading and constant resolution points. By implementing gc-safe points within the interpreter, the system is guaranteed to become gc-safe within discrete periods of time.

### 14.4.2 Memory references in the CVM

The CVM uses a method of pointer indirection to perform pointer accounting tasks and to ensure no pointers become invisible to the garbage collector. There are two interfaces supported by the CVM. The direct memory interface provides direct access to the heap. Primarily the virtual machine interpreter uses this interface. Accessing pointers through the direct memory interface is always gc-unsafe. The second interface is the indirect memory interface. This method of accessing the heap is always gc-safe. Code running outside of the virtual machine interpreter should always use the indirect memory interface. Class loading and the JNI are examples that would use the indirect memory interface.

## 14.5    SUMMARY

The two virtual machines defined within the J2ME architecture provide for the characteristics defined in the configuration specifications. Each configuration has different needs and requirements that are reflected in their virtual machines. One of the primary concerns with battery-powered devices has to do with power consumption. Both of the J2ME virtual machines take into account the fact that they may need to run on a battery-powered device and must be conservative about how many CPU cycles are consumed to handle its responsibilities. Memory is also a driving issue behind the J2ME runtime environments. Small devices require small, efficient runtime engines. The J2ME virtual machines are optimized to be effective in small heap spaces. Finally, the portability factor of the reference implementations allows manufacturers and vendors to support J2ME quickly.

**CHAPTER 15**

# Related technologies

J2ME technology is still in its infancy. Indeed, the hardware platforms and communication systems that support J2ME applications have just recently, within the last five years, become commercially viable, widely accessible, and an important part of the business world and our personal lives. We are all still learning what is possible and how to apply the technological possibilities to problems and needs. Think about it. How long have you owned your cellular telephone? Do you own a PDA and how long have you had it? Moreover, there has been and will continue to be an enormous amount of movement in the "hot" personal information and communications products that people have been attracted to and use. For example, sales of Palm OS systems accounted for over 85 percent of the handheld market as late as February 2001.[1] But in June of 2001, Reuters reported that Palm was expected to lose that lead to Compaq's iPaq, at least in terms of revenue, some time during the summer of 2001.[2] The race for producing good products that capture consumer attention and market share is unlikely to abate in the near future.

Given the tumultuous nature of the consumer electronics and embedded device industry, it should come as no surprise that many companies are also competing to

---

[1]   The Standard, "Palm Losing Grip on Market Share," April 20, 2001.

[2]   Reuters, "Compaq iPaq will top Palm in market share, survey says," June 17, 2001.

build better and more convenient services for these devices. Vendors and organizations providing these solutions are scrambling to keep up with the demand. The need for standards, such as J2ME, has never been more apparent. However, standards take time to become established and time to gain acceptance. With the void of widely accepted and practiced standards, consumers demand solutions. Solutions demand innovation regardless of the state of the standards, and, as we have seen, J2ME is still evolving and growing. Today, there are plenty of choices when contemplating the development of an application on consumer electronic or embedded devices. Sometimes, J2ME is not the right choice or even an available choice depending on the nature of the application.

In this chapter, we explore some of the competing, supporting, and ancillary technologies and products that are often talked about in J2ME circles. We discuss each product in light of its relationship to J2ME.

It is impossible, in a single chapter, to cover all of the technologies and products in the typical J2ME developer's radar screen. First of all, it is impossible to know them all, and second it is likely that, like the devices themselves, some of the hot development technologies and products of today will be gone tomorrow and replaced with products that were not known at the time this text was written. However, this chapter provides an insight into available options and areas to explore in preparation for your own development efforts.

## 15.1  J2ME IMPLEMENTATIONS

Sun has produced the reference implementation for the released J2ME specifications, but they are not the only producers. In fact, the Sun reference implementation often leaves developers wanting for a virtual machine with better performance and smaller footprint. There are already several implementations of the various J2ME specifications and more surely to follow.

### 15.1.1  esmertec's Jbed

In chapters 8 through 10, we took you through the world of developing applications for Palm OS using Jbed Micro Edition CLDC, esmertec's IDE and virtual machine for developing applications in CLDC and KJava. esmertec claims that their virtual machine is up to fifty times faster than other virtual machines.

esmertec also produces Jbed Profile for MID. This is an implementation of J2ME CLDC and MIDP. esmertec is a member of the PDAP Expert Group. So it can be expected that esmertec will have an implementation of the CLDC and PDAP when the new PDAP specification is available. Again, more information about esmertec and their Jbed products is available at: www.esmertec.com

By the way, we should mention that the Jbed product provides more tools and utilities than were shown in this text. For example, Jbed provides a means to run and debug the application running on the emulator while still communicating with and providing information to the Jbed IDE. This is an especially important and time-saving feature while building J2ME applications.

### 15.1.2 Motorola's Embedded Reference Implementation (MERI)

Motorola serves and leads the Java Community Process Expert Group that developed the MIDP specification. It should then come as no surprise that Motorola has developed an implementation of the CLDC and MIDP specification. Motorola claims that their Embedded Reference Implementation (MERI) was the first Sun-certified implementation. While already available on Motorola's iDen Model i85 and Accompli Model 6288, as well as the 008 cellular telephones today, MERI can be ported to other equipment. Information on Motorola J2ME products and cell phones is available at:www.motorola.com/java

## 15.2  THE OTHER SUN SPECIFICATIONS

There was life on consumer electronics and embedded devices before J2ME, even at Sun Microsystems. In the first chapter, you were told how Java started as a programming language for consumer electronics. Alongside J2ME, there have been a couple of other Java specifications and implementations prepared by Sun for putting Java on consumer electronics and embedded devices.

### 15.2.1 PersonalJava

PersonalJava (not a typo, there is no space between Personal and Java), also called the PersonalJava Application Environment (PJAE), is a Java application environment and Java virtual machine that was developed before J2ME and was written for personal, consumer and mobile devices, which is much the same space J2ME intends to provide for today. In fact, marketing literature from Sun suggests that PersonalJava was developed for web phones, digital set-top boxes, personal digital assistants, and car navigational systems. Information on PersonalJava is available from Sun Microsystems at: java.sun.com/products/personaljava

Initially released around January 1998, PersonalJava is based on JDK 1.1.8. PersonalJava is guided by the PersonalJava API Specification, which is currently at version 1.2a. According to Sun, it will be transitioned into the CDC and Personal Profile in the near future.

While PersonalJava is essentially JDK 1.1.8, there have been a couple of modifications to the specification requiring that PJAE contain some of the SDK 1.2 APIs. As of the 1.2 version of the PersonalJava specification, additional security has been added to comply with Java 2 SDK, Standard Edition, version 1.2.2 security. PJAE also now requires support for Java Native Interface 1.2.2. There are a few classes that are specific to the PJAE API. For example, a set of PJAE-specific classes in com.sun.util are provided for creating and managing timer events.

In addition to inclusion of certain SDK 1.2 APIs, there are several "optionally" supported APIs. These are features that are not absolutely required, per the specification, but allow the specification implementer to provide if desired. However, if the implementer does choose to provide a given "optional" feature, then the implementation must support it completely per the standard edition JDK API.

As a subset of the older JDK, developers are usually most disappointed that PersonalJava application graphical user interfaces are built using a slightly modified version of the old Abstract Windowing Toolkit (AWT). Java developers familiar with the latest version of Java, usually also lament that many of their favorite collection classes (ArrayList, Collection, HashMap, HashSet, Iterator, List, ListIterator, Map, and Set) are only unsupported optional classes.

While intended to have a far-reaching impact, the reference implementation of PersonalJava is supported on only three processors today, namely, the MIPS (R4000 Compatible), StrongARM, and Hitachi's SH3/SH4. However, with the popularity of many Windows CE devices that use these processors (such as Compaq's iPaq, which uses the StrongARM processor), and with the continued delays in the release and implementation of CDC and Personal and Foundational Profiles, PersonalJava has a place in today's small device Java applications. Given that Sun plans to migrate PersonalJava to the CDC and Personal Profile, there is a sense among the development community that PJAE is at least a platform that has a future, albeit a moving future, in small device application development.

Several vendors offer PersonalJava integrated development environments to include Borland's JBuilder and Metrowerks' CodeWarrior. Furthermore, and just as importantly, there are several vendors offering implementations of the PJAE specification. Some of the known commercially available PersonalJava implementations are covered in alphabetical order as follows:

### JV-Lite2 by ACCESS

JV-Lite2, available in three editions, implements PersonalJava, EmbeddedJava and J2ME CLDC specification. JV-Lite runs off several real-time operating systems to include those listed below:

- Linux

- VxWorks

- ITRON

Along with claims of having an extremely compact virtual machine, JV-Lite2 includes Access's own "Windows-based Abstract Virtual Environment (WAVE)" which is a simple window manager allowing for easier porting to various platforms. Information about JV-Lite2 can be obtained from: www.access.co.jp/english/products/jv.html

### Jeode by Insignia

The Jeode platform complies with and is an implementation of both the PersonalJava and EmbeddedJava specifications. Information on Jeode is available at: www.insignia.com/java_enabled.htm.

Insignia claims that Jeode's value comes in accelerated performance, which is due in part to their patented compiling techniques, robust memory management due to superior garbage collection, and the ability to configure and tune the platform for specific devices. Jeode runs on the following list of operating systems and processors:

**Table 15.1    Insignia's Jeode supported operating systems and platforms.**

| Operating Systems | Processors |
|---|---|
| Windows CE | ARM |
| Windows NT | MIPS |
| VxWorks | x86 |
| Linux | Hitachi SuperH-3/4 |
| ITRON | Motorola PowerPC |
| Nucleus | |
| BSDi Unix | |
| PSOS | |

## Kada Mobile Platform by Kada Systems

Kada Systems has developed its line of products to operate under a fully upwardly compatible set of specifications. Kada's platform is a full JDK 1.1.8 implementation and therefore compliant with the PersonalJava API. But the Kada API also includes additional packages not included or optional in PersonalJava such as java.math, and soon will offer RMI and the java.beans packages. Kada is expected to release support for J2ME and MIDP in the near future.

Kada is currently available for Palm OS, Windows CE, and Windows platforms and is being ported to EPOC and RIM systems in the near future. To learn more about Kada, visit www.kadasystems.com.

## PersonalJava for OS-9 by RadiSys/Microware

OS-9 is a real time operating system (RTOS) for embedded systems. In particular OS-9 is available for a host of processors including x86, PowerPC, StrongARM, ARM, SuperH, MIPS, and IXP1200. Therefore, as its name implies, PersonalJava for OS-9 is a PersonalJava implementation for use on top of the OS-9 RTOS. Microware has become a division of RadiSys Corporation. Contact RadiSys or Microware through the following web site locations: www.radisys.com and www.microware.com/Products/Software/java.html.

## CrEme by NSIcom

NSIcom calls CrEme an "augmented" Java virtual machine. CrEme is a PersonalJava implementation designed specifically to run on the Microsoft Windows CE operating system. Information is available at: www.nsicom.com/products/creme.asp.

### intent Java Technology Edition, by Tao Group

Tao Group's intent Java virtual machine implements the PersonalJava specification. intent JTE, according to Tao Group, is a fast and smaller footprint Java environment, which comes from a patented translation mechanism used in place of a Just-in-Time (JIT) compiler. More information can be obtained from their website at: tao-group. com/2/tao/index.html.

intent is supported on the following processors and operating systems.

**Table 15.2   Operating systems and platforms that support intent JTE by Tao Group**

| Operating Systems | Processors |
|---|---|
| Windows CE/PocketPC | ARM |
| Windows NT, 95, 98, 2000 | StrongARM |
| Epoc | MIPS |
| Linux | x86 |
| Embedded Linux | ColdFire |
| VxWorks | Motorola M-core/Power PC |
| Elate | Hitachi SuperH-3/4 |
| | ST40 |
| | NEC V850 |

### Personal Jworks by Wind River

Wind River is the creator of VxWorks, an embedded real-time operating system (RTOS) used in a multitude of products such as networking equipment, medical scanners and monitors, printers, fax machines, and so forth. Personal JWorks is a PersonalJava implementation that works in the VxWorks RTOS. More information about VxWorks and JWorks is available at: www.windriver.com/products

### Kaffe

Kaffe is billed as the only open source and independent implementation of Personal-Java. Along with support for various operating systems (see the list below), Kaffe is particularly popular for use with PocketLinux. Both Kaffe and PocketLinux are developed by Transvirtual Technologies, Inc. Information and a copy of Kaffe is available at: www.kaffe.org

Operating systems supported by Kaffe include the following:

- Windows NT/CE/...
- Linux
- Solaris
- FreeBSD
- DOS

## 15.2.2    EmbeddedJava

Software destined for embedded devices such as instrumentation, factory automation equipment, facsimile machines, network routers and switches, plus low-end mobile phones, usually operates under very strict resource constraints and is created to fulfill very specific tasks. In many cases, the software has a limited, if any, user interface. Living inside a device, embedded software is often referred to as black-box software, since its exposure to the outside world, after being created, is severely limited if exposed at all. Whereas third-party (not the device manufacturer or end user) developers often create J2ME applications, EmbeddedJava applications are usually going to be created and deployed by the original equipment manufacturers (OEM) of the device.

The memory footprint, power consumption, and security requirements are just some of the limiting factors associated with embedded applications. EmbeddedJava is the Java environment established to handle the software needed for the insides of devices. EmbeddedJava is also called the Embedded Java Application Environment or EJAE and is based on the even older JDK 1.1.7 API minus applets (all EmbeddedJava programs must run as applications).

Like PersonalJava, EmbeddedJava is guided by a specification; the latest released version is EmbeddedJava 1.1. Unlike PersonalJava, however, EmbeddedJava will not be rolled into J2ME, but it is likely that it will be further integrated with other Java technologies like Jini, as discussed in section 15.4.3.

Because of the constraints on embedded applications, the EJAE allows for the APIs to be completely configured for the requirements of the application. Therefore, while EmbeddedJava is based on the JDK 1.1.7, the Java packages, classes, methods, and fields are completely configurable, meaning that any unnecessary items can be removed for a particular device, its real-time operating system and/or applications. To assist in streamlining the application for a device, EJAE provides three tools that an application is fed through before placing the application on the device. A JavaFilter builds the list of fields and methods used by the Java platform necessary to run a Java application. Using the list generated by the JavaFilter, the JavaCodeCompact tool reduces the application down to its required essentials. Finally, the JavaDataCompact tool links in additional resource and data files such as HTML, images, sound, and so forth. The result of this process is a compact executable image that is loaded on a device's ROM or RAM.

Along with some of the previously mentioned vendors such as Insignia and ACCESS that support both PersonalJava and EmbeddedJava, there are several other vendors that provide EmbeddedJava implementations or tools for various real time operating systems. Consult Sun's EmbeddedJava web site (java.sun.com/products/ embeddedjava/) for more information on EmbeddedJava and those organizations working with EmbeddedJava systems.

## 15.3 NON-J2ME ALTERNATIVES

Other vendors and organizations have been wrestling with Java on small devices outside of the J2ME specification. Some started before J2ME began. While J2ME hopes to someday provide a ubiquitous specification for Java developers looking to provide Java applications on all consumer electronics and embedded devices, this is not the case today. There are many competing products and environments. Therefore, some of the non-J2ME Java platforms may be the way to go if you are looking to develop an application today.

### 15.3.1 ChaiVM by Hewlett-Packard

HP's ChaiVM is an implementation of the JDK 1.1.8 API (with some class libraries such as `java.security` and the `java.util.jar` packages supported at the JDK 2.0 level) designed to run on resource-constrained devices such as HP's own Jornada. HP claims that one of the biggest values offered by ChaiVM is its ChaiFreezeDry technology that loads the Java class libraries at runtime or dynamically during runtime using up to fifty percent less RAM space than other virtual machines.

ChaiVM is available on a relatively limited number of platforms (see the following list), but applications developed with the ChaiVM are also upwardly compatible with PersonalJava. The source for information about ChaiVM is: www.hp.com/go/embedded

ChaiVM supports certain operating system and platform combinations. These include:

- Windows NT/x86
- Red Hat Linux/x86
- Window CE or Pocket PC/ Hitachi SuperH-3

### 15.3.2 IBM's VisualAge Micro Edition

In all fairness, IBM's VisualAge Micro Edition (VAME) now deserves a place under both the non-reference J2ME implementations and non-J2ME headings in this chapter. However, when initially introduced, VAME was not compliant with the J2ME specifications. While VAME contains an implementation of the CLDC and MIDP class libraries and can be used to create CLDC and MIDP-compliant applications today, it can still be used to create Java applications for a host of hardware and operating system platforms that are not yet supported by J2ME.

Underlying IBM's implementation of Java for small devices is the J9 virtual machine. The J9 virtual machine was based on the JDK 1.2.2 specification. It supports JNI (see section 15.4.2) and can be configured with application and class files in an executable file format for storing and execution in device ROM. J9 is available for the platforms and operating systems listed in table 15.6.

Based on IBM's line of VisualAge programming tools, VAME is also an IDE providing a code repository and version control, code assistance, and some testing capabilities. With VAME and J9, IBM allows for two application development approaches.

**Table 15.3  Operating systems and platforms supported by IBM's J9.**

| Operating Systems | Processors |
|---|---|
| AIX | x86 |
| Linux | MIPS |
| ITRON | PowerPC |
| OSE | Hitachi SuperH-3/4 |
| Palm OS | Sparc |
| PocketPC | ARM/StrongARM |
| QNX/Neutrino/RTP | Motorola 68K |
| Solaris | |
| Windows | |
| Windows CE | |

If a standard exists and the API is provided, such as with CLDC and MIDP, one can develop an application under this standard and also take advantage of IBM's virtual machine which is faster and smaller than the reference implementation. On the other hand, where the standards and specification are not yet available, IBM may offer the developer a means to write a Java application for the desired target devices. For example, IBM provides a means to write a Java application capable of running on a Palm OS device using base classes and calls to the Palm OS directly.

Notice, in the following HelloWorld example for a Palm OS device using VAME, the application's use of the operating system calls (identified by OS in front of the method calls). This example is shown running in figure 15.1.

**Figure 15.1**
The VAME HelloWorld application is depicted here running on IBM's J9 virtual machine in a Palm OS device. VAME allows developers to make native OS calls at the expense of portability.

```java
import com.ibm.oti.palmos.*;

public class HelloWorld implements OSConsts {

 public static void main(String[] args) throws InterruptedException {

    CharPtr title = new CharPtr("HelloW orld Demo");

    FormType mainForm = OS.FrmNewForm(0,title,0,0,160,160,0,0,0,0);   ❶
    title.dispose();
    PtrPtr formPP = PtrPtr.fromValue(mainForm.getCPointer());

    CharPtr text3 = new CharPtr("Howdie!");
    OS.FrmNewLabel(formPP, 0, text3, 10, 40, 1);   ❶
    text3.dispose();

    CharPtr buttonText = new CharPtr("Exit");
    ControlType buttonControl = OS.CtlNewControl(formPP, 0, buttonCtl,
      buttonText, 125, 100, 30, 15, 1, 0, ctrue);   ❶
    buttonText.dispose();

    mainForm.setCPointer(formPP.getPointerAt(0));
    OS.FrmDrawForm(mainForm);
    OS.FrmSetActiveForm(mainForm);   ❶

    EventType event = new EventType();
    while (true) {
        Thread.yield();
        OS.EvtGetEvent(event, -1);   ❶
        int eType = event.getEType();
        if (OS.SysHandleEvent(event) == ctrue)   ❶
            continue;
        OS.CtlHandleEvent(buttonControl, event);   ❶
        if (eType == appStopEvent || eType == ctlSelectEvent){
            break;
        }
    }
    OS.FrmEraseForm(mainForm);
    OS.FrmDeleteForm(mainForm);
    OS.FrmCloseAllForms();
    event.dispose();
    formPP.dispose();
 }
}
```

❶ **The OS calls are calls to the underlying Palm OS which VAME supports**

With this power comes the responsibility to know how to use it. You must take care and consideration when determining whether to use native device features because it is likely that these features will not port or port easily to the next device. However, where the alternative is to write in a language other than Java, IBM's VAME and J9 may be a nice alternative. More information about VAME, J9 and IBM's efforts in products for small devices is available at www.oti.com.

### 15.3.3　Waba by Wabasoft

Waba is not Java according to both its makers and Sun Microsystems. However, its syntax and behavior is a subset of Java and so therefore can be learned easily by Java developers. In fact, to develop Waba programs you can use your favorite Java development environment and put the WabaSDK classes that are used to develop and debug Waba applications in the classpath of the tool.

Waba is free under the GNU license agreement and has its own virtual machine, the WabaVM, which runs on Palm OS and Windows CE devices. However, as the WabaVM source code is available, others have ported the WabaVM to a number of other platforms. This source code can also be used to build in native functions.

A simple HelloWorld program in Waba is listed as follows:

```
import waba.ui.*;
import waba.fx.*;

public class HelloWorld extends MainWindow {
    public void onPaint(Graphics g) {
        g.setColor(0,0,0);
        g.drawText("Hello World", 10,10);
    }
}
```

While not strictly Java, for those looking to write an application that is portable between the two most popular operating systems of PDAs today, namely Palm OS and Windows CE, Waba may be an alternative worth looking into. More information is available at www.wabasoft.com.

## 15.4　RELATED JAVA TECHNOLOGIES

While J2ME is the set of specifications used to guide application development on consumer and embedded application development, there are other Java technologies that help support this type software development. These are considered "non-J2ME" technologies in that these technologies are guided by their own specifications and not J2ME configurations and profiles. However, it is likely that, in developing J2ME applications, an application will utilize one of these technologies, or, as a developer, you are likely to at least come in contact with these technologies in designing and developing your applications.

### 15.4.1　Java Card

Credit card-sized plastic cards are now being outfitted with a microprocessor or a memory chip. There are several types of smart card devices. Smart cards with an integrated circuit microprocessor can actually process data stored on the card. Other integrated circuit cards require the assistance of a reader for processing, but contain a fixed set of processing instructions for manipulating data stored on the card. Smart cards are finding their way into many applications, and you may actually own some smart cards without knowing it. Several credit card companies have started using smart cards in place of standard magnetic strip credit cards. Government agencies are using smart cards in place of standard identification cards such as driver's licenses, and mass transit systems are replacing coin or token-operated fare systems with smart card applications. Smart cards hold all the necessary functions and data on the card. Therefore, unlike magnetic strip styled credit cards, these cards do not require access to remote systems or data during the time of a transaction. They can also, typically, store more information than the standard magnetic strip card.

Java Card defines the use of Java in smart card devices and applications. In some Java technology circles, Java Card is actually considered part of J2ME. In fact, there have been documents on Sun's own web site that have lumped Java Card with J2ME. However, Java Card is guided by its own specification and the current Java Card specification is version 2.1.1.

The Java Card specification defines a special kind of applet, a class that extends `javacard.framework.Applet`, which is part of a Java Card framework. When a Java Card, containing one or more applets, is inserted or somehow presented to a card reader, called a card acceptance device (CAD), the Java Card virtual machine is running and the reader identifies an applet it wishes to communicate with. The CAD then sends the applet a series of commands to execute. Communication between the applet and the reader are transmitted in the form of application protocol data units (APDU). An applet replies to each APDU by giving the CAD the result of the operation and optionally data as a result of the operation. The Java Card specification and more information about this technology can be found at java.sun.com/products/javacard.

### 15.4.2  Java Native Interface

The world and its software does not run entirely on Java. In a report by ZDNet,[3] the number of Java programmers is expected to overtake the number of C/C++ programmers sometime in 2002. Java's popularity not withstanding, there are still a lot of software applications written in other languages. Furthermore, there are times when an application should be written in some other language. For example, the speed of the application may dictate that the application or a part of it is written in the device's native assembly language.

The Java Native Interface (JNI) allows Java applications to access other code through a standardized programming interface. There are several reasons why this may be necessary.

- The Java class library does not provide platform-dependent features that are required in the Java application.

- Access to an application written in another language is desired from inside a Java application.

- A critical feature needs to be implemented in a low-level language such as the system's assembly language.

---

[3]  ZDNet, eWeek, "Study: Java to overtake C/C++ in 2002," August 16, 2001.

JNI is an interface, which is to say that JNI is actually provided through the Java language constructs. A Java developer wanting to access a non-Java method, for example, would create a wrapper class containing the desired external native method. The class might look something like the following:

```
public class OutsideWorld {
  {
  static
    {
    //load the appropriate native library
    System.loadLibrary("OutsideWorld");
    }
  public static native int someMethod(int anArg);
}
```

In this simple example, the native method called `someMethod` may be a C++ method located in the OutsideWorld Dynamically Linked Library (DLL). Native methods are brought into the Java environment with a `System.loadLibrary` method call and then used inside of the Java application as if just another Java method. Of course, applications that use JNI must be concerned with portability. The native method, whether it be a C++ method, assembly language application, or operating system feature, may not be available on every platform to which the Java application can be ported.

JNI is part of the Java 2 SDK, but it is also guided by its own specification. JNI 1.1 is the current JNI specification. As one might imagine, JNI is of great interest to the J2ME community. The reason is that for developers of applications to a very wide spectrum of devices, JNI can sometimes be the only way to take advantage of the platform-specific features and software.

Unfortunately, J2ME does not always support JNI. The CDC does support JNI, but the CLDC does not. JNI was thought to be too big to add to the footprint-constrained CLDC. There were also concerns about its effect on security. However, it is believed that Sun and others are investigating a lightweight JNI implementation for smaller devices. As an alternative to JNI today, native code for a particular device can be added into the CLDC's virtual machine (usually the KVM), that is, native code that is going to be called from the virtual machine must be linked directly into the virtual machine at compile time. This is not an easy or straightforward task, and even Sun recommends avoiding this approach in their J2ME white papers.[4]

You will find more information about JNI under the documents section of the current version of the SDK on Sun's web site. For example, JNI under version 1.3 of the SDK would be at:java.sun.com/j2se/1.3/docs/guide/jni.

---

[4] "Java 2 Platform Micro Edition (J2ME) Technology for Creating Mobile Devices," Sun Microsystems, Whitepaper, May 19, 2000.

### 15.4.3  Jini

How often have you bought new software or a new device such as a printer or scanner for your home or office computer or network, rushed home to use it, only to spend hours trying to get it running? Computer systems and networks are complicated pieces of equipment. Even as so-called industry experts, it is impossible to understand all the various operating systems, communication protocols, and layers of our computer systems and ancillary hardware.

Jini technology (usually pronounced like Jeannie in "I Dream of Jeannie"), a distributed computing technology developed by Sun Microsystems, is an architecture for having a hardware, software, or other system resource identify itself and its services on a network or computer system in a commonly understood language. The means used for publishing services is actually a Java object that implements a service API. Clients find needed services by looking for the appropriate published service object. The service object can instruct the client on how to communicate with it. All clients then communicate with services via a "service protocol." A service implementer, whether it is the printer manufacturer, or a developer of a software system such as a general ledger application, must then build in the mechanism to translate the service API requests into the required protocols and APIs of the actual service.

Jini is referred to as the "instant-on" connection technology. The idea is that a device or resource should be able to be quickly introduced and made immediately available to the community, usually a network of systems, for use. The idea is that this should also happen without the need for the community to know the service's location, and the community should be able to cope with changes such as removal of the service over time. How many times have you had to take a printer offline for general maintenance, only to have to spend more time hooking it back into the network when the maintenance was complete? In Sun's own terminology, Jini "federates" computers, devices, and other resources into a virtual single system from a client's perspective.

So how does J2ME relate to Jini? Jini could run on top of J2ME allowing small mobile and wireless devices to become users or providers of service on the network. J2ME brings Java to small consumer electronics and embedded devices. Jini uses Java objects as its means to publish and communicate with services. At its core, Jini utilizes RMI as its communications protocol, and with the introduction of the RMI Profile, particularly for the CDC, Jini could be used directly in conjunction with J2ME.

On a more fundamental plane, Jini technology is based on a concept known as the surrogate architecture. The surrogate architecture is the basic architecture for a device or resource to identify itself to or interact with other devices on a network. While RMI and all of Jini may not be available on all platforms or for all profiles and configurations in the near future, the surrogate architecture does provide the blueprints for designing the same or similar services for these devices and resources.

More information on Jini and the surrogate architecture is available at the following web sites: jini.org and www.sun.com/jini.

### 15.4.4 JavaPhone and Java TV APIs

Both the JavaPhone and Java TV APIs are vertical extensions to PersonalJava and EmbeddedJava. As PersonalJava is expected to migrate toward the Personal Profile, it is anticipated that these two APIs will one day be vertical extensions of the J2ME configurations and profile specifications.

The JavaPhone API has been developed to work with two new types of client telephony devices: namely the wireless smart phones and the Internet screen phones. Wireless smart phones are intended to be the personal planner and communication device of the future. Smart phones will bring voice communications, e-mail, fax capability, two-way radio communications, paging, Internet access, PDA styled scheduling, and planning and many other functions that cell phones, PDAs, pagers and computers share today together into one device. Internet screen phones are essentially two-way video screens and optional keyboards hooked up to the Internet to allow for more personal and direct personal or business communications on line. The JavaPhone API brings Java to these devices.

Digital television may be the next big thing in home entertainment. In particular, this technology brings interactive content to our televisions. The Java TV API provides a means to write Java programs to control the televisions and set-top boxes providing this new digital entertainment. The Java API could allow digital television to provide viewers with features including electronic programming guides (EPG), the ability to select and view videos on demand, network games, the ability to choose from which camera to watch a multi-camera-angle ball game, and much more.

Java, through the JavaPhone and Java TV API is attractive to the manufacturers of telephone and digital home entertainment equipment because of its strength on most hardware systems. Namely, Java provides platform independence, security, and dynamic upgrade capabilities. More information on the JavaPhone and Java TV APIs is available through Sun at: java.sun.com/products/javaphone and java.sun.com/products/javatv.

## 15.5    NON-JAVA ALTERNATIVES

If portability is not an issue, then developing applications on small devices using Java may not necessarily be the way to go. Certainly, Java has advantages that go beyond portability. Java is a good object-oriented language, offers security features that other languages do not have and is widely accepted, which means it is usually easier to find a developer to help build or maintain a Java application. But there are downsides as well. Because Java requires a virtual machine, Java developers are sometimes waiting for the virtual machine and API to be developed for the target platform. Throughout this book, we have noted gaps in J2ME coverage. Because Java is run as a set of byte codes that must be interpreted by a virtual machine at runtime, performance is almost always a consideration. The virtual machine does not help when worrying about the size of the application as well. While some vendors strip away the unnecessary classes, fields and methods in a Java application destined for a small device, not all do and this means the runtime environment is carrying around a lot of weight waiting for instructions that will never come. So let's take a brief look at some of the more popular alternatives to Java application development for consumer electronics and embedded devices.

### 15.5.1 WAP/WML

When no processing or data storage are required on the device, you may want to consider using the Wireless Application Protocol and Wireless Markup Language to build your application. WAP is a set of specifications for developing web-like applications that run over wireless networks. WML is one part of WAP that specifies how document pages are annotated to convey information around the wireless network. WML is analogous to HTML in the Internet and World Wide Web arena. In fact, WAP and WML are used to link wireless devices to the Internet by translating Internet data to be displayed on the screen of a mobile/wireless device like a cell phone or PDA device. The translator between the WAP world and the Internet is a WAP Gateway. Many of today's cellular telephones and PDA devices provide "WAP browsers" or are WAP-enabled which means they are capable of accessing the Internet (at least the portion of the Internet that can be put in WML format).

And just like JavaScript or VBScript for the Internet, WML has its own scripting language called WMLScript that allows for more interactive applications on these WAP devices. For example, popular WAP/WML applications allow their users to order books, concert tickets or CDs over their WAP-enabled cellular phones.

WAP faces many challenges and its standard has been slow to be adopted. The small screens, key pad entry system, and slow bandwidth associated with WAP systems make WAP an unlikely means to access much information or applications off the Internet. Furthermore, using WAP requires the device to make a call in order to connect and receive the needed information. This is an unwelcome cost on the user's monthly service bill. Finally, providers of services and information on the Internet must "WAP-ize" their website if they want to be able to offer WAP devices any content. This requires maintaining multiple versions of a website which can be costly.

There are literally hundreds of web sites containing information about WAP and WML. A good place to start is with the industry association that leads the development of the WAP standards, the WAP Forum at: www.wapforum.org. You may also wish to refer to *Dynamic WAP Application Development* by Manning Publications.

### 15.5.2 Other languages

Most of the software built for devices today is not built using Java. If you are the manufacturer of a device, such as Palm, you are probably not all that concerned that your software also runs very nicely on Windows CE devices.

C++, C, and Visual Basic are the most popular development languages for the various devices available today. Many of the IDEs already offer versions or editions of their popular tools for creating applications on the more popular devices like Palm OS or Windows CE. Metrowerks' CodeWarrior is available for various processors and platform operating systems, and Microsoft provides Visual Basic and Visual C++ optimized for a number of embedded environments as well as its own Windows CE operating system. For more information on developing applications for small devices in other programming languages, you may want to start with the following two URLs: www.microsoft.com/windows/embedded and www.palmos.com/dev.

## 15.6 DATA STORAGE AND SYNCHRONIZATION

As mentioned in chapter 11, one of the more difficult issues in dealing with mobile and wireless applications is how and where to store the information, and how to keep the information synchronized when the data is on multiple devices. A number of databases are now being offered on small devices. Many of these are much smaller adaptations from the larger enterprise systems with which developers are already well acquainted. This usually makes for a less steep learning curve. Unfortunately, not all of these databases can be accessed through the J2ME APIs.

XML has become the world's de facto standard for describing and communicating data in a platform-independent way. XML is slowly working its way into the realm of small devices and their applications. XML, however, is not seen as a small, fast, or lightweight data mechanism, even in the world of enterprise systems. This same problem is only compounded in the world of consumer electronics and embedded devices.

### 15.6.1 Data storage

Many of today's popular database systems are available for small platforms. Connecting to and using these databases may be difficult in Java. Java Database Connectivity (JDBC) is the standard API for connecting to databases in more traditional Java client or server applications. However, neither the CDC nor the CLDC contain support for JDBC. The `java.sql` package (the home of the classes and interfaces that make up the JDBC API) is optionally provided in PersonalJava implementations. Therefore, the first step in using one of these databases is to find a Java environment that contains the `java.sql` package and provides for JDBC. Even where JDBC may be available, an appropriate driver is also required by the application to use the JDBC API. This is usually an easier problem to solve since the database vendor often provides the driver.

A critical factor in the usefulness of a database engine is its ability to link up and exchange data with the enterprise database system that coordinates disbursement of data to small devices. Depending on the vendor, some of the database engines come with a tool to help synchronize them with enterprise database systems. Others do not provide this luxury and require the developer to determine how best to keep any data distributed to devices synchronized. All of the databases listed here provide some form of data synchronization with their "mother" databases.

### Cloudscape

Cloudscape is a pure Java object-relational database that can be run on all sizes of platforms from servers to handhelds. Implemented as a library of Java classes, Cloudscape has a footprint of a little more than 2 megabytes and requires JDBC to access the database. Cloudscape was a separate business unit of Informix, another of the large database vendors, but was recently purchased by IBM. www.cloudscape.com

### Oracle Lite

Oracle9*i* Lite is a lightweight cousin of Oracle9i, but built from the ground up for small, resource-constrained platforms. It is available for Palm OS, Microsoft PocketPC/Windows 95/98/NT/2000, and Symbian EPOC platforms. Connection to Oracle9*i* Lite is accomplished via JDBC and Oracle9*i* Lite's ultrathin native JDBC driver. Oracle claims that its Lite database requires as little as one MB of memory even in its most complete configuration. www.oracle.com/ip/deploy/database/oracle9i/9ilite

### Pointbase Micro

Pointbase is a pure Java database with versions that also run on various sized platforms from servers down to small devices. Its Micro version advertises that it is based on the J2ME as well as J2SE architecture. Pointbase Micro deploys in a single Jar file and has a footprint of less than 45 KB. A subset of the JDBC API with SQL is used to get access and update data.

As a pure Java solution, the database should port to a platform running Java, but it has been specifically tested on Windows, Windows CE/Pocket PC, Symbian EPOC, Palm OS, Motorola and iDen platforms. www.pointbase.com

### UltraLite

Sybase's entry in the small device database market is UltraLite, with a footprint of about 150 KB. It is available in C and Java, and the Java port has two versions, one at the JDK 1.2 level and another for Java 1.1 systems. Access to the database is via JDBC. The JDBC driver and database runtime environment are packaged together in a single jar file. UltraLite is available for EPOC, Palm OS, VxWorks, and Windows CE/Pocket PC platforms. www.sybase.com

## 15.6.2   A data synchronization standard, SyncML

Some data is placed on a device as reference information for periodic lookups and examination. The care and management of this information is relatively easy, requiring the device to simply receive periodic updates on occasion. On the other hand, data that is more regularly retrieved from an enterprise database system, updated and then returned, requires a great deal of coordination, or more appropriately, synchronization. As discussed in chapters 11 and 12, synchronizing data on mobile and wireless devices can be quite complicated because there is no way of knowing when, if ever, data put on a mobile/remote device is going to be returned.

Many of the major commercial database engines today, such as those listed in the previous section, offer a means to synchronize data between their database servers and client databases on devices such as laptops, consumer electronics and embedded devices. However, each vendor implements synchronization in a unique manner. Many of the device manufactures also have proprietary applications and protocols for updating information such as address books, calendars, and so forth.

SyncML is an open industry initiative for devising universal synchronization standards, a "synchronization protocol," that works across all types of databases, networks and platforms. This protocol enables mobile devices to synchronize with any networked data and, likewise, any networked data to be synchronized with the mobile device. SyncML sponsor participants include Ericsson, IBM, Lotus, Matsushita, Motorola, Nokia, Openwave, Starfish Software and Symbian. These sponsors hope to produce a protocol that can synchronize most any data and can:

- work in a wireless and wired fashion

- support many different transport protocols (such as HTTP, Wireless Session Protocol, TCP/IP, OBEX, SMTP, POP3, and others) for the fundamental communications of information

- enable access from many different applications on all sizes and shapes of resource-constrained devices

- utilize existing Web and Internet technologies where possible.

This last bullet point is interesting because the initiative has taken the position that "to the extent possible, the protocol should use XML to represent data being exchanged during a synchronization session."[5] More information and the latest SyncML specifications are available at: www.syncml.org

### 15.6.3 XML

When data must be transported between systems, whether through the Internet or wirelessly, the universal data transport markup language has become the Extensible Markup Language (XML). XML is to data what Java is to programming languages. It is a platform independent language for describing and transmitting data.

While ubiquitous to data exchanged on the Web, especially in a business-to-business (B2B) environment, XML creates some problems for the mobile device developer. First, the structure of XML data and the tools usually needed to handle and manipulate XML data does not always avail itself to be used in resource-constrained devices. XML, by its nature, describes the data it also represents. While extremely useful to the users of the data, the extra data may not be something that the devices can handle. Furthermore, most of the leading XML parsers, by themselves, would bust the

---

[5] "Building an Industry-Wide Mobile Data Synchronization Protocol," Version 1.0, SyncML Whitepaper.

memory budget of many of the small devices in the J2ME arena. Finally, XML parsers are notoriously slow parts of many applications. Given the resource constraints of many small devices, the performance issues are further exacerbated.

However, a number of third parties have developed XML or an XML-subset API for use in resource-constrained Java environments. Below are some of the known efforts underway to bring XML to the micro Java platform.

## kXML

kXML is an open source XML API available from the Enhydra community. kXML is a non-validating, incremental parser that has optional DOM (called kDOM) and WBXML/WML support. In its minimal configuration, kXML is around 16 KB in size. You can obtain a copy of kXML at: www.kxml.org

**VALIDATING VS. NON-VALIDATING PARSERS** One of the many ways that XML parsers are differentiated is by whether the parser is a validating or non-validating parser. A validating parser compares an XML document's definition (otherwise known as its document type definition or schema) against its contents to ensure the data in the document is actually organized according to the definition. Obviously, this requires more work on the part of the parser, and will slow the parsing process down, but the application has the benefit of working with documents it can more easily accept and trust in terms of data organization and content.

A non-validating parser does not check the validity of the data against a definition. All a non-validating parser will do for an application is ensure that it is "well-formed." This means that the parser will only check that the XML document follows the general standards of an XML document (tags are present, opened and closed appropriately, and so forth).

## NanoXML

Another open source XML parser is NanoXML. Originally built for standard Java environments, it is a non-validating, single-step, parser written by Marc De Scheemaecker. NanoXML has been ported for smaller environments, like that of J2ME applications, and comes in three flavors.

NanoXML/Java is an XML-compliant standard parser capable of both parsing and writing XML. NanoXML/SAX is the SAX adapter for the standard NanoXML/Java version. Finally, there is NanoXML/Lite. This last version is the version intended for use in small devices. Whereas NanoXML/Java's footprint stands at a small 32 KB, Nano XML/Lite is a minuscule 5 KB.

More information and a download of NanoXML is available from nanoxml. sourceforge.net.

**SINGLE STEP VS. INCREMENTAL PARSERS**

Another differentiating component of XML parsers on the market today is in how they parse a document: either in a single-step or incrementally. A single-step parser performs its work in a single process. It reads the entire document into memory and parses it in a single operation, returning a tree of objects. An incremental parser, on the other hand, parses an XML document a piece at a time.

Single-step parsers can be advantageous if a document, held in memory, needs to be parsed several times. However, large documents can be problematic for single-step parsers to handle, especially on memory-constrained small devices. Incremental parsers can deal with large documents more easily but require more work to track or follow where the parser is with a document.

### TinyXML

Like NanoXML, TinyXML was initially developed for more standard Java applications by Tom Gibara. Christian Sauer has ported a special version to work in the J2ME CLDC environment. Available under GNU public license, TinyXML has a footprint of less than 10 KB. It is a non-validating parser and more information on it is available at www.gibaradunn.srac.org/tiny/index.shtml.

## 15.7 *J2ME SUPPLEMENTARY TECHNOLOGY*

As J2ME, in most cases, is a minimal Java platform for which to build applications for resource-constrained devices, there have been (and undoubtedly will continue to be) a burgeoning market for third-party vendors to provide platform components and facilities through J2ME. Below are some of the known products and vendors to date.

### 15.7.1 GUI, kAWT

One of the more lackluster elements of J2ME development is the graphical user interface. This is due, in part, to the fact that most small devices have very limited screens. Also, J2ME is required to address the lowest common denominator and the lowest common denominator in the world of user interfaces can be quite limiting.

However, a number of groups are working to develop additional user interface components (those that would augment J2ME UI components) or replacement user interface components and packages for the micro Java world. This should come as little surprise to the Java community since the same thing happened with the maturity of the standard Java environment. In fact, several organizations, including Sitraka (formerly KL Group, with a web site at www.sitraka.com), have carved a niche market for themselves in providing graphical user interface components for today's Java applications.

The kAWT project, started by Michael Kroll and Stefan Haustein of Germany a few years ago, set out to develop a graphical user interface API that was more portable yet similar to Java's AWT. Today, the kAWT runs on top of the CLDC and is available for Palm OS and various RIM pager systems. A version is also available on the MIDP platforms. Several IDE's have also been licensed to use kAWT. Jbed and VAME are among the IDEs that now offer kAWT with versions of their tools.

The kAWT supports an event listener like that in AWT and is upwardly compatible with the AWT in the J2SE. In fact a version of the kAWT is also available for SDK 1.2 environments. Today, Michael and Stefan serve on the PDA profile expert group. More information on kAWT is available at www.kawt.de.

### 15.7.2 Web browsing, Kbrowser

4thpass has developed a 100% Java browser for J2ME-enabled phones and PDAs. They claim their "microbrowser" is the smallest such browser in the industry with a minimal footprint of 64 KB. This browser is designed to carry out the standard browser tasks on very resource-constrained devices and it supports the standard protocols (HTTP, WAP) in a secure manner, if desired. Kbrowser can also be used to download Java applications, such as Midlets in a wireless fashion right to the devices. This type technology and software has great potential in solving application distribution issues to systems that are far-reaching, mobile and not very accessible. Get more information on Kbrowser from www.4thpass.com/kbrowser.

### 15.7.3 Encryption, Bouncy Castle

Data being transmitted, especially when transmitted wirelessly, is subject to interception and misuse. Therefore, the need to secure that information is creating a demand for cryptography and security API packages.

The Legion of Bouncy Castle has developed a Java Cryptography Extension (version 1.2) compliant lightweight cryptography API in Java that works in all Java environments including J2ME. The lightweight version intended for use with the J2ME is less than 450kB (for the entire set of MIDP version classes).

More information about Bouncy Castle and their crypto API is available from www.bouncycastle.org.

## 15.8 SUMMARY

J2ME is growing in popularity. However, there are many circumstances, platforms and types of applications to which a J2ME solution cannot or should not be applied. For these types of environments, as we have seen in this chapter, there are plenty of Java and non-Java alternatives.

Furthermore, J2ME is, like its bigger brothers J2SE and J2EE, a platform from which to build Java applications. It does not comprise the entire set of components you will ever need to build your award winning applications. A growing industry of J2ME and other micro Java environment component and tool vendors are starting to provide some very nice capabilities that can give your application development efforts a head start. As with other Java environments, we can expect more of these efforts as J2ME specifications are strengthened and expanded.

# APPENDIX A

## J2ME development tools

There are a number of integrated development environments (IDEs) and development tools that directly support J2ME development today. In this appendix, we provide a list of the known products. Some of these tools support development in all the Java editions (J2EE, J2SE, and J2ME). Many of the tools are produced by tool manufacturers that support a whole line of development environments that include tools for developing software for large and small devices as well as for developing software in different programming languages. The list here focuses on products directly supporting J2ME development.

We do not endorse or disparage any of the tools listed in this appendix. In fact, all have their particular strengths and weaknesses. For that matter, as we have shown in this text, one does not have to have a development environment or tool to develop J2ME applications. A simple text editor and the necessary compilers, preverifiers, and converters are all that is required to start building your J2ME applications. The purpose of these products, as with all development environments and tools, is to help you produce better products or make the process of developing software easier and faster.

The products listed here may or may not fulfill that mission depending on your background and your project. As with most things in life, we recommend you try before you buy.

| Product | Vendor | Web Site |
| --- | --- | --- |
| BlackBerry Java Development Environment (JDE) | Research in Motion | developers.rim.net |
| CodeWarrior for Java | Metrowerks | www.metrowerks.com |
| Forte for Java | Sun Microsystems | www.sun.com/forte/ffj |
| Java2 Platform Micro Edition (J2ME) Wireless Toolkit | Sun Microsystems | java.sun.com/products/j2mewtoolkit |
| Jbed IDE | esmertec | www.esmertec.com |
| JBuilder and JBuilder MobileSet | Borland | www.borland.com |
| VisualAge Micro Edition | IBM | www.oti.com |
| WHITEboard SDK | Zucotto Wireless | www.zucotto.com/whiteboard/index.html |

# J2ME resources

Birdstep
www.birdstep.com

CDC/CVM Homepage
java.sun.com/products/cdc

CLDC/KVM Homepage
java.sun.com/products/cldc

Cloudscape
www.cloudscape.com

Enhydra
www.enhydra.org

esmertec (Jbed)
www.esmertec.com

Insignia Solutions (Jeode)
www.insignia.com

J2ME Homepage
java.sun.com/j2me

Java Community Process Specifications
jcp.org/jsr/all/index.jsp

Kada Systems
www.kadasystems.com

Kaffe Homepage
www.kaffe.org

kAWT
www.trantor.de/kawt/index.html

kSoap
ksoap.enhydra.org

KVM Forum
forums.java.sun.com/forum.jsp?forum=50

KVM Interest Group
archives.java.sun.com/archives/kvm-interest.html

KXML
www.kxml.org

Metrowerks (CodeWarrior)
www.metrowerks.com/desktop/java

Micro Java Network
www.microjava.com

MIDP Homepage
java.sun.com/products/midp

Motorola Developer Resources
developers.motorola.com/developers

NanoXML
nanoxml.sourceforge.net

Nokia
www.nokia.com

Oracle (OracleLite)
www.oracle.com/ip/deploy/database/oracle9i/9ilite/index.html/content.html

Palm
www.palm.com

PersonalJava Forum
forums.java.sun.com/forum.jsp?forum=56

PersonalJava Homepage
java.sun.com/products/personaljava

PointBase
www.pointbase.com

SAX Homepage
sax.sourceforge.net

Sybase (iAnywhere)
www.sybase.com/solutions/mobilewireless

TinyXML
www.gibaradunn.srac.org/tiny/index.shtml

Transvirtual (PocketLinux/Kaffe)
www.transvirtual.com

Wireless Developer (Sun)
wireless.java.sun.com

Wireless Developer Network
www.wirelessdevnet.com

WirelessDeveloper.com
www.wirelessdeveloper.com

# APPENDIX C

# *Java and J2ME history*

While being familiar with Java's history and evolution may not help you write a J2ME application, it can certainly help you as you try to understand how J2ME was put together or why a feature may or may not be included in the API. Knowing the history can also help you as you read documentation or information that may be a little outdated. Without historical background, terminology or product references will be hard to put into perspective with the current environment. This appendix outlines the history and development of Java and places J2ME in this context.

## C.1   OAK AND THE GREEN PROJECT

Java was developed in the early to mid-1990s. Actually, Java, or more appropriately Oak as Java was first called, was a by-product of Sun's Green Project. The goal of the Green Project was to develop a set of networked consumer electronic devices that could be programmed from a device similar to a personal digital assistant. The Green Project team (the Green team) believed digitally controlled consumer devices (TV, VCR, video disc players, etc.) and computer technologies were starting to come together. However, the Green team was confounded in their efforts because the diverse set of devices they wanted to connect all used different hardware and programming firmware. A single programming language to handle their needs was not available and efforts to modify languages such as C++ to handle their requirements proved inadequate. Therefore, one of their first tasks in developing their network of consumer electronic devices was to develop a single operating environment that allowed software to run on a multitude of devices. Thus, believe it or not, Java was born, not out of a need to run as a platform-independent language on thousands of server and client computers as it does today. Instead, it had humble beginnings as a means to network and program home entertainment equipment. In a way, early micro-Java was the start of the whole Java effort.

Early Java, or Oak, was loosely based on a stripped-down C++ to work and provide the absolute necessities in the limited spaces of the chips employed by consumer devices. Even then, its goal was to provide developers with a means to easily support an ever-changing and evolving set of hardware.

Additionally, Oak had to satisfy two other major concerns. It had to be reliable and secure. For a consumer electronic device to be successful, it could not rely on resetting or rebooting as a general practice. Programming errors had to be minimized in order to improve reliability. And because the goal was to network these consumer electronic devices, there was a fear that these devices could intentionally or unintentionally harm other systems on the network. Therefore security was also a prime ingredient in Oak.

By the middle of 1992, the Green team introduced a PDA-like handheld device for controlling a home entertainment system. The device, called *7 (Star7), had an animated and interactive touch screen pad. Although this device did not turn out to be commercially successful, the technology developed by the Green team proved to be extremely useful and profitable because of the arrival and expansion of another set of technologies: the Internet and the World Wide Web.

## C.2 *JAVA AND THE INTERNET*

The National Center for Supercomputing Applications released Mosaic in 1993. Considered the first successful Web browser, Mosaic allowed people to use the Internet in a powerful, visual way and eventually paved the way for the World Wide Web.

By 1994, the developers of Java saw the applicability of their new language in this new medium. The requirement for reliable and secure software applications that could be written once for an undetermined number of potential computer systems fit perfectly with Java's original design for consumer electronic devices. Quickly, Java's applet technology was born. With appropriate Java runtime support configured for the target platform and hidden in the Web browser on the client system, the relatively small application called the Java applet was, and still is today, capable of being written once and run almost anywhere.

With a foothold in its use with the Internet and World Wide Web and a renewed reason for being, Java expanded to serve in almost every nook and cranny of current software development. Its versatility, many features, and, of course, platform independence have made Java a major component of modern software technology.

**JAVA VS. JDK**    In discussing the evolution of Java, we need to clarify the terms "Java" and "Java platform" and the "JDK," now called the "SDK."

Java and the SDK have become synonymous. However, in reality Java "the language" should be viewed as a separate entity from Sun's reference implementation of the language and developer's kit that have traditionally shared the same version number. Java or, as Sun likes to refer to it, the Java platform, is the abstract language and specification that surrounds the language. The SDK is Sun's product and an implementation of the specification that is used by software engineers to create applications. If you prefer, the Java platform is conceptual and the SDK is physical.

You might have noticed from the last paragraph that the SDK is "an" implementation, not necessarily "the" implementation. In theory, if not practice, many other organizations could provide their own implementation of the Java platform. In fact some organizations such as IBM and Hewlett-Packard provide their own compilers and virtual machines. For more information on the differences between Java and the SDK, see Sun's web site at java.sun.com/products/jdk/1.2/java2.html.

For the purposes of this book, any reference to Java and a version number refers to both the Java specification and Sun's SDK unless explicitly stated.

## C.3   *EVOLUTION OF JAVA*

On May 23, 1995, Sun officially released Java. The first public release of the Java Development Kit (JDK) was version 1.02. Amazingly, Java's core architecture and programming language have not changed substantially. However, Sun has released two additional major releases and several minor releases of Java and the corresponding JDK since its first public release.

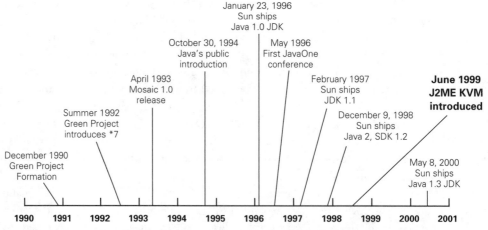

**Figure C.1**   **As this timeline depicts, Java was developed in the early 1990s, publicly introduced in the mid 1990s, and has been reintroduced, through J2ME, to consumer electronic and embedded devices in the late 1990s.**

### C.3.1     Java 1.02

As the first public release, Java 1.02 attempted to offer a best-of-breed programming language, borrowing ideas and trying to avoid the mistakes of its predecessor languages. Java was intended to look a lot like C++ while also providing many of the key features available in programming languages such as Smalltalk, Eiffel, and other object-oriented languages.

Java 1.02 introduced a new object-oriented programming language that provided a platform-neutral development environment that produced applications that were considered more secure and reliable than applications produced with other programming languages. As previously mentioned, its platform independence was able to shine through in new groundbreaking features, such as the Java applet, that were important to the development of the early Internet. Yet, like all first releases, Java 1.02 had some notable shortcomings as well.

### C.3.2     Java 1.1

In many cases, a second release of something in the software industry implies fixing that which was discovered broken, or not quite right, by the users in the first release. Java 1.1, including all the subsequent 1.1.x (Sun released 8 minor releases from 1.1.1 to 1.1.8) "minor" releases, did fix many shortcomings, but it also introduced many new features. In fact, the version number associated with Java's second major release is a real misnomer. The 1.1 version of Java included many substantial additions.

Along with performance enhancements and API enhancements in the event model, networking, and input/output (IO) support, the 1.1.x releases were monumental in the new APIs they introduced. These include server-side programming, Java database connectivity (JDBC), a new component model (JavaBeans), Reflection, and Java Native Interface to name a few.

### C.3.3     Java 2

With the introduction of Java 2, Sun made a stronger distinction between the Java platform and the JDK. In fact, they even changed the name of the Java Development Kit to the Software Development Kit (SDK). The Java language and specification jumped version numbers from Java 1.1 to Java 2. The development kit and runtime were renamed but kept the original version number progression. So what was the JDK became the Java 2 SDK, Standard Edition version 1.2 or just plain SDK 1.2 for short.

Along with the name and packaging realignment, the new SDK 1.2 offered many enhancements to the existing API, along with a few important new features such as a new set of collection classes and a new set of GUI components (the GUI components were actually introduced as an add-on package in late Java 1.1.x releases but made a permanent part of the SDK 1.2). Of course, Java 2 also brought a split in the "editions" of Java.

### C.3.4    SDK 1.3

The latest SDK release from Sun as of this writing is version 1.3. SDK 1.3 once again has presented Java developers with a number of enhancements and improvements to the existing APIs while introducing several features. Technologies such as the Common Object Request Broker Architecture (CORBA) and the Java Naming Directory Interface (JNDI), which were available through extension packages in previous versions, became part of the standard SDK in version 1.3. New APIs, like the sound API, were also added to SDK 1.3.

### C.3.5    Java 3 coming soon?

So will there be a Java 3? The SDK continues to undergo refinement. SDK 1.4 is expected to be released in 2002. What about an update in the Java specification? It would seem logical that unless Java 2 is perfect, we can expect a new version of Java at some point in the future. Watch your favorite Java information source for the latest from Sun and others.

### C.3.6    Java today

With the three editions and the numerous packages, it is hard to find a software development need that is not covered or at least partially addressed by Java 2 or a Java 2 add-on module. In less than five years, Java has made its way into almost every personal computer via almost every Web browser and in less than two years it has captured an estimated 90% of the application server market. In 1998, there were an estimated 7 million Java users. Today there are over 400 Java users groups worldwide and countless millions using Java technology. Sometime in the year 2002, Java is expected to surpass C++ as the predominate programming language. The term ubiquity can be overused, but it just might apply to Java in the world of software engineering today.

## C.4    ORIGINS OF J2ME

We have already discussed the early history and beginning of Java, which in reality is also the early beginning of J2ME. More recently, however, Sun has reintroduced J2ME as an important technology for small devices. During this reintroduction, some terminology and early product names were used that are generally not used or seen in reference material today.

You may encounter old J2ME terminology in early specifications or other older technical documents, and therefore you may want to be familiar with J2ME history in order to know what its current name or rendition is in "modern" J2ME. Furthermore, this history gives you some indication of where the technology has been in hopes that you may glean some indication of where J2ME technology is heading.

## C.4.1 Micro-Java rebirth

In June of 1999, at the 1999 JavaOne conference, Sun introduced the three platform editions of Java: the J2SE, J2EE, and J2ME. Sun also introduced a preview version of the KVM or K Virtual Machine.

The K has come to stand for Kilobyte, but its actual representation has been clouded over the past few years. According to various news groups, rumor has it that the K actually stood for "Kauai" (one of the Hawaiian islands that happens to produce coffee), which was the name of the KVM development project.

The KVM was developed in cooperation with several companies, most notably Motorola, 3COM, Bull, Fujitsu, Matsushita (Panasonic), Mitsubishi Electric, NEC, NTT DoCoMo, and Siemens. At the conference, the KVM was demonstrated on what was then 3COM's Palm Pilot. Since then, 3COM has spun off Palm as a separate entity. Palm, Inc. now controls the Palm device. To demonstrate this new virtual machine, Sun used a class API called KJava that provides the graphical user interface and database classes necessary to build applications for Palm OS (Palm operating system) devices. Those lucky enough to be at the conference were offered the KVM, Java class API and KJava classes (in a com.sun.kjava package) to put on their own personal devices to take home and try out.

## C.4.2 Early access versions of J2ME

In October of 1999, Sun provided the first release of the KVM. It was called the KVM Early Access Version 0.1 or DR4 for Developers Release 4. Still very much in the prototypical stage, Sun released several point releases of the KVM, Java API, and KJava classes for development of Palm OS applications through the remainder of 1999 and into 2000.

### *The first configuration*

Shortly after the preview release of the KVM, the J2ME community began its re-organization of the J2ME platform. Realizing that a single virtual machine and class API would probably not suffice for such a vast range of devices, an architecture of configurations and profiles emerged. We discuss the various configurations and profiles in chapters 2–10.

The J2ME architecture was developed through a series of specifications in Sun's Java Community Process (JCP). And, in fact, the JCP continues to develop and refine all of Java to include the J2ME platform today.

The first full release of a configuration was made available in May of 2000. The Connected, Limited Device Configuration (J2ME CLDC 1.0) provided J2ME developers with the first fully-supported J2ME platform. This release was also called the "Final Candidate for Shipment" version or FCS since it was considered the final release of the work that started with the KVM preview version.

The first configuration provided the first real J2ME reference implementation of Java running on small devices, but it also introduced another issue. A configuration provides the basic class API, but it alone does not provide many of the necessary classes to produce a full application on a device like the Palm. So the first configuration lacked the tools necessary to allow developers to develop a fully supported application for the Palm device. What to do?

Sun decided to continue to use the KJava API on top of the first configuration. As an unsupported and a soon to be replaced API, the KJava classes were meant to serve as a tool for testing and demonstrating the early J2ME technology. However, it was the only API that allowed developers to build an application.

### The first profile

The first reference implementation of a profile was released, in early access form, in July 2000. It is called the Mobile Information Device Profile (MIDP). Its FCS, version 1.0, became available in September 2000. However, as we saw in chapter 2, the MIDP is for the development of applications for cellular telephones and pagers. As a result, Palm and other PDA developers were stuck with KJava and are still waiting for a profile of their own.

## C.4.3 J2ME's continuing evolution

By the summer of 2000, a more clear and definitive picture on the evolution of J2ME specifications and related technologies emerged from Sun and the JCP. To date, not all of the specifications have been completed and even fewer have been implemented. However, progress is being made and more profiles are anticipated in the very near future. In fact, work is already underway to improve some of the current specifications and implementations. Additional Java technologies are also being woven into the edition.

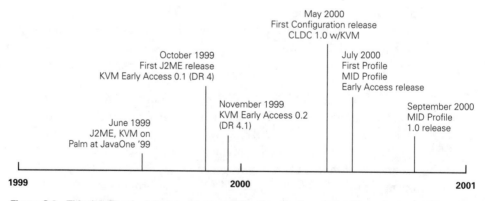

**Figure C.2** This timeline depicts the various specification versions and releases during J2ME's early creation and evolution. Today, there are more than a half-dozen specifications associated with J2ME.

### C.4.4 J2ME today

J2ME technology, like all Java platforms, is constantly changing and improving. The JCP allows for each edition of Java and each Java technology to expand and improve to better meet the needs of the development community it supports.

J2ME is still growing and some might say maturing. Along with evolution of the J2ME specifications, there are many other Java and non-Java technologies that are impacting and impacted by J2ME. It will take some time to find out exactly how all this technology fits together.

# APPENDIX D

# J2ME Wireless Toolkit

The J2ME Wireless Toolkit is partial IDE and emulator all-in-one for developing CLDC/MIDP applications. Developed by Sun Microsystems, the Wireless Toolkit is not the reference implementation of the CLDC/MIDP, but rather is an entire development environment providing J2ME developers with a means to create, package and test their CLDC/MIDP applications. In this appendix, we will re-examine the MIDP Hello World application developed in chapter 4 using the toolkit. This appendix is meant to provide a quick overview of the toolkit. More information about the J2ME Wireless Toolkit and its options and features is available from the Sun web site as well as the documentation that comes with the product. Other MIDP applications covered in this text can also be developed using the toolkit given the basic steps shown here.

## D.1   DOWNLOADING THE WIRELESS TOOLKIT

The J2ME Wireless Toolkit is available from Sun Microsystems web site at java.sun.com/products/j2mewtoolkit/download.html. The current available version of the J2ME Wireless Toolkit at this writing is 1.0.3. A copy of the toolkit is available for Microsoft Windows 98, NT and 2000 platforms as well as Linux and Solaris operating systems. However, the toolkits available for the Linux and Solaris platforms are not officially supported by Sun. A version for Windows XP is available but not tested at the time of this writing. Windows 95 does not support the J2ME Wireless Toolkit.

In addition to the toolkit, which we discuss in a moment, you will need the Java 2 Standard Edition SDK (version 1.3.0 or greater) that can be obtained from java.sun.com/ j2se/1.3/download-windows.html. The J2ME Wireless Toolkit requires 30 MB of disk space and 64 MB of RAM to run.

## D.2 INSTALLING THE J2ME WIRELESS TOOLKIT

For the sake of brevity, we will assume you already have the SDK installed on your system. If not, please install the Java 2 SDK, Standard Edition, version 1.3.0 or higher before installing the J2ME Wireless Toolkit.

What you get in the download from the Sun J2ME Wireless Toolkit web site is a self-extracting executable called j2me_wireless_toolkit-1_0_3-win.exe. Your version number or operating system type may vary depending on when you access the download site and the operating system version you desire. Execute this file by either double clicking on its icon in a file listing display or select the Run... option from the Start button on your Windows operating system, then browse to the file. You should be greeted with a screen that looks similar to the picture in figure D.1.

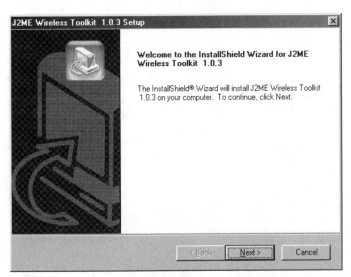

**Figure D.1    After starting the downloaded J2ME Wireless Toolkit installation executable obtained from Sun's web site, the installation should start with a screen that looks similar to this display (version 1.0.3).**

The installation program will guide you through a series of prompts to assist you in the installation process. By default, the application will install into a directory called J2mewtk.

Once the application is installed properly, along with the appropriate icons on your desktop, you should have a set of J2ME Wireless Toolkit directories on your hard drive. Some of directories that are placed on your hard drive and their general purpose are listed in the following table:

**Table D.1**   The directory structure of the J2ME Wireless Toolkit that contains the necessary files and executables to run the toolkit as well as the applications you develop.

| Directory | Purpose |
| --- | --- |
| \apps | Directory containing the demo applications provided with the toolkit as well as the future home for applications you create |
| \bin | Batch and .exe files of the J2ME Wireless Toolkit |
| \docs | The J2ME Wireless Toolkit documentation directory containing the Users Guide among other documents |
| \lib | The CLDC and MIDP API class files which are used during the compiling and preverifying of your applications |
| \wtklib | Emulator device property files |

## D.3   HELLO WORLD PROJECT REVISITED

In chapter 4, we created a simple Hello World MIDlet to demonstrate the MIDP technology and to get familiar with how to create MIDP applications. We will reuse the code from chapter 4 to demonstrate how to build an MIDP application using the J2ME Wireless Toolkit. The HiSmallWorld MIDlet from chapter 4 is listed below.

```
import javax.microedition.midlet.MIDlet;
import javax.microedition.lcdui.*;

public class HiSmallWorld extends MIDlet {
  private TextBox textbox;
  public HiSmallWorld() {
    textbox = new TextBox("", "Hi Small World!", 20, 0);
  }

  public void startApp() {
    Display.getDisplay(this).setCurrent(textbox);
  }

  public void pauseApp() {
  }

  public void destroyApp(boolean unconditional) {
  }

}
```

### D.3.1   Starting the toolkit

The J2ME Wireless Toolkit provides for a host of tools to help you build your application. The KToolBar is a graphically oriented user interface tool for accessing most of the tools provided in the toolkit. After installing the J2ME Wireless Toolkit, the KToolBar should be a program listed in the Programs of your desktop (under version 1.0.3, you will find it under Start –> Programs –> J2ME Wireless Toolkit 1.0.3). Clicking

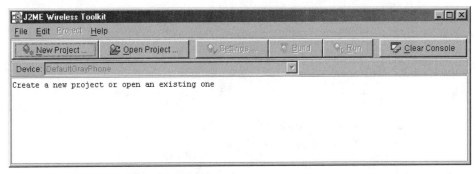

**Figure D.2  The KToolBar allows developers to configure, compile, preverify, package, and test MIDP applications.**

on KToolBar will start the application and you should see a window like that depicted in figure D.2.

This application allows you to create and configure projects, build or package your applications and run your applications in various emulators. Applications in this instance, as we shall see, mean MIDlet suites.

## D.3.2  Creating a project

Development in the KToolBar is accomplished via a project. A project is a collection of MIDlets in a MIDlet suite. Before writing, packaging or testing any code, the MIDlet code must be established as part of a project. To create a new project, push the New Project… button on the top left hand corner of the KToolBar window. A New Project window will display, requesting you to provide a Project Name and MIDlet Class Name (see figure D.3).

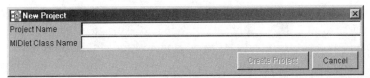

**Figure D.3  A new project name and associated first MIDlet are entered in this window that displays after pushing the New Project… button on the KToolBar.**

Enter the name of your MIDlet suite in the Project Name field. In the case of our Hello World example, we enter the name SmallWorldSuite. In the MIDlet Class Name field enter the name of the first MIDlet you want to be part of the suite. In this example, our first and only MIDlet will be the HiSmallWorld class. Once you enter these names and press the Create Project button on this window, a Settings for project "SmallWorldSuite" should display as seen in figure D.4. These are the settings or attributes for our project, MIDlet suite and all the MIDlets in the suite. We discuss these attributes in the next section so don't hit either the OK or Cancel button quite yet.

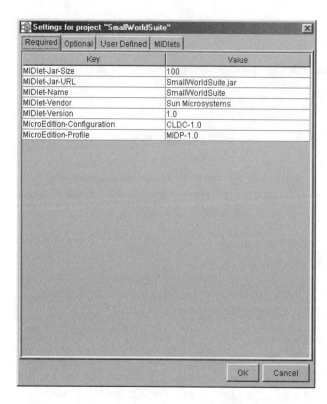

**Figure D.4**
**When creating a new project, settings for the project, MIDlet suite and associated MIDlets are provided in this window.**

Once the OK button on this window is pushed, a new J2ME Wireless Toolkit project is created. Pay particular attention to the text displayed in the main KToolBar window after a project is created. Move, but do not cancel the Settings window so that you can see the KToolBar window. As in our example shown in figure D.5, the toolkit indicates the directories being used by your new project. In particular, it tells you where to place your MIDlet application code and associated files. We will need this information later so it is a good idea to take note of these directories now.

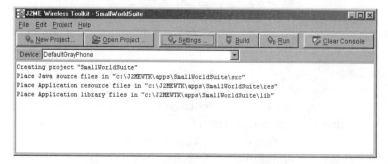

**Figure D.5** Note the directories that the toolkit specifies for source code, resource and library files. These will be used later on in the application development.

## D.3.3 Editing the project settings

The Settings for project "SmallWorldSuite" window acts as an editor for the attributes found in the MIDlet and MIDlet suite JAD and manifest files. If you push the tabs at the top of this window, you will see the various attributes that can be set for the MIDlet suite or individual MIDlet. For example, if you push on the MIDlets tab, you will see a table listing the MIDlets in our SmallWorldSuite (see figure D.6).

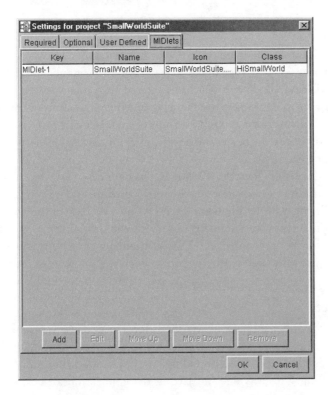

**Figure D.6**
**The MIDlets associated with the project and MIDlet suite are listed in the MIDlets tab on the Settings window.**

In our particular case, we do not yet have an icon for our HiSmallWorld MIDlet. So let's change this to indicate that the MIDlet has no icon. Click on the only row in the table and push the Edit button. In the window provided (see figure D.7), remove the SmallWorldSuite.png text that is in the Icon text field and press the OK button. Once you have entered the settings to your liking and push the OK button, the appropriate files (JAD and manifest) are modified by KToolBar and the project is created. After the project has been created, you can return to the project settings by pushing the Settings button on the KToolBar.

As can be seen by the Settings window, there are several attributes in the project. Once you have had a chance to get your first MIDlet up and running with the J2ME Wireless Toolkit, we suggest you read the documentation on the tool and play with these attributes.

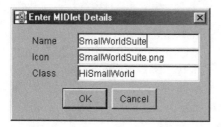

**Figure D.7**
**This window allows you to change the attributes of each MIDlet in the MIDlet suite.**

### D.3.4 Entering the Java code

The J2ME Wireless Toolkit does not come with a text editor. Therefore, you will need to use your favorite editor to type in the `HiSmallWorld` class code from page 466 into a HiSmallWorld.java file. Once you have entered the code into a text file, the KToolBar does tell you where to save the file. Namely, if you recall from the project's creation, the KToolBar informed us that Java source code for our project should be placed in a certain directory. In our example, this directory was c:\J2MEWTK\apps\ SmallWorldSuite\src (see figure D.5).

Each project in the J2ME Wireless Toolkit has its own directory, which is usually kept in the \apps subdirectory of the toolkit's main directory. If you peruse to the SmallWorldSuite directory under the \apps directory now, you will already see a directory structure that includes a \bin directory. Likewise, the \bin directory contains the manifest and JAD files for our tutorial suite. We will not have to edit these files directly since the KToolBar provides the Settings window which will allow us to set attributes via the tool.

### D.3.5 Building a project

With the project or MIDlet suite set up via the KToolBar and the Java code entered and saved to the appropriate directory, we are ready to compile, preverify, and jar our code. This part of the project is called "building" the application. In the J2ME Wireless Toolkit, compiling, preverifying, and jarring the application all occur with the push of a button (provided there are no bugs in your code).

To build your MIDlet suite, push the Build button on the KToolBar. If your application build is successful, you will see text displayed in the KToolBar panel that indicates "Build complete." If there were errors in your code, this same window will display messages indicating problems. You will then have to go back to your text editor and attempt to fix the code.

### D.3.6 Running a project

It is easy to compile, preverify and jar your application. It is equally easy to run and test your MIDlet suite in an emulator. In fact, with the J2ME Wireless Toolkit, you can test your application in a number of emulators. Located just below the New Project... button on the KToolBar is a Device drop-down box. Select this drop-down box and pick any one of a number of device emulators as shown in figure D.8.

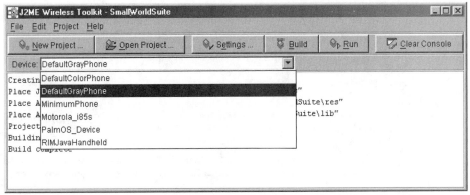

**Figure D.8** The default list of emulation devices offered in the J2ME Wireless Toolkit allows you to test your MIDlet suite on any number of devices. More device emulators can be added to the J2ME Wireless Toolkit. See the documentation on the J2ME Wireless Toolkit for how to add emulators.

Notice that even the Palm OS device is listed. We will discuss Palm OS emulation a little later. For now, pick any one of the various cell phone emulators listed in the drop-down.

With your favorite phone emulator selected from the Device list, push the Run button on the KToolBar. If all goes well, an emulator window running your MIDlet suite containing the HiSmallWorld MIDlet should display as in figure D.9.

You can close the emulator at any time, or start more emulators to simulate many HiSmallWorld MIDlets all running at one time. This can be advantageous when you want to test your networking applications as discussed in chapter 7. Remember, the HiSmallWorld MIDlet does not yet have any event handling capabilities—you will need to see chapter 5 for that—so you must power off the emulator to close the MIDlet application.

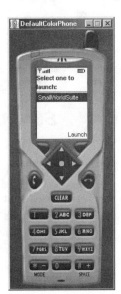

**Figure D.9**
**The SmallWorldSuite's**
**HiSmallWorld MIDlet**
**running in the**
**DefaultColorPhone**
**emulator.**

### D.3.7 Palm OS Emulator

The J2ME Wireless Toolkit has been designed to allow for the addition of new emulators in the future. In fact, the J2ME Wireless Toolkit is already prepared to interact with the Palm OS Emulator if it is available on your system.

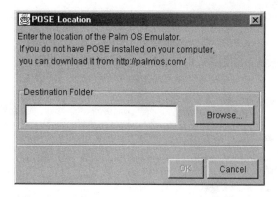

**Figure D.10**
**Attempting to run a MIDlet suite with the Palm OS as the selected emulation device results in the KToolBar requesting the location of your emulator.**

If you attempt to run the SmallWorldSuite with the Palm OS Emulator selected as the emulation device, you will be requested by the KToolBar to provide the location of the POSE on your system (see figure D.10). If you supply the location of the POSE in this window, then your MIDP applications will run as though we had developed MIDP for Palm OS applications.

### D.3.8    Operating from the command line

The KToolBar provides a convenient graphical user interface to the tools offered by the J2ME Wireless Toolkit. However, the J2ME Wireless Toolkit is really an assembly of tools for creating and testing J2ME MIDP applications. These tools can be utilized from the command line as opposed to the KToolBar. Instructions for running the various tools are available in the J2ME Wireless Toolkit documentation.

## D.4    SUMMARY

In this book, we have provided you with the ins and outs of MIDP application development. There is a growing number of development tools and IDEs and various products on the market to assist you in developing MIDlets and MIDlet suites. Because it is free and has the capabilities to be tied to other Java development products such as Forte by Sun Microsystems, the J2ME Wireless Toolkit is a popular development tool used by the J2ME community.

# index